TOMARE!

止まれ

[STOP!]

You're going the wrong way!

Manga is a completely different type of reading experience.

To start at the *beginning*, go to the *end*!

That's right! Authentic manga is read the traditional Japanese way—from right to left. Exactly the *opposite* of how American books are read. It's easy to follow: Just go to the other end of the book, and read each page—and each panel—from right side to left side, starting at the top right. Now you're experiencing manga as it was meant to be!

THE WALLFLOWER
YAMATONADESHIKO SHICHIHENGE

13

Tomoko Hayakawa

TRANSLATED AND ADAPTED BY
David Ury

LETTERED BY
Dana Hayward

DEL REY

BALLANTINE BOOKS • NEW YORK

The Wallflower, volume 13 is a work of fiction. Names, characters, places, and incidents are the products of the author's imagination or are used fictitiously. Any resemblance to actual events, locales, or persons, living or dead, is entirely coincidental.

A Del Rey Trade Paperback Original

Published in the United States by Del Rey Books, an imprint of The Random House Publishing Group, a division of Random House Inc., New York.

Publication rights arranged through Kodansha, Ltd.

First published in Japan in 2005 by Kodansha Ltd., Tokyo, as *Yamatonadeshiko Shichihenge.*

ISBN 978-0-345-49557-0

Printed in the United States of America

www.delreymanga.com

9 8 7 6 5 4 3 2 1

Translator and adaptor—David Ury
Lettering—Dana Hayward

Contents

A Note from the Author

♥ I know it's a little late, but it's time for me to introduce myself. I was born on March 3rd, 19xx. my blood type is AB. I'm single and I live in Tokyo. I'm kind of a loser. The things I love most in this world are my cat, Ten, and, of course, Kiyoharu. ♥ My hobby is checking out cute guys and girls. I love comedies, but I hate sports. I hate exercise. I collect skeleton and skull stuff. To be continued (probably).

—Tomoko Hayakawa

Honorifics Explained

Throughout the Del Rey Manga books, you will find Japanese honorifics left intact in the translations. For those not familiar with how the Japanese use honorifics and, more important, how they differ from American honorifics, we present this brief overview.

Politeness has always been a critical facet of Japanese culture. Ever since the feudal era, when Japan was a highly stratified society, use of honorifics—which can be defined as polite speech that indicates relationship or status—has played an essential role in the Japanese language. When addressing someone in Japanese, an honorific usually takes the form of a suffix attached to one's name (example: "Asuna-san"), is used as a title at the end of one's name or appears in place of the name itself (example: "Negi-sensei," or simply "Sensei!").

Honorifics can be expressions of respect or endearment. In the context of manga and anime, honorifics give insight into the nature of the relationship between characters. Many English translations leave out these important honorifics, and therefore distort the feel of the original Japanese. Because Japanese honorifics contain nuances that English honorifics lack, it is our policy at Del Rey not to translate them. Here, instead, is a guide to some of the honorifics you may encounter in Del Rey Manga.

-san: This is the most common honorific, and is equivalent to Mr., Miss, Ms., Mrs. It is the all-purpose honorific and can be used in any situation where politeness is required.

-sama: This is one level higher than "-san." It is used to confer great respect.

-dono: This comes from the word "tono," which means "lord." It is an even higher level than "-sama" and confers utmost respect.

-kun: This suffix is used at the end of boys' names to express familiarity or endearment. It is also sometimes used by men among friends, or when addressing someone younger or of a lower station.

-chan: This is used to express endearment, mostly toward girls. It is also used for little boys, pets, and even among lovers. It gives a sense of childish cuteness.

Bozu: This is an informal way to refer to a boy, similar to the English terms "kid" and "squirt."

Sempai/Senpai: This title suggests that the addressee is one's senior in a group or organization. It is most often used in a school setting, where underclassmen refer to their upperclassmen as "sempai." It can also be used in the workplace, such as when a newer employee addresses an employee who has seniority in the company.

Kohai: This is the opposite of "sempai," and is used toward underclassmen in school or newcomers in the workplace. It connotes that the addressee is of a lower station.

Sensei: Literally meaning "one who has come before," this title is used for teachers, doctors, or masters of any profession or art.

-[blank]: This is usually forgotten in these lists, but it is perhaps the most significant difference between Japanese and English. The lack of honorific means that the speaker has permission to address the person in a very intimate way. Usually, only family, spouses, or very close friends have this kind of permission. Known as *yobisute*, it can be gratifying when someone who has earned the intimacy starts to call one by one's name without an honorific. But when that intimacy hasn't been earned, it can be very insulting.

THE wallFLOWER
YAMATONADESHIKO SHICHIHENGE
ヤマトナデシコ七変化♡

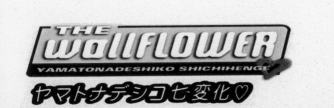

CONTENTS

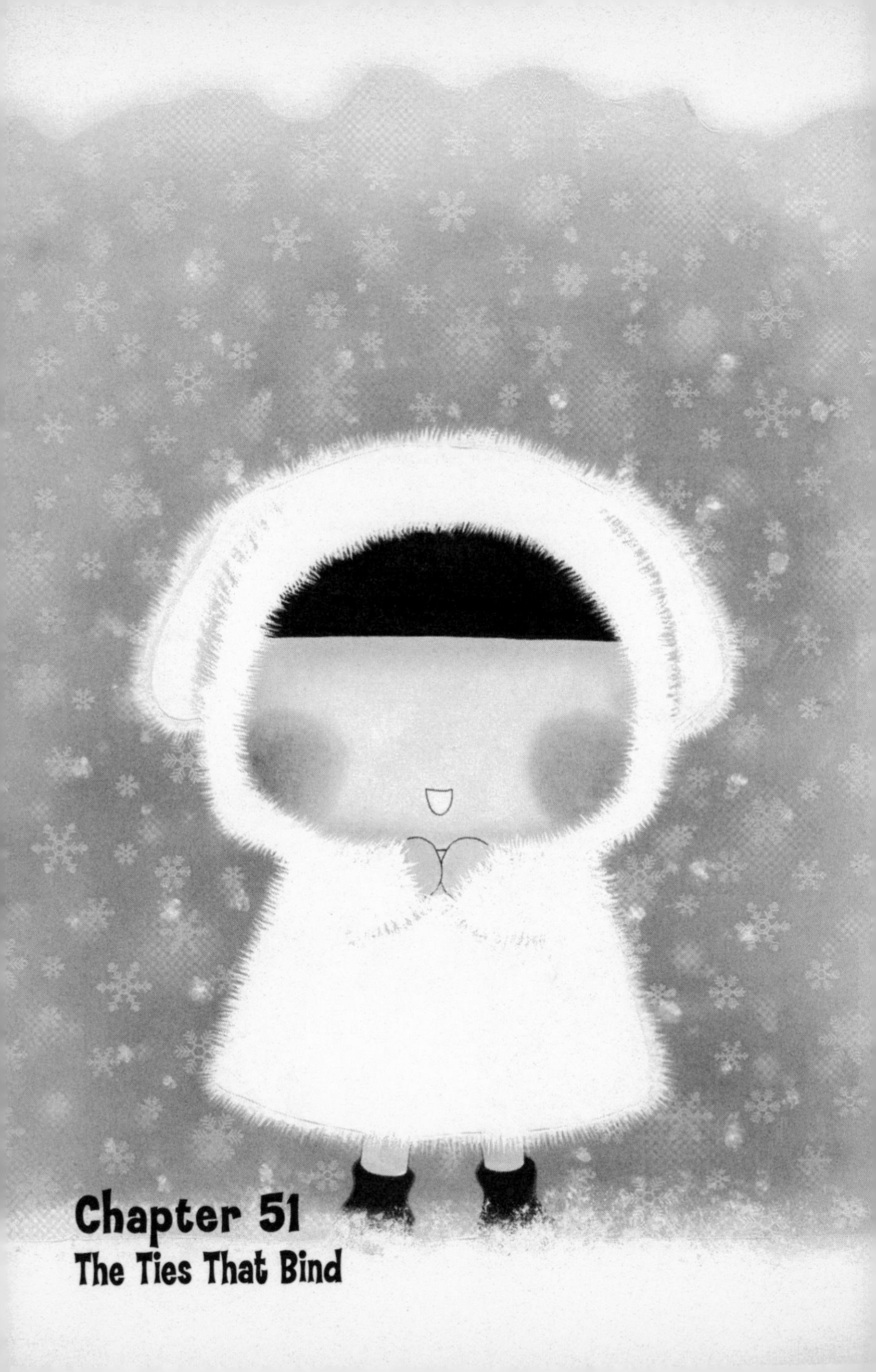

Chapter 51
The Ties That Bind

THE WALLFLOWER'S BEAUTIFUL CAST OF CHARACTERS (?)

SUNAKO IS A DARK LONER WHO LOVES HORROR MOVIES. WHEN HER AUNT, THE LANDLADY OF A BOARDINGHOUSE, LEAVES TOWN WITH HER BOYFRIEND, SUNAKO IS FORCED TO LIVE WITH FOUR HANDSOME GUYS. SUNAKO'S AUNT MAKES A DEAL WITH THE BOYS, WHICH CAUSES NOTHING BUT HEADACHES FOR SUNAKO: "MAKE SUNAKO INTO A LADY, AND YOU CAN LIVE RENT FREE."

SUNAKO HAS BEEN LIVING HER LIFE AT HER OWN PACE AS THE FOUR GUYS LOOK ON. EVEN SUNAKO'S AUNT, THE LANDLADY, HAS LEARNED OF SUNAKO'S LIFE OF DARKNESS. THE CHANCES OF SUNAKO ACTUALLY BECOMING A "LADY" SEEM TO BE GROWING SLIMMER BY THE DAY.

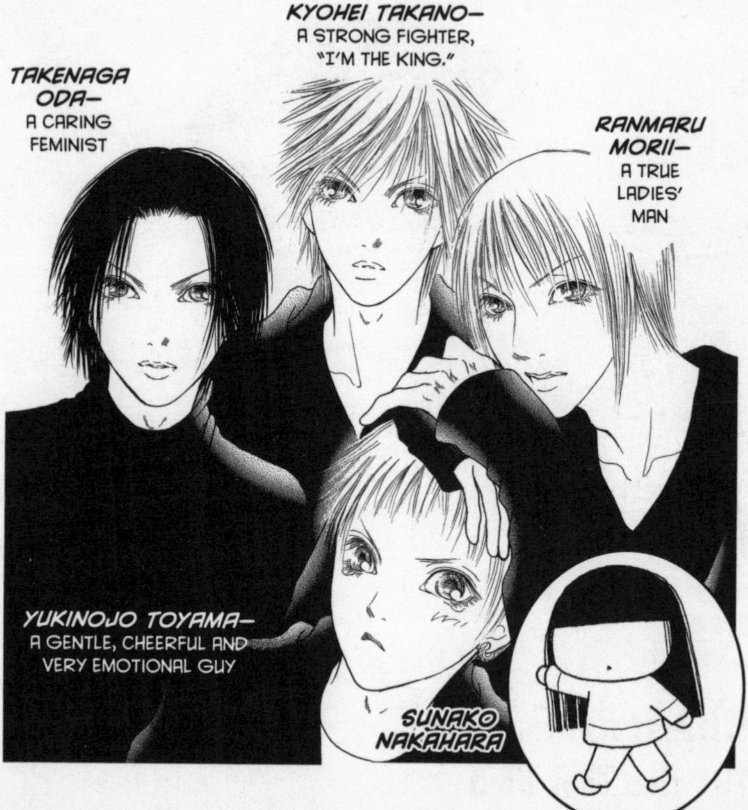
KYOHEI TAKANO— A STRONG FIGHTER, "I'M THE KING."
TAKENAGA ODA— A CARING FEMINIST
RANMARU MORII— A TRUE LADIES' MAN
YUKINOJO TOYAMA— A GENTLE, CHEERFUL AND VERY EMOTIONAL GUY
SUNAKO NAKAHARA

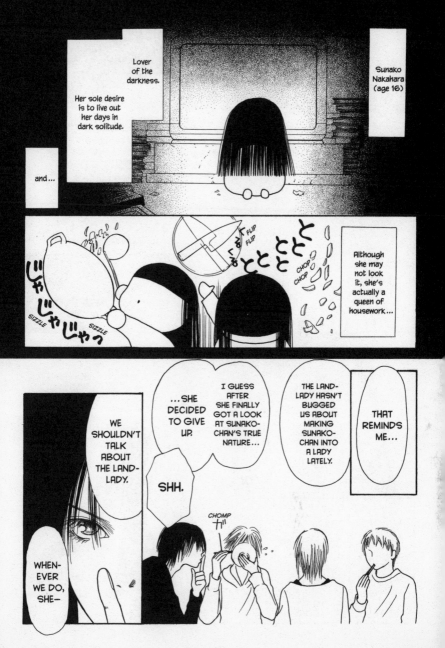

Sunako Nakahara (age 16)
Lover of the darkness.
Her sole desire is to live out her days in dark solitude.
and...
Although she may not look it, she's actually a queen of housework...
とととと
CHOP CHOP
FLIP FLIP
じゃじゃじゃっ
SIZZLE SIZZLE
THAT REMINDS ME...
THE LAND-LADY HASN'T BUGGED US ABOUT MAKING SUNAKO-CHAN INTO A LADY LATELY.
I GUESS AFTER SHE FINALLY GOT A LOOK AT SUNAKO-CHAN'S TRUE NATURE...
...SHE DECIDED TO GIVE UP.
SHH.
WE SHOULDN'T TALK ABOUT THE LAND-LADY.
CHOMP
ガ
WHEN-EVER WE DO, SHE—

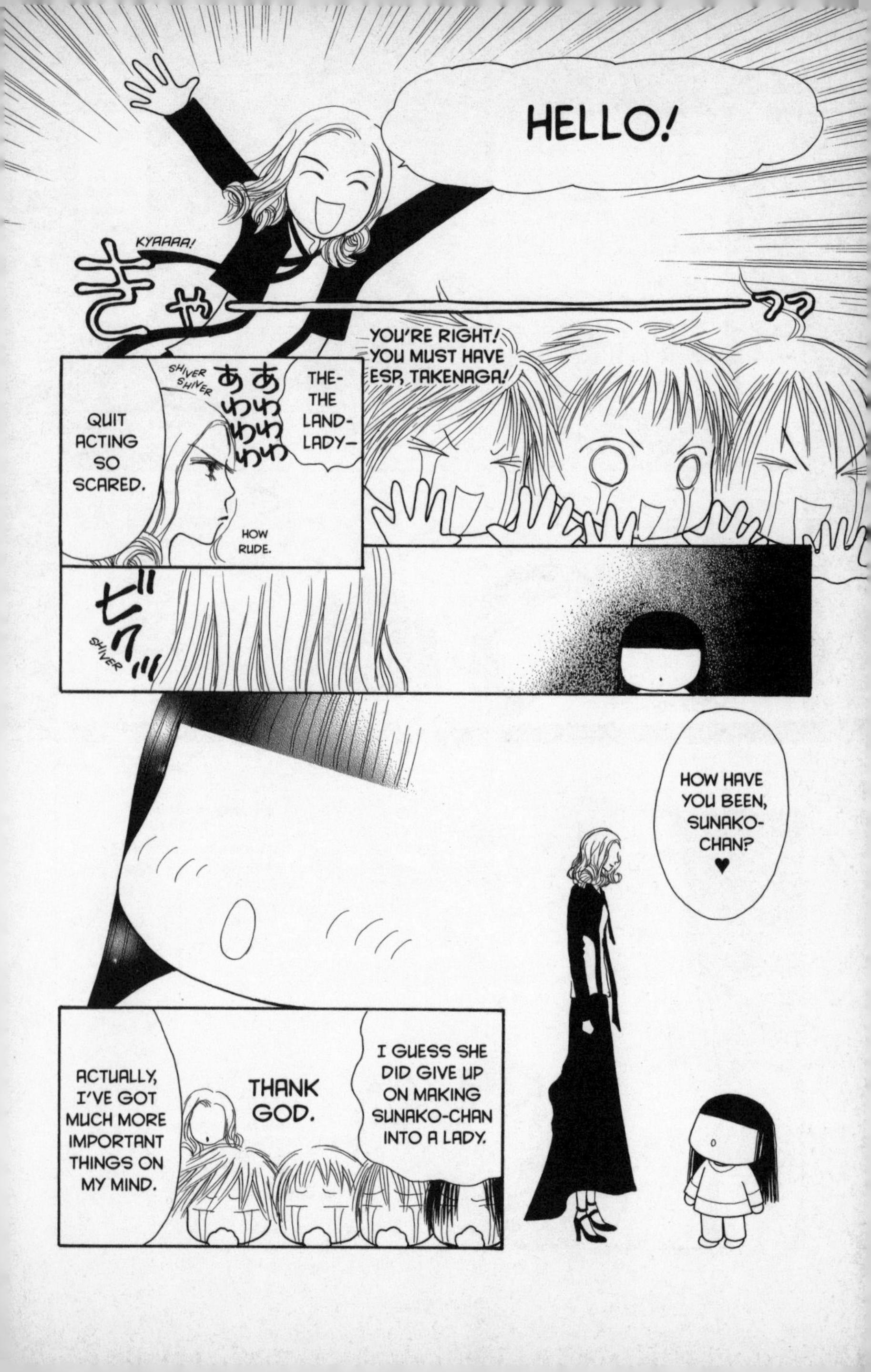
HELLO!
KYAAAA!
YOU'RE RIGHT! YOU MUST HAVE ESP, TAKENAGA!
THE- THE LAND-LADY—
SHIVER SHIVER
QUIT ACTING SO SCARED.
HOW RUDE.
SHIVER
HOW HAVE YOU BEEN, SUNAKO-CHAN? ♥
I GUESS SHE DID GIVE UP ON MAKING SUNAKO-CHAN INTO A LADY.
THANK GOD.
ACTUALLY, I'VE GOT MUCH MORE IMPORTANT THINGS ON MY MIND.

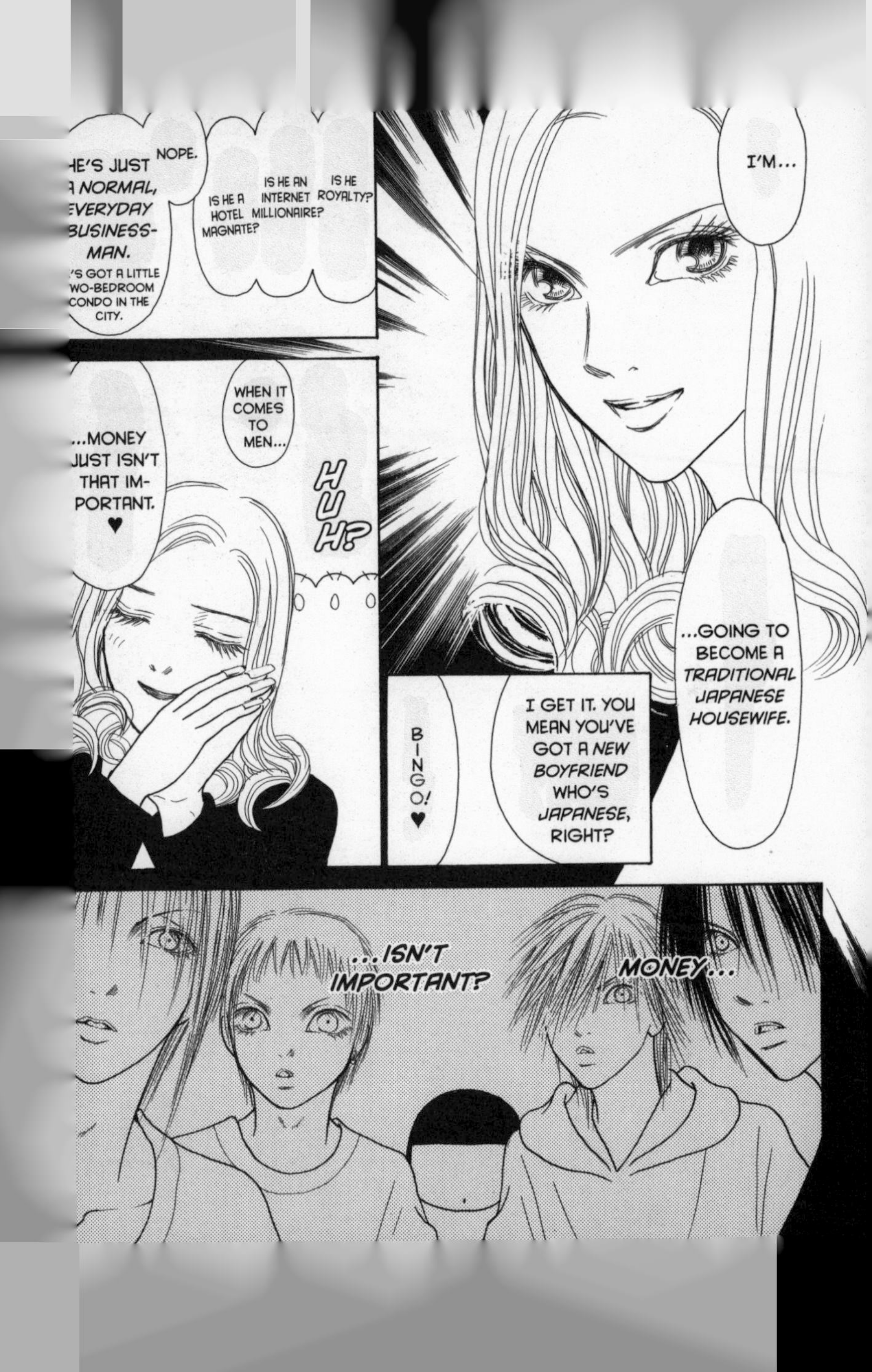
I'M...
...GOING TO BECOME A TRADITIONAL JAPANESE HOUSEWIFE.
I GET IT. YOU MEAN YOU'VE GOT A NEW BOYFRIEND WHO'S JAPANESE, RIGHT?
BINGO! ♥
IS HE ROYALTY?
IS HE AN INTERNET MILLIONAIRE?
IS HE A HOTEL MAGNATE?
NOPE.
HE'S JUST A NORMAL, EVERYDAY BUSINESS-MAN.
'S GOT A LITTLE WO-BEDROOM CONDO IN THE CITY.
WHEN IT COMES TO MEN...
...MONEY JUST ISN'T THAT IM-PORTANT. ♥
HUH?
MONEY...
...ISN'T IMPORTANT?

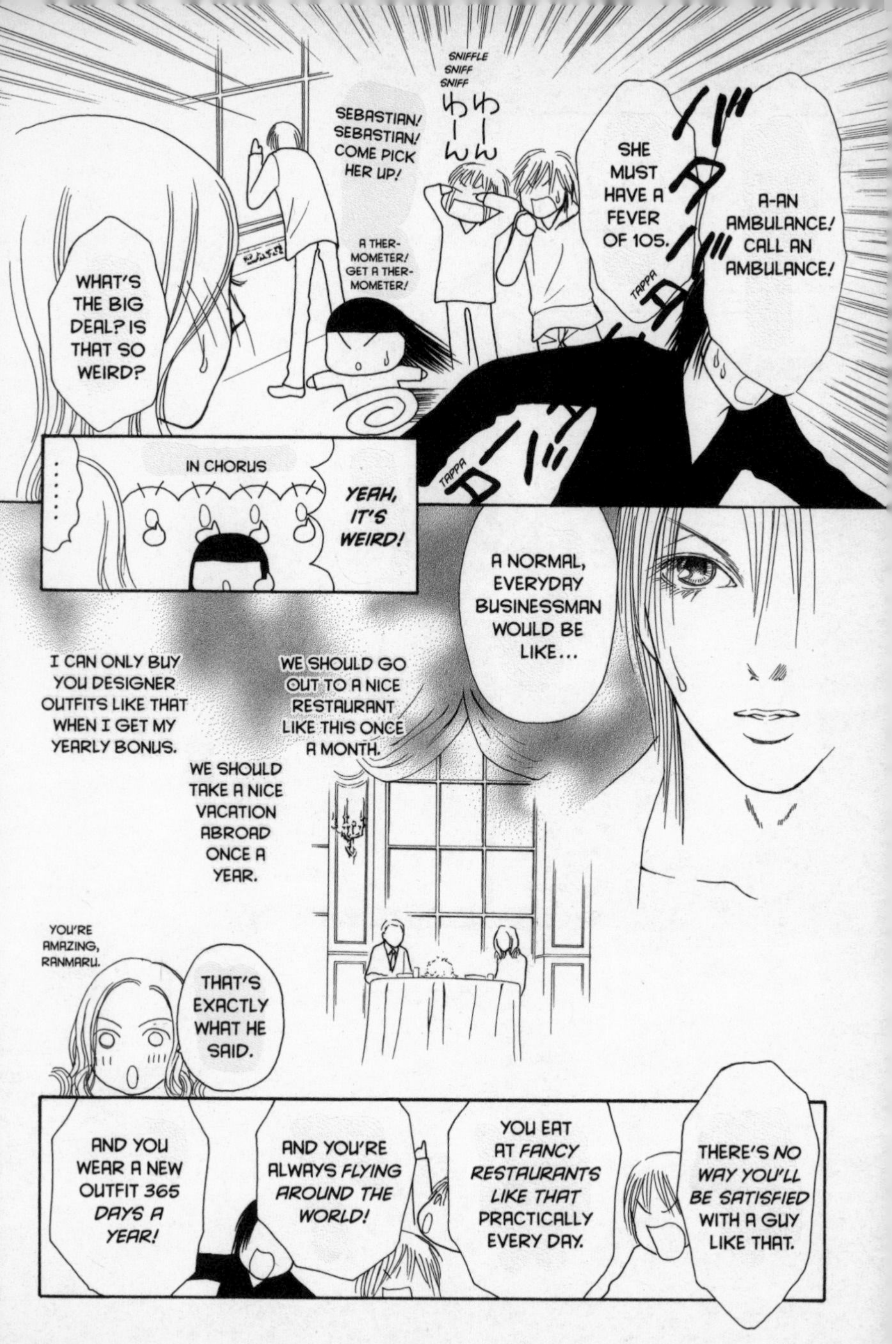
A-AN AMBULANCE! CALL AN AMBULANCE!
SHE MUST HAVE A FEVER OF 105.
TAPPA
TAPPA
SNIFFLE SNIFF SNIFF
わーん わーん
SEBASTIAN! SEBASTIAN! COME PICK HER UP!
A THERMOMETER! GET A THERMOMETER!
WHAT'S THE BIG DEAL? IS THAT SO WEIRD?
YEAH, IT'S WEIRD!
IN CHORUS
......
A NORMAL, EVERYDAY BUSINESSMAN WOULD BE LIKE...
WE SHOULD GO OUT TO A NICE RESTAURANT LIKE THIS ONCE A MONTH.
I CAN ONLY BUY YOU DESIGNER OUTFITS LIKE THAT WHEN I GET MY YEARLY BONUS.
WE SHOULD TAKE A NICE VACATION ABROAD ONCE A YEAR.
THAT'S EXACTLY WHAT HE SAID.
YOU'RE AMAZING, RANMARU.
THERE'S NO WAY YOU'LL BE SATISFIED WITH A GUY LIKE THAT.
YOU EAT AT FANCY RESTAURANTS LIKE THAT PRACTICALLY EVERY DAY.
AND YOU'RE ALWAYS FLYING AROUND THE WORLD!
AND YOU WEAR A NEW OUTFIT 365 DAYS A YEAR!

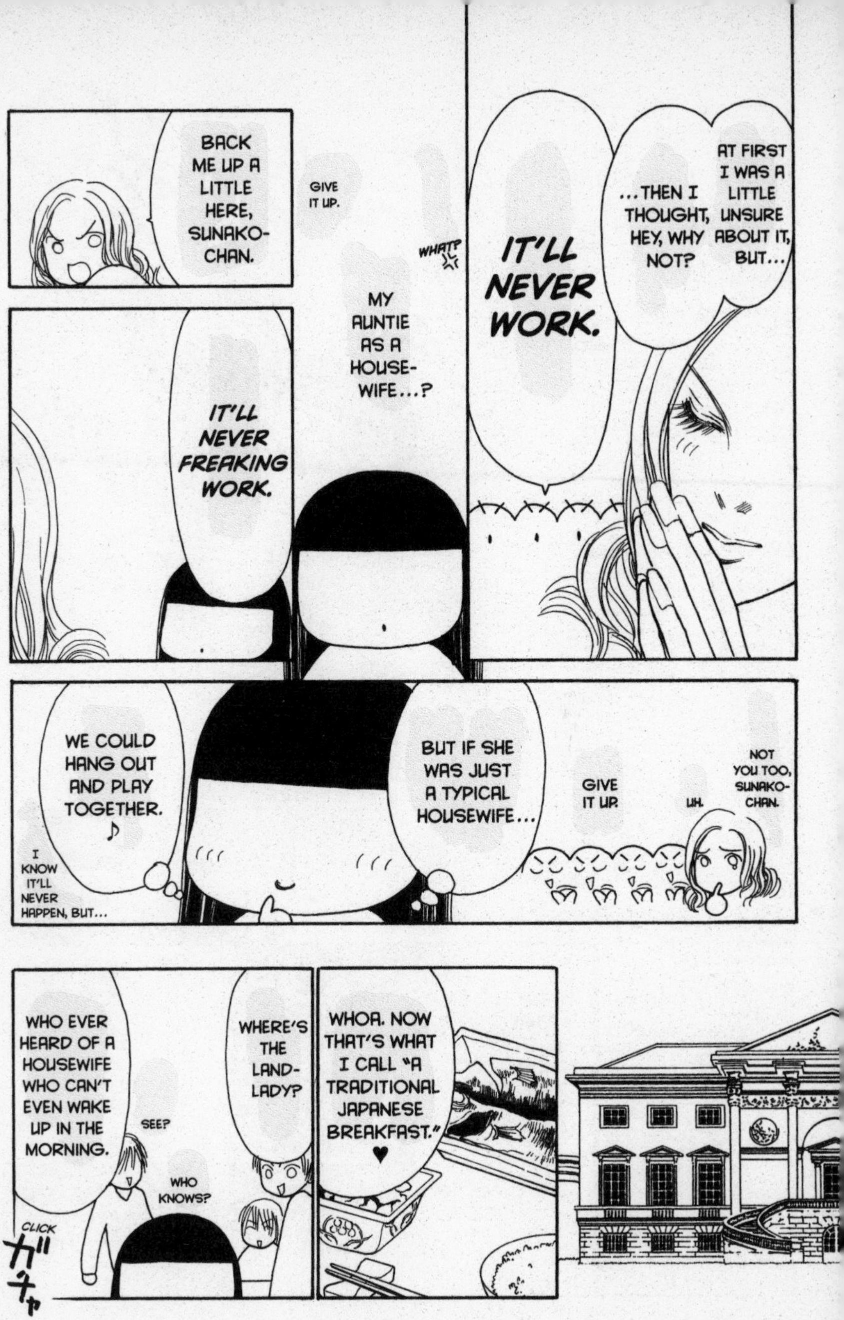
AT FIRST I WAS A LITTLE UNSURE ABOUT IT, BUT...
...THEN I THOUGHT, HEY, WHY NOT?
IT'LL NEVER WORK.
WHAT?!
BACK ME UP A LITTLE HERE, SUNAKO-CHAN.
GIVE IT UP.
MY AUNTIE AS A HOUSE-WIFE...?
IT'LL NEVER FREAKING WORK.
NOT YOU TOO, SUNAKO-CHAN.
UH.
GIVE IT UP.
BUT IF SHE WAS JUST A TYPICAL HOUSEWIFE...
WE COULD HANG OUT AND PLAY TOGETHER. ♪
I KNOW IT'LL NEVER HAPPEN, BUT...
WHOA. NOW THAT'S WHAT I CALL "A TRADITIONAL JAPANESE BREAKFAST." ♥
WHERE'S THE LAND-LADY?
WHO EVER HEARD OF A HOUSEWIFE WHO CAN'T EVEN WAKE UP IN THE MORNING.
SEE?
WHO KNOWS?
CLICK
ガチャ

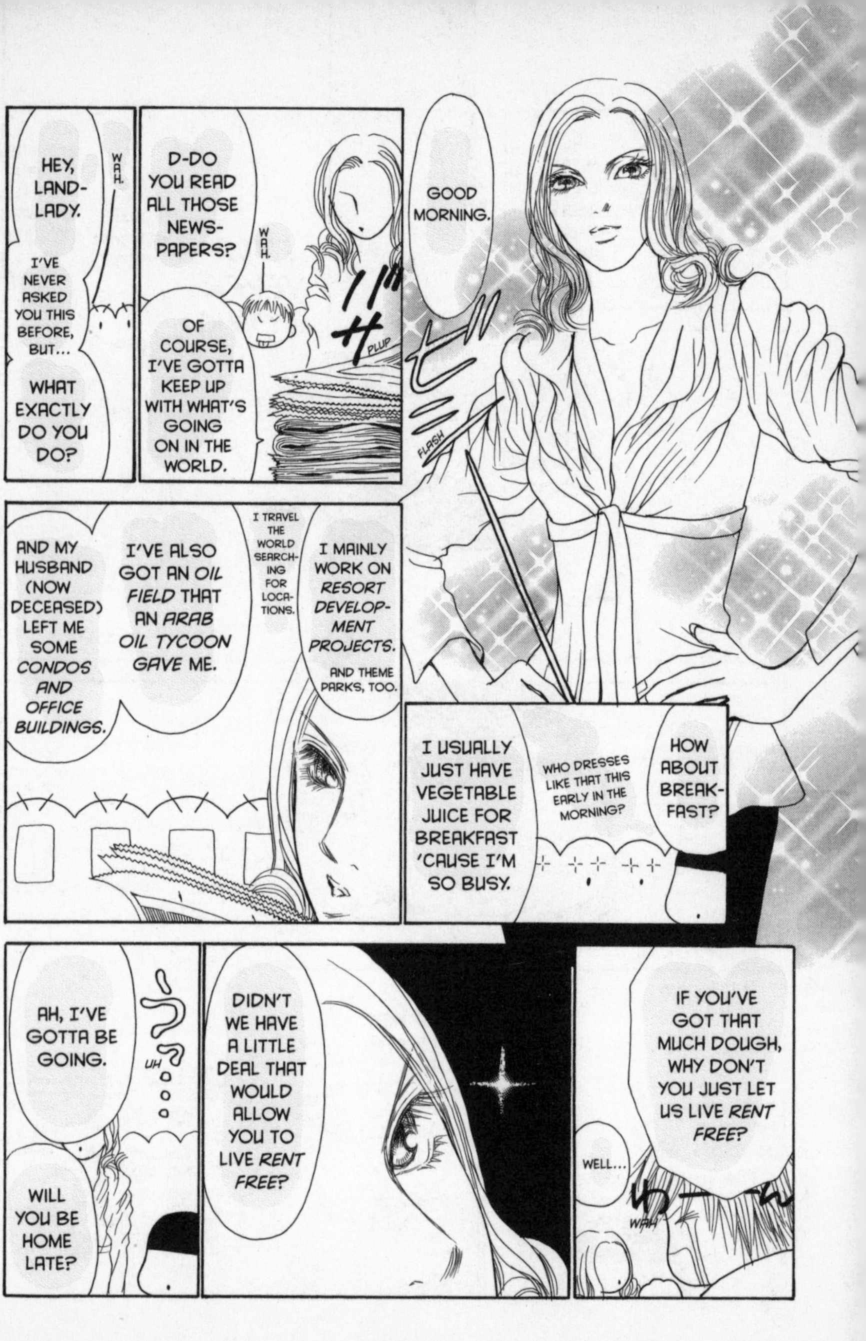
GOOD MORNING.
FLASH
D-DO YOU READ ALL THOSE NEWS-PAPERS?
WAH.
PLUP
OF COURSE, I'VE GOTTA KEEP UP WITH WHAT'S GOING ON IN THE WORLD.
HEY, LAND-LADY.
WAH.
I'VE NEVER ASKED YOU THIS BEFORE, BUT...
WHAT EXACTLY DO YOU DO?
HOW ABOUT BREAK-FAST?
WHO DRESSES LIKE THAT THIS EARLY IN THE MORNING?
I USUALLY JUST HAVE VEGETABLE JUICE FOR BREAKFAST 'CAUSE I'M SO BUSY.
I MAINLY WORK ON *RESORT DEVELOP-MENT PROJECTS.*
AND THEME PARKS, TOO.
I TRAVEL THE WORLD SEARCH-ING FOR LOCA-TIONS.
I'VE ALSO GOT AN *OIL FIELD* THAT AN *ARAB OIL TYCOON GAVE* ME.
AND MY HUSBAND (NOW DECEASED) LEFT ME SOME *CONDOS AND OFFICE BUILDINGS.*
IF YOU'VE GOT THAT MUCH DOUGH, WHY DON'T YOU JUST LET US LIVE *RENT FREE?*
WELL...
WAH
DIDN'T WE HAVE A LITTLE DEAL THAT WOULD ALLOW YOU TO LIVE *RENT FREE?*
AH, I'VE GOTTA BE GOING.
UH
WILL YOU BE HOME LATE?

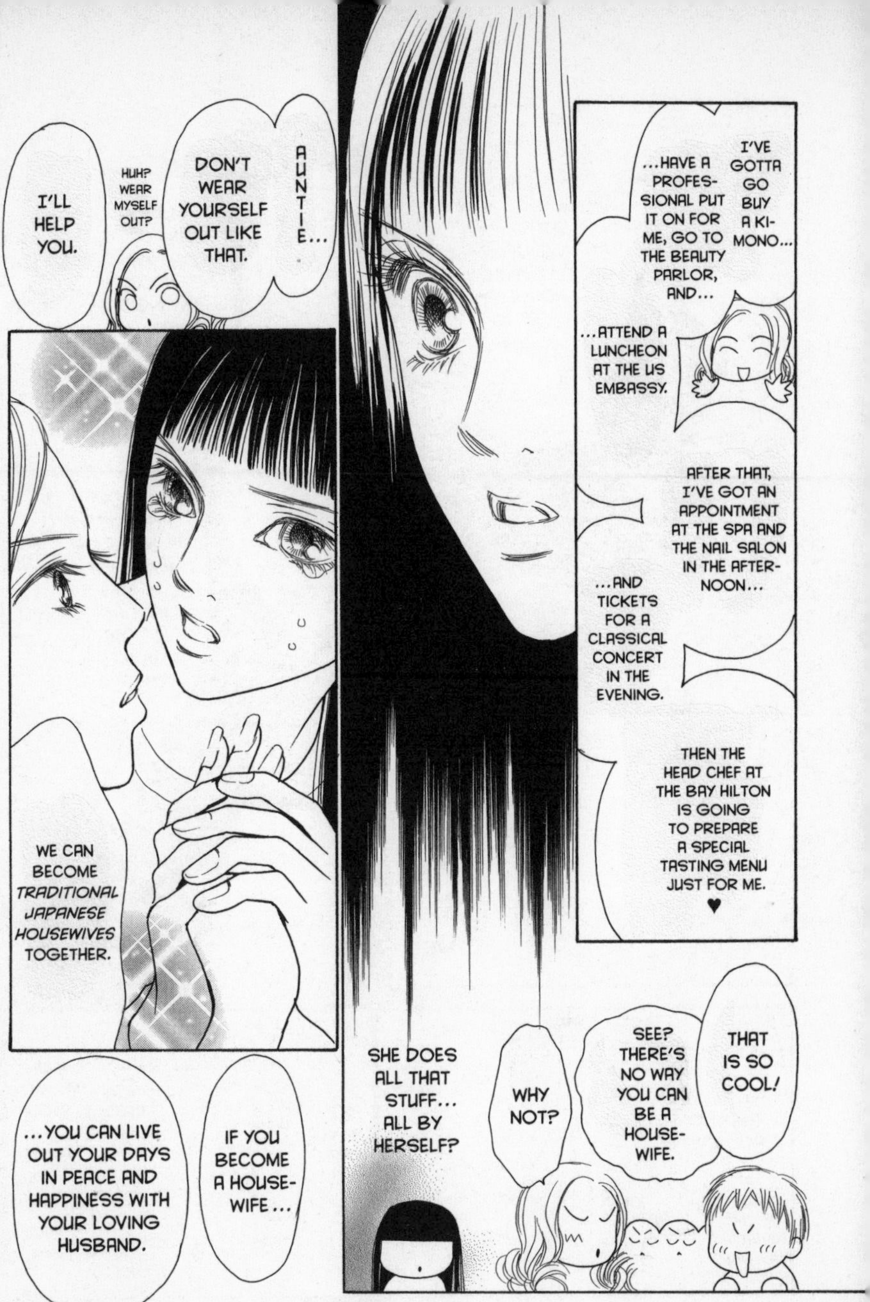
I'VE GOTTA GO BUY A KI-MONO...
...HAVE A PROFES-SIONAL PUT IT ON FOR ME, GO TO THE BEAUTY PARLOR, AND...
...ATTEND A LUNCHEON AT THE US EMBASSY.
AFTER THAT, I'VE GOT AN APPOINTMENT AT THE SPA AND THE NAIL SALON IN THE AFTER-NOON...
...AND TICKETS FOR A CLASSICAL CONCERT IN THE EVENING.
THEN THE HEAD CHEF AT THE BAY HILTON IS GOING TO PREPARE A SPECIAL TASTING MENU JUST FOR ME. ♥
THAT IS SO COOL!
SEE? THERE'S NO WAY YOU CAN BE A HOUSE-WIFE.
WHY NOT?
SHE DOES ALL THAT STUFF... ALL BY HERSELF?
AUNTIE...
DON'T WEAR YOURSELF OUT LIKE THAT.
HUH? WEAR MYSELF OUT?
I'LL HELP YOU.
WE CAN BECOME *TRADITIONAL JAPANESE HOUSEWIVES* TOGETHER.
IF YOU BECOME A HOUSE-WIFE...
...YOU CAN LIVE OUT YOUR DAYS IN PEACE AND HAPPINESS WITH YOUR LOVING HUSBAND.

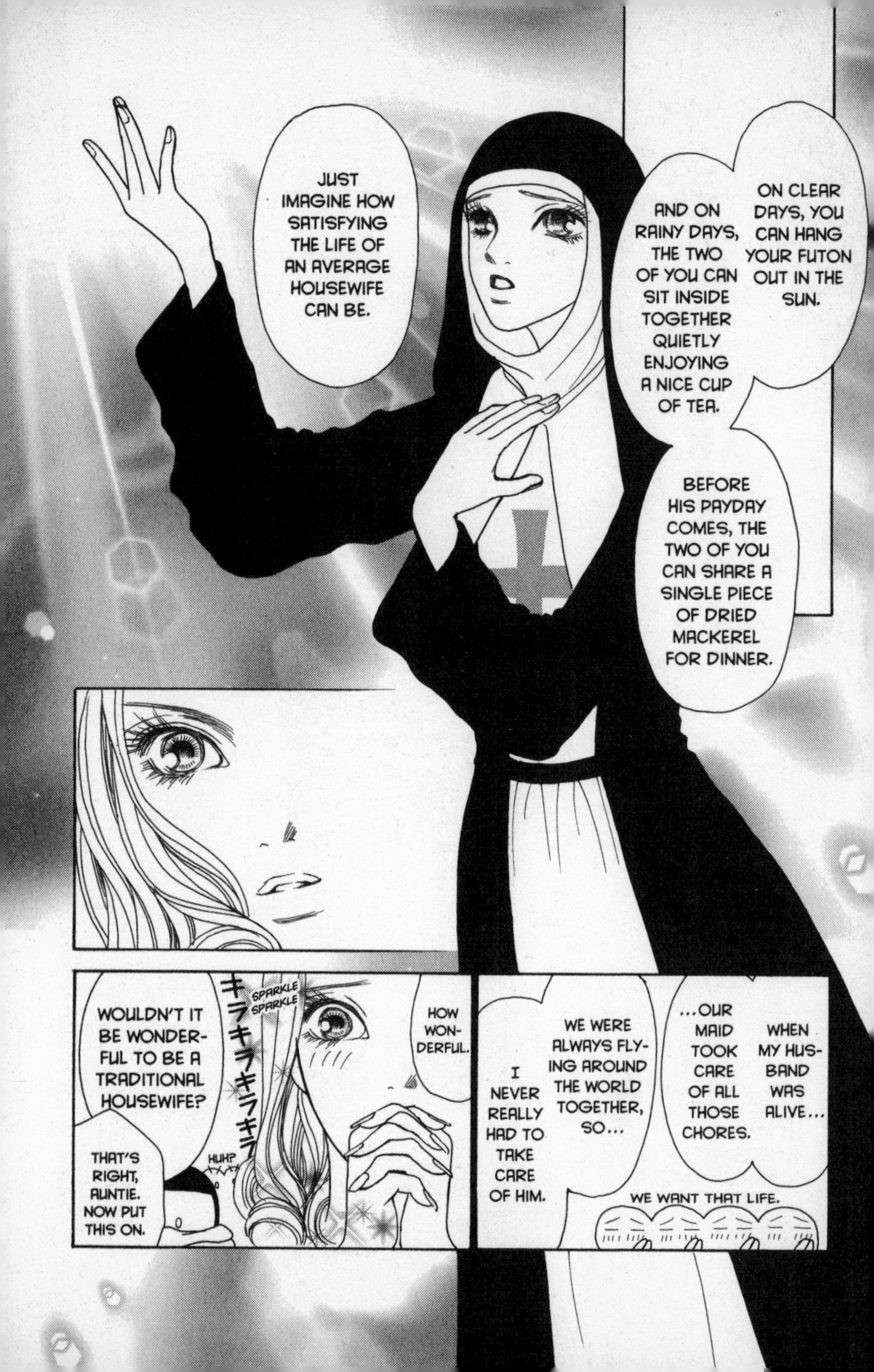
ON CLEAR DAYS, YOU CAN HANG YOUR FUTON OUT IN THE SUN.
AND ON RAINY DAYS, THE TWO OF YOU CAN SIT INSIDE TOGETHER QUIETLY ENJOYING A NICE CUP OF TEA.
JUST IMAGINE HOW SATISFYING THE LIFE OF AN AVERAGE HOUSEWIFE CAN BE.
BEFORE HIS PAYDAY COMES, THE TWO OF YOU CAN SHARE A SINGLE PIECE OF DRIED MACKEREL FOR DINNER.
WHEN MY HUS-BAND WAS ALIVE...
...OUR MAID TOOK CARE OF ALL THOSE CHORES.
WE WERE ALWAYS FLY-ING AROUND THE WORLD TOGETHER, SO...
I NEVER REALLY HAD TO TAKE CARE OF HIM.
WE WANT THAT LIFE.
HOW WON-DERFUL.
キラキラキラキラ
SPARKLE SPARKLE
WOULDN'T IT BE WONDER-FUL TO BE A TRADITIONAL HOUSEWIFE?
HUH?
THAT'S RIGHT, AUNTIE. NOW PUT THIS ON.

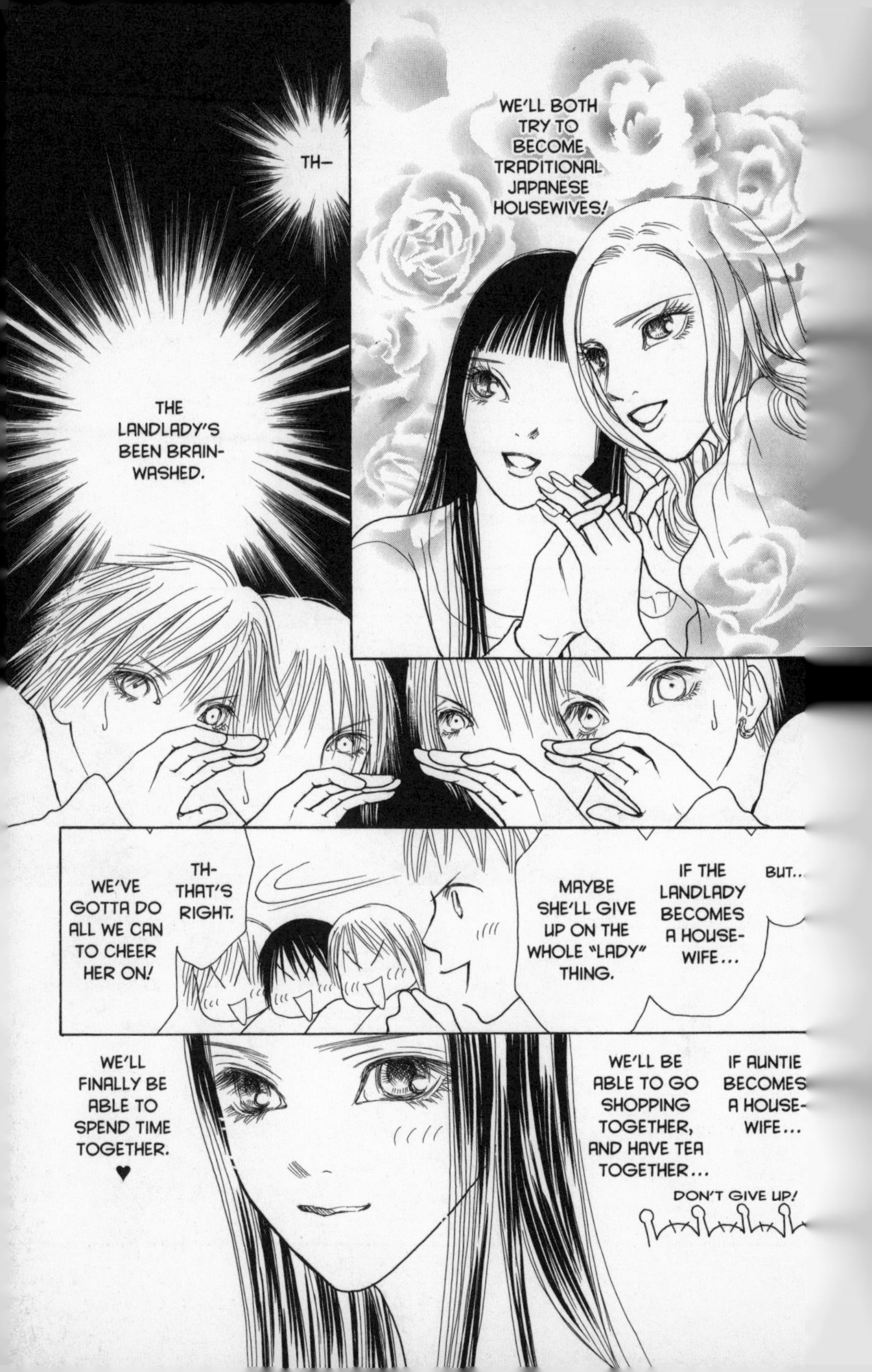
WE'LL BOTH TRY TO BECOME TRADITIONAL JAPANESE HOUSEWIVES!
TH—
THE LANDLADY'S BEEN BRAIN-WASHED.
BUT...
IF THE LANDLADY BECOMES A HOUSE-WIFE...
MAYBE SHE'LL GIVE UP ON THE WHOLE "LADY" THING.
TH-THAT'S RIGHT.
WE'VE GOTTA DO ALL WE CAN TO CHEER HER ON!
IF AUNTIE BECOMES A HOUSE-WIFE...
WE'LL BE ABLE TO GO SHOPPING TOGETHER, AND HAVE TEA TOGETHER...
DON'T GIVE UP!
WE'LL FINALLY BE ABLE TO SPEND TIME TOGETHER. ♥

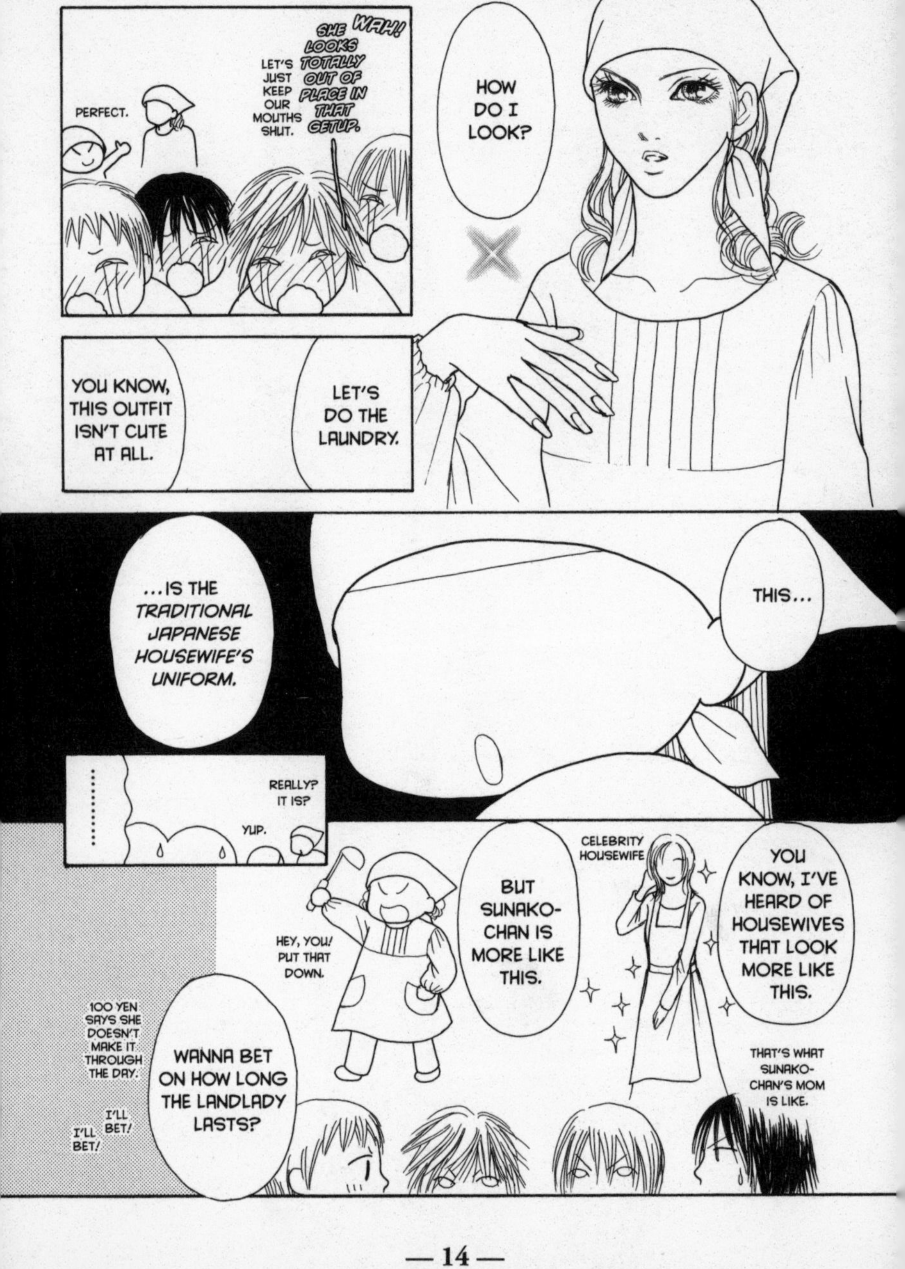
HOW DO I LOOK?
WAH! SHE LOOKS TOTALLY OUT OF PLACE IN THAT GETUP.
LET'S JUST KEEP OUR MOUTHS SHUT.
PERFECT.
LET'S DO THE LAUNDRY.
YOU KNOW, THIS OUTFIT ISN'T CUTE AT ALL.
THIS...
...IS THE *TRADITIONAL JAPANESE HOUSEWIFE'S UNIFORM.*
REALLY? IT IS?
YUP.
....
YOU KNOW, I'VE HEARD OF HOUSEWIVES THAT LOOK MORE LIKE THIS.
CELEBRITY HOUSEWIFE
BUT SUNAKO-CHAN IS MORE LIKE THIS.
HEY, YOU! PUT THAT DOWN.
THAT'S WHAT SUNAKO-CHAN'S MOM IS LIKE.
WANNA BET ON HOW LONG THE LANDLADY LASTS?
100 YEN SAYS SHE DOESN'T MAKE IT THROUGH THE DAY.
I'LL BET!
I'LL BET!

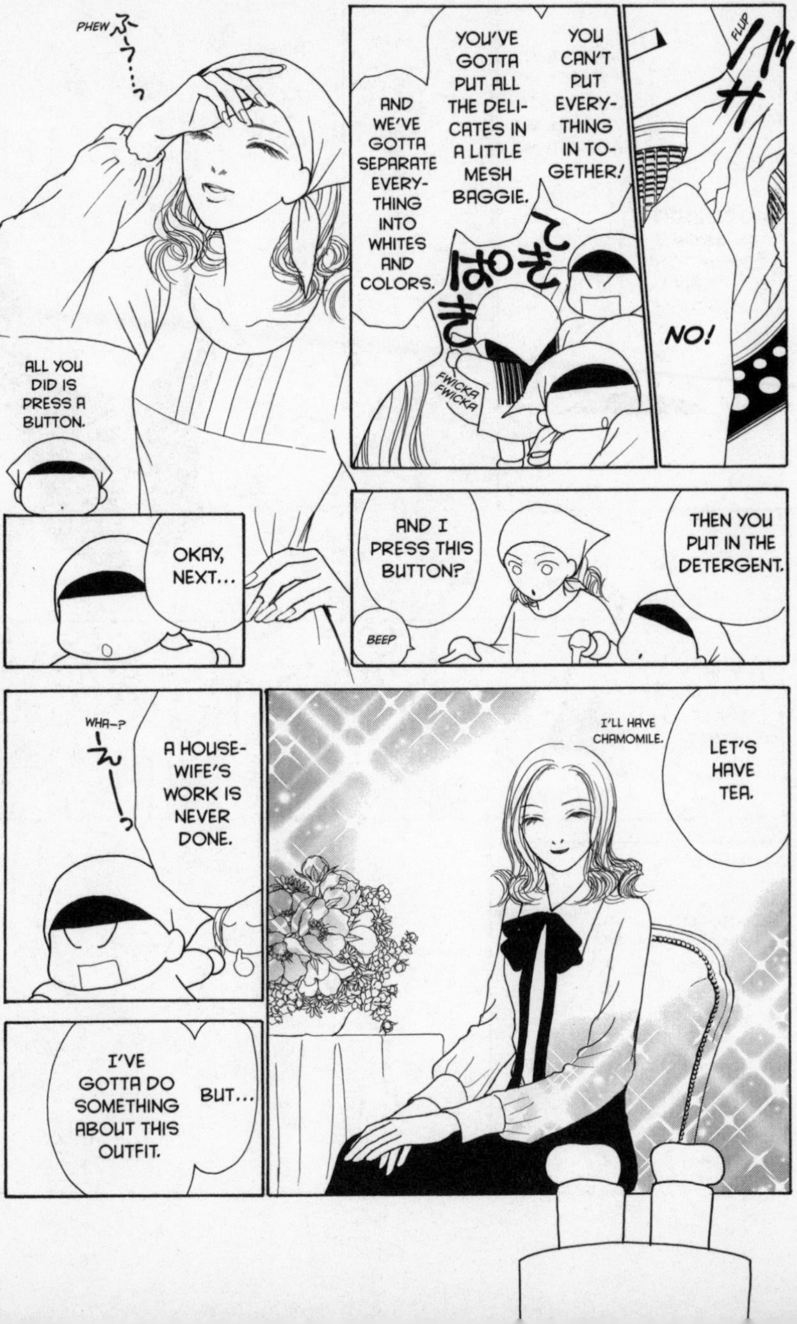
FLUP
NO!
YOU CAN'T PUT EVERYTHING IN TOGETHER!
YOU'VE GOTTA PUT ALL THE DELICATES IN A LITTLE MESH BAGGIE.
AND WE'VE GOTTA SEPARATE EVERYTHING INTO WHITES AND COLORS.
FWICKA FWICKA
PHEW
ALL YOU DID IS PRESS A BUTTON.
THEN YOU PUT IN THE DETERGENT.
AND I PRESS THIS BUTTON?
BEEP
OKAY, NEXT...
LET'S HAVE TEA.
I'LL HAVE CHAMOMILE.
WHA-?
A HOUSEWIFE'S WORK IS NEVER DONE.
BUT...
I'VE GOTTA DO SOMETHING ABOUT THIS OUTFIT.

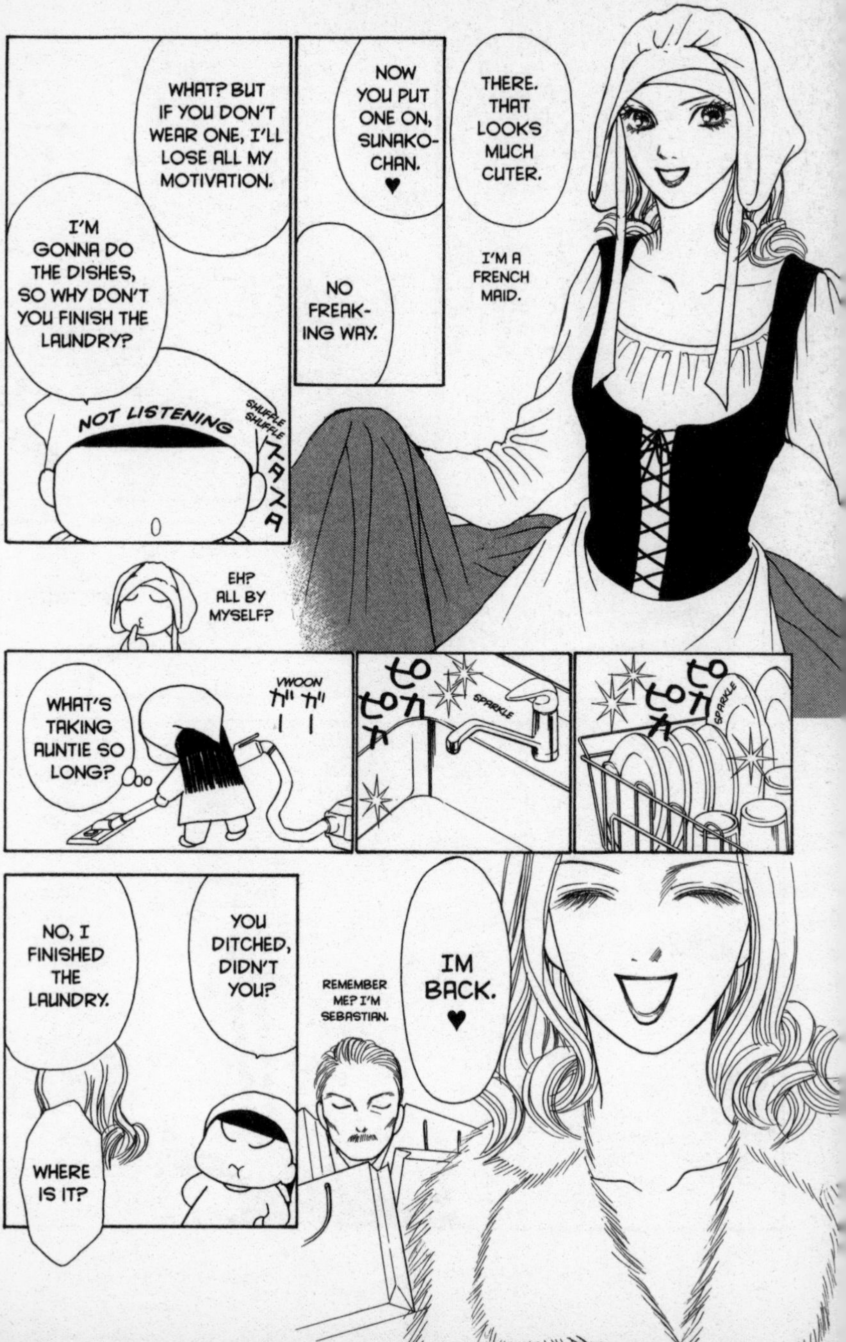
THERE. THAT LOOKS MUCH CUTER.
I'M A FRENCH MAID.
NOW YOU PUT ONE ON, SUNAKO-CHAN. ♥
NO FREAKING WAY.
WHAT? BUT IF YOU DON'T WEAR ONE, I'LL LOSE ALL MY MOTIVATION.
I'M GONNA DO THE DISHES, SO WHY DON'T YOU FINISH THE LAUNDRY?
NOT LISTENING
SHUFFLE SHUFFLE
スタスタ
EH? ALL BY MYSELF?
ピカピカ
SPARKLE
ピカピカ
SPARKLE
VWOON
ガーガー
WHAT'S TAKING AUNTIE SO LONG?
IM BACK. ♥
REMEMBER ME? I'M SEBASTIAN.
YOU DITCHED, DIDN'T YOU?
NO, I FINISHED THE LAUNDRY.
WHERE IS IT?

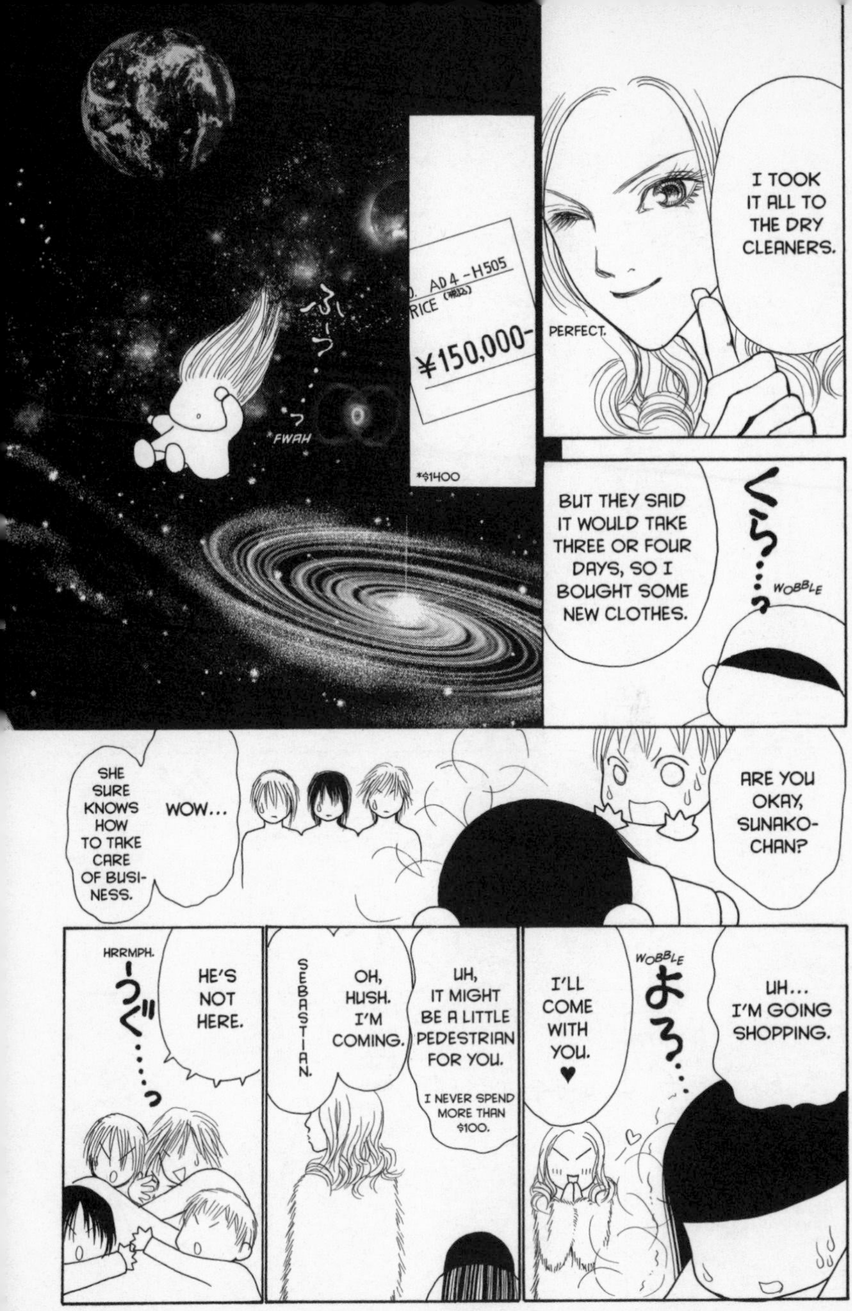
I TOOK IT ALL TO THE DRY CLEANERS.
PERFECT.
AD4-H505
¥150,000-
*$1400
BUT THEY SAID IT WOULD TAKE THREE OR FOUR DAYS, SO I BOUGHT SOME NEW CLOTHES.
くら…っ
WOBBLE
ふーっ
FWAH
ARE YOU OKAY, SUNAKO-CHAN?
WOW…
SHE SURE KNOWS HOW TO TAKE CARE OF BUSI-NESS.
UH… I'M GOING SHOPPING.
よろ…
WOBBLE
I'LL COME WITH YOU. ♥
UH, IT MIGHT BE A LITTLE PEDESTRIAN FOR YOU.
I NEVER SPEND MORE THAN $100.
OH, HUSH. I'M COMING.
SEBASTIAN.
HE'S NOT HERE.
うぐ…っ
HRRMPH.

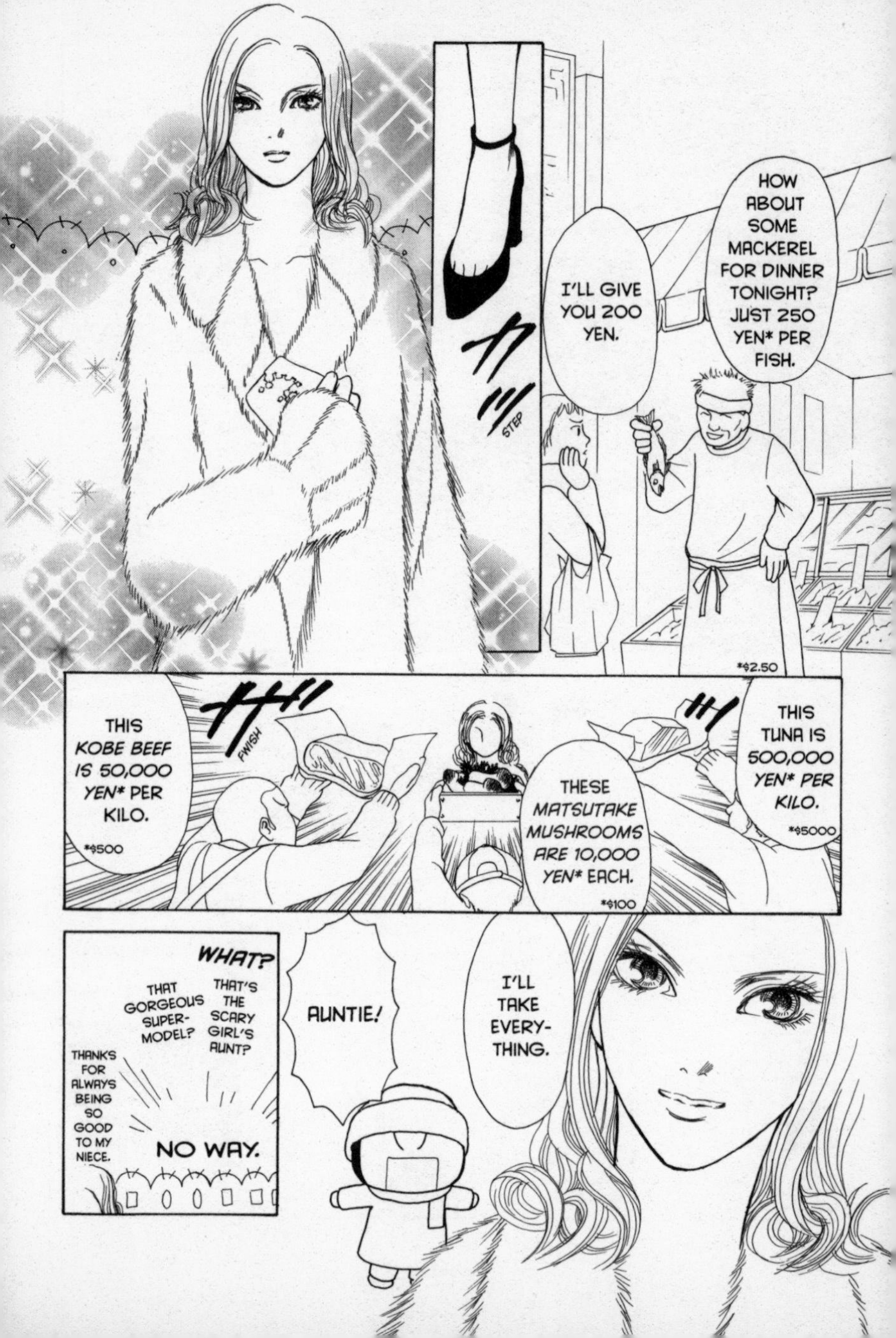
HOW ABOUT SOME MACKEREL FOR DINNER TONIGHT? JUST 250 YEN* PER FISH.
I'LL GIVE YOU 200 YEN.
*$2.50
STEP
THIS TUNA IS 500,000 YEN* PER KILO.
*$5000
THESE MATSUTAKE MUSHROOMS ARE 10,000 YEN* EACH.
*$100
FWISH
THIS KOBE BEEF IS 50,000 YEN* PER KILO.
*$500
I'LL TAKE EVERY-THING.
AUNTIE!
WHAT?
THAT'S THE SCARY GIRL'S AUNT?
THAT GORGEOUS SUPER-MODEL?
THANKS FOR ALWAYS BEING SO GOOD TO MY NIECE.
NO WAY.

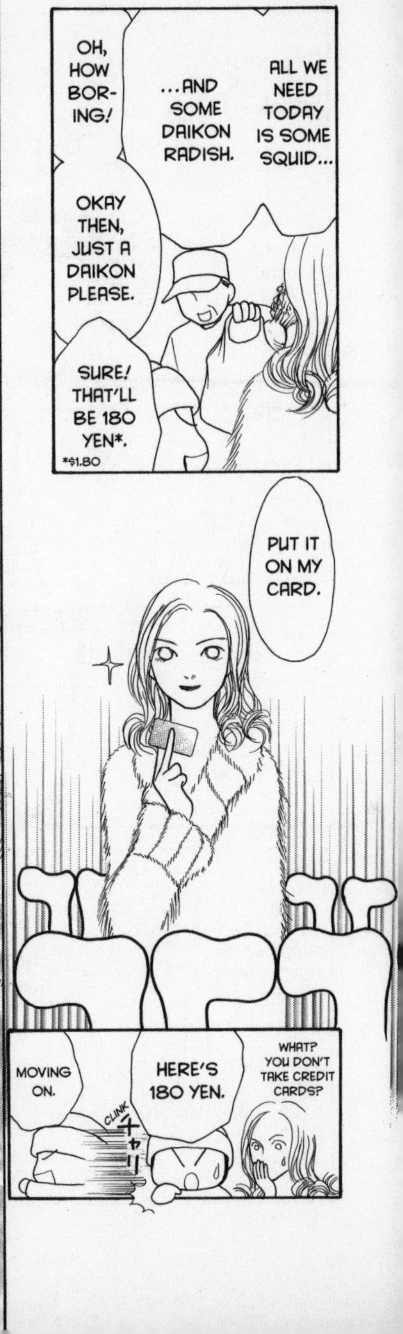
ALL WE NEED TODAY IS SOME SQUID...
...AND SOME DAIKON RADISH.
OH, HOW BOR-ING!
OKAY THEN, JUST A DAIKON PLEASE.
SURE! THAT'LL BE 180 YEN*.
*$1.80
PUT IT ON MY CARD.
WHAT? YOU DON'T TAKE CREDIT CARDS?
HERE'S 180 YEN.
CLINK
MOVING ON.
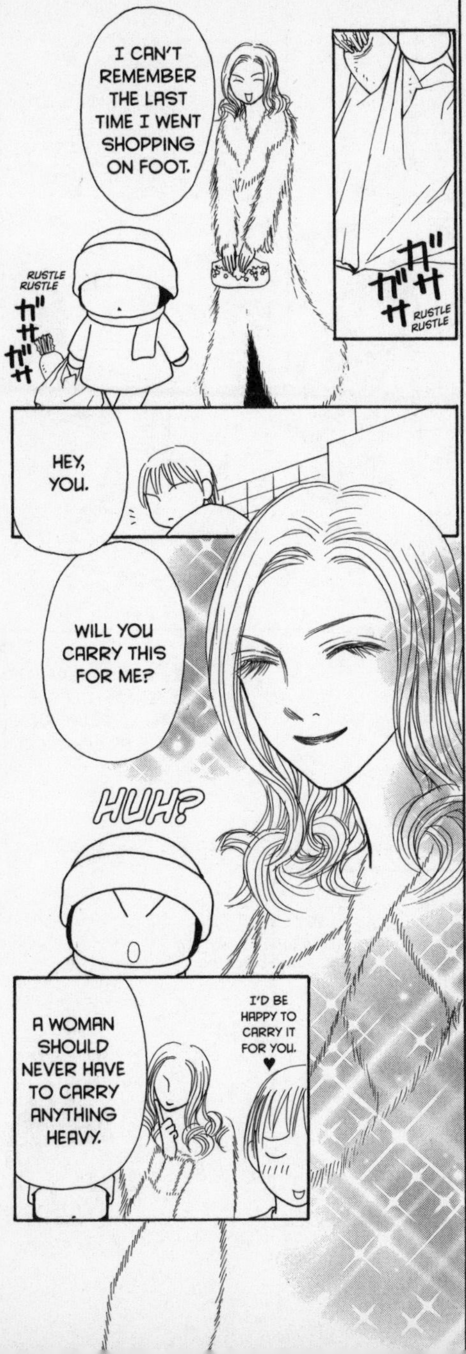
ガサガサ
RUSTLE RUSTLE
I CAN'T REMEMBER THE LAST TIME I WENT SHOPPING ON FOOT.
RUSTLE RUSTLE
ガサガサ
HEY, YOU.
WILL YOU CARRY THIS FOR ME?
HUH?
I'D BE HAPPY TO CARRY IT FOR YOU. ♥
A WOMAN SHOULD NEVER HAVE TO CARRY ANYTHING HEAVY.

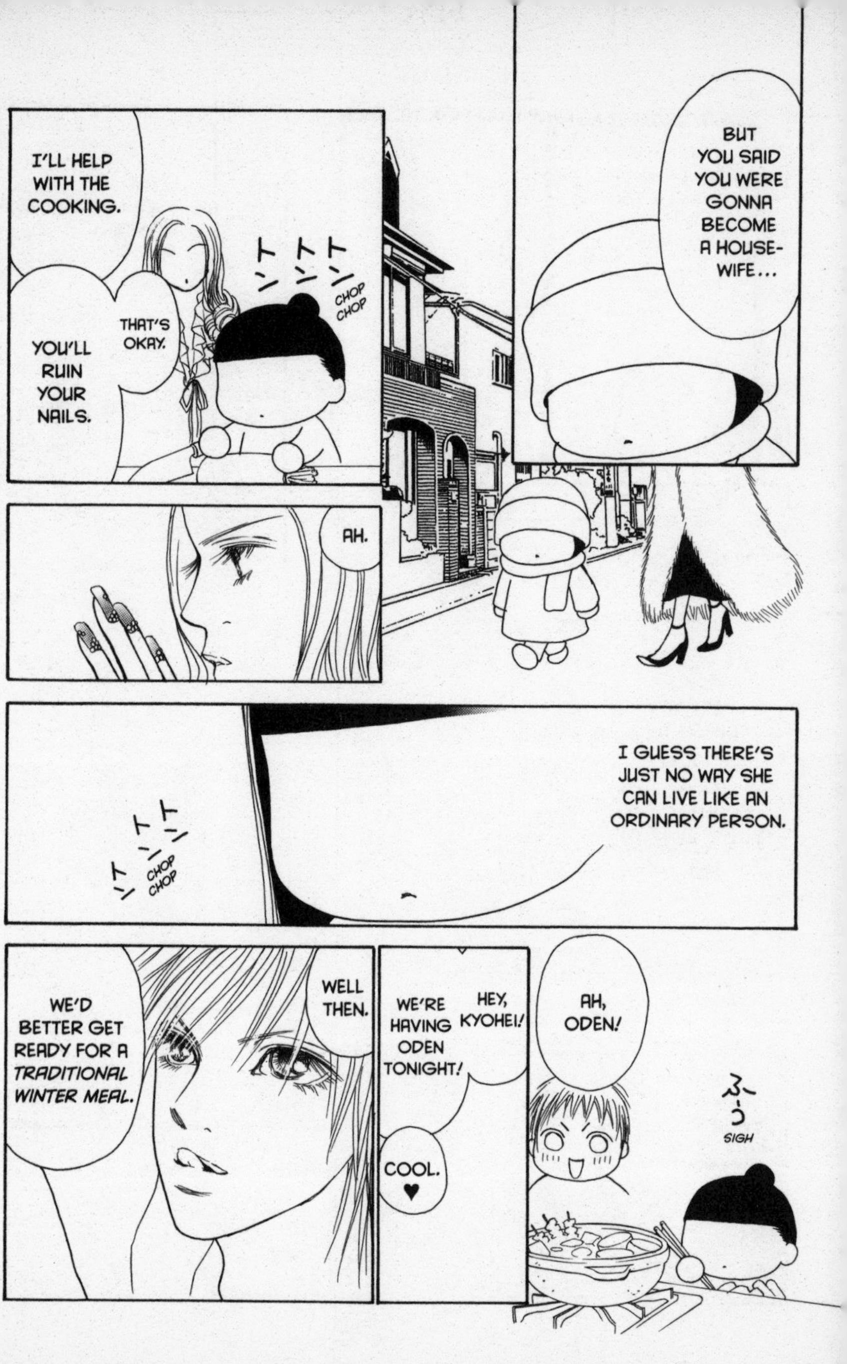
BUT YOU SAID YOU WERE GONNA BECOME A HOUSE-WIFE…
I'LL HELP WITH THE COOKING.
トントン
CHOP CHOP
THAT'S OKAY.
YOU'LL RUIN YOUR NAILS.
AH.
I GUESS THERE'S JUST NO WAY SHE CAN LIVE LIKE AN ORDINARY PERSON.
トントン
CHOP CHOP
AH, ODEN!
ふーっ
SIGH
HEY, KYOHEI!
WE'RE HAVING ODEN TONIGHT!
COOL. ♥
WELL THEN.
WE'D BETTER GET READY FOR A *TRADITIONAL* WINTER MEAL.

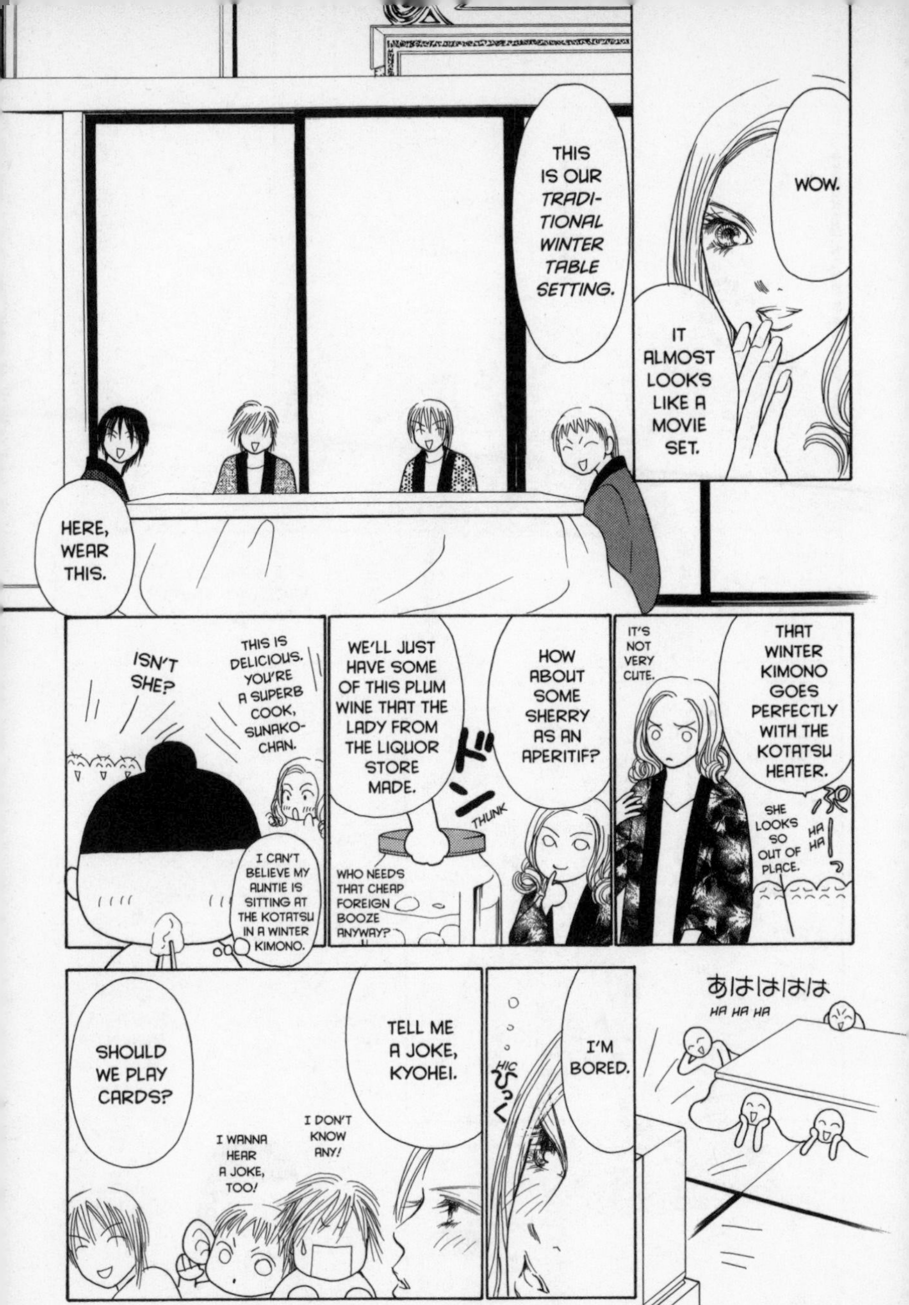
WOW.
IT ALMOST LOOKS LIKE A MOVIE SET.
THIS IS OUR TRADITIONAL WINTER TABLE SETTING.
HERE, WEAR THIS.
THAT WINTER KIMONO GOES PERFECTLY WITH THE KOTATSU HEATER.
IT'S NOT VERY CUTE.
SHE LOOKS SO OUT OF PLACE.
HA HA
HOW ABOUT SOME SHERRY AS AN APERITIF?
WE'LL JUST HAVE SOME OF THIS PLUM WINE THAT THE LADY FROM THE LIQUOR STORE MADE.
ドン
THUNK
WHO NEEDS THAT CHEAP FOREIGN BOOZE ANYWAY?
THIS IS DELICIOUS. YOU'RE A SUPERB COOK, SUNAKO-CHAN.
ISN'T SHE?
I CAN'T BELIEVE MY AUNTIE IS SITTING AT THE KOTATSU IN A WINTER KIMONO.
あははは
HA HA HA
I'M BORED.
ひっく
HIC
TELL ME A JOKE, KYOHEI.
I DON'T KNOW ANY!
I WANNA HEAR A JOKE, TOO!
SHOULD WE PLAY CARDS?

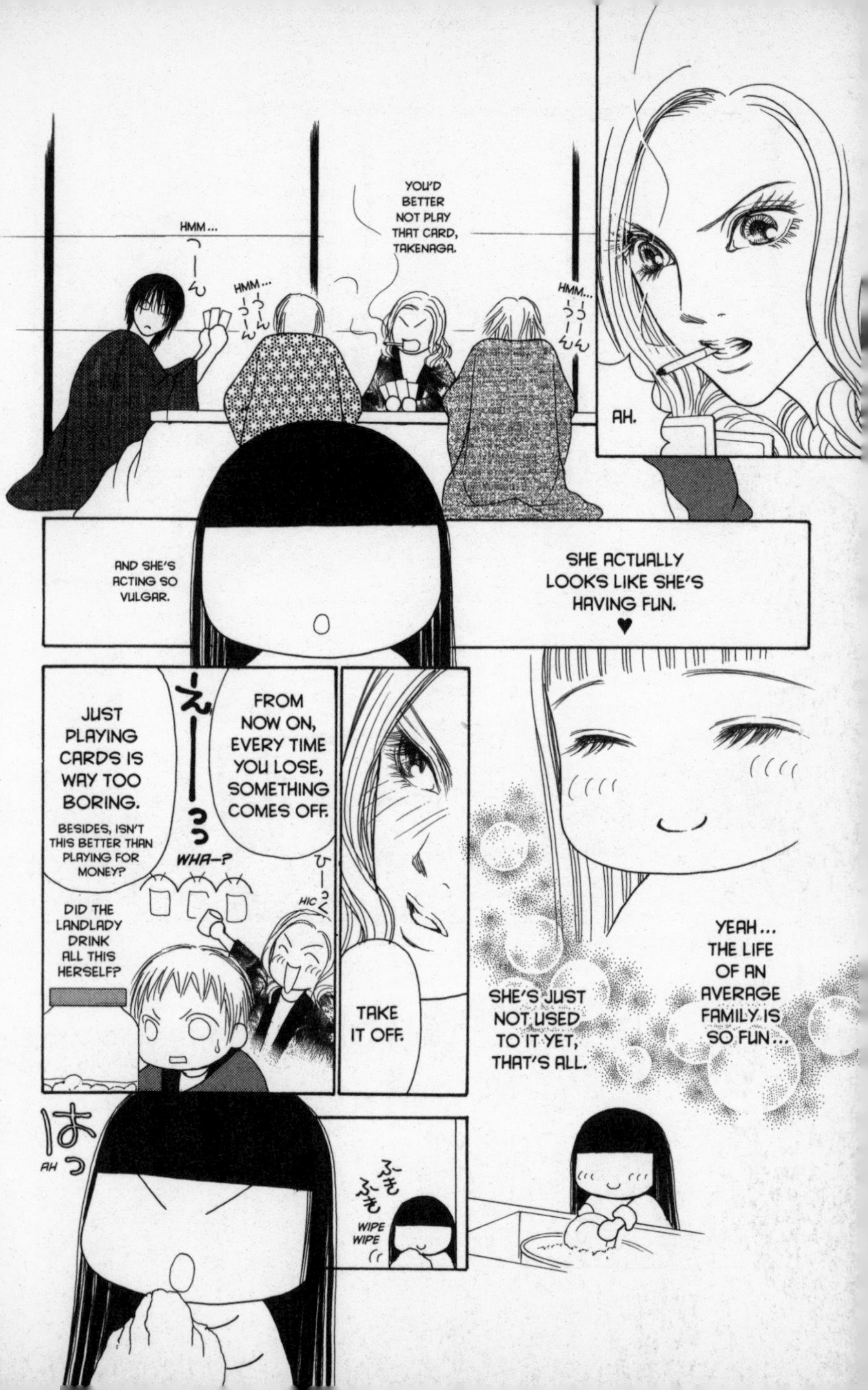
AH.
YOU'D BETTER NOT PLAY THAT CARD, TAKENAGA.
HMM...
HMM...
HMM...
SHE ACTUALLY LOOKS LIKE SHE'S HAVING FUN. ♥
AND SHE'S ACTING SO VULGAR.
YEAH... THE LIFE OF AN AVERAGE FAMILY IS SO FUN...
SHE'S JUST NOT USED TO IT YET, THAT'S ALL.
TAKE IT OFF.
FROM NOW ON, EVERY TIME YOU LOSE, SOMETHING COMES OFF.
JUST PLAYING CARDS IS WAY TOO BORING.
BESIDES, ISN'T THIS BETTER THAN PLAYING FOR MONEY?
WHA-?
HIC
DID THE LANDLADY DRINK ALL THIS HERSELF?
WIPE WIPE
AH

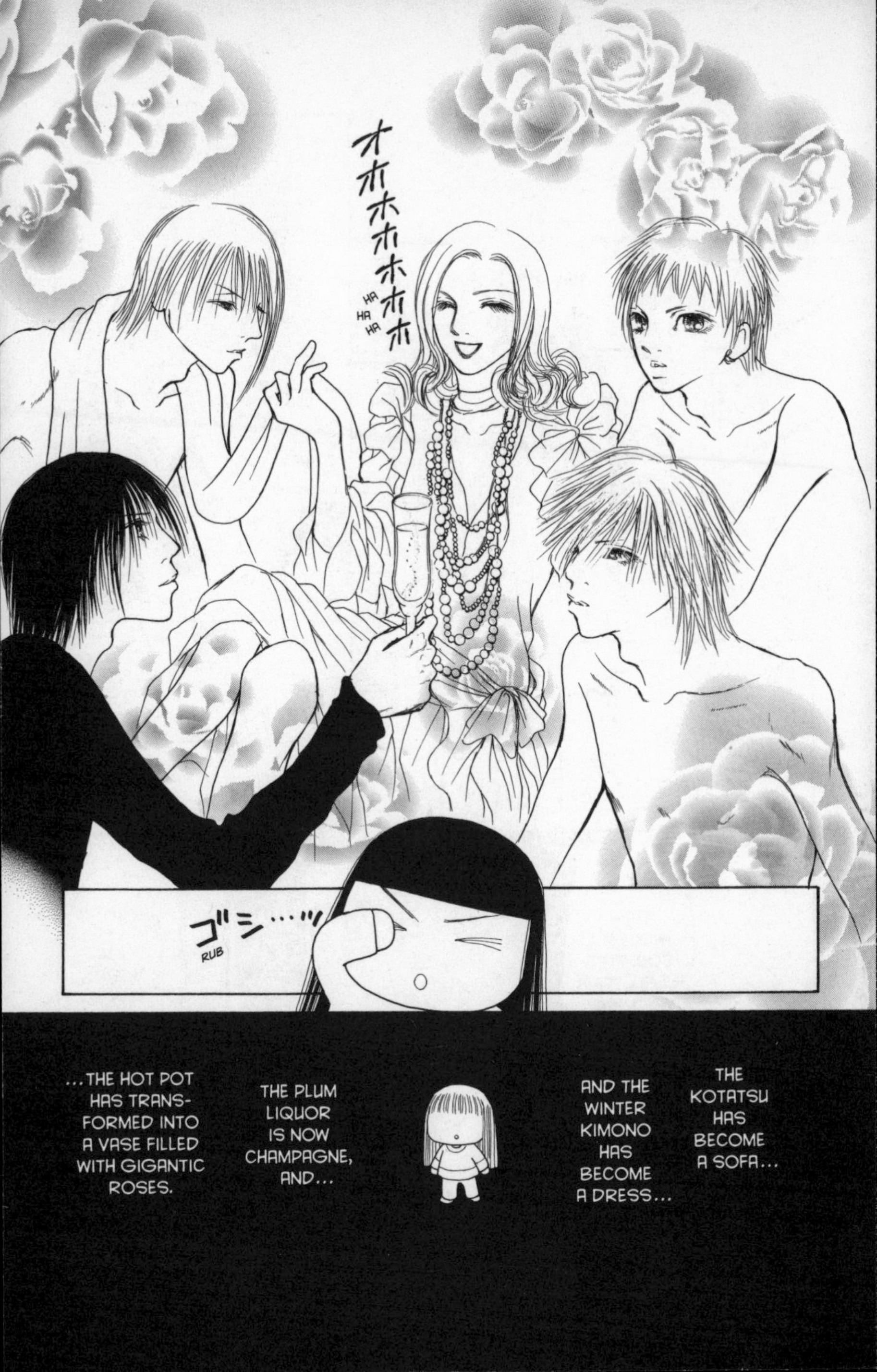
オホホホホホホ
HA HA HA
ゴシ…ッ
RUB
THE KOTATSU HAS BECOME A SOFA…
AND THE WINTER KIMONO HAS BECOME A DRESS…
THE PLUM LIQUOR IS NOW CHAMPAGNE, AND…
…THE HOT POT HAS TRANSFORMED INTO A VASE FILLED WITH GIGANTIC ROSES.

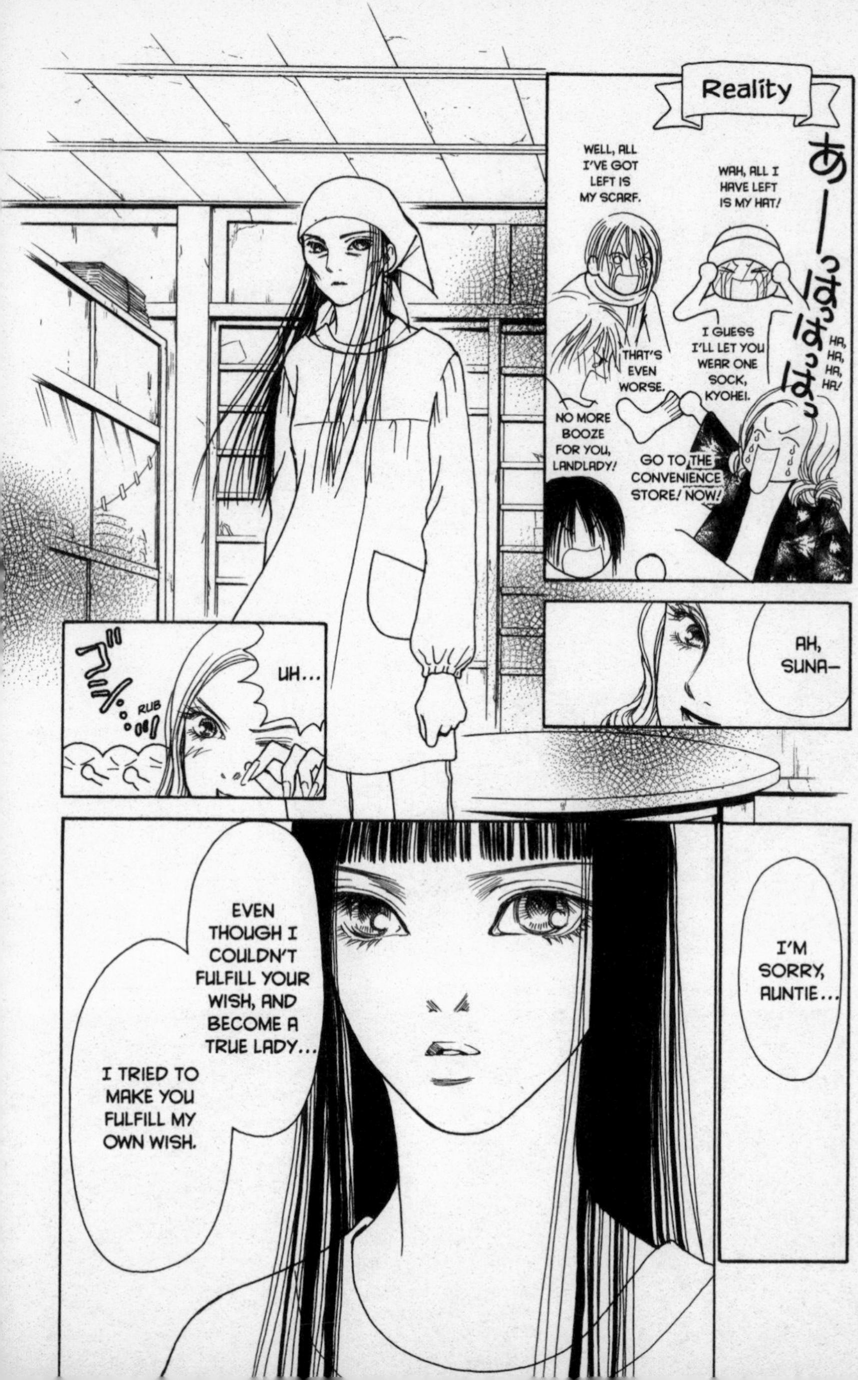

Reality
あーっはっはっはっ
WAH, ALL I HAVE LEFT IS MY HAT!
HA, HA, HA, HA!
WELL, ALL I'VE GOT LEFT IS MY SCARF.
I GUESS I'LL LET YOU WEAR ONE SOCK, KYOHEI.
THAT'S EVEN WORSE.
GO TO THE CONVENIENCE STORE! NOW!
NO MORE BOOZE FOR YOU, LANDLADY!
AH, SUNA—
UH...
RUB
I'M SORRY, AUNTIE...
EVEN THOUGH I COULDN'T FULFILL YOUR WISH, AND BECOME A TRUE LADY...
I TRIED TO MAKE YOU FULFILL MY OWN WISH.

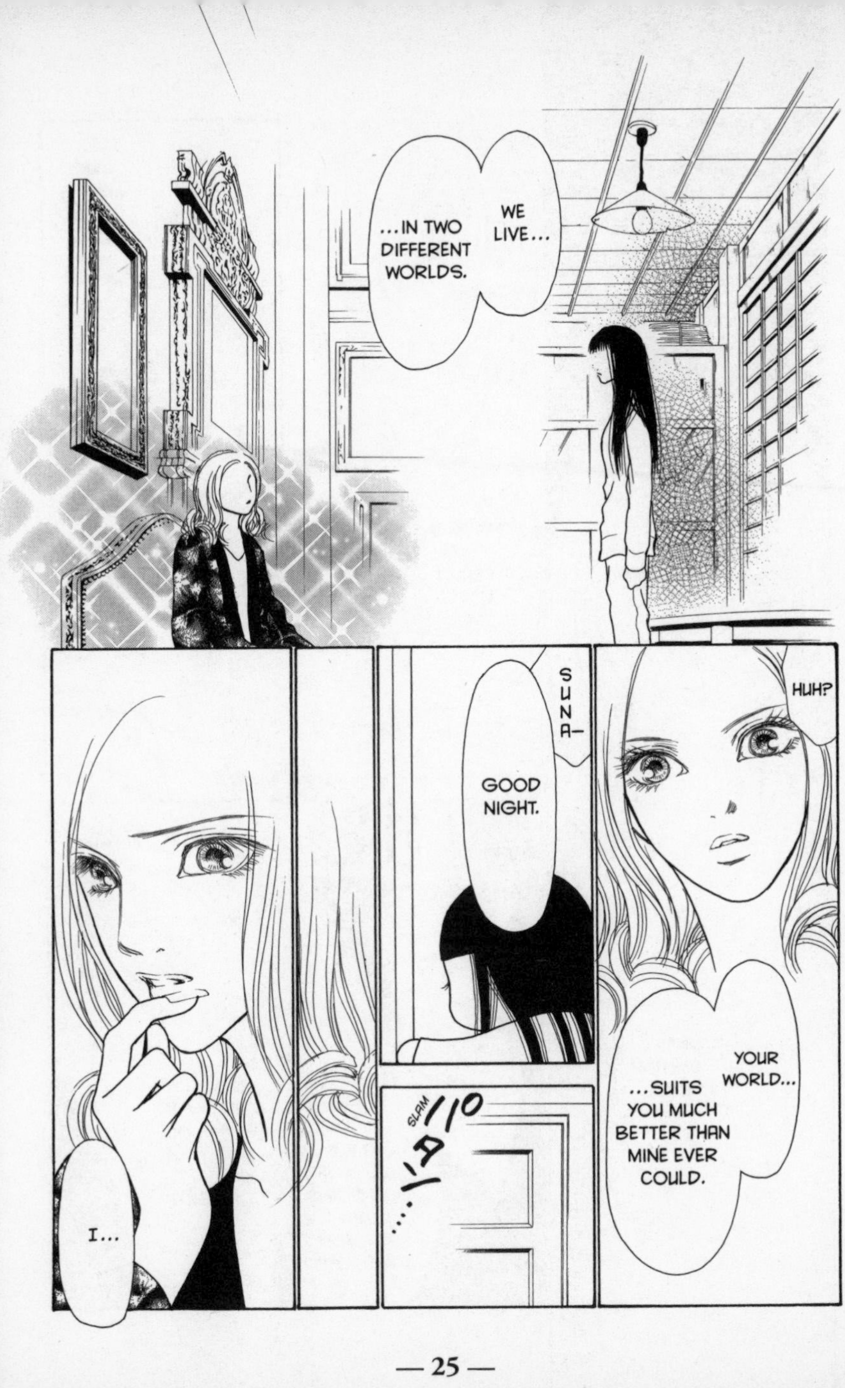
WE LIVE...
...IN TWO DIFFERENT WORLDS.
HUH?
YOUR WORLD...
...SUITS YOU MUCH BETTER THAN MINE EVER COULD.
SUNA—
GOOD NIGHT.
SLAM
I...

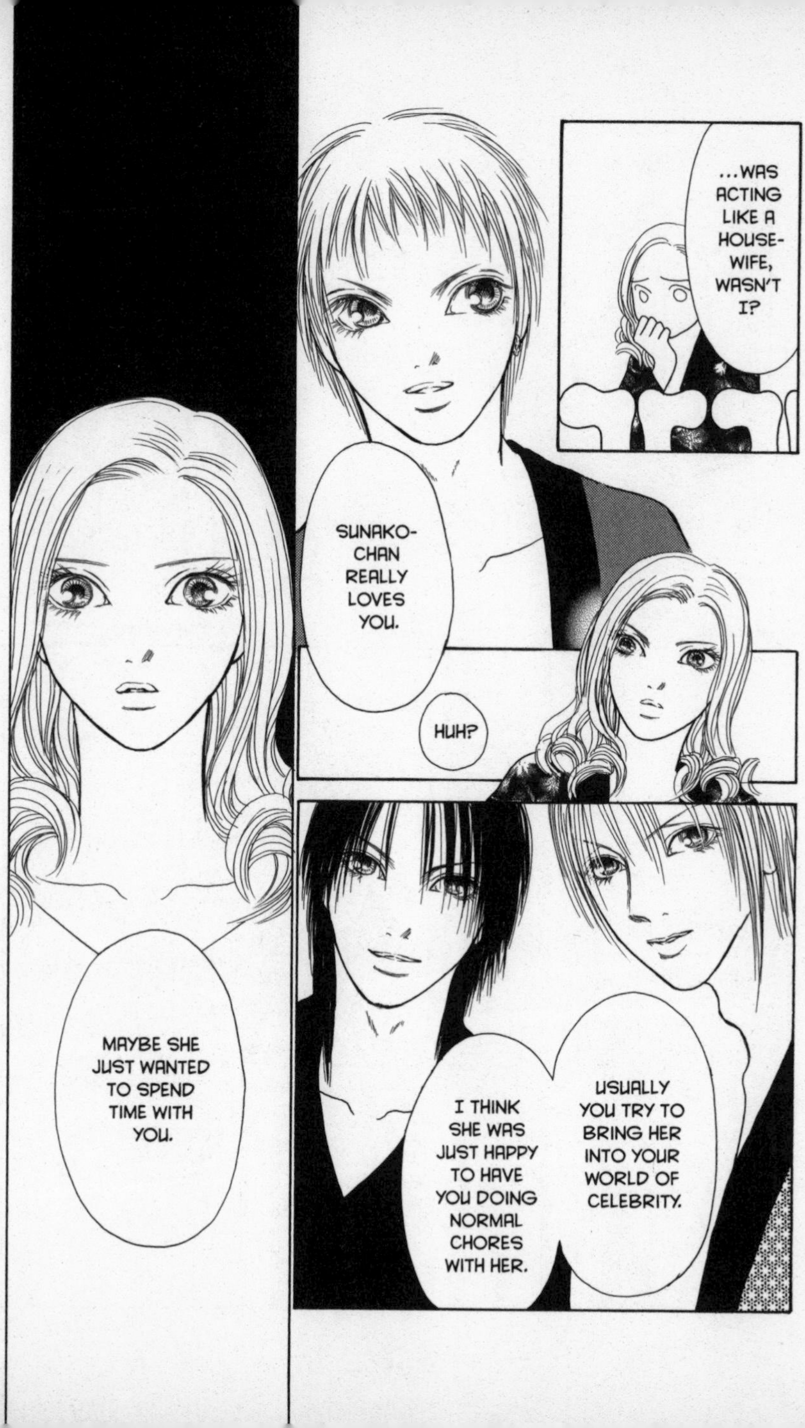
...WAS ACTING LIKE A HOUSE-WIFE, WASN'T I?
SUNAKO-CHAN REALLY LOVES YOU.
HUH?
USUALLY YOU TRY TO BRING HER INTO YOUR WORLD OF CELEBRITY.
I THINK SHE WAS JUST HAPPY TO HAVE YOU DOING NORMAL CHORES WITH HER.
MAYBE SHE JUST WANTED TO SPEND TIME WITH YOU.

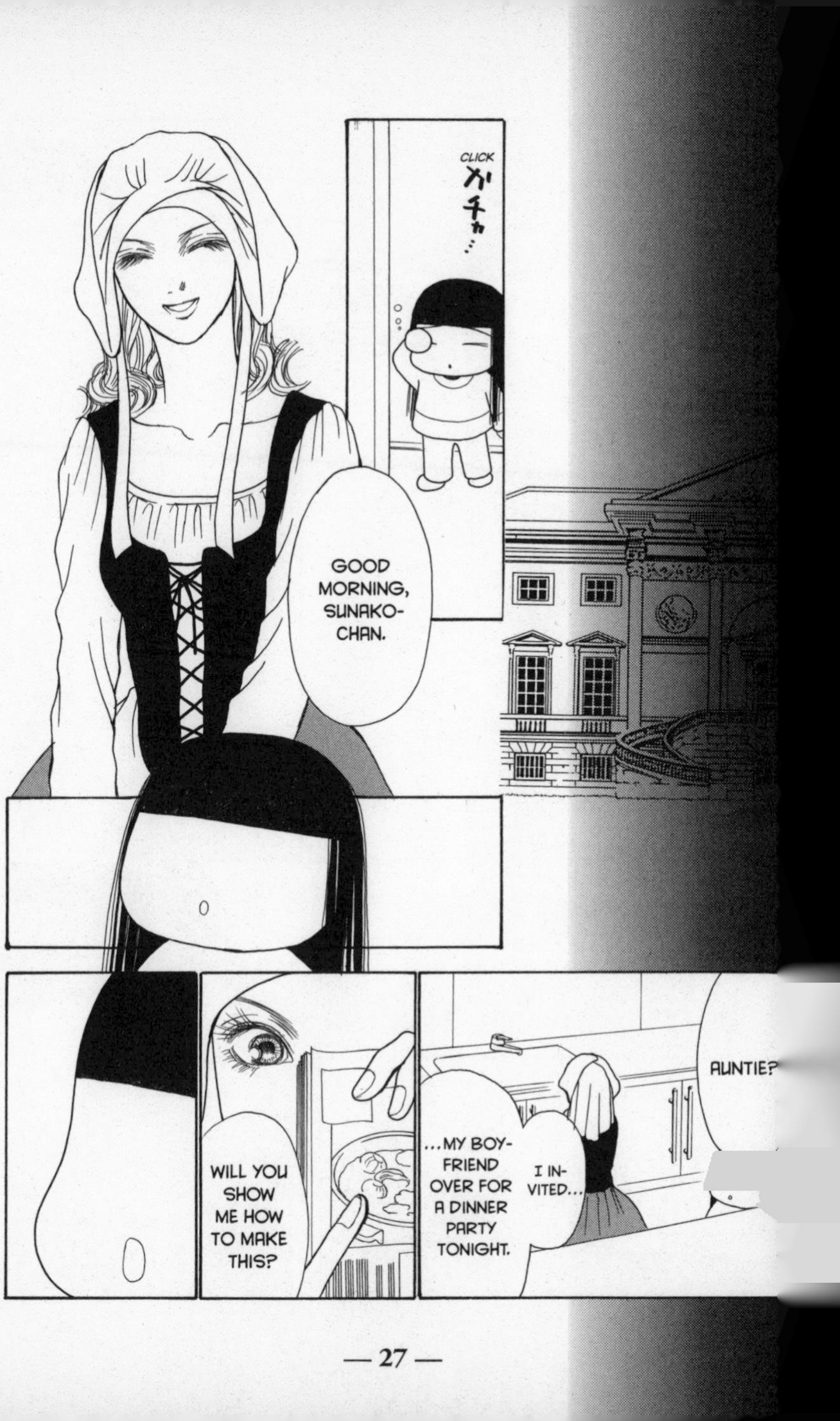
CLICK
ガチャ…
GOOD MORNING, SUNAKO-CHAN.
AUNTIE?
I IN-VITED...
...MY BOY-FRIEND OVER FOR A DINNER PARTY TONIGHT.
WILL YOU SHOW ME HOW TO MAKE THIS?

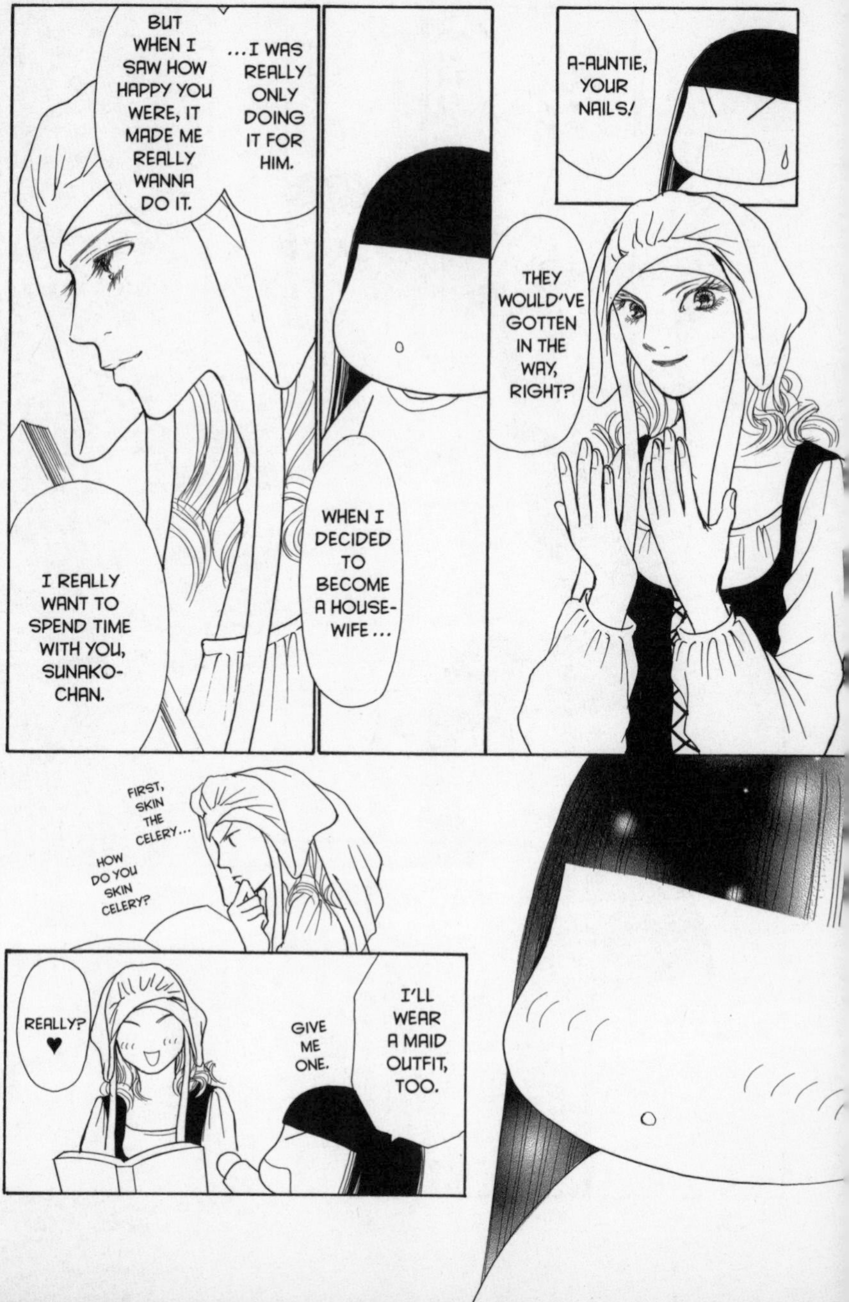
A-AUNTIE, YOUR NAILS!
THEY WOULD'VE GOTTEN IN THE WAY, RIGHT?
WHEN I DECIDED TO BECOME A HOUSE-WIFE...
...I WAS REALLY ONLY DOING IT FOR HIM.
BUT WHEN I SAW HOW HAPPY YOU WERE, IT MADE ME REALLY WANNA DO IT.
I REALLY WANT TO SPEND TIME WITH YOU, SUNAKO-CHAN.
FIRST, SKIN THE CELERY...
HOW DO YOU SKIN CELERY?
I'LL WEAR A MAID OUTFIT, TOO.
GIVE ME ONE.
REALLY? ♥

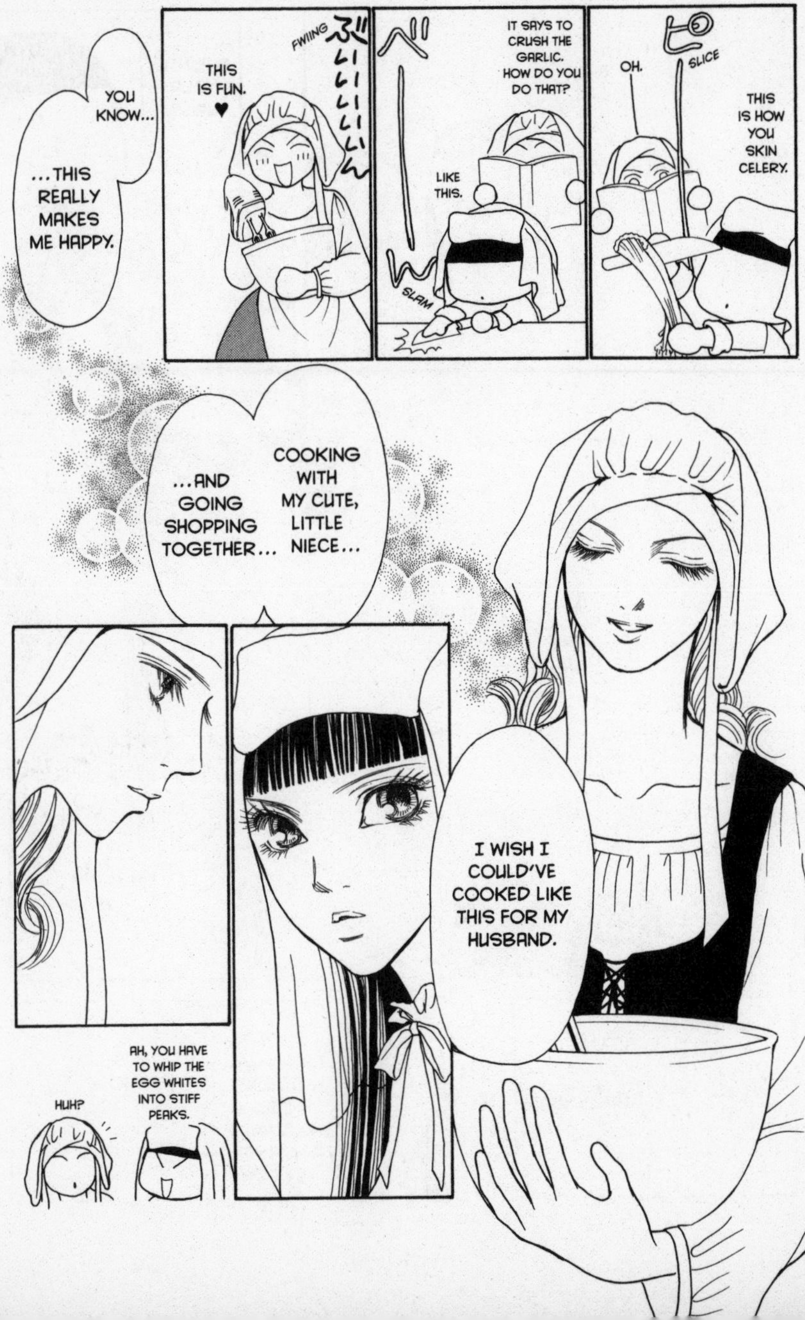
OH.
SLICE
THIS IS HOW YOU SKIN CELERY.
IT SAYS TO CRUSH THE GARLIC. HOW DO YOU DO THAT?
LIKE THIS.
SLAM
FWIING
THIS IS FUN. ♥
YOU KNOW...
...THIS REALLY MAKES ME HAPPY.
COOKING WITH MY CUTE, LITTLE NIECE...
...AND GOING SHOPPING TOGETHER...
I WISH I COULD'VE COOKED LIKE THIS FOR MY HUSBAND.
AH, YOU HAVE TO WHIP THE EGG WHITES INTO STIFF PEAKS.
HUH?

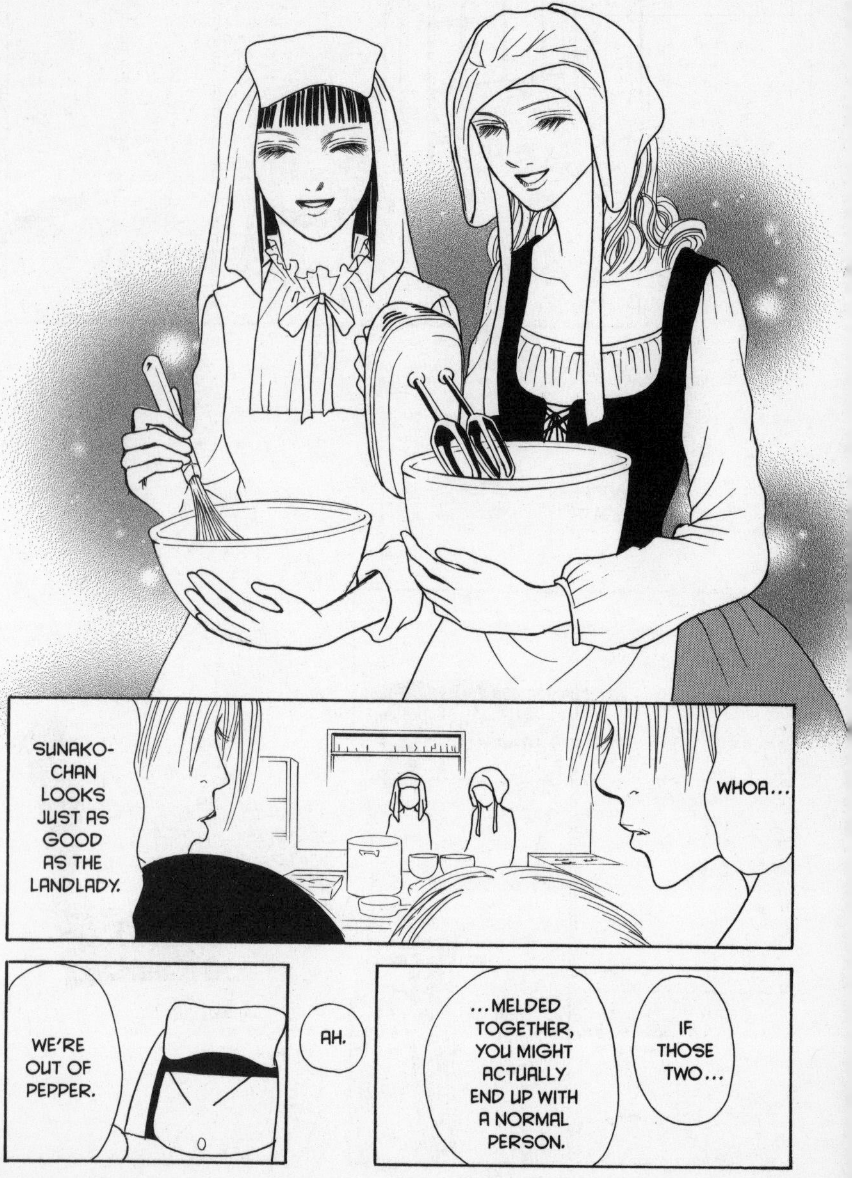
WHOA...
SUNAKO-CHAN LOOKS JUST AS GOOD AS THE LANDLADY.
IF THOSE TWO...
...MELDED TOGETHER, YOU MIGHT ACTUALLY END UP WITH A NORMAL PERSON.
AH.
WE'RE OUT OF PEPPER.

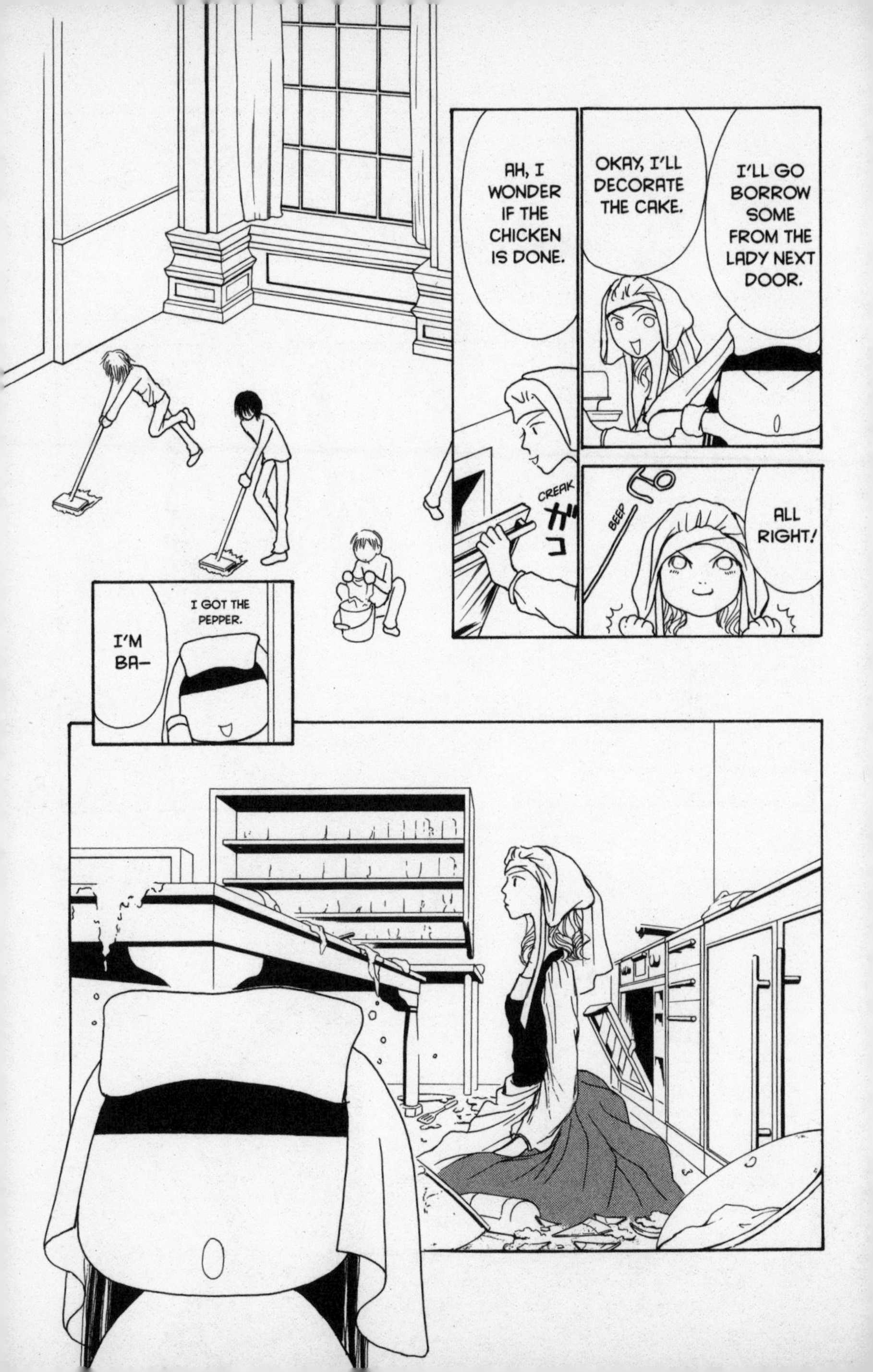

I'LL GO BORROW SOME FROM THE LADY NEXT DOOR.
OKAY, I'LL DECORATE THE CAKE.
AH, I WONDER IF THE CHICKEN IS DONE.
CREAK
ガコ
BEEP
ALL RIGHT!
I GOT THE PEPPER.
I'M BA—

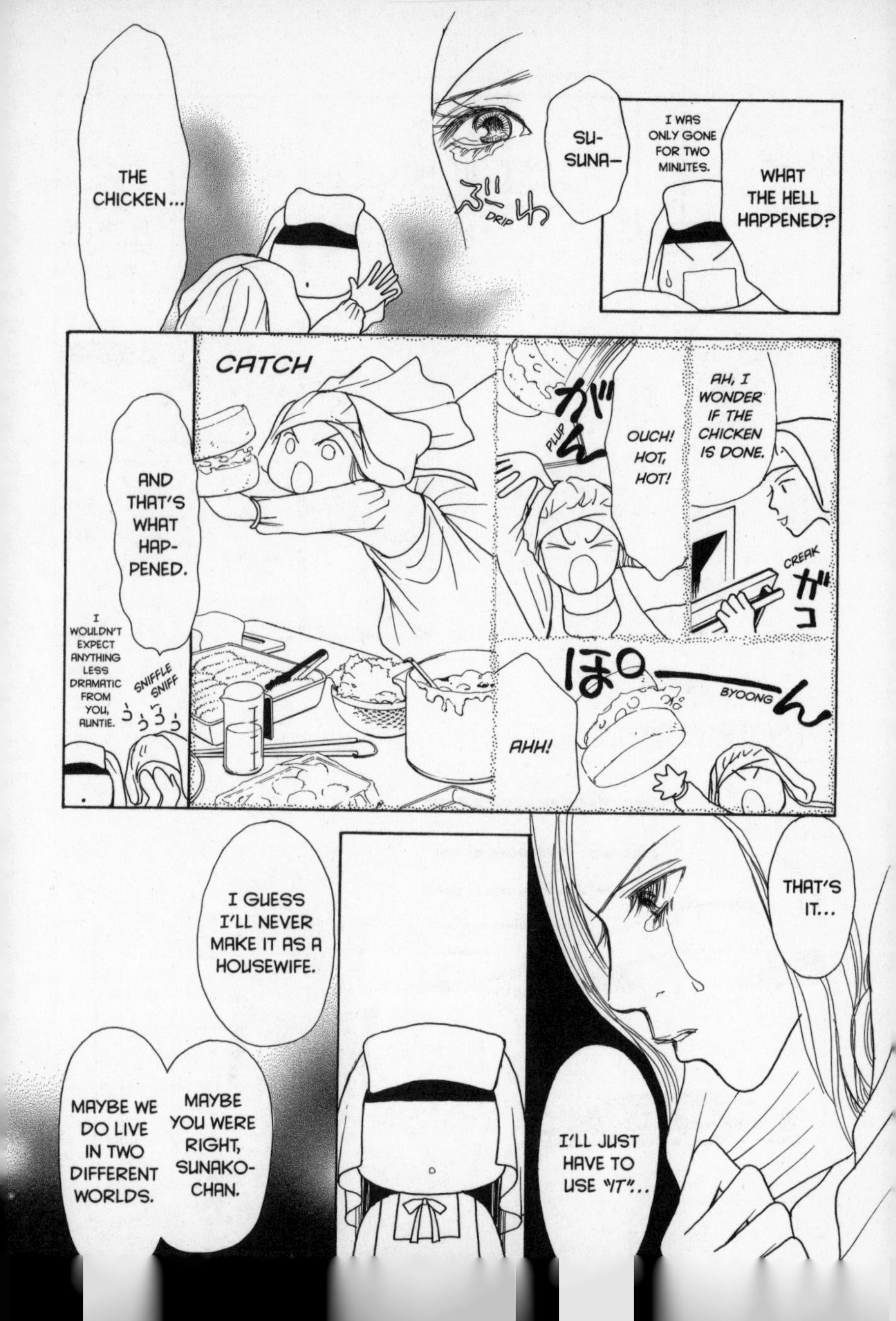
WHAT THE HELL HAPPENED?
I WAS ONLY GONE FOR TWO MINUTES.
SU- SUNA—
DRIP
THE CHICKEN...
AH, I WONDER IF THE CHICKEN IS DONE.
CREAK
ガコ
OUCH! HOT, HOT!
PLIP
がん
BYOONG
AHH!
CATCH
AND THAT'S WHAT HAP- PENED.
I WOULDN'T EXPECT ANYTHING LESS DRAMATIC FROM YOU, AUNTIE.
SNIFFLE SNIFF
THAT'S IT...
I'LL JUST HAVE TO USE "IT"...
I GUESS I'LL NEVER MAKE IT AS A HOUSEWIFE.
MAYBE YOU WERE RIGHT, SUNAKO-CHAN.
MAYBE WE DO LIVE IN TWO DIFFERENT WORLDS.

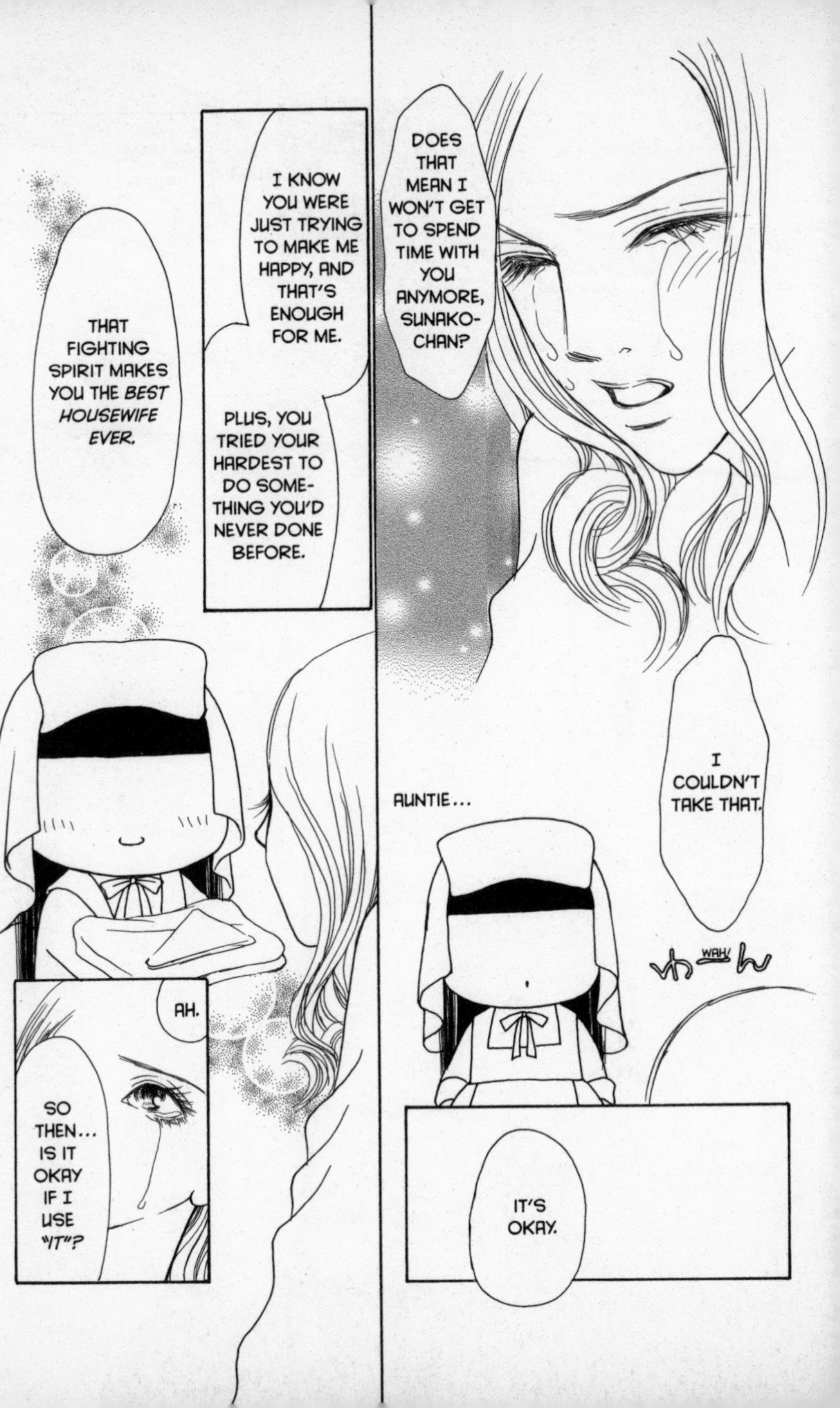
I KNOW YOU WERE JUST TRYING TO MAKE ME HAPPY, AND THAT'S ENOUGH FOR ME.
PLUS, YOU TRIED YOUR HARDEST TO DO SOME-THING YOU'D NEVER DONE BEFORE.
THAT FIGHTING SPIRIT MAKES YOU THE *BEST HOUSEWIFE* EVER.
AH.
SO THEN... IS IT OKAY IF I USE *"IT"*?
DOES THAT MEAN I WON'T GET TO SPEND TIME WITH YOU ANYMORE, SUNAKO-CHAN?
I COULDN'T TAKE THAT.
WAH!
AUNTIE...
IT'S OKAY.

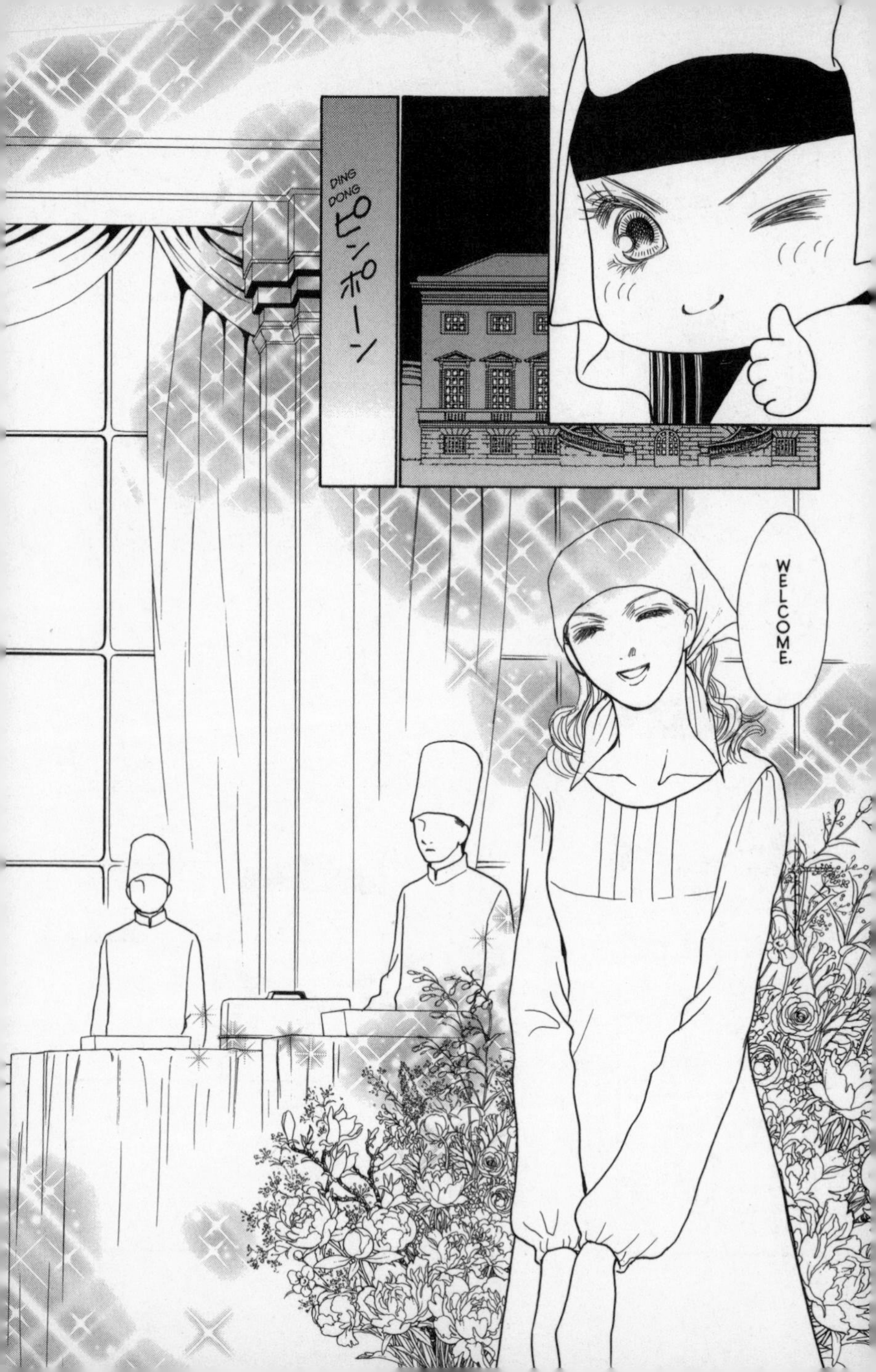
DING DONG
ピンポーン
WELCOME.

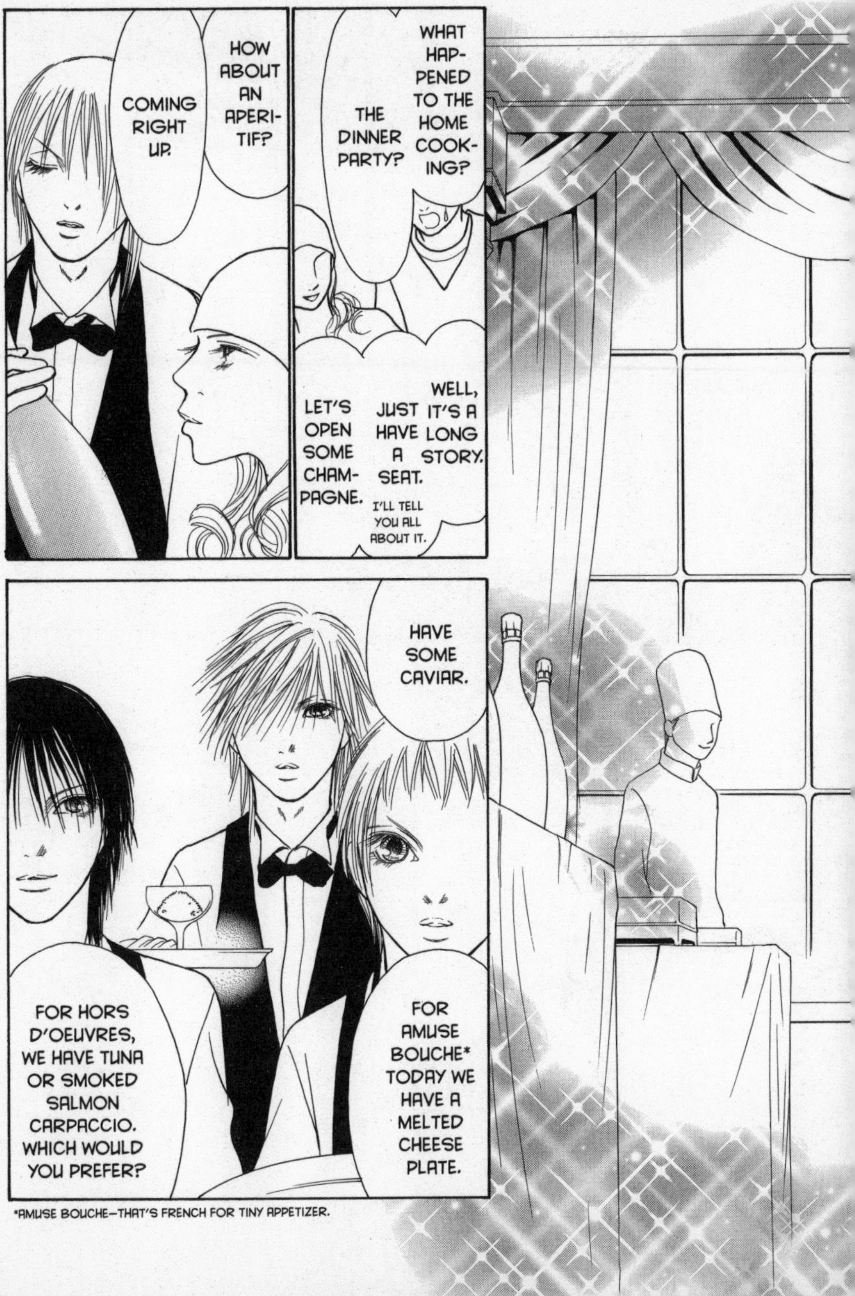
WHAT HAPPENED TO THE HOME COOKING?
THE DINNER PARTY?
WELL, IT'S A LONG STORY.
JUST HAVE A SEAT.
LET'S OPEN SOME CHAMPAGNE.
I'LL TELL YOU ALL ABOUT IT.
HOW ABOUT AN APERITIF?
COMING RIGHT UP.
HAVE SOME CAVIAR.
FOR AMUSE BOUCHE* TODAY WE HAVE A MELTED CHEESE PLATE.
FOR HORS D'OEUVRES, WE HAVE TUNA OR SMOKED SALMON CARPACCIO. WHICH WOULD YOU PREFER?

*AMUSE BOUCHE—THAT'S FRENCH FOR TINY APPETIZER.

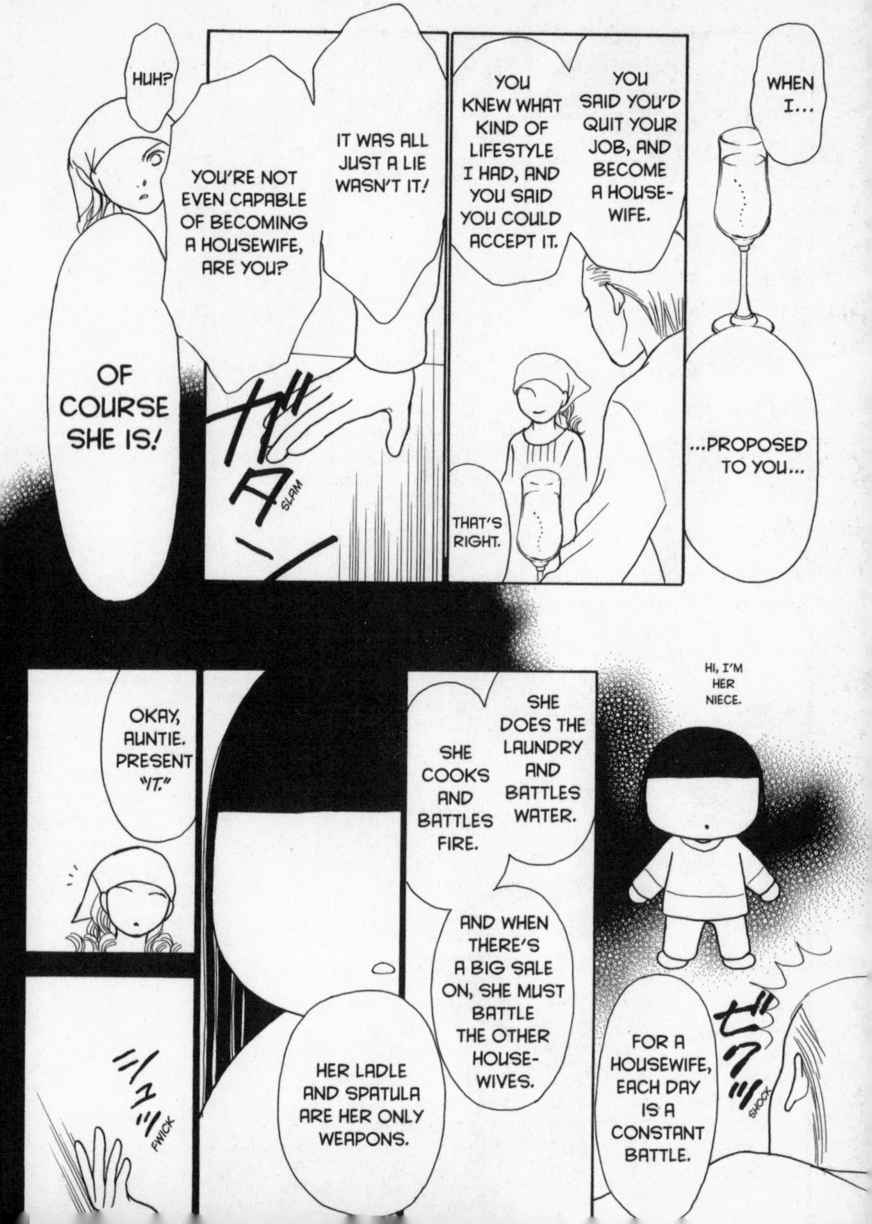
WHEN I...
...PROPOSED TO YOU...
YOU SAID YOU'D QUIT YOUR JOB, AND BECOME A HOUSEWIFE.
YOU KNEW WHAT KIND OF LIFESTYLE I HAD, AND YOU SAID YOU COULD ACCEPT IT.
THAT'S RIGHT.
IT WAS ALL JUST A LIE WASN'T IT!
YOU'RE NOT EVEN CAPABLE OF BECOMING A HOUSEWIFE, ARE YOU?
SLAM
HUH?
OF COURSE SHE IS!
HI, I'M HER NIECE.
FOR A HOUSEWIFE, EACH DAY IS A CONSTANT BATTLE.
SHOCK
SHE DOES THE LAUNDRY AND BATTLES WATER.
SHE COOKS AND BATTLES FIRE.
AND WHEN THERE'S A BIG SALE ON, SHE MUST BATTLE THE OTHER HOUSE-WIVES.
HER LADLE AND SPATULA ARE HER ONLY WEAPONS.
OKAY, AUNTIE. PRESENT "IT."
FWICK

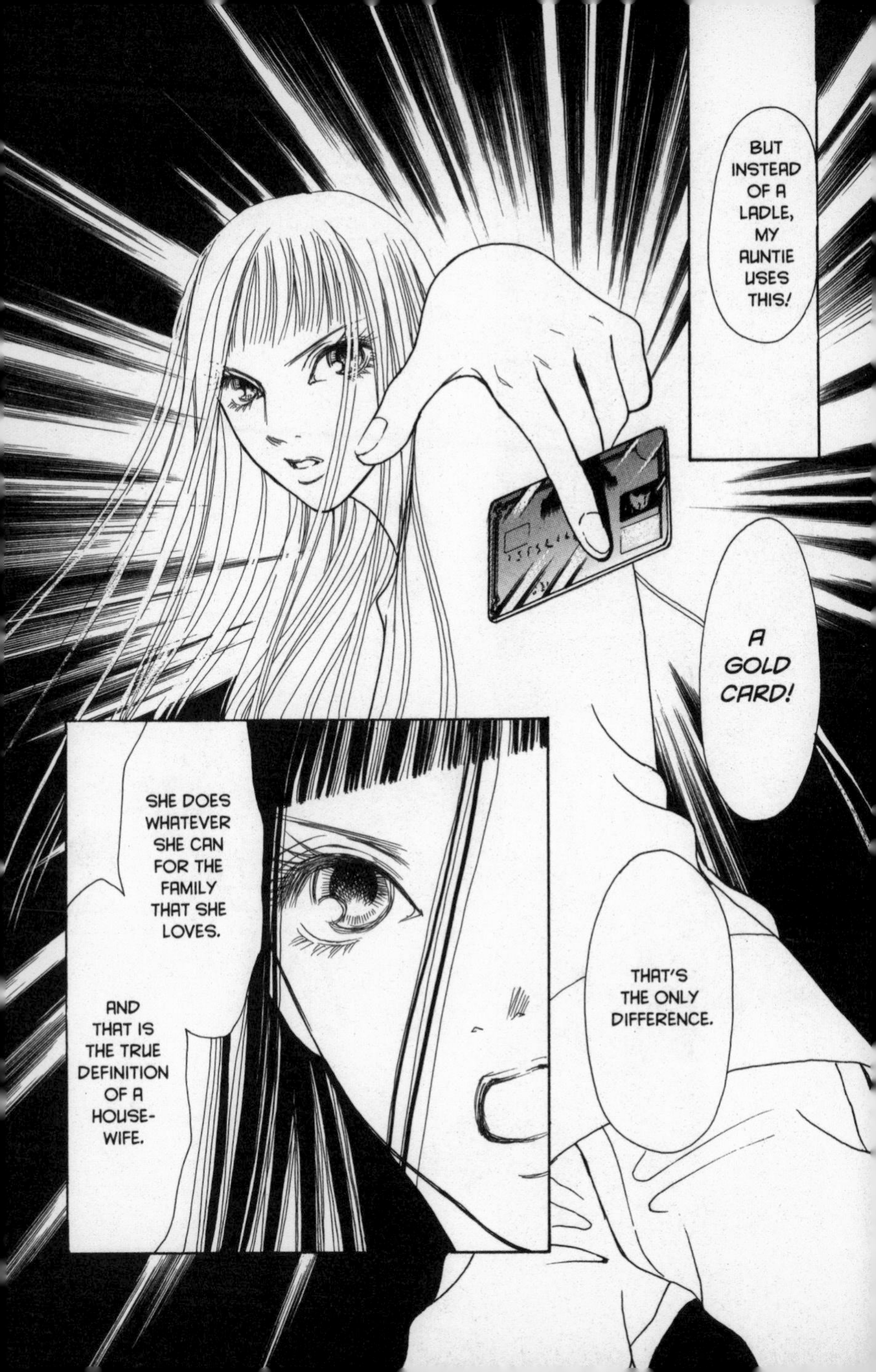
BUT INSTEAD OF A LADLE, MY AUNTIE USES THIS!
A GOLD CARD!
THAT'S THE ONLY DIFFERENCE.
SHE DOES WHATEVER SHE CAN FOR THE FAMILY THAT SHE LOVES.
AND THAT IS THE TRUE DEFINITION OF A HOUSE-WIFE.

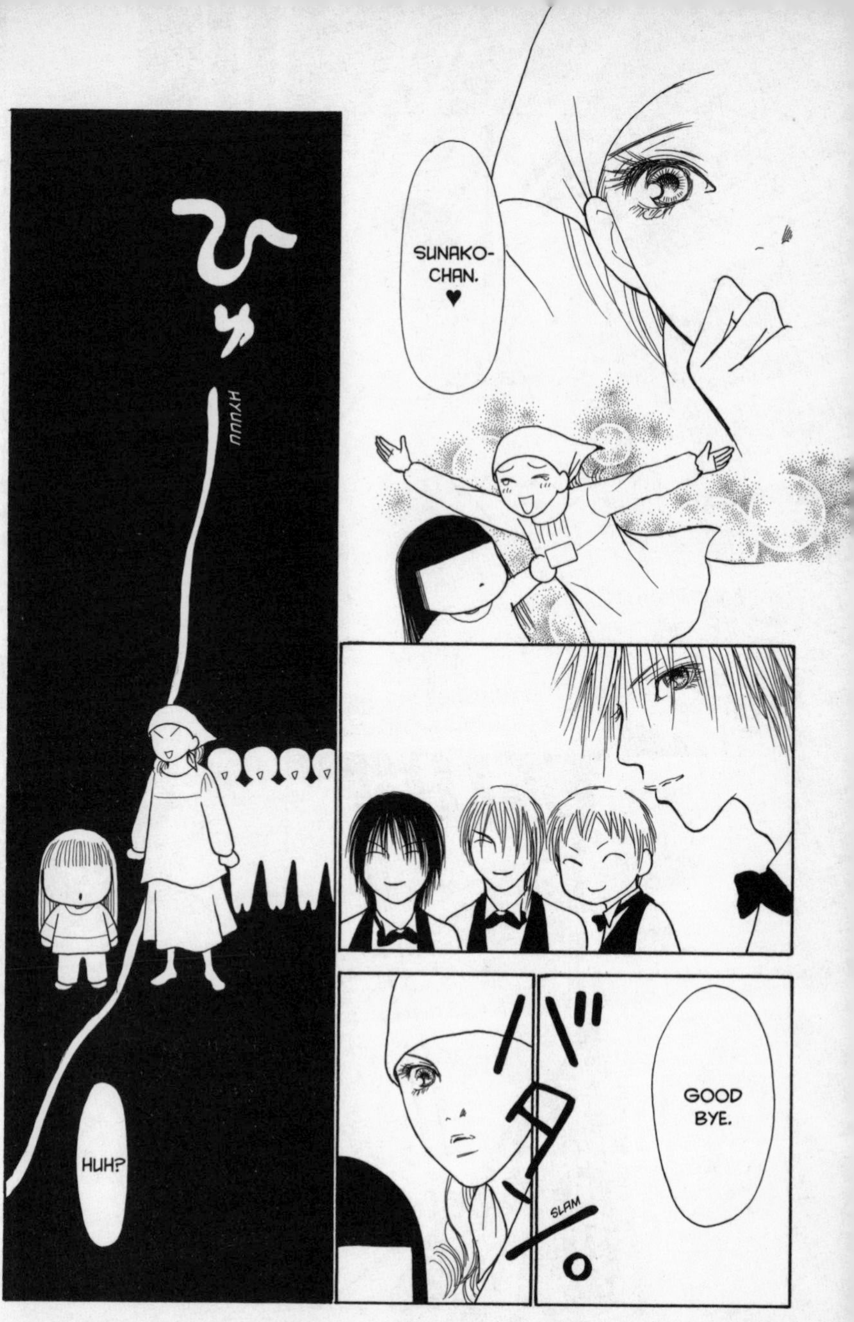
SUNAKO-CHAN. ♥
GOOD BYE.
SLAM
HYUUU
HUH?

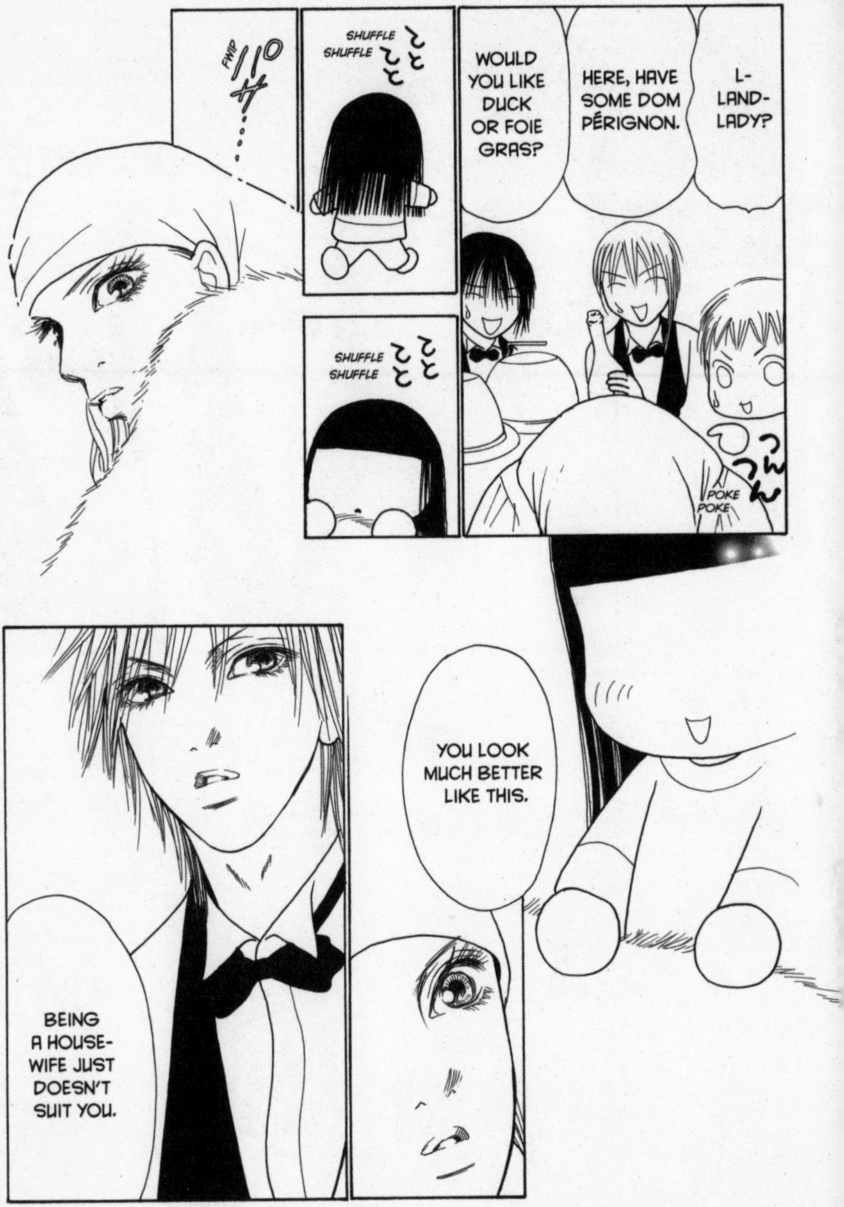
L-
LAND-
LADY?
HERE, HAVE SOME DOM PÉRIGNON.
WOULD YOU LIKE DUCK OR FOIE GRAS?
POKE POKE
SHUFFLE SHUFFLE
SHUFFLE SHUFFLE
FWIP
YOU LOOK MUCH BETTER LIKE THIS.
BEING A HOUSE-
WIFE JUST DOESN'T SUIT YOU.

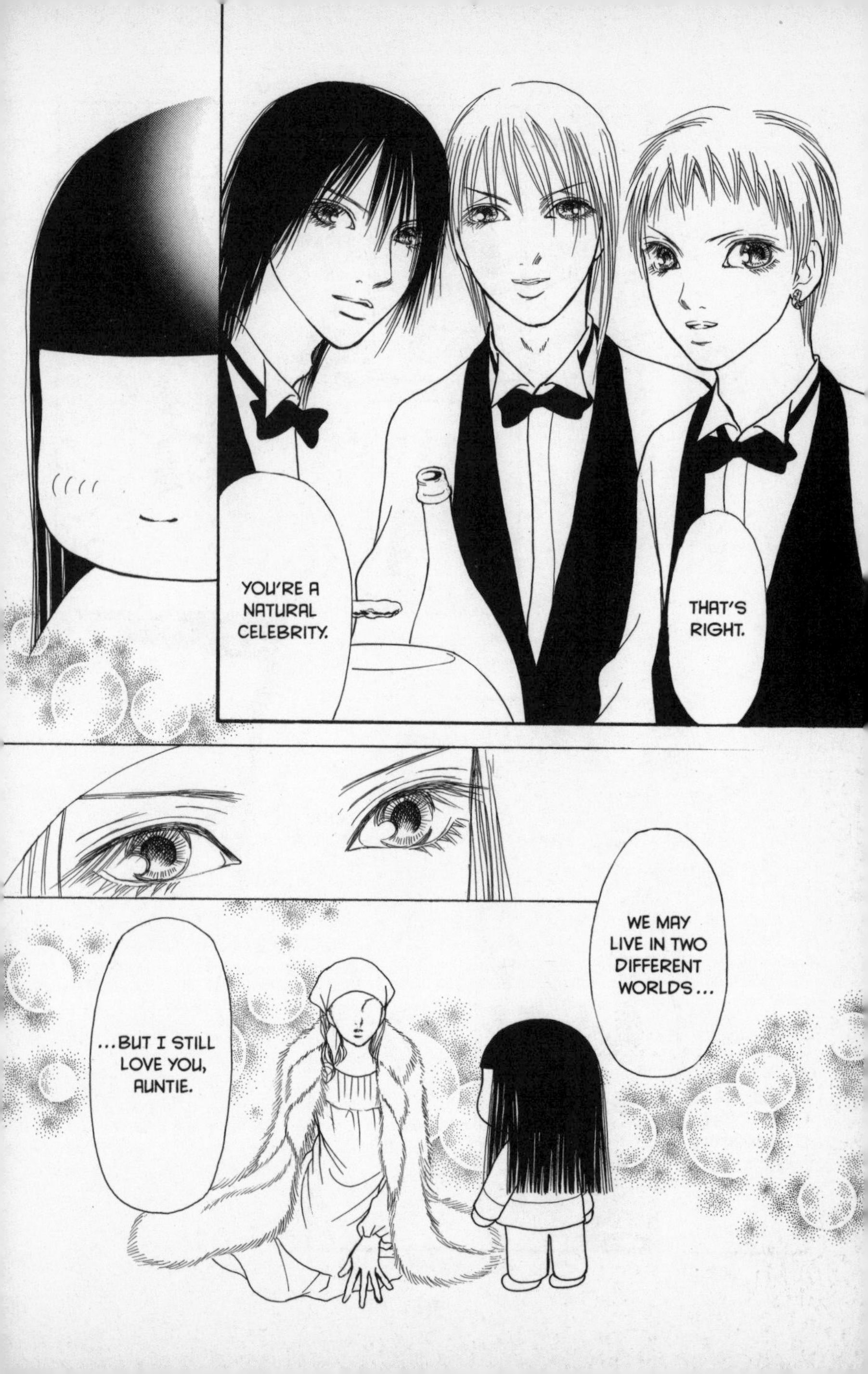
THAT'S RIGHT.
YOU'RE A NATURAL CELEBRITY.
WE MAY LIVE IN TWO DIFFERENT WORLDS...
...BUT I STILL LOVE YOU, AUNTIE.

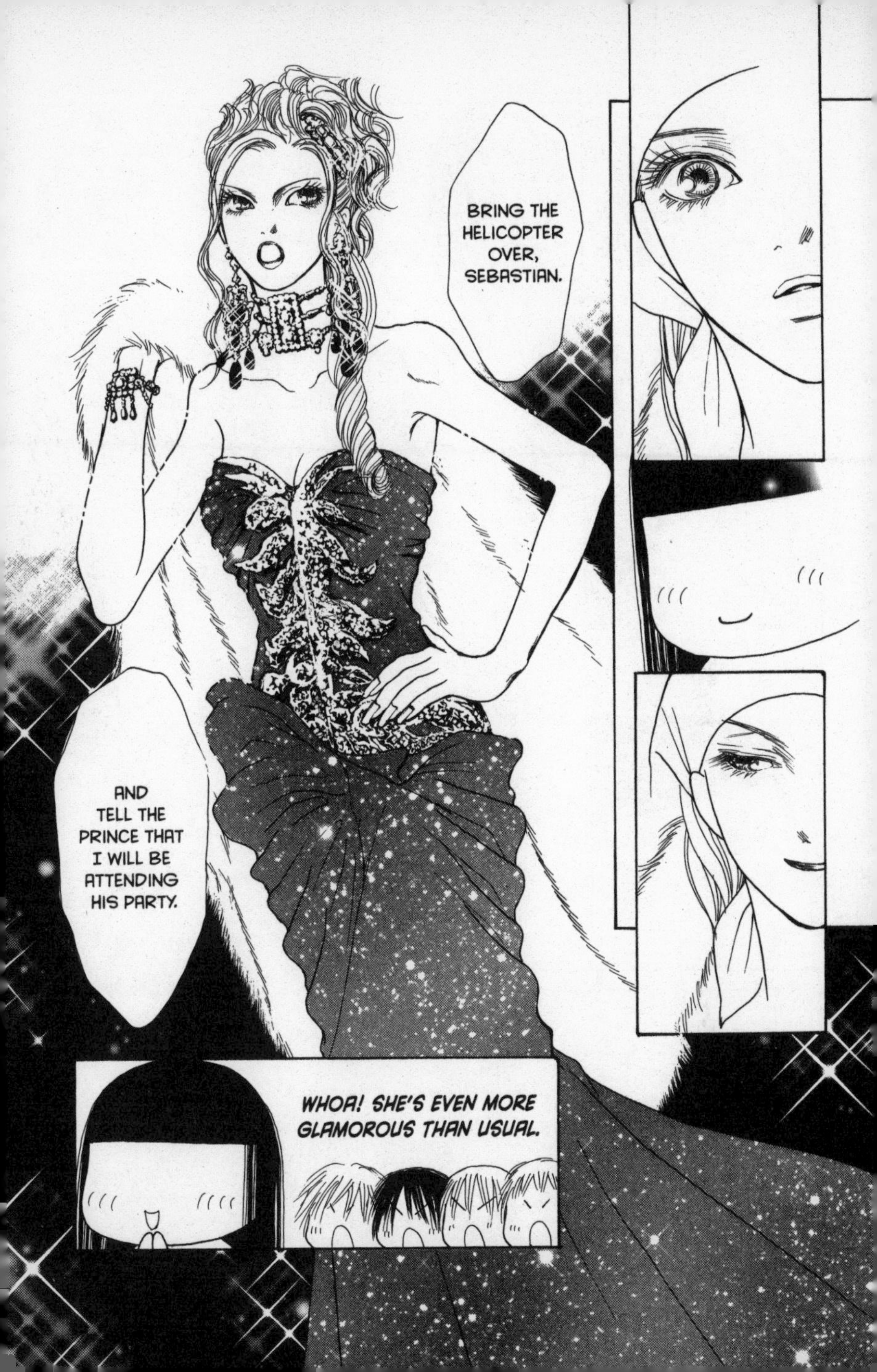
BRING THE HELICOPTER OVER, SEBASTIAN.
AND TELL THE PRINCE THAT I WILL BE ATTENDING HIS PARTY.
WHOA! SHE'S EVEN MORE GLAMOROUS THAN USUAL.

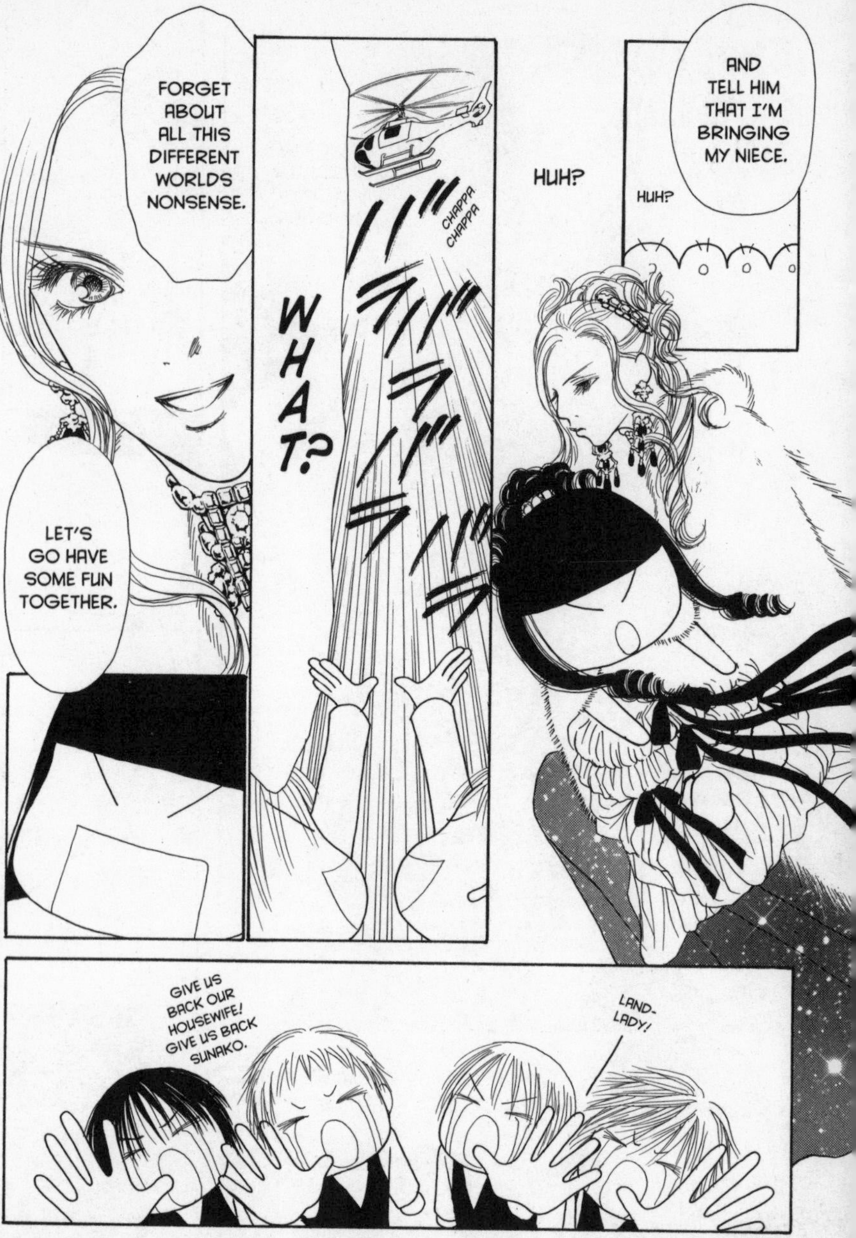
AND TELL HIM THAT I'M BRINGING MY NIECE.
HUH?
HUH?
CHAPPA CHAPPA
WHAT?
FORGET ABOUT ALL THIS DIFFERENT WORLDS NONSENSE.
LET'S GO HAVE SOME FUN TOGETHER.
LAND-LADY!
GIVE US BACK OUR HOUSEWIFE! GIVE US BACK SUNAKO.

Chapter 52
The Brilliant Accident

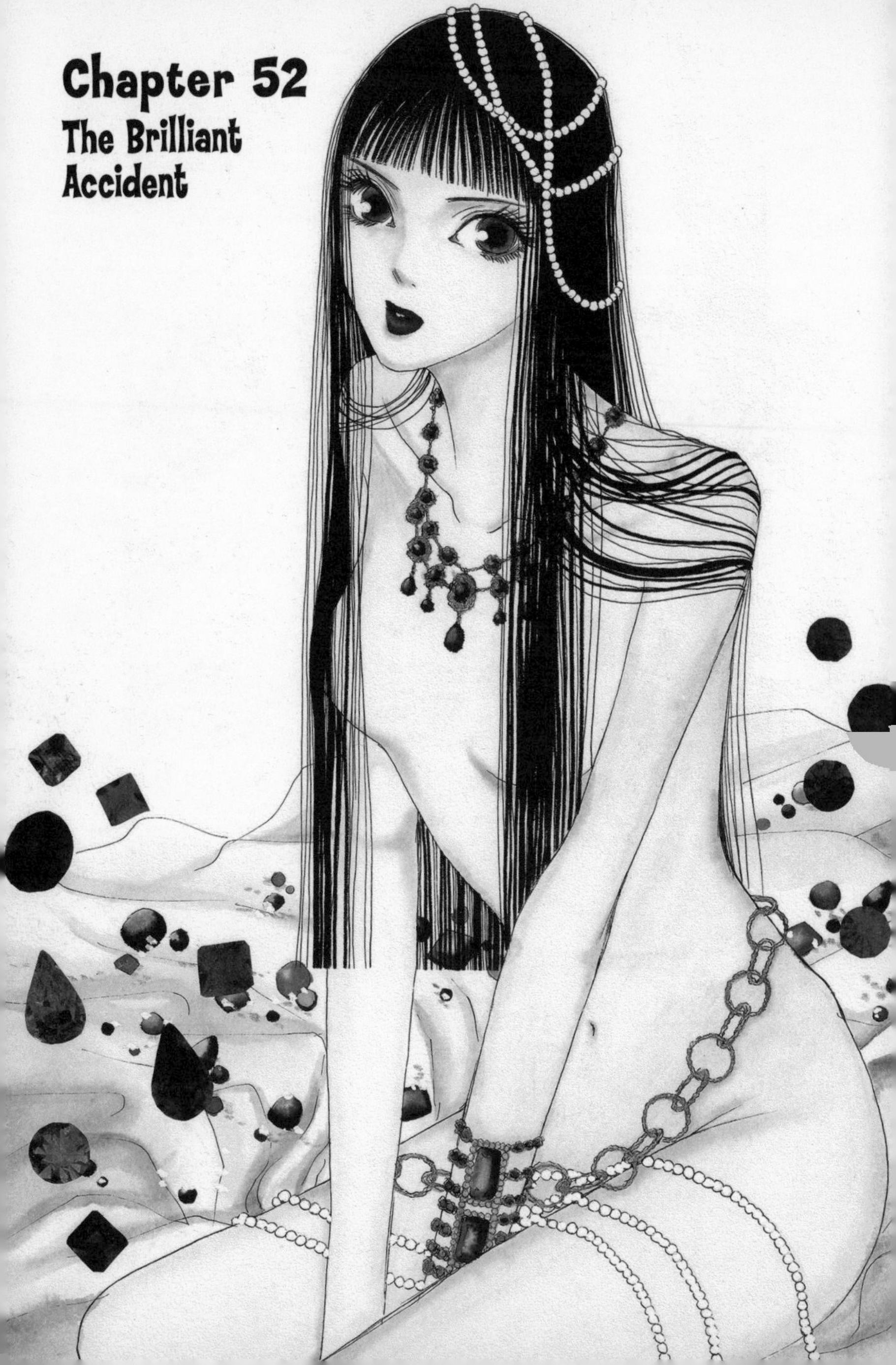

I HAVE ABSOLUTELY NO MEMORY OF WHAT I WAS
DOING WHILE I WROTE THIS STORY, SO THERE'S
NO "BEHIND THE SCENES"....

I WONDER WHY I DON'T REMEMBER ANYTHING.

THE BONUS PAGES ARE JAM-PACKED, AND THERE WASN'T ANY ROOM FOR PHOTOS OF TEN.
SO I'LL PUT ONE HERE. ♥

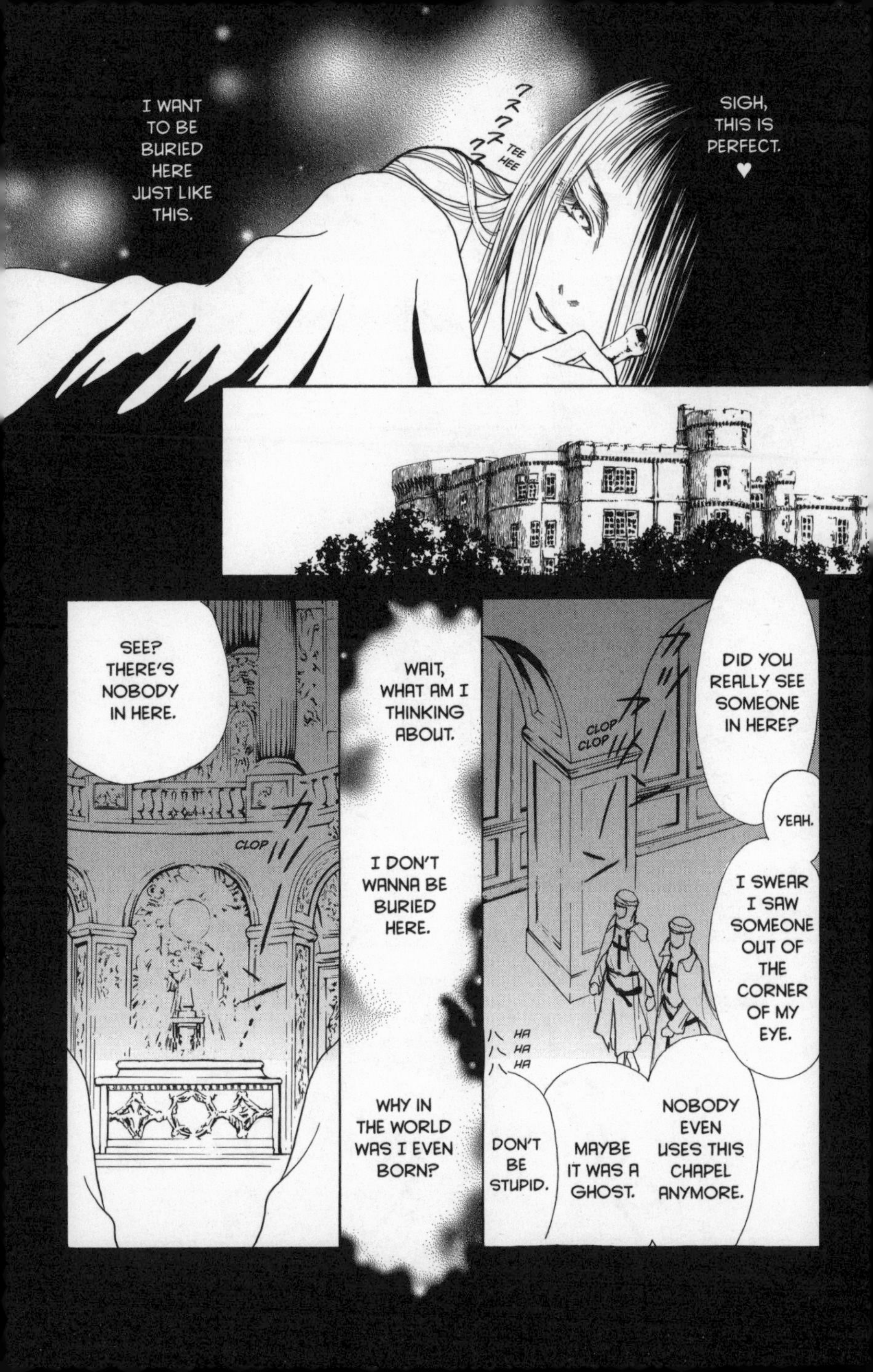
SIGH, THIS IS PERFECT. ♥
TEE HEE
I WANT TO BE BURIED HERE JUST LIKE THIS.
DID YOU REALLY SEE SOMEONE IN HERE?
CLOP CLOP
YEAH.
I SWEAR I SAW SOMEONE OUT OF THE CORNER OF MY EYE.
HA HA HA
NOBODY EVEN USES THIS CHAPEL ANYMORE.
MAYBE IT WAS A GHOST.
DON'T BE STUPID.
WAIT, WHAT AM I THINKING ABOUT.
I DON'T WANNA BE BURIED HERE.
WHY IN THE WORLD WAS I EVEN BORN?
SEE? THERE'S NOBODY IN HERE.
CLOP

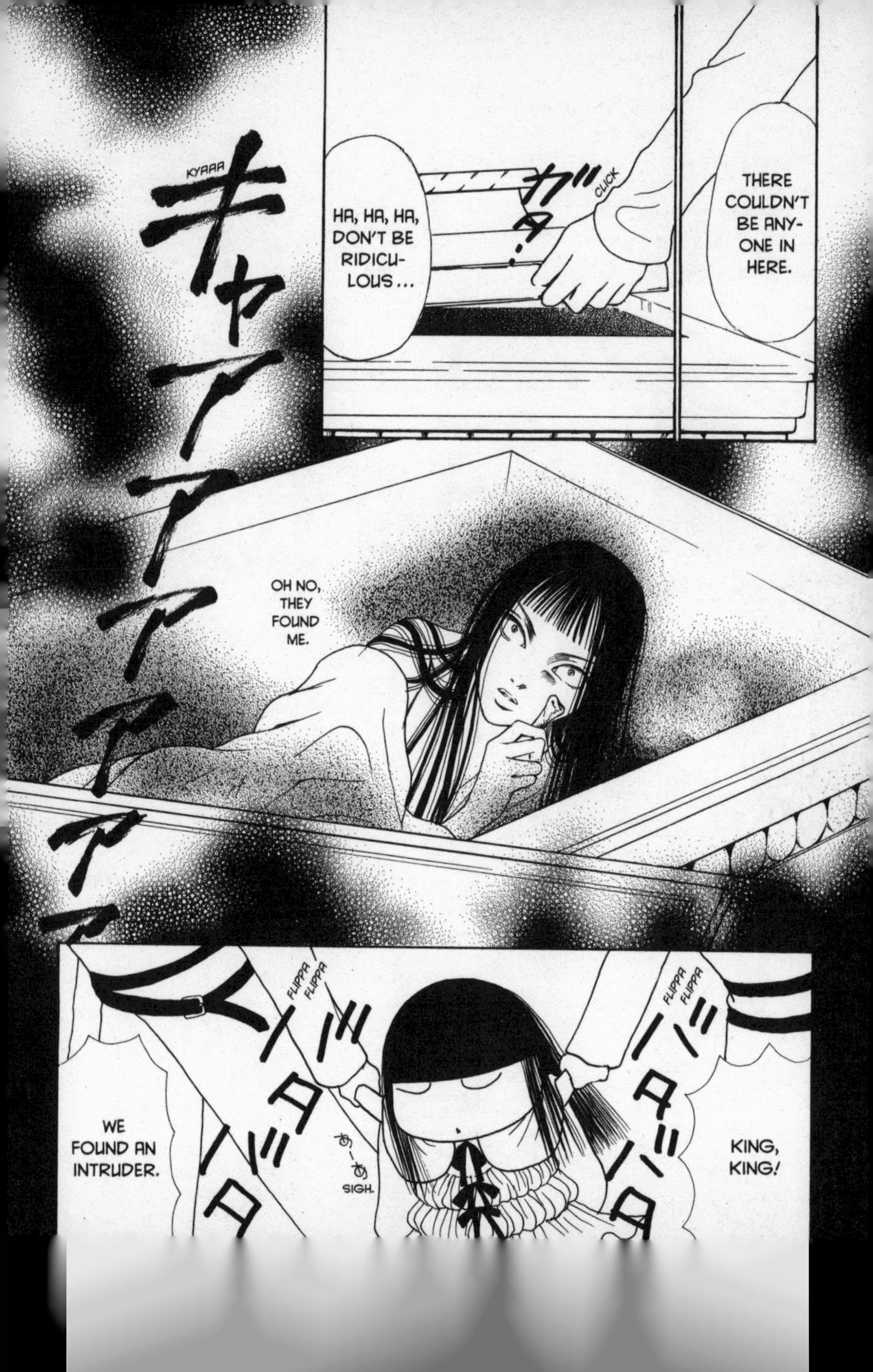
THERE COULDN'T BE ANY-ONE IN HERE.
CLICK
HA, HA, HA, DON'T BE RIDICULOUS...
KYAAA
OH NO, THEY FOUND ME.
KING, KING!
FLIPPA FLIPPA
FLIPPA FLIPPA
SIGH.
WE FOUND AN INTRUDER.

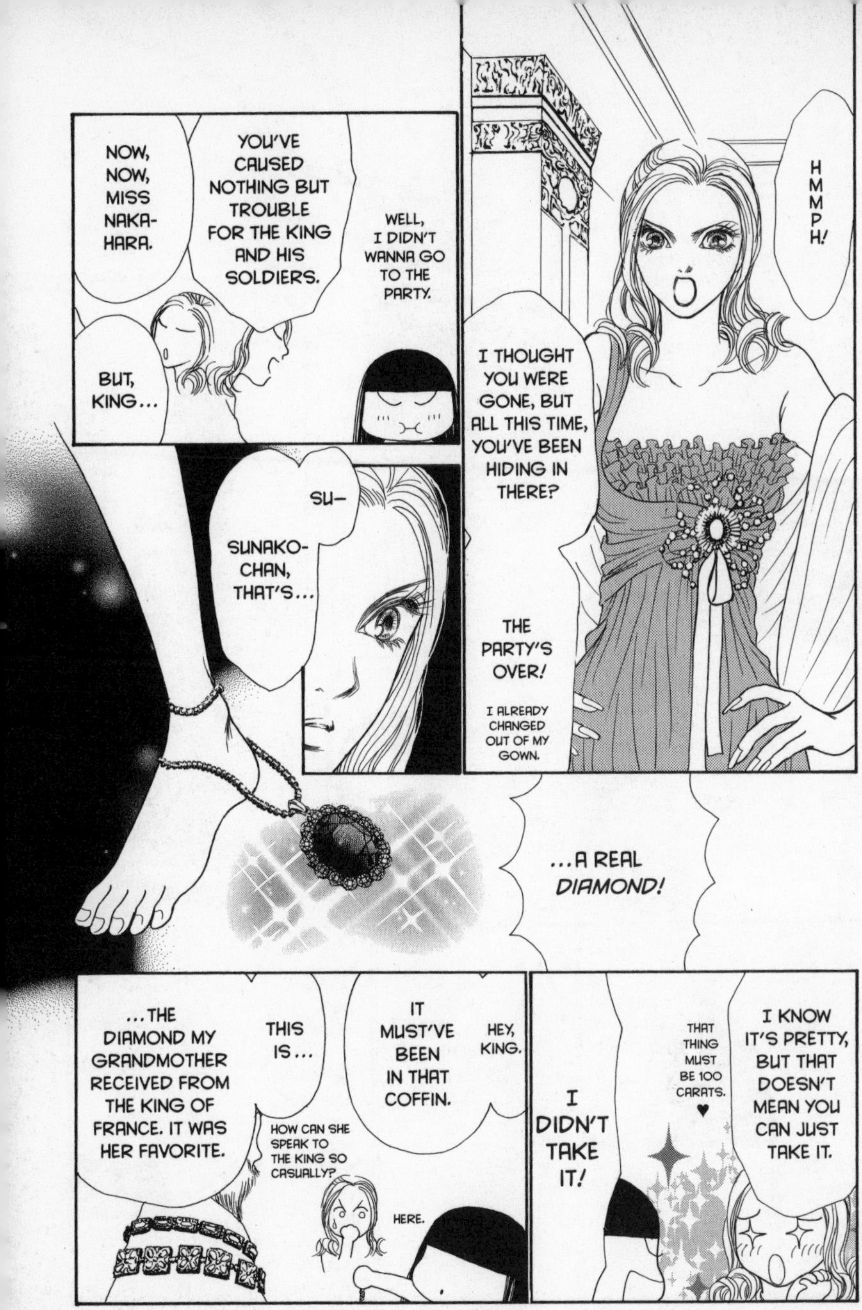
HMMPH!
I THOUGHT YOU WERE GONE, BUT ALL THIS TIME, YOU'VE BEEN HIDING IN THERE?
THE PARTY'S OVER!
I ALREADY CHANGED OUT OF MY GOWN.
WELL, I DIDN'T WANNA GO TO THE PARTY.
YOU'VE CAUSED NOTHING BUT TROUBLE FOR THE KING AND HIS SOLDIERS.
NOW, NOW, MISS NAKA-HARA.
BUT, KING...
SU–
SUNAKO-CHAN, THAT'S...
...A REAL DIAMOND!
I KNOW IT'S PRETTY, BUT THAT DOESN'T MEAN YOU CAN JUST TAKE IT.
THAT THING MUST BE 100 CARATS. ♥
I DIDN'T TAKE IT!
HEY, KING.
IT MUST'VE BEEN IN THAT COFFIN.
HERE.
THIS IS...
...THE DIAMOND MY GRANDMOTHER RECEIVED FROM THE KING OF FRANCE. IT WAS HER FAVORITE.
HOW CAN SHE SPEAK TO THE KING SO CASUALLY?

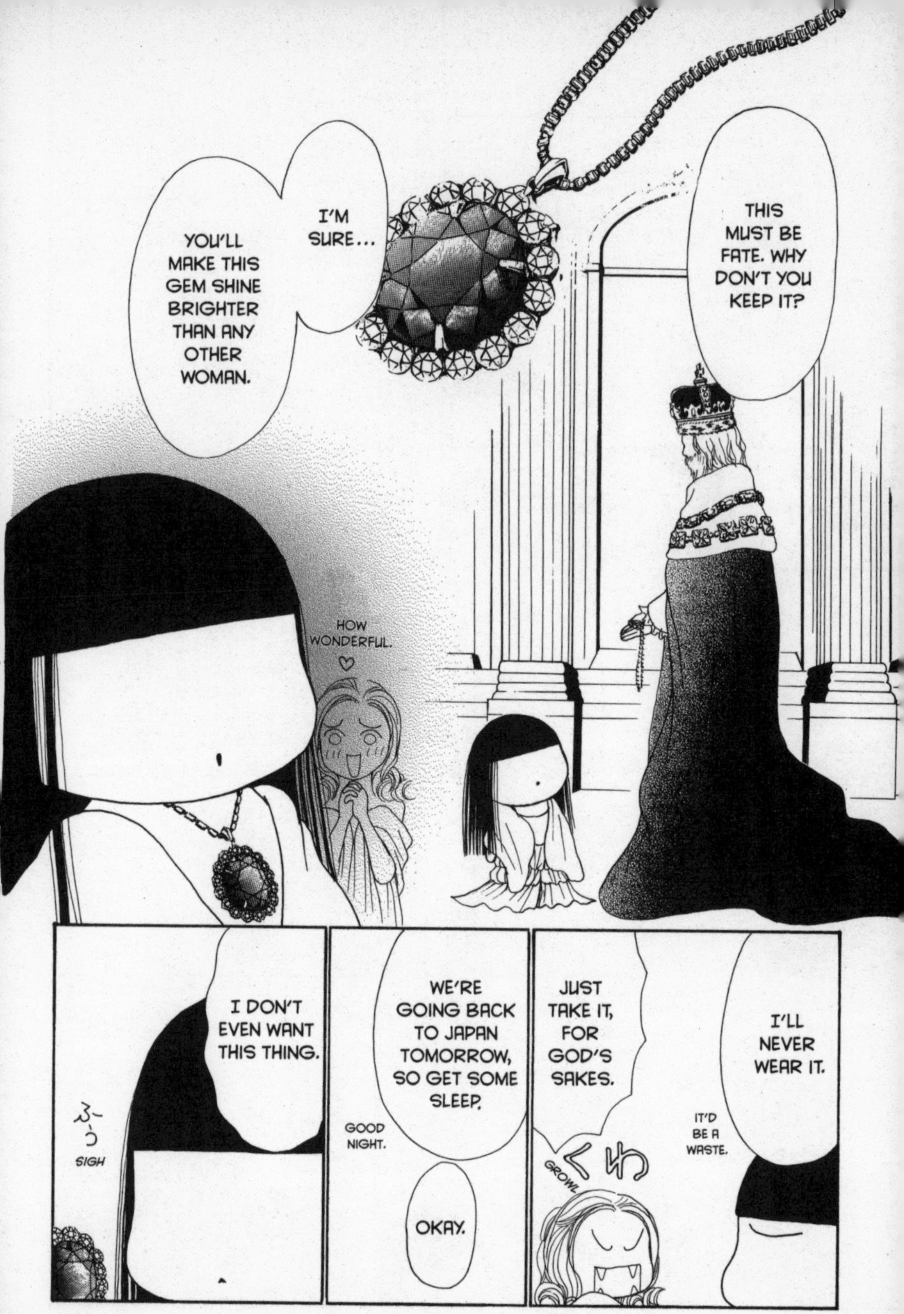
THIS MUST BE FATE. WHY DON'T YOU KEEP IT?
I'M SURE...
YOU'LL MAKE THIS GEM SHINE BRIGHTER THAN ANY OTHER WOMAN.
HOW WONDERFUL. ♡
I'LL NEVER WEAR IT.
IT'D BE A WASTE.
JUST TAKE IT, FOR GOD'S SAKES.
くわ
GROWL
WE'RE GOING BACK TO JAPAN TOMORROW, SO GET SOME SLEEP.
GOOD NIGHT.
OKAY.
I DON'T EVEN WANT THIS THING.
ふーっ
SIGH

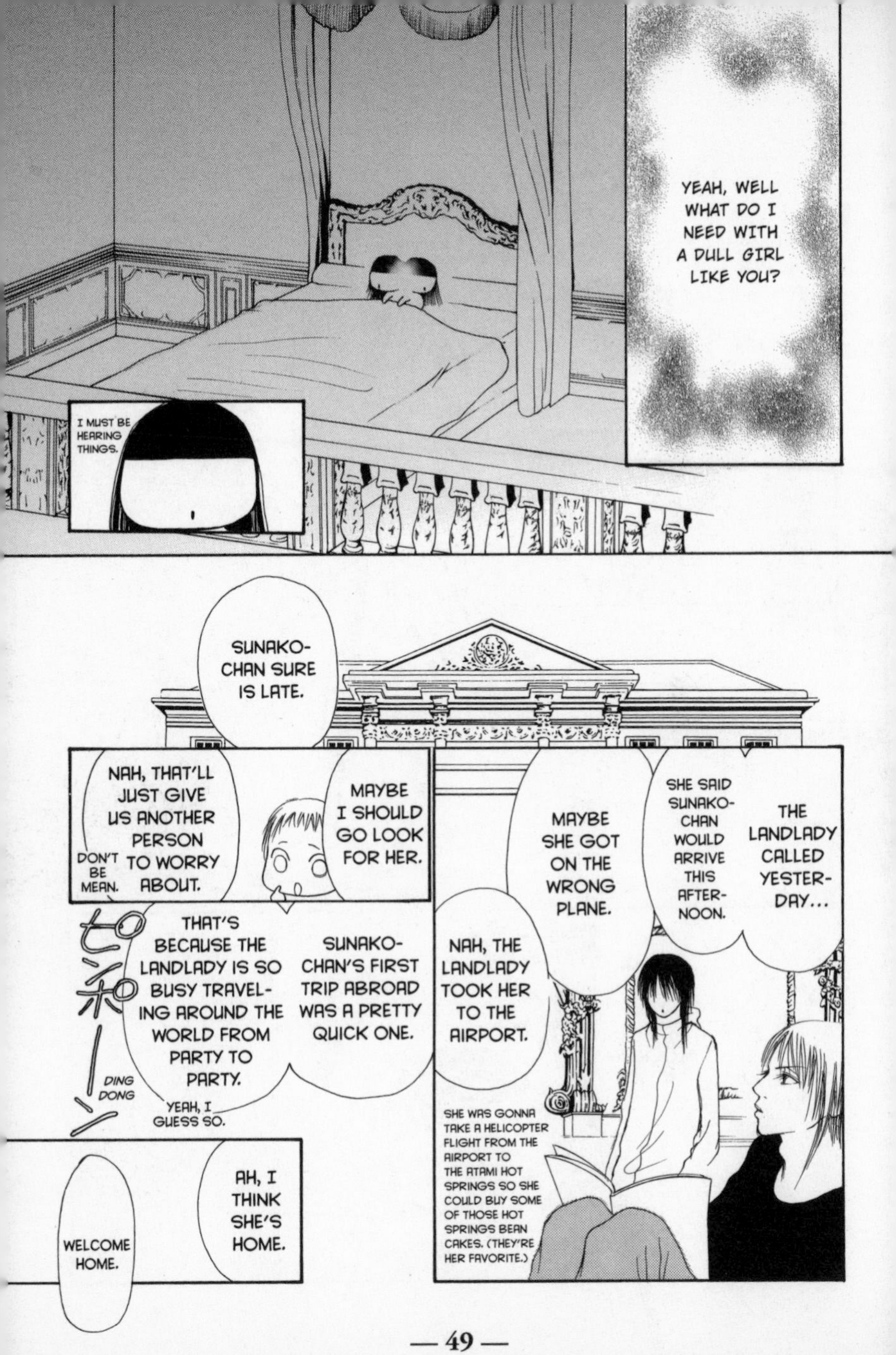
YEAH, WELL WHAT DO I NEED WITH A DULL GIRL LIKE YOU?
I MUST BE HEARING THINGS.
SUNAKO-CHAN SURE IS LATE.
THE LANDLADY CALLED YESTER-DAY...
SHE SAID SUNAKO-CHAN WOULD ARRIVE THIS AFTER-NOON.
MAYBE SHE GOT ON THE WRONG PLANE.
NAH, THE LANDLADY TOOK HER TO THE AIRPORT.
SHE WAS GONNA TAKE A HELICOPTER FLIGHT FROM THE AIRPORT TO THE ATAMI HOT SPRINGS SO SHE COULD BUY SOME OF THOSE HOT SPRINGS BEAN CAKES. (THEY'RE HER FAVORITE.)
MAYBE I SHOULD GO LOOK FOR HER.
NAH, THAT'LL JUST GIVE US ANOTHER PERSON TO WORRY ABOUT.
DON'T BE MEAN.
SUNAKO-CHAN'S FIRST TRIP ABROAD WAS A PRETTY QUICK ONE.
THAT'S BECAUSE THE LANDLADY IS SO BUSY TRAVEL-ING AROUND THE WORLD FROM PARTY TO PARTY.
YEAH, I GUESS SO.
DING DONG
AH, I THINK SHE'S HOME.
WELCOME HOME.

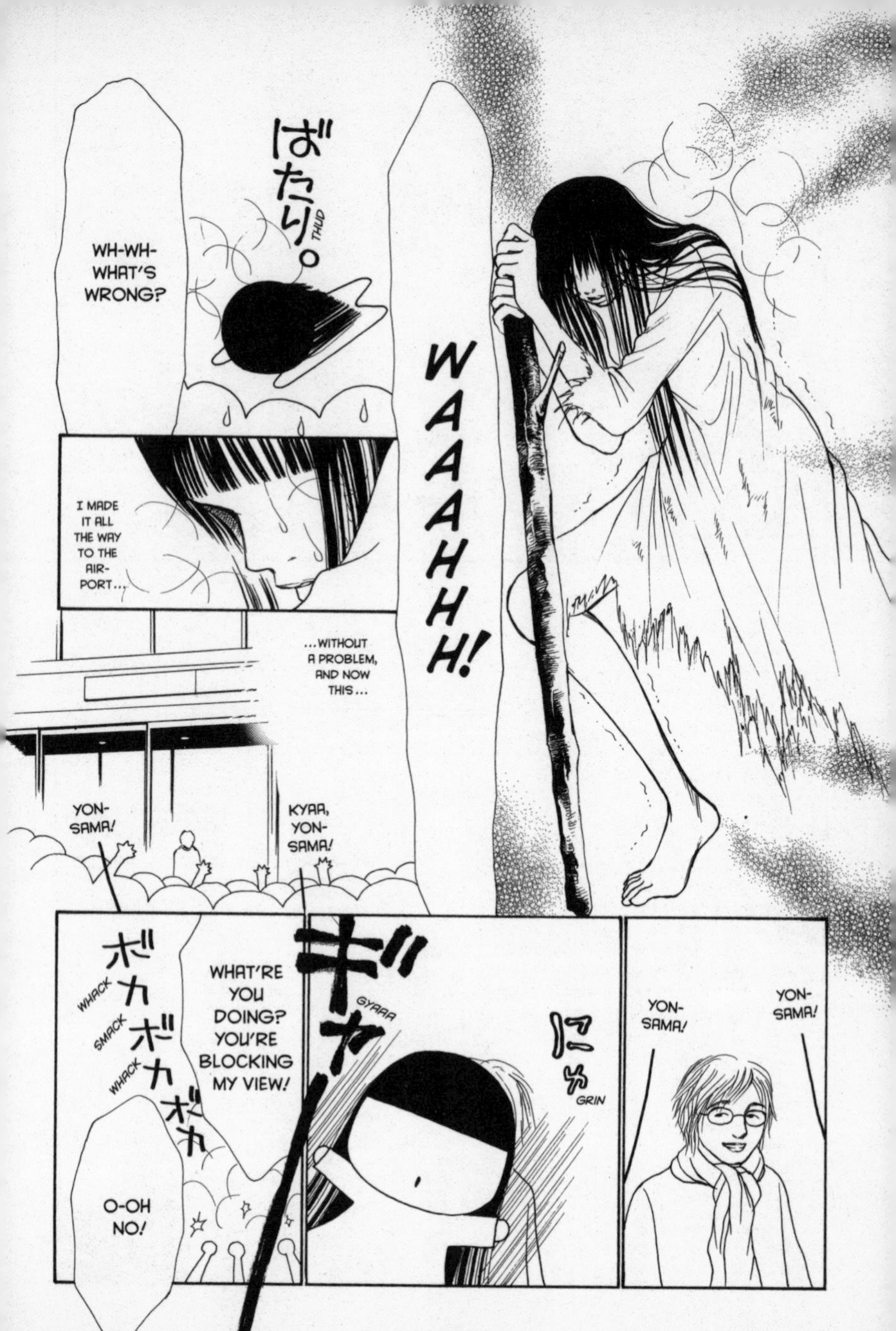
WAAAAHHH!
ばたり。
THUD
WH-WH-WHAT'S WRONG?
I MADE IT ALL THE WAY TO THE AIR-PORT...
...WITHOUT A PROBLEM, AND NOW THIS...
KYAA, YON-SAMA!
YON-SAMA!
YON-SAMA!
YON-SAMA!
にゃ
GRIN
ギャ
GYAAA
WHAT'RE YOU DOING? YOU'RE BLOCKING MY VIEW!
ボカボカボカボカ
WHACK SMACK WHACK
O-OH NO!

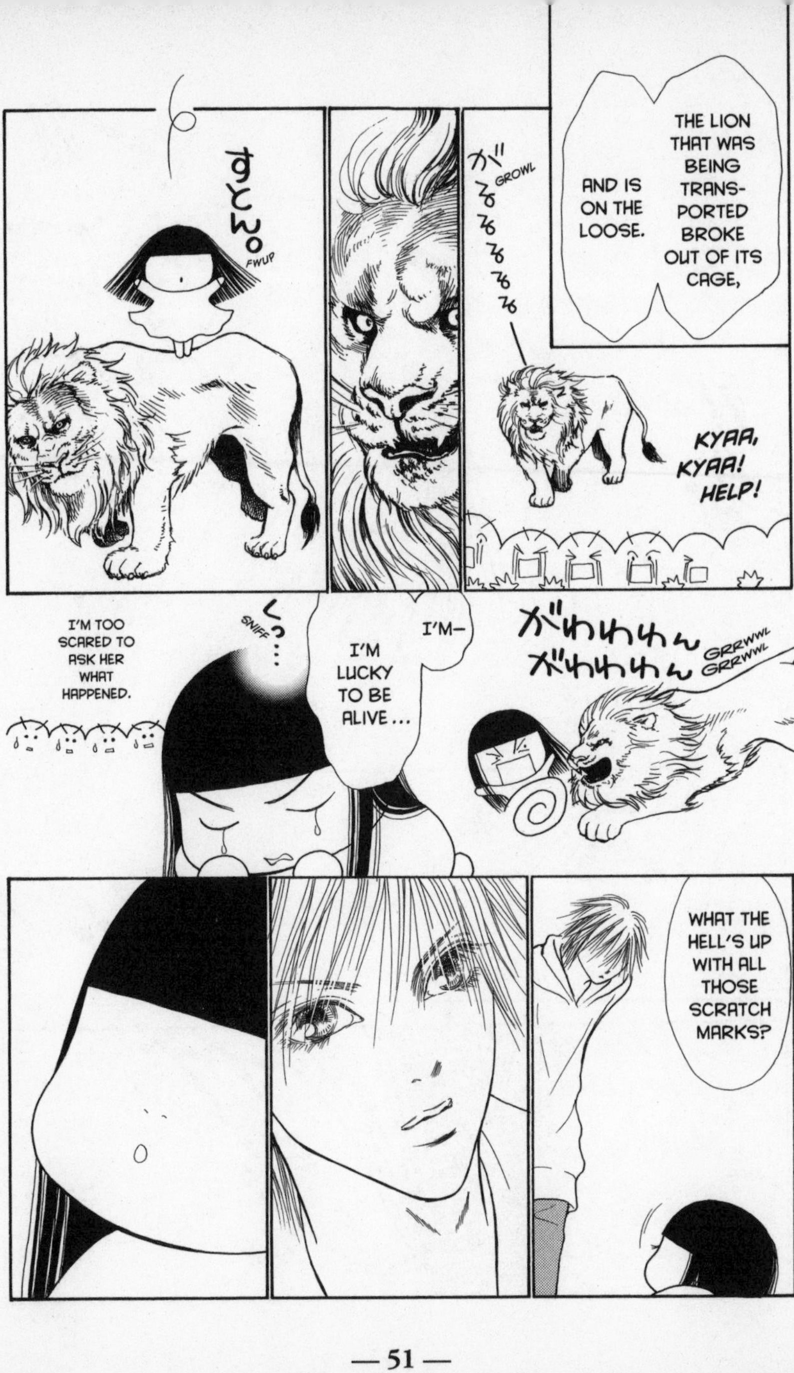
THE LION THAT WAS BEING TRANS-PORTED BROKE OUT OF ITS CAGE,
AND IS ON THE LOOSE.
がるるるるる
GROWL
KYAA, KYAA! HELP!
すとん。
FWUP
がわわわん がわわわん
GRRWWL GRRWWL
I'M—
I'M LUCKY TO BE ALIVE…
くっ…
SNIFF
I'M TOO SCARED TO ASK HER WHAT HAPPENED.
WHAT THE HELL'S UP WITH ALL THOSE SCRATCH MARKS?

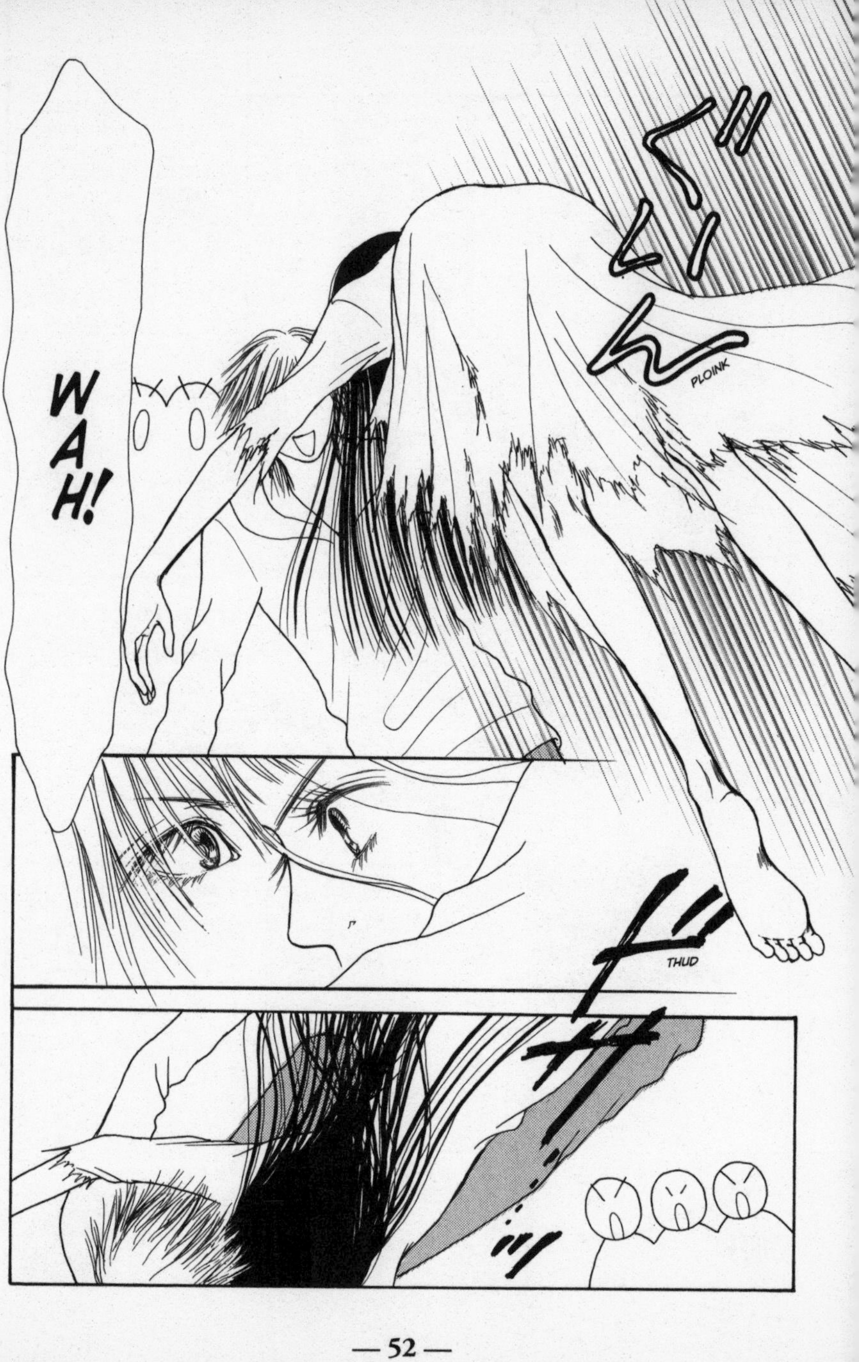
PLOINK
WAH!
THUD

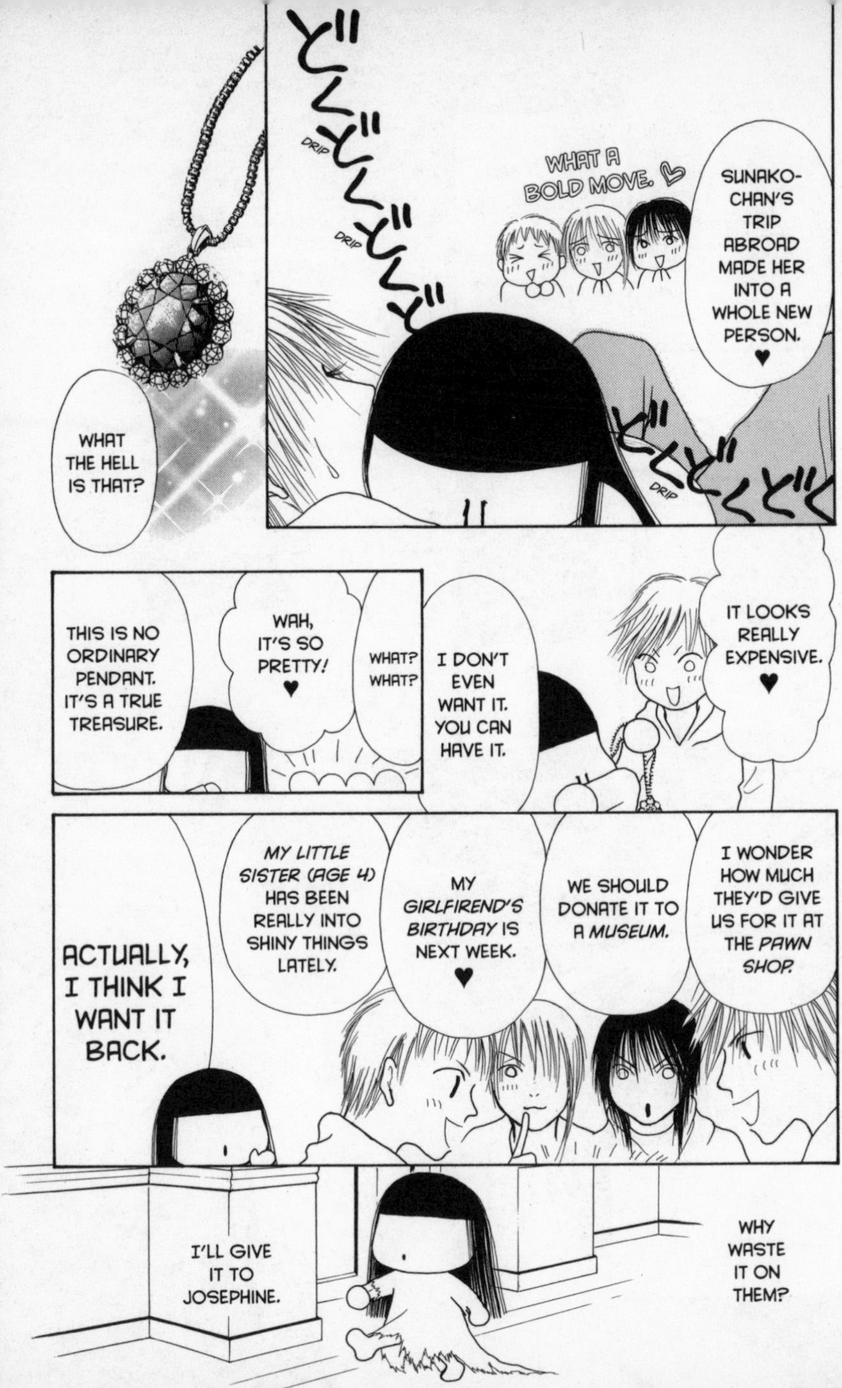
SUNAKO-CHAN'S TRIP ABROAD MADE HER INTO A WHOLE NEW PERSON. ♥
WHAT A BOLD MOVE. ♡
どくどくどくど
DRIP
DRIP
どくどくどく
DRIP
WHAT THE HELL IS THAT?
IT LOOKS REALLY EXPENSIVE. ♥
I DON'T EVEN WANT IT. YOU CAN HAVE IT.
WHAT? WHAT?
WAH, IT'S SO PRETTY! ♥
THIS IS NO ORDINARY PENDANT. IT'S A TRUE TREASURE.
I WONDER HOW MUCH THEY'D GIVE US FOR IT AT THE PAWN SHOP.
WE SHOULD DONATE IT TO A MUSEUM.
MY GIRLFIREND'S BIRTHDAY IS NEXT WEEK. ♥
MY LITTLE SISTER (AGE 4) HAS BEEN REALLY INTO SHINY THINGS LATELY.
ACTUALLY, I THINK I WANT IT BACK.
WHY WASTE IT ON THEM?
I'LL GIVE IT TO JOSEPHINE.

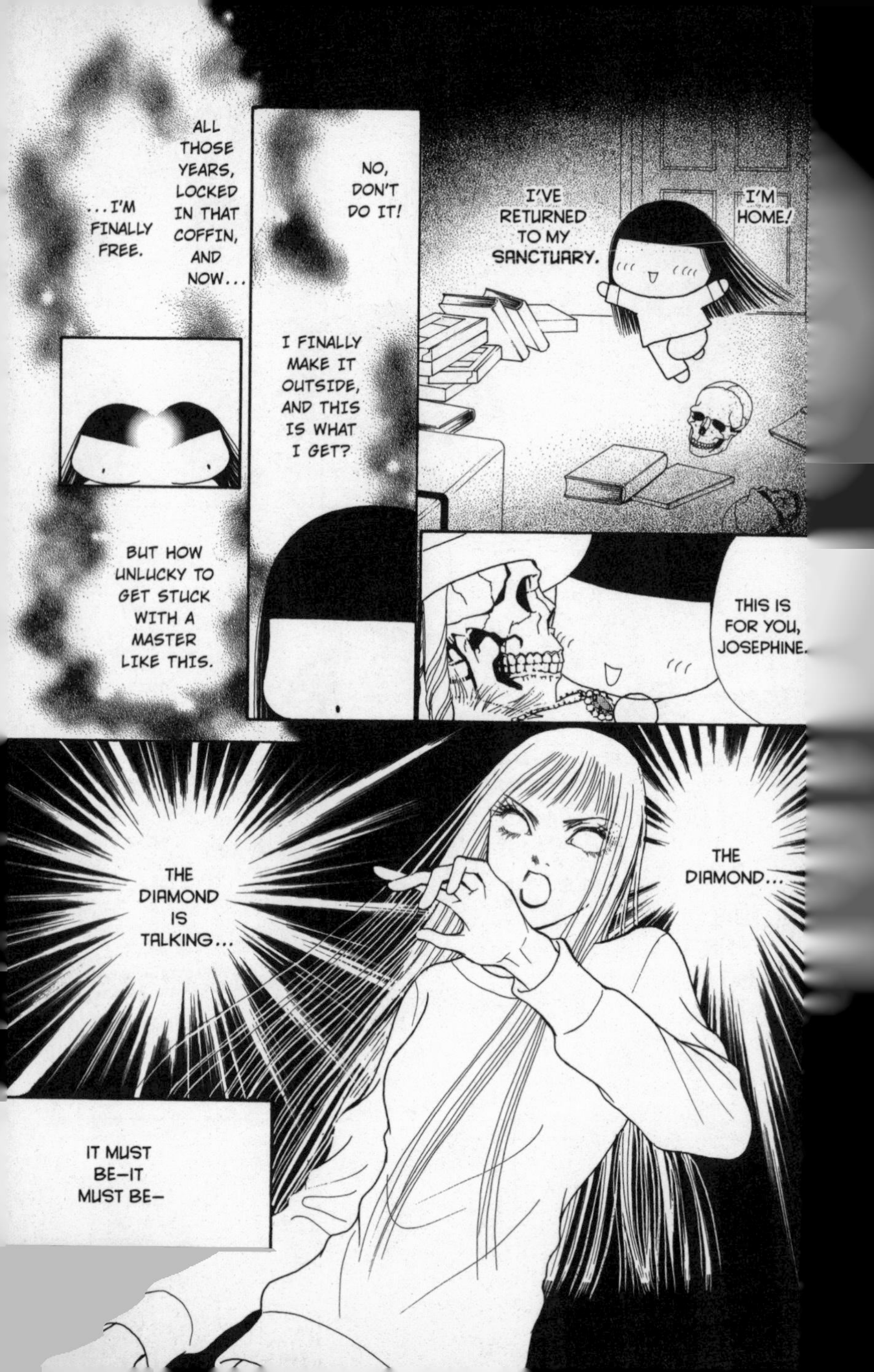
I'M HOME!
I'VE RETURNED TO MY SANCTUARY.
THIS IS FOR YOU, JOSEPHINE.
NO, DON'T DO IT!
I FINALLY MAKE IT OUTSIDE, AND THIS IS WHAT I GET?
ALL THOSE YEARS, LOCKED IN THAT COFFIN, AND NOW...
...I'M FINALLY FREE.
BUT HOW UNLUCKY TO GET STUCK WITH A MASTER LIKE THIS.
THE DIAMOND...
THE DIAMOND IS TALKING...
IT MUST BE—IT MUST BE—

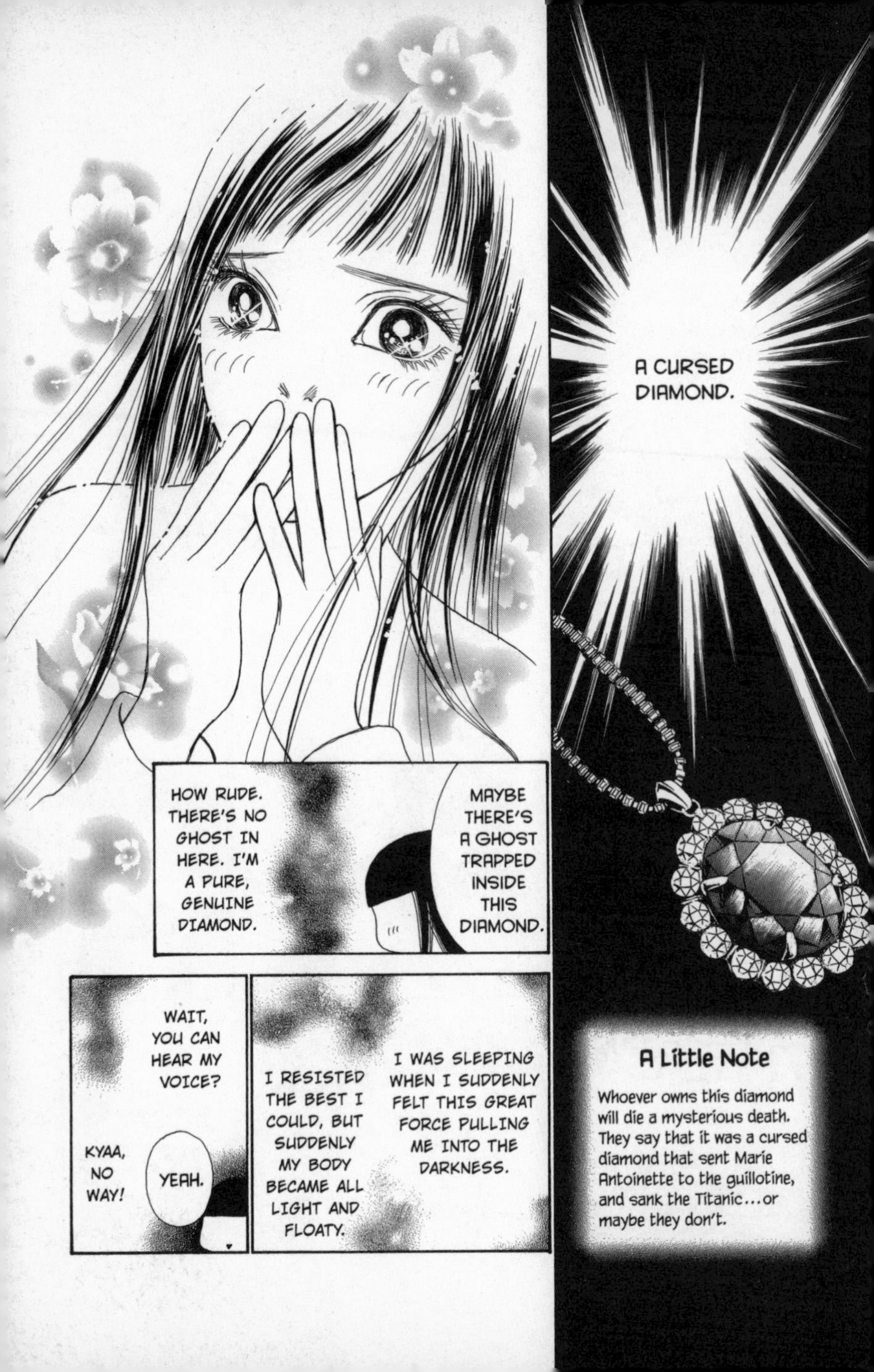
A CURSED DIAMOND.
A Little Note
Whoever owns this diamond will die a mysterious death. They say that it was a cursed diamond that sent Marie Antoinette to the guillotine, and sank the Titanic...or maybe they don't.
MAYBE THERE'S A GHOST TRAPPED INSIDE THIS DIAMOND.
HOW RUDE. THERE'S NO GHOST IN HERE. I'M A PURE, GENUINE DIAMOND.
I WAS SLEEPING WHEN I SUDDENLY FELT THIS GREAT FORCE PULLING ME INTO THE DARKNESS.
I RESISTED THE BEST I COULD, BUT SUDDENLY MY BODY BECAME ALL LIGHT AND FLOATY.
WAIT, YOU CAN HEAR MY VOICE?
YEAH.
KYAA, NO WAY!

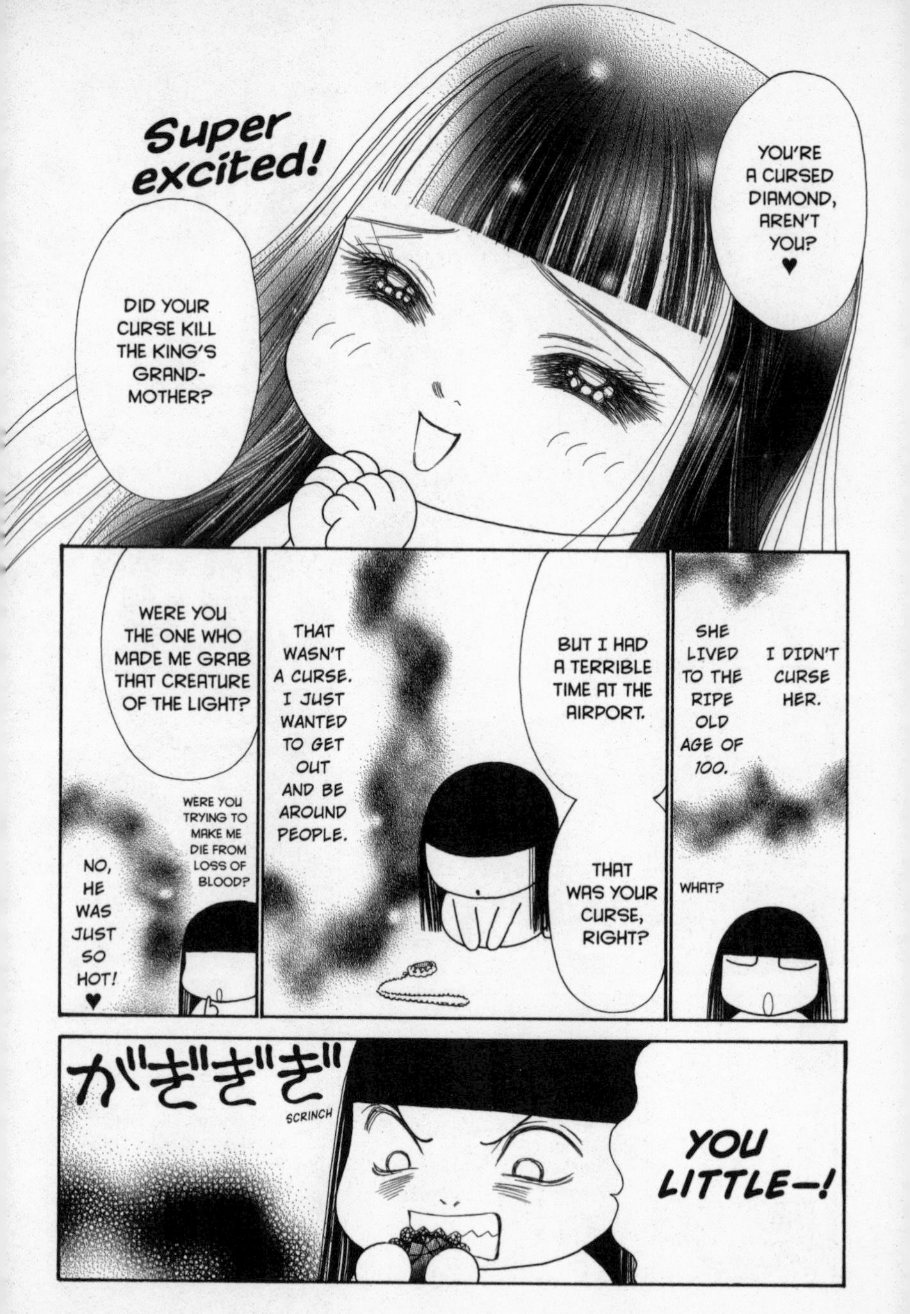
YOU'RE A CURSED DIAMOND, AREN'T YOU? ♥
Super excited!
DID YOUR CURSE KILL THE KING'S GRAND-MOTHER?
I DIDN'T CURSE HER.
SHE LIVED TO THE RIPE OLD AGE OF 100.
WHAT?
BUT I HAD A TERRIBLE TIME AT THE AIRPORT.
THAT WAS YOUR CURSE, RIGHT?
THAT WASN'T A CURSE. I JUST WANTED TO GET OUT AND BE AROUND PEOPLE.
WERE YOU THE ONE WHO MADE ME GRAB THAT CREATURE OF THE LIGHT?
WERE YOU TRYING TO MAKE ME DIE FROM LOSS OF BLOOD?
NO, HE WAS JUST SO HOT! ♥
YOU LITTLE—!
がぎぎぎ
SCRINCH

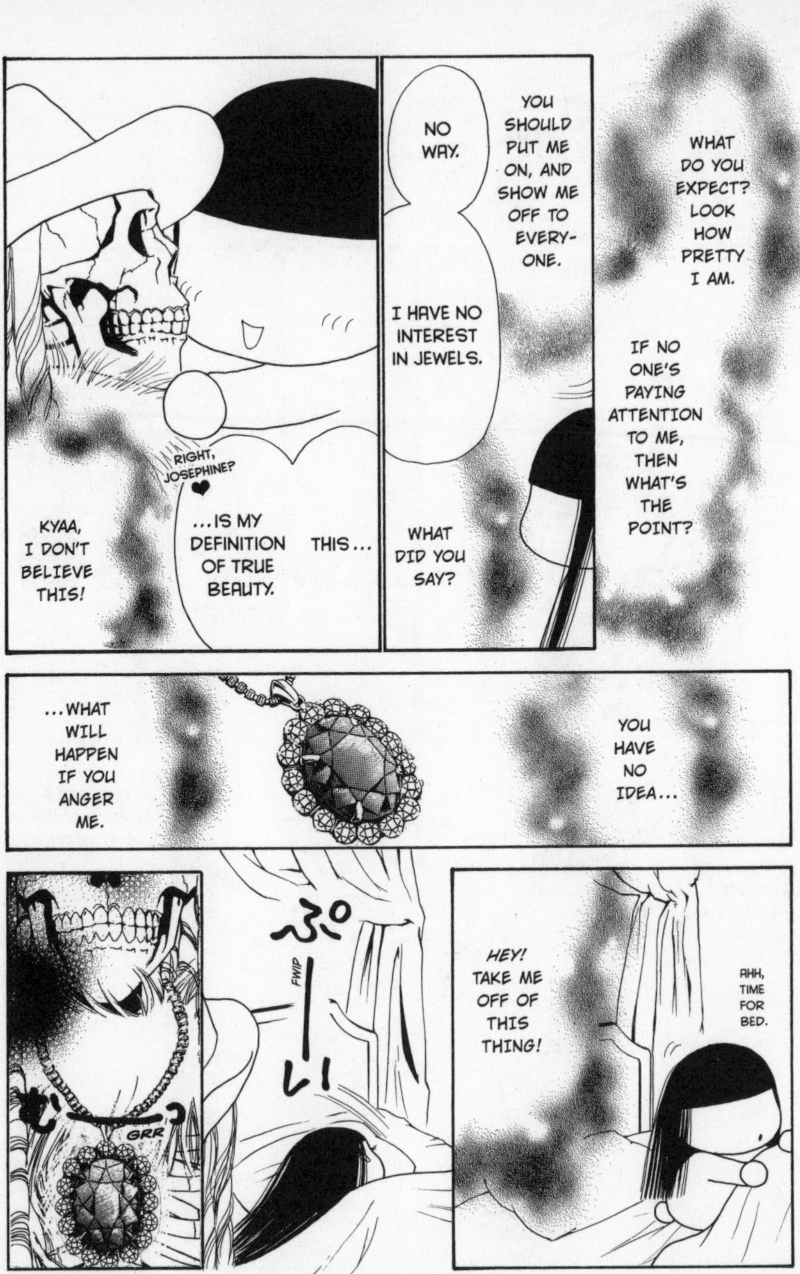
WHAT DO YOU EXPECT? LOOK HOW PRETTY I AM.
IF NO ONE'S PAYING ATTENTION TO ME, THEN WHAT'S THE POINT?
YOU SHOULD PUT ME ON, AND SHOW ME OFF TO EVERY-ONE.
NO WAY.
I HAVE NO INTEREST IN JEWELS.
WHAT DID YOU SAY?
THIS...
...IS MY DEFINITION OF TRUE BEAUTY.
RIGHT, JOSEPHINE? ❤
KYAA, I DON'T BELIEVE THIS!
YOU HAVE NO IDEA...
...WHAT WILL HAPPEN IF YOU ANGER ME.
AHH, TIME FOR BED.
HEY! TAKE ME OFF OF THIS THING!
ぷーい
FWIP
GRR

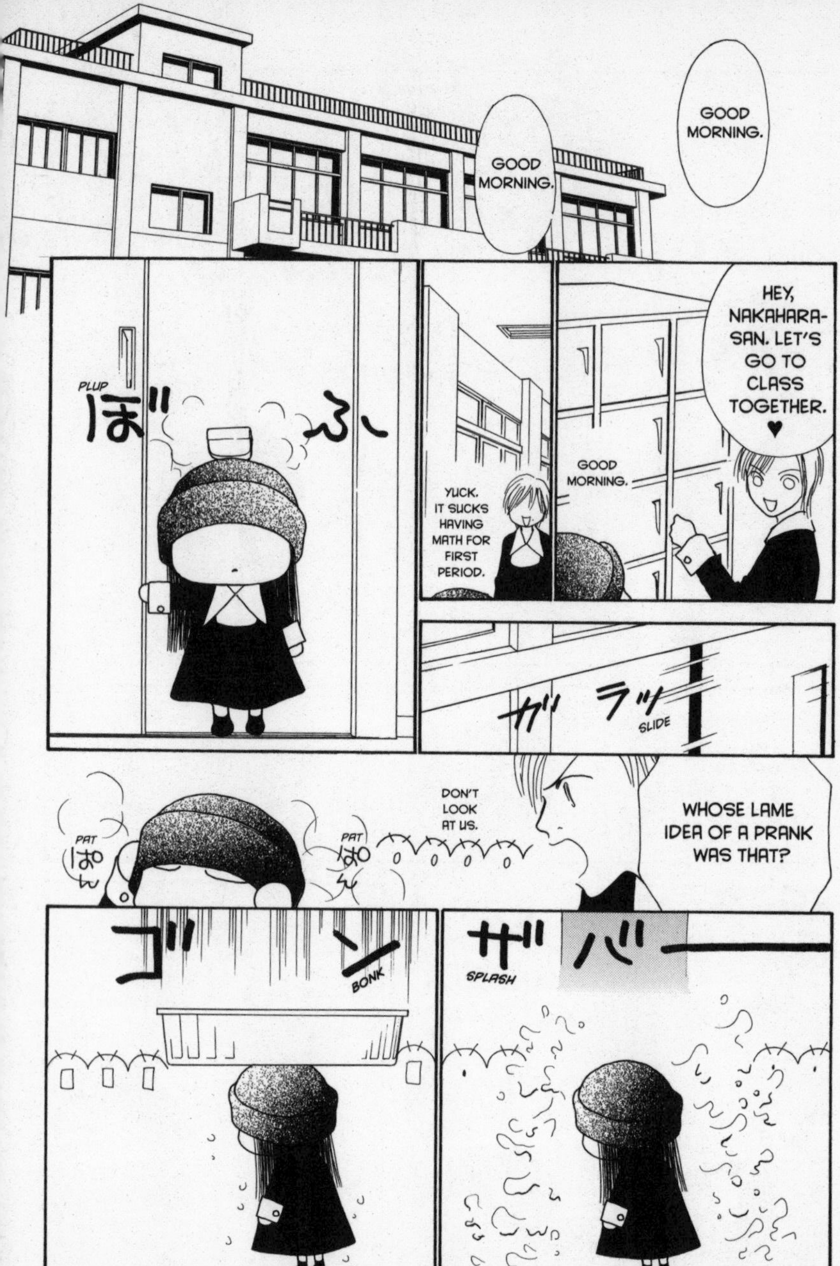
GOOD MORNING.
GOOD MORNING.
HEY, NAKAHARA-SAN. LET'S GO TO CLASS TOGETHER. ♥
GOOD MORNING.
YUCK. IT SUCKS HAVING MATH FOR FIRST PERIOD.
ガラッ
SLIDE
PLUP
ぼふ
WHOSE LAME IDEA OF A PRANK WAS THAT?
DON'T LOOK AT US.
PAT
ぽん
PAT
ぽん
ザバー
SPLASH
ゴン
BONK

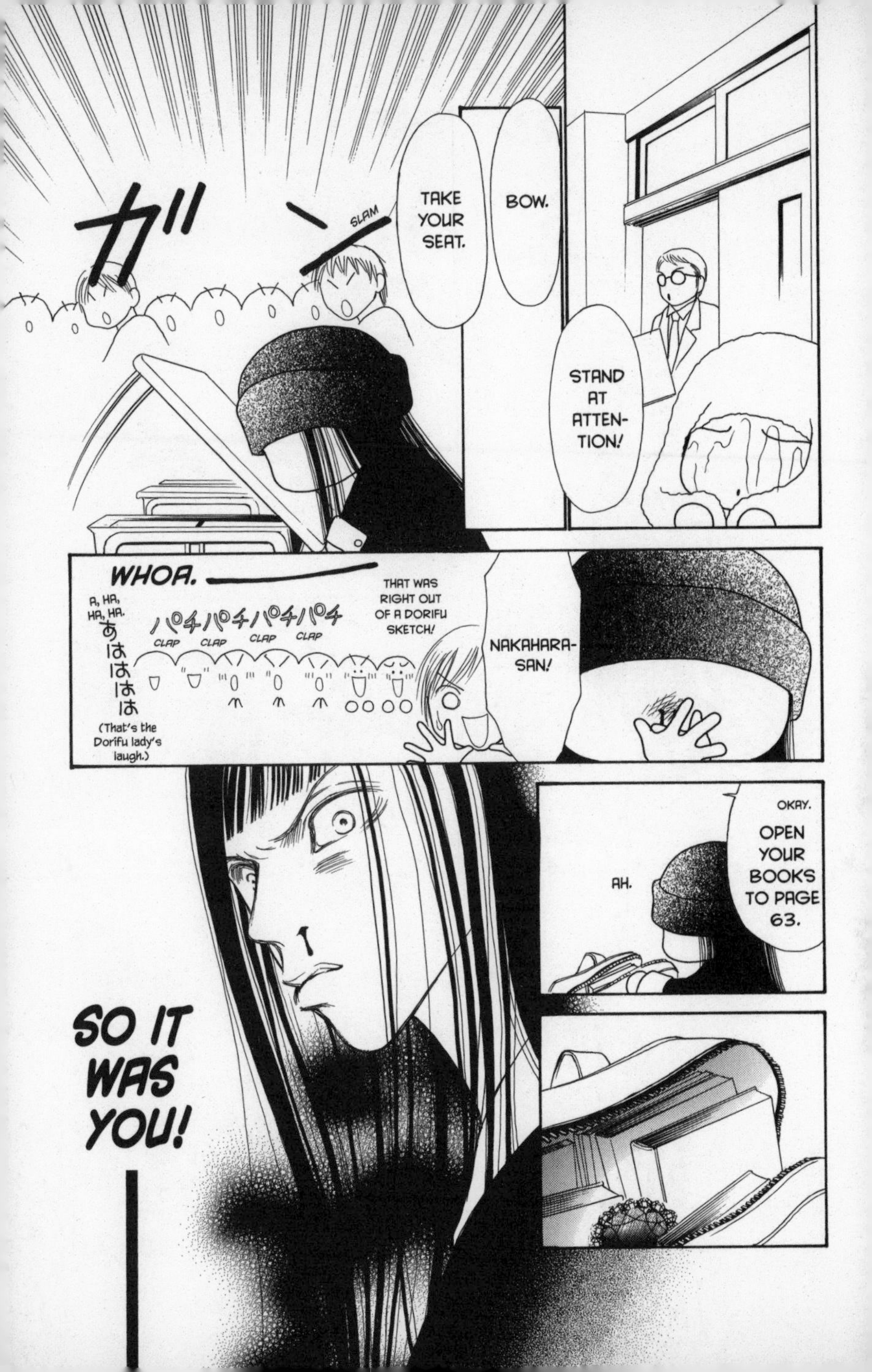
STAND AT ATTENTION!
BOW.
TAKE YOUR SEAT.
ガン
SLAM
NAKAHARA-SAN!
THAT WAS RIGHT OUT OF A DORIFU SKETCH!
WHOA.
パチパチパチパチ
CLAP CLAP CLAP CLAP
A, HA, HA, HA.
あははは
(That's the Dorifu lady's laugh.)
OKAY. OPEN YOUR BOOKS TO PAGE 63.
AH.
SO IT WAS YOU!

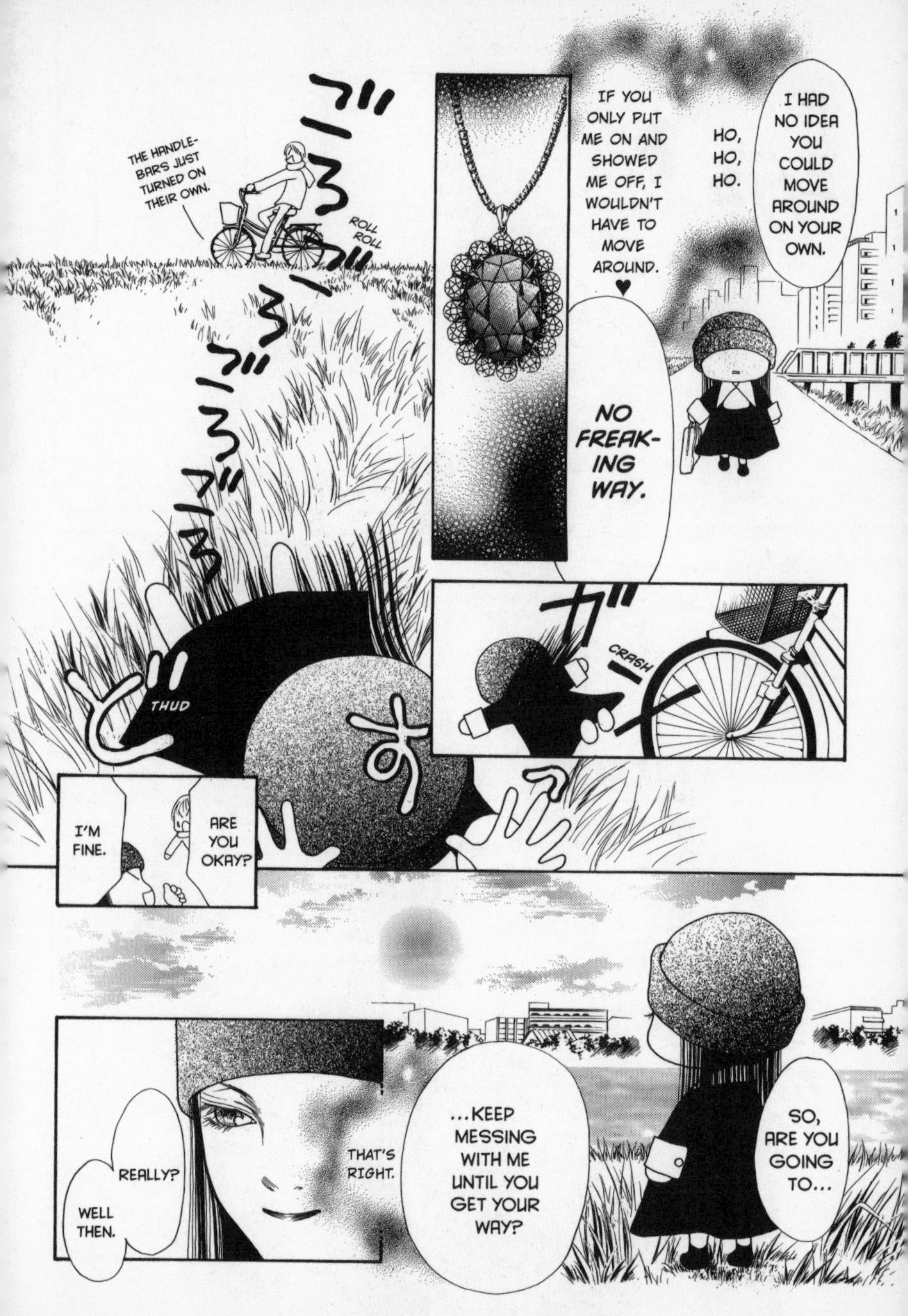
I HAD NO IDEA YOU COULD MOVE AROUND ON YOUR OWN.
HO, HO, HO.
IF YOU ONLY PUT ME ON AND SHOWED ME OFF, I WOULDN'T HAVE TO MOVE AROUND. ♥
NO FREAKING WAY.
THE HANDLE-BARS JUST TURNED ON THEIR OWN.
ROLL ROLL
CRASH
THUD
ARE YOU OKAY?
I'M FINE.
SO, ARE YOU GOING TO...
...KEEP MESSING WITH ME UNTIL YOU GET YOUR WAY?
THAT'S RIGHT.
REALLY?
WELL THEN.

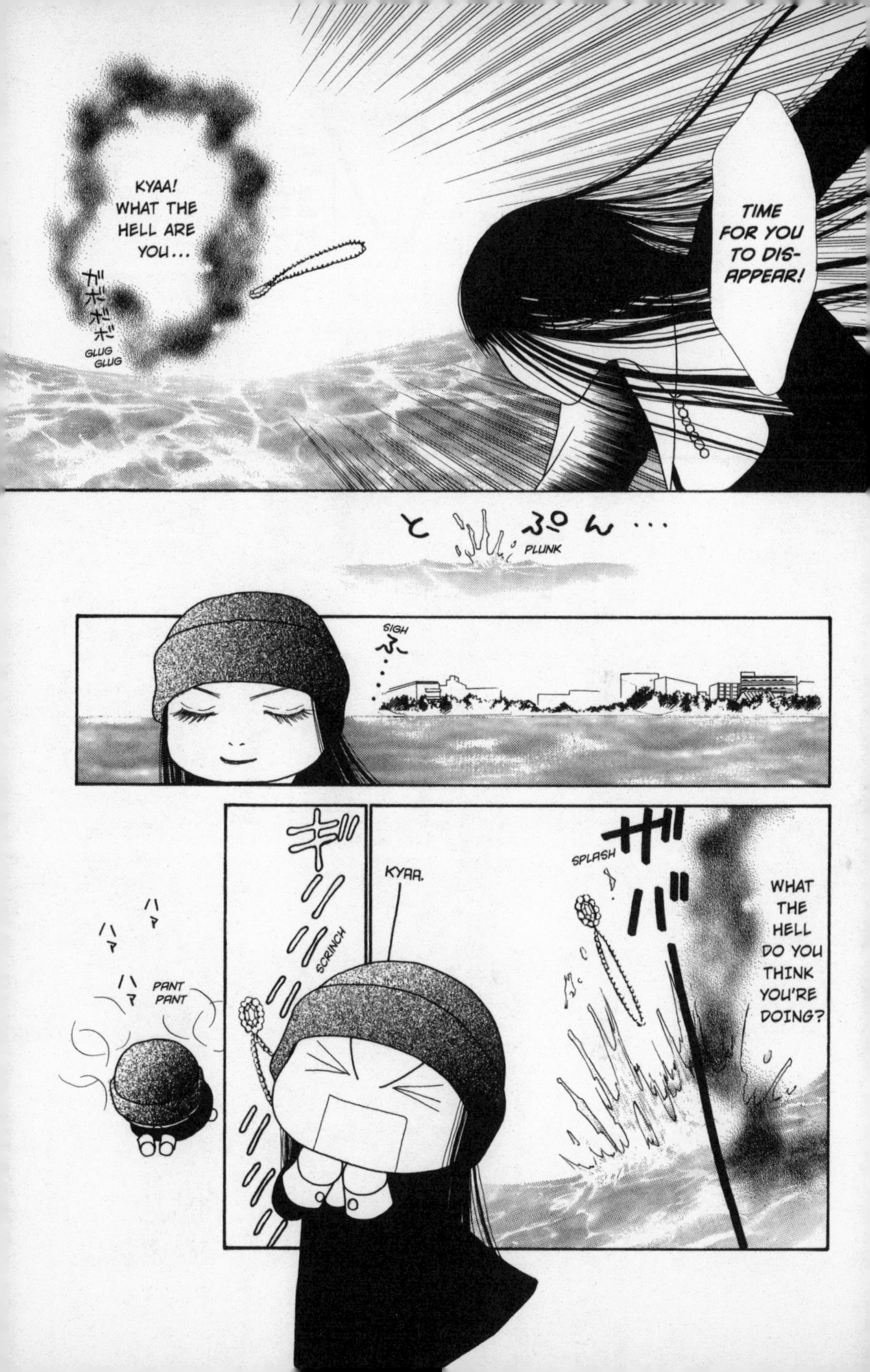
TIME FOR YOU TO DIS-APPEAR!
KYAA! WHAT THE HELL ARE YOU...
ガボガボ
GLUG GLUG
とぷん…
PLUNK
SIGH
ふ…
ザバ
SPLASH
WHAT THE HELL DO YOU THINK YOU'RE DOING?
ギリ
SCRINCH
KYAA.
ハァハァハァ
PANT PANT

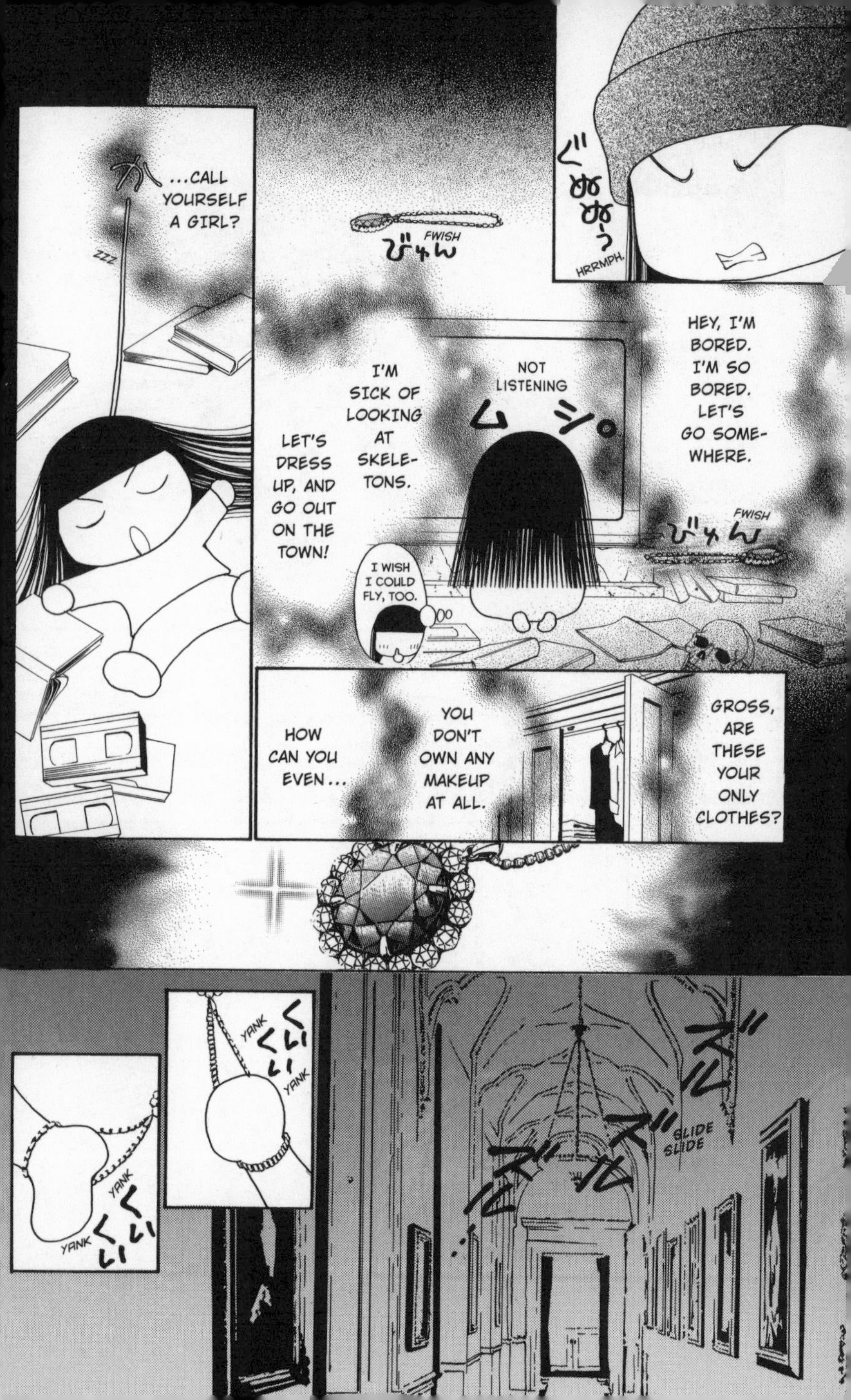
ぐぬぬぬぅ
HRRMPH.
HEY, I'M BORED. I'M SO BORED. LET'S GO SOMEWHERE.
びゅん
FWISH
NOT LISTENING
ムシ。
I'M SICK OF LOOKING AT SKELETONS.
LET'S DRESS UP, AND GO OUT ON THE TOWN!
I WISH I COULD FLY, TOO.
GROSS, ARE THESE YOUR ONLY CLOTHES?
YOU DON'T OWN ANY MAKEUP AT ALL.
HOW CAN YOU EVEN...
びゅん
FWISH
...CALL YOURSELF A GIRL?
ZZZ
ズルズル
SLIDE SLIDE
くいくいくい
YANK
YANK
くいくいくい
YANK
YANK

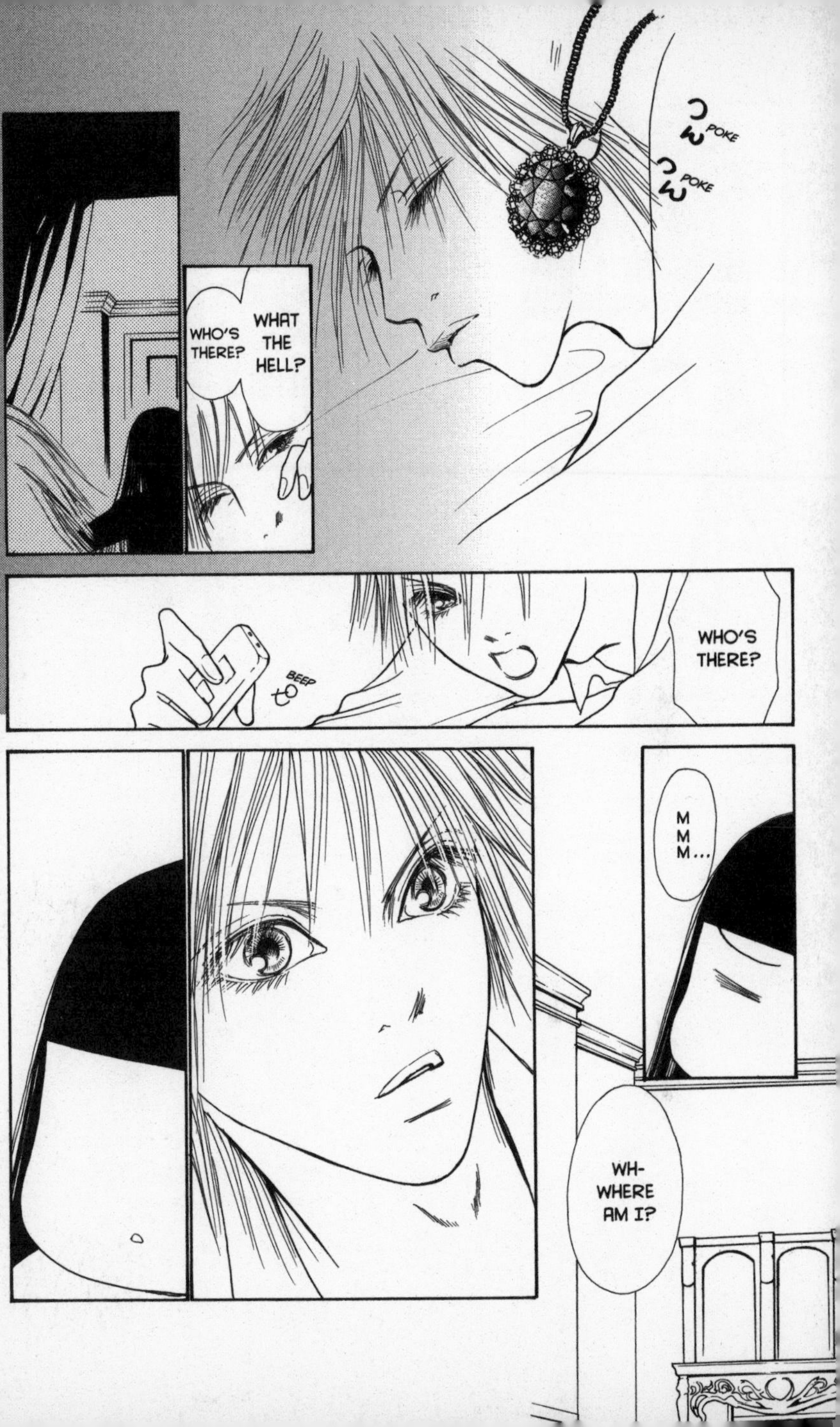
POKE
POKE
WHAT THE HELL?
WHO'S THERE?
WHO'S THERE?
BEEP
MMM...
WH- WHERE AM I?

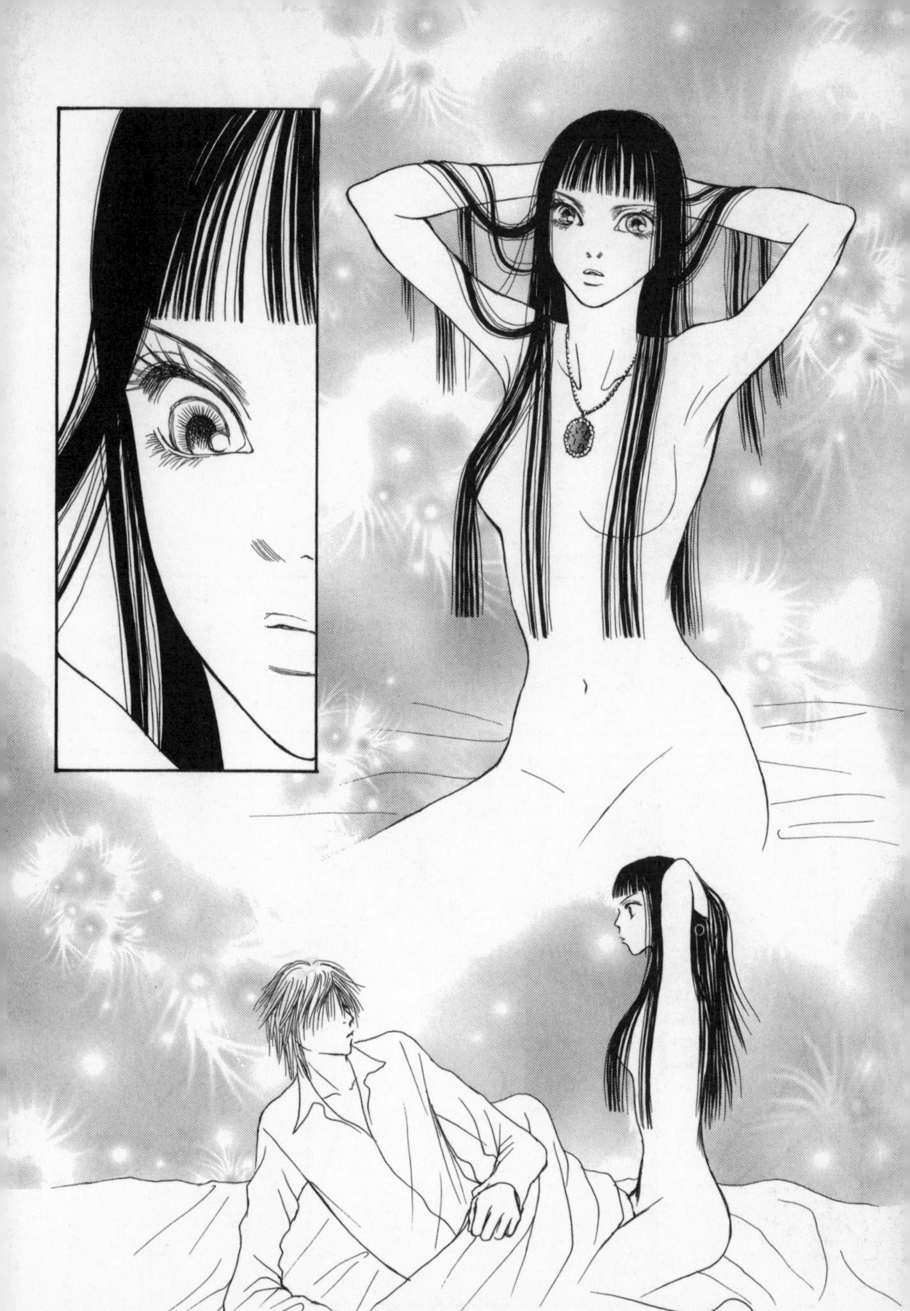

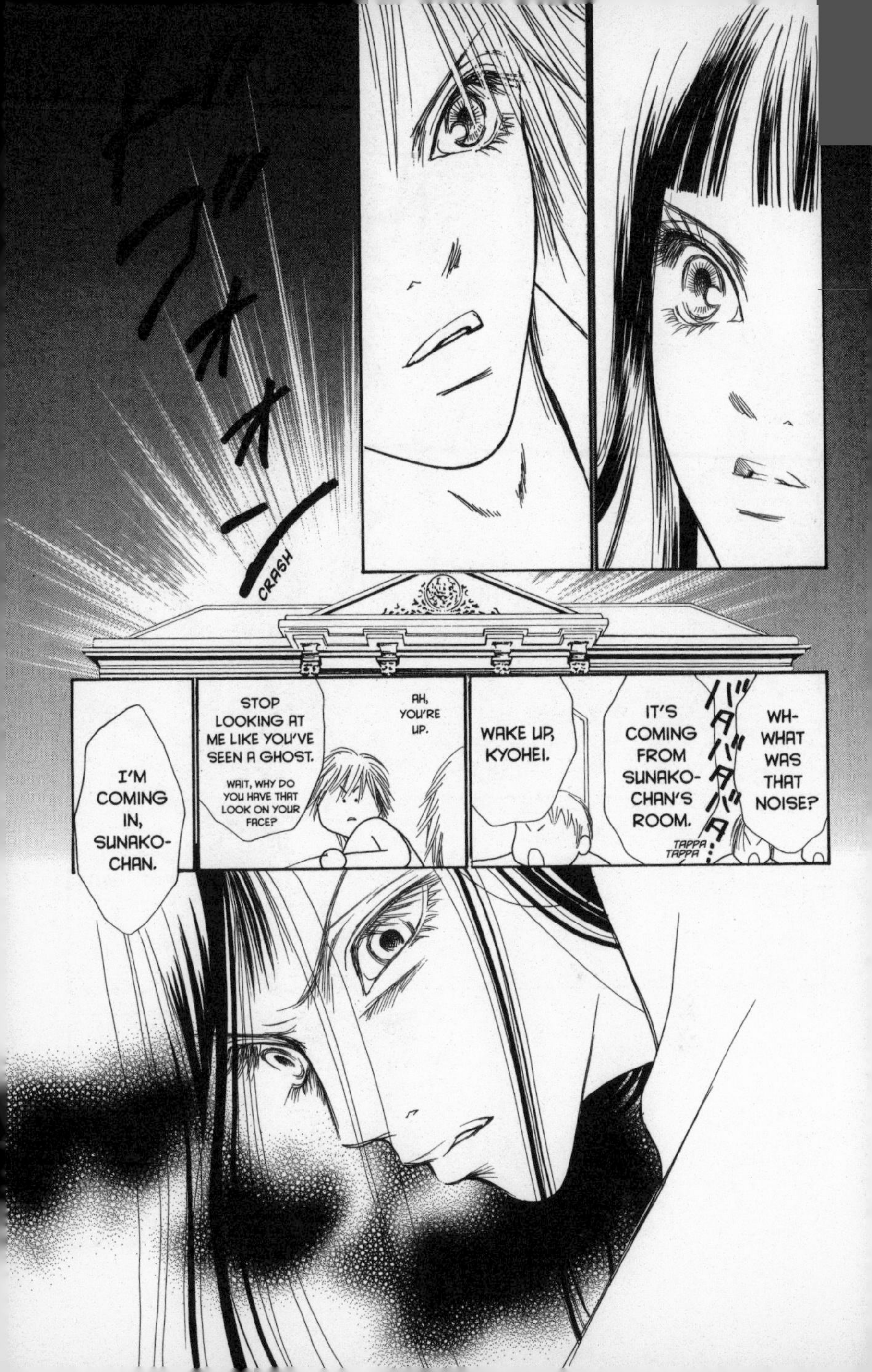
CRASH
WH- WHAT WAS THAT NOISE?
IT'S COMING FROM SUNAKO-CHAN'S ROOM.
TAPPA TAPPA...
WAKE UP, KYOHEI.
AH, YOU'RE UP.
STOP LOOKING AT ME LIKE YOU'VE SEEN A GHOST.
WAIT, WHY DO YOU HAVE THAT LOOK ON YOUR FACE?
I'M COMING IN, SUNAKO-CHAN.

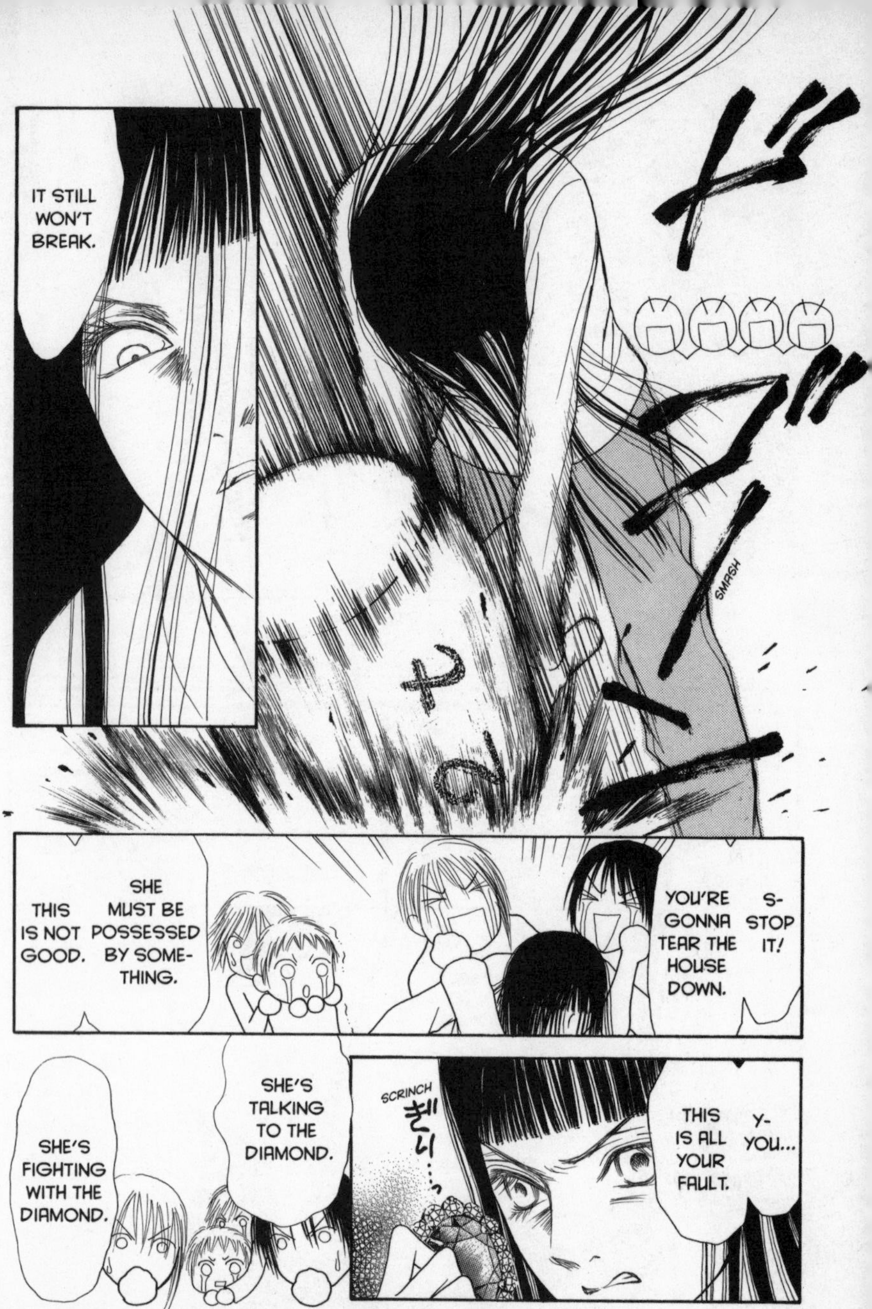
SMASH
IT STILL WON'T BREAK.
S-STOP IT!
YOU'RE GONNA TEAR THE HOUSE DOWN.
SHE MUST BE POSSESSED BY SOMETHING.
THIS IS NOT GOOD.
Y-YOU...
THIS IS ALL YOUR FAULT.
SCRINCH
SHE'S TALKING TO THE DIAMOND.
SHE'S FIGHTING WITH THE DIAMOND.

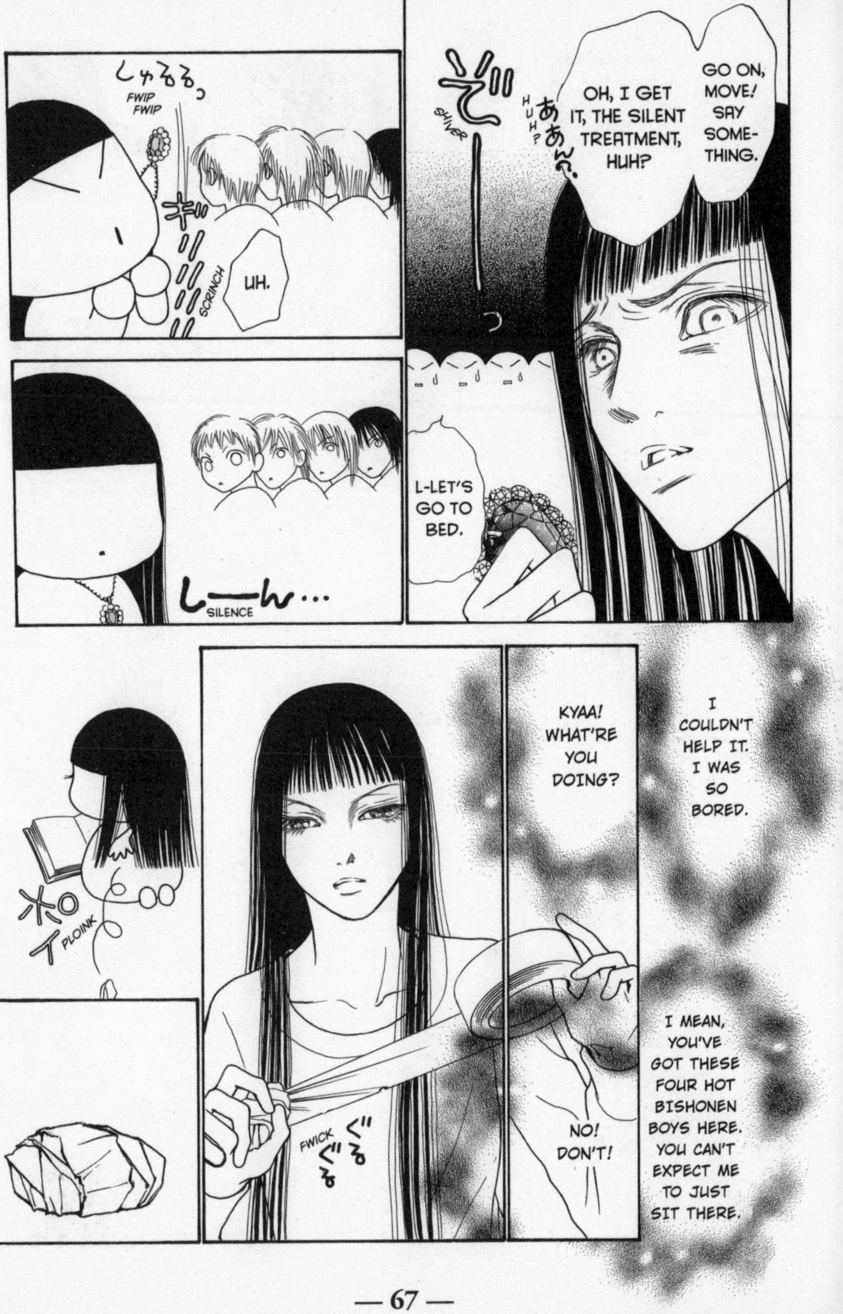
GO ON, MOVE! SAY SOMETHING.
OH, I GET IT, THE SILENT TREATMENT, HUH?
HUH?
SHIVER
L-LET'S GO TO BED.
FWIP FWIP
SCRINCH
UH.
SILENCE
I COULDN'T HELP IT. I WAS SO BORED.
KYAA! WHAT'RE YOU DOING?
I MEAN, YOU'VE GOT THESE FOUR HOT BISHONEN BOYS HERE. YOU CAN'T EXPECT ME TO JUST SIT THERE.
NO! DON'T!
FWICK
PLOINK

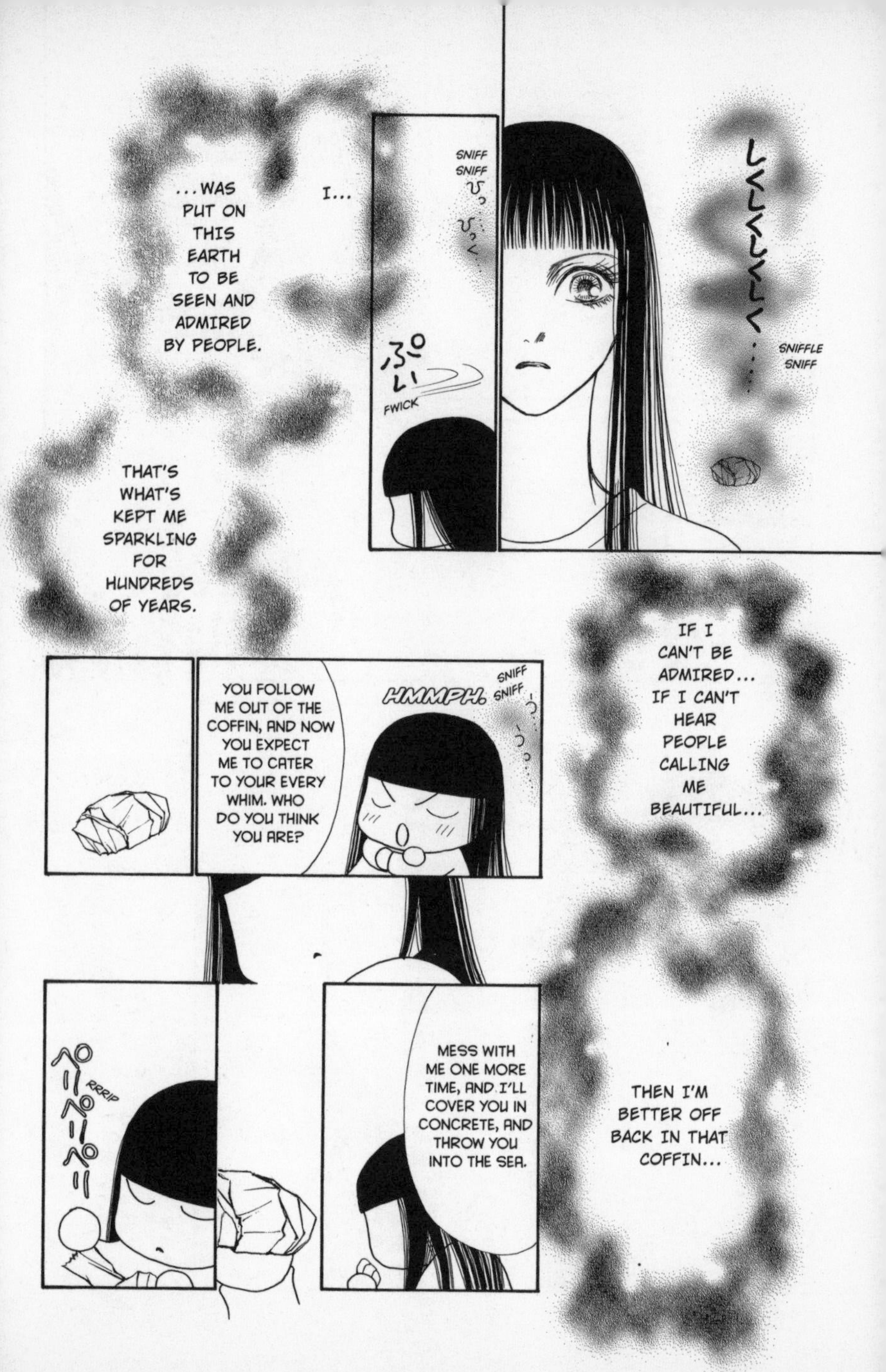
しくしくしくしく……
SNIFFLE SNIFF
SNIFF SNIFF
ぷい
FWICK
I...
...WAS PUT ON THIS EARTH TO BE SEEN AND ADMIRED BY PEOPLE.
THAT'S WHAT'S KEPT ME SPARKLING FOR HUNDREDS OF YEARS.
IF I CAN'T BE ADMIRED... IF I CAN'T HEAR PEOPLE CALLING ME BEAUTIFUL...
HMMPH.
SNIFF SNIFF
YOU FOLLOW ME OUT OF THE COFFIN, AND NOW YOU EXPECT ME TO CATER TO YOUR EVERY WHIM. WHO DO YOU THINK YOU ARE?
THEN I'M BETTER OFF BACK IN THAT COFFIN...
MESS WITH ME ONE MORE TIME, AND I'LL COVER YOU IN CONCRETE, AND THROW YOU INTO THE SEA.
ペーペーペー
RRRIP

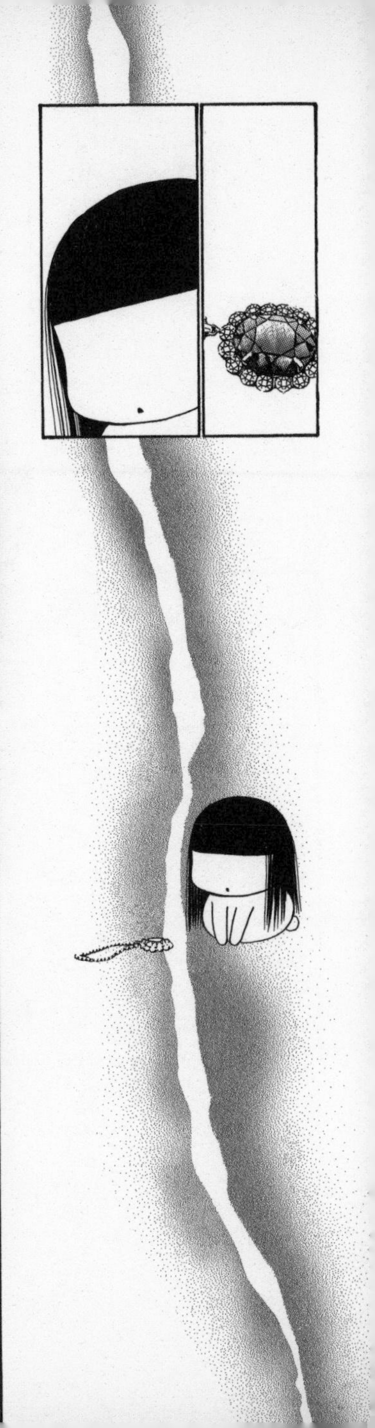

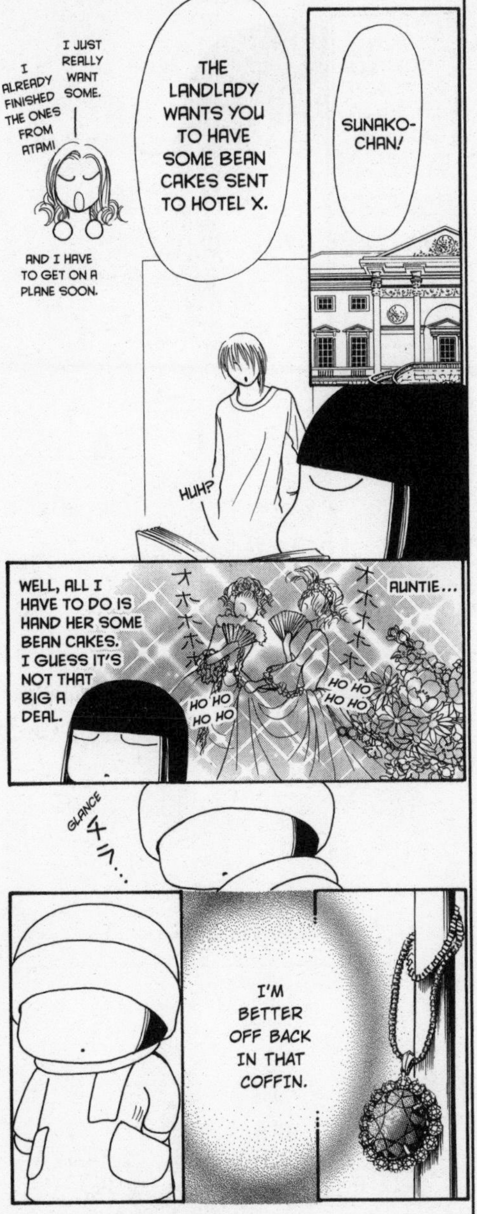
SUNAKO-CHAN!
THE LANDLADY WANTS YOU TO HAVE SOME BEAN CAKES SENT TO HOTEL X.
I JUST REALLY WANT SOME.
I ALREADY FINISHED THE ONES FROM ATAMI
AND I HAVE TO GET ON A PLANE SOON.
HUH?
AUNTIE...
オホホホホ
HO HO HO HO
オホホホホ
HO HO HO HO
WELL, ALL I HAVE TO DO IS HAND HER SOME BEAN CAKES. I GUESS IT'S NOT THAT BIG A DEAL.
GLANCE
チラ…
I'M BETTER OFF BACK IN THAT COFFIN.

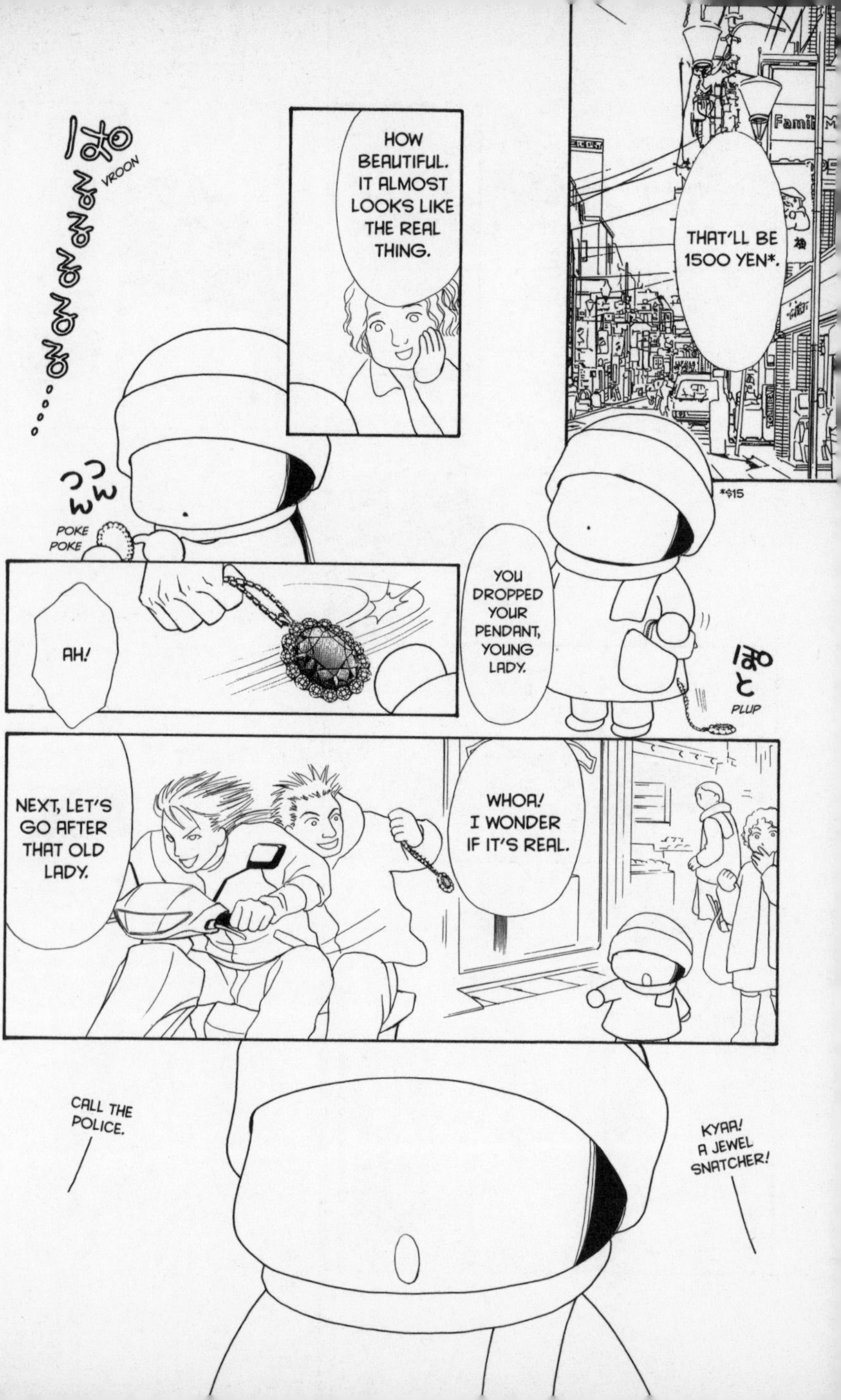

THAT'LL BE 1500 YEN*.
*$15
HOW BEAUTIFUL. IT ALMOST LOOKS LIKE THE REAL THING.
VROON
POKE POKE
YOU DROPPED YOUR PENDANT, YOUNG LADY.
ぽと
PLUP
AH!
WHOA! I WONDER IF IT'S REAL.
NEXT, LET'S GO AFTER THAT OLD LADY.
KYAA! A JEWEL SNATCHER!
CALL THE POLICE.

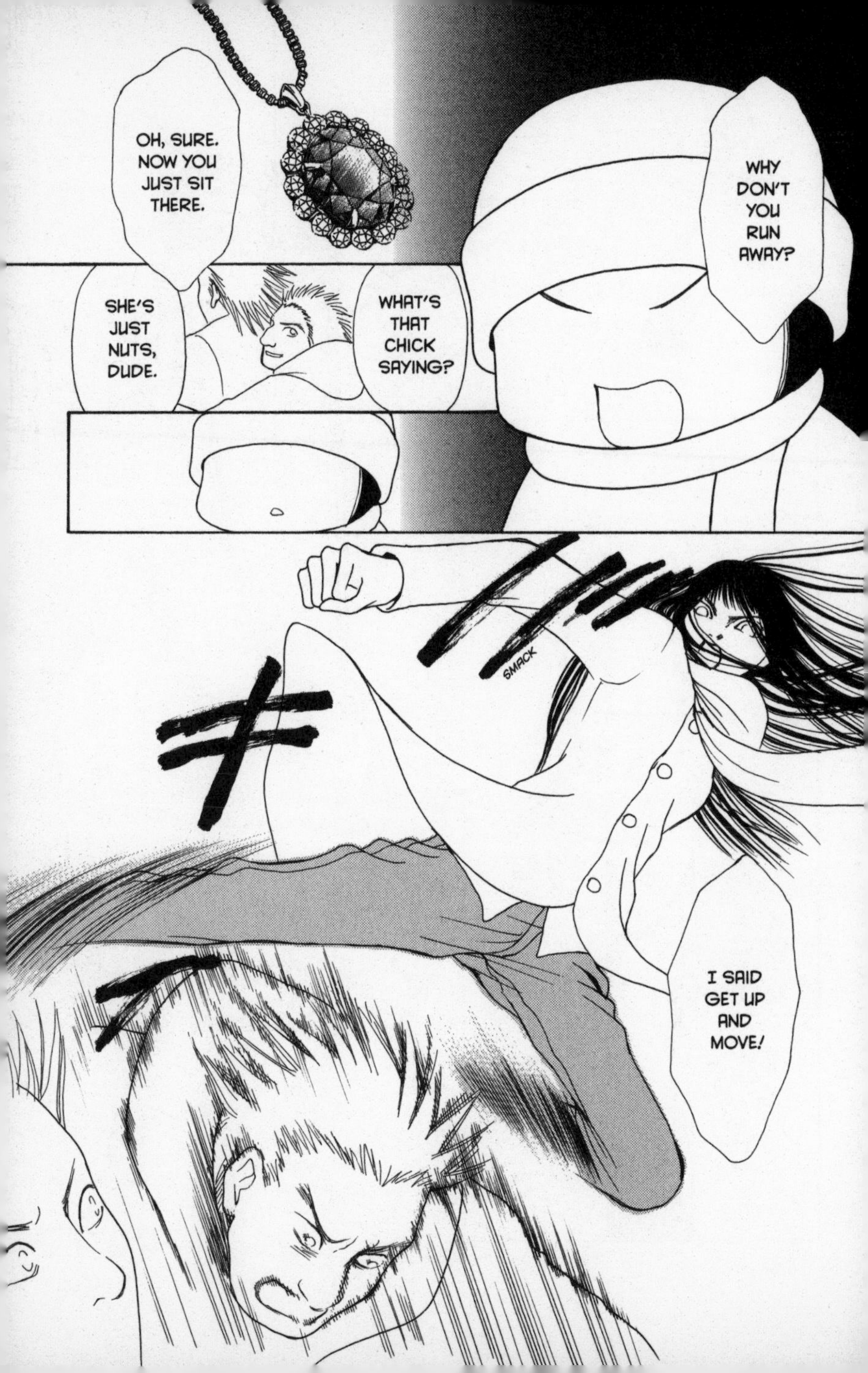
WHY DON'T YOU RUN AWAY?
OH, SURE. NOW YOU JUST SIT THERE.
WHAT'S THAT CHICK SAYING?
SHE'S JUST NUTS, DUDE.
SMACK
I SAID GET UP AND MOVE!

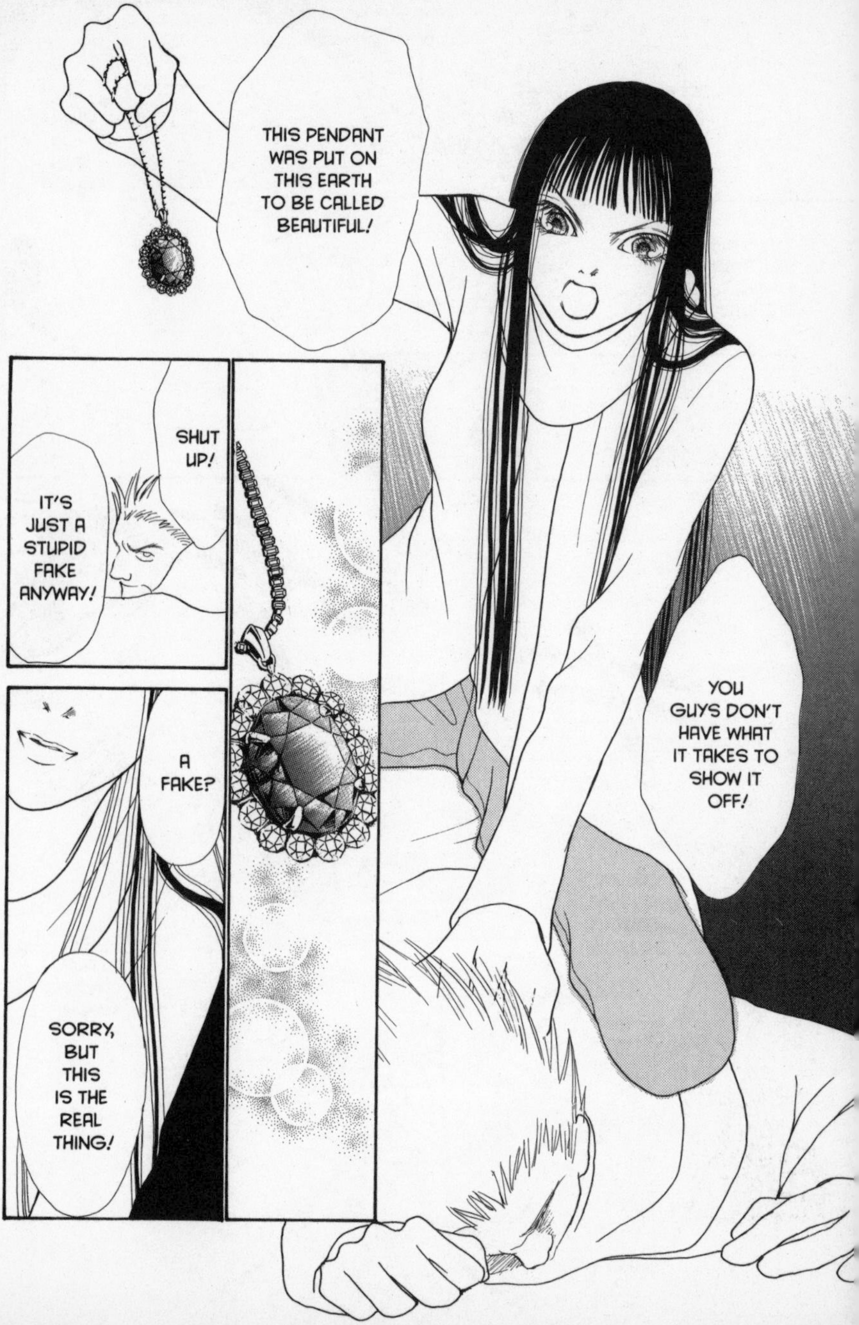
THIS PENDANT WAS PUT ON THIS EARTH TO BE CALLED BEAUTIFUL!
YOU GUYS DON'T HAVE WHAT IT TAKES TO SHOW IT OFF!
SHUT UP!
IT'S JUST A STUPID FAKE ANYWAY!
A FAKE?
SORRY, BUT THIS IS THE REAL THING!

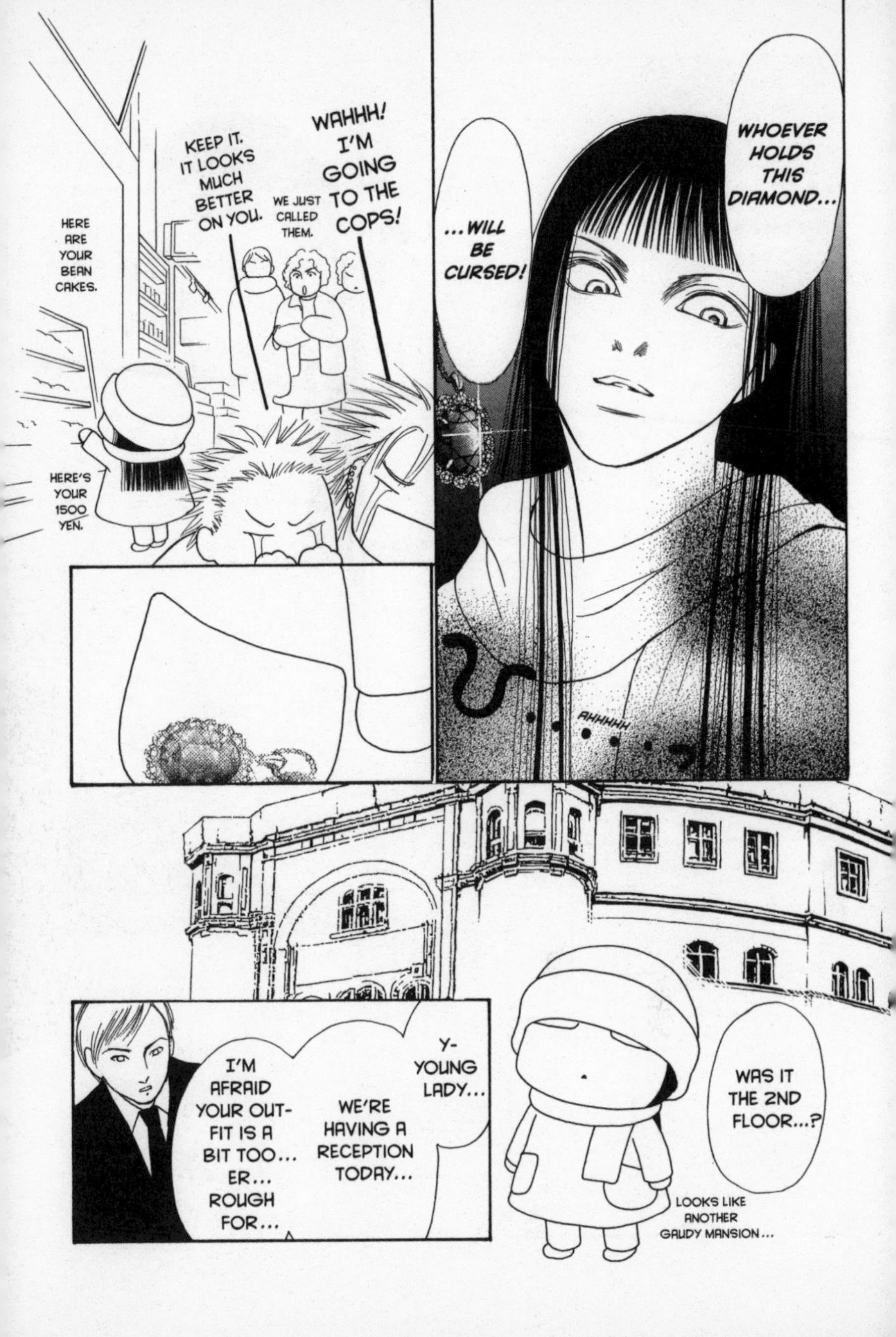
WHOEVER HOLDS THIS DIAMOND...
...WILL BE CURSED!
AHHHHH
WAHHH! I'M GOING TO THE COPS!
WE JUST CALLED THEM.
KEEP IT. IT LOOKS MUCH BETTER ON YOU.
HERE ARE YOUR BEAN CAKES.
HERE'S YOUR 1500 YEN.
WAS IT THE 2ND FLOOR...?
LOOKS LIKE ANOTHER GAUDY MANSION...
Y-YOUNG LADY...
WE'RE HAVING A RECEPTION TODAY...
I'M AFRAID YOUR OUT-FIT IS A BIT TOO... ER... ROUGH FOR...

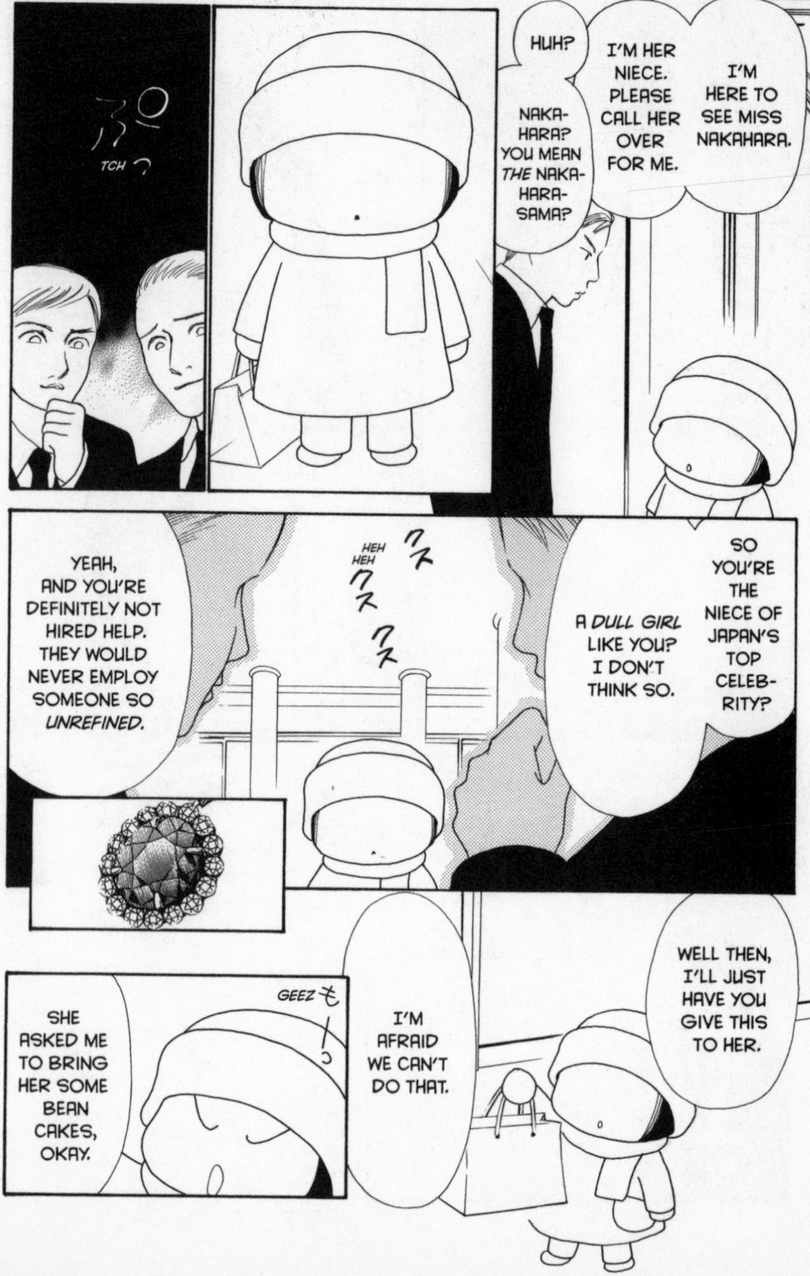
I'M HERE TO SEE MISS NAKAHARA.
I'M HER NIECE. PLEASE CALL HER OVER FOR ME.
HUH?
NAKA-HARA? YOU MEAN *THE* NAKA-HARA-SAMA?
TCH
SO YOU'RE THE NIECE OF JAPAN'S TOP CELEB-RITY?
A *DULL GIRL* LIKE YOU? I DON'T THINK SO.
HEH HEH
YEAH, AND YOU'RE DEFINITELY NOT HIRED HELP. THEY WOULD NEVER EMPLOY SOMEONE SO *UNREFINED*.
WELL THEN, I'LL JUST HAVE YOU GIVE THIS TO HER.
I'M AFRAID WE CAN'T DO THAT.
GEEZ
SHE ASKED ME TO BRING HER SOME BEAN CAKES, OKAY.

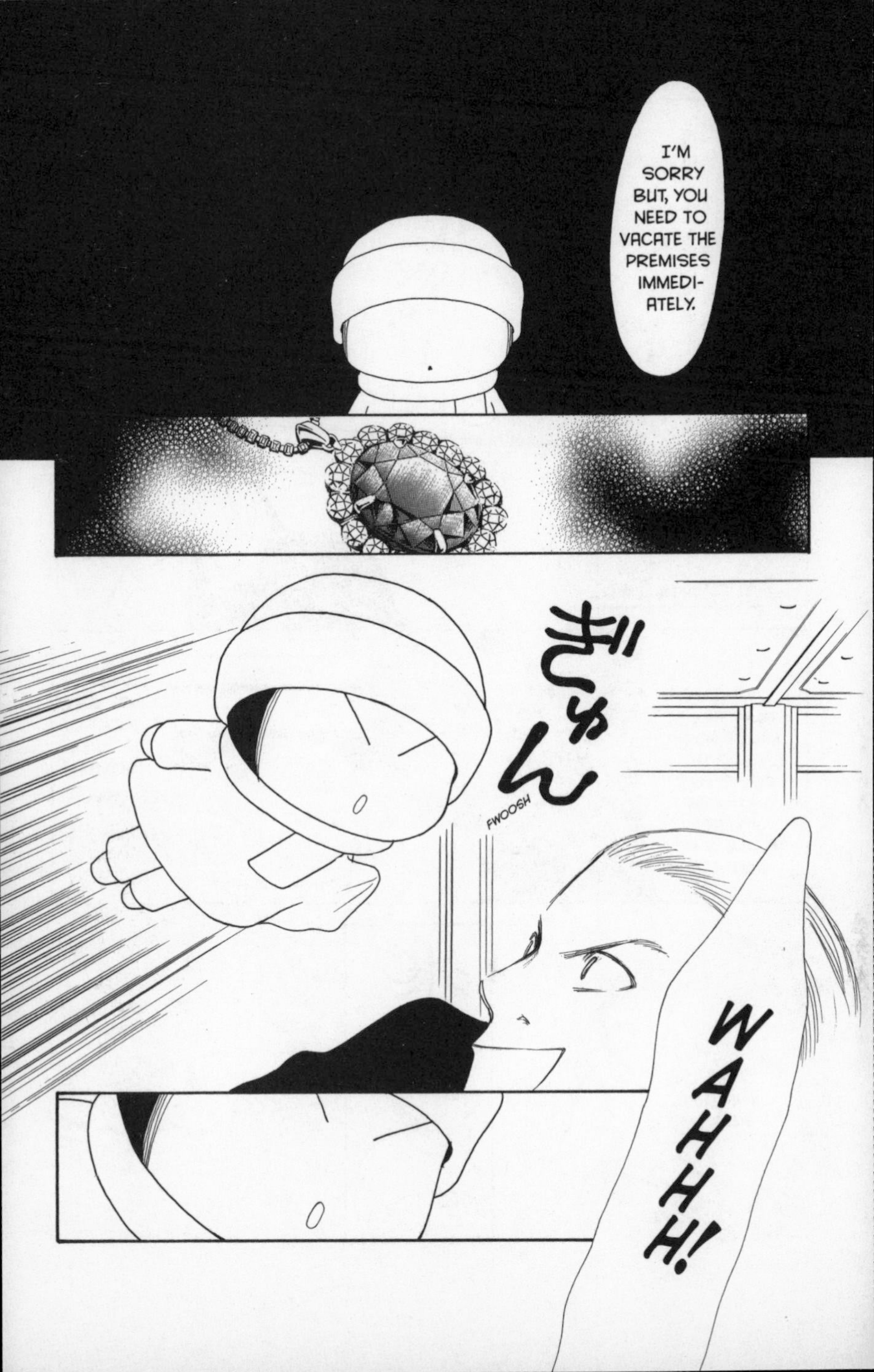
I'M SORRY BUT, YOU NEED TO VACATE THE PREMISES IMMEDI-ATELY.
ぎゅん
FWOOSH
WAHHH!

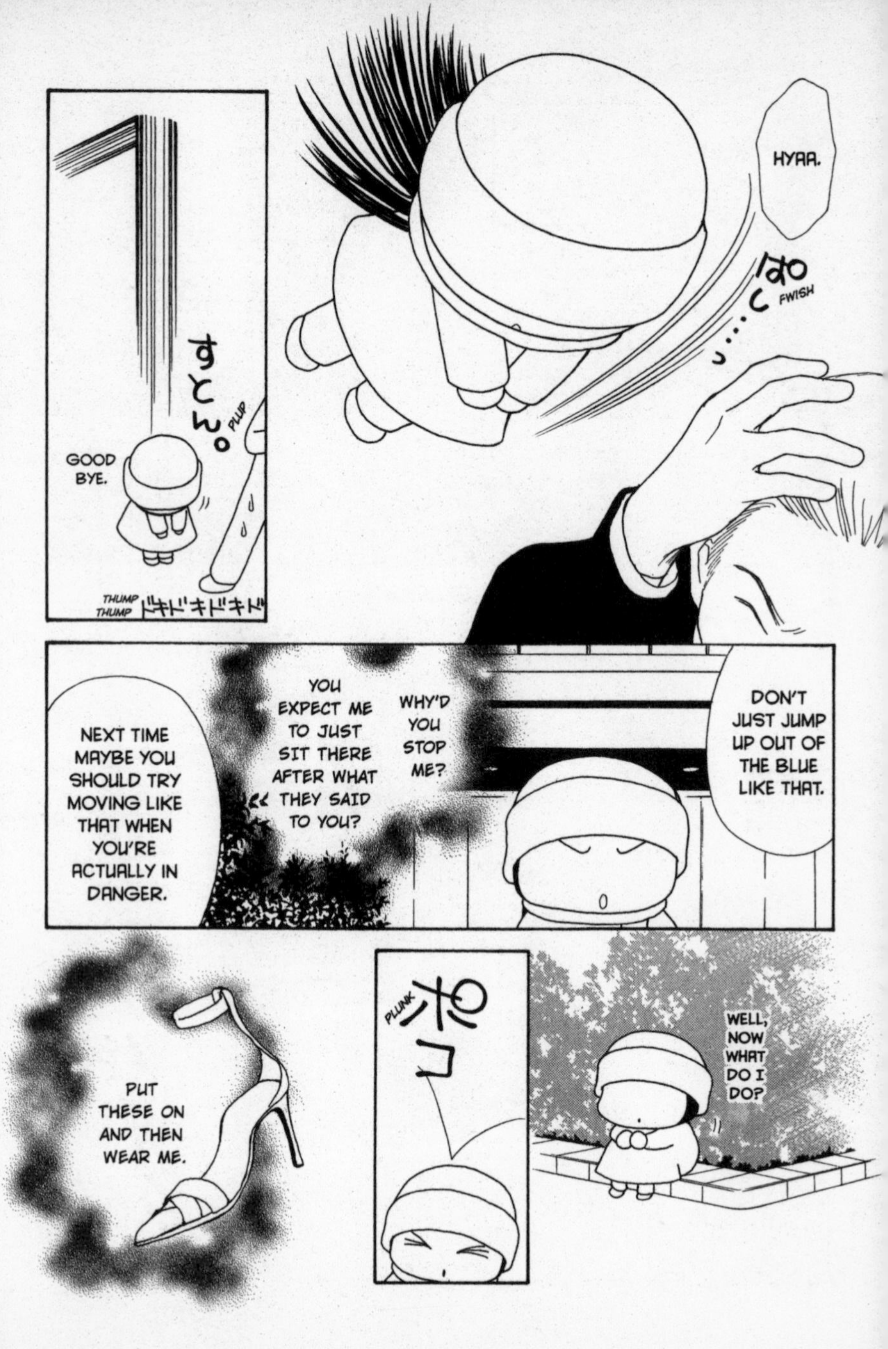
HYAA.
FWISH
すとん。
PLUP
GOOD BYE.
THUMP THUMP
ドキドキドキド
DON'T JUST JUMP UP OUT OF THE BLUE LIKE THAT.
WHY'D YOU STOP ME?
YOU EXPECT ME TO JUST SIT THERE AFTER WHAT THEY SAID TO YOU?
NEXT TIME MAYBE YOU SHOULD TRY MOVING LIKE THAT WHEN YOU'RE ACTUALLY IN DANGER.
WELL, NOW WHAT DO I DO?
ポコ
PLUNK
PUT THESE ON AND THEN WEAR ME.

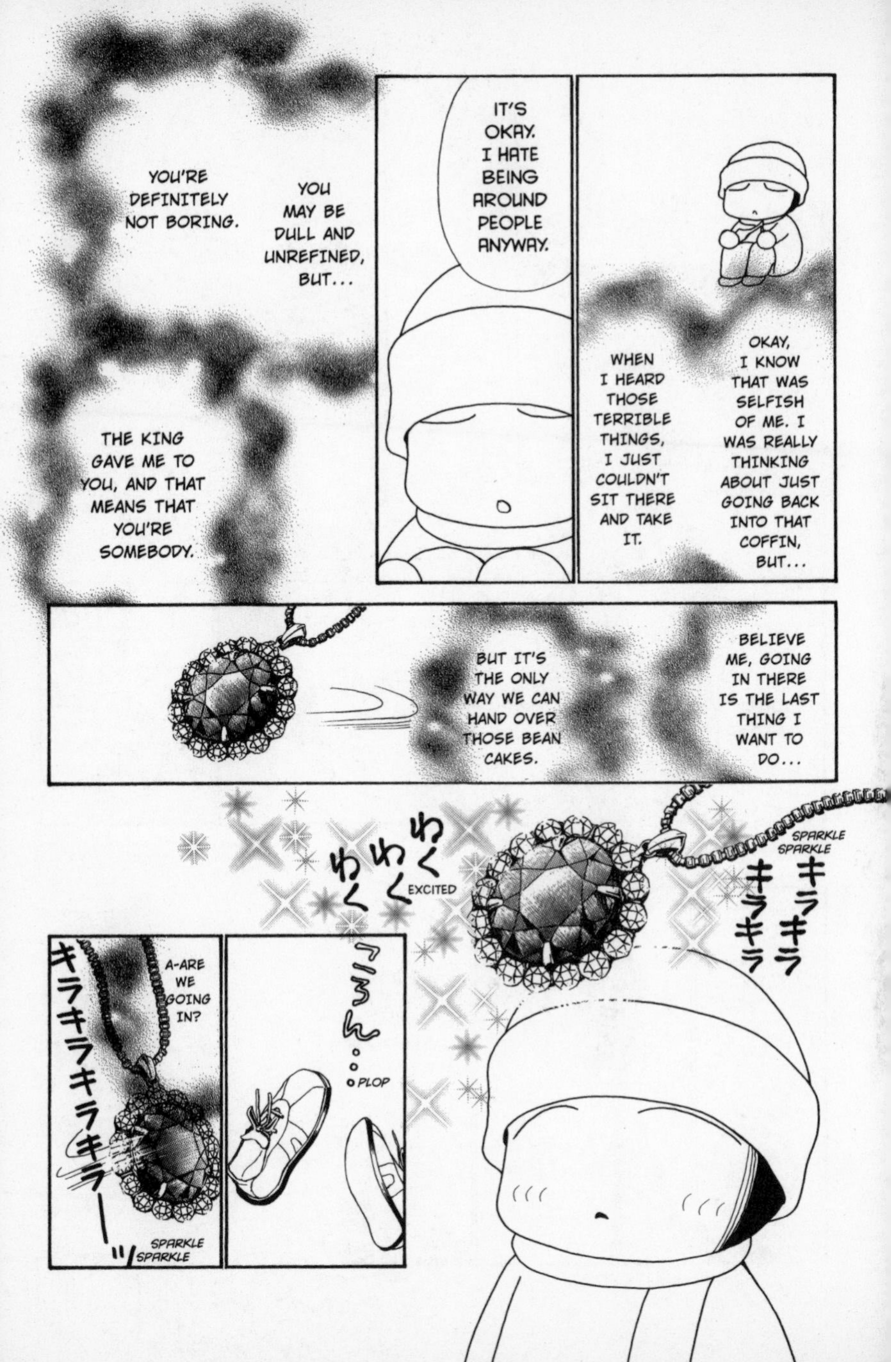

OKAY, I KNOW THAT WAS SELFISH OF ME. I WAS REALLY THINKING ABOUT JUST GOING BACK INTO THAT COFFIN, BUT...
WHEN I HEARD THOSE TERRIBLE THINGS, I JUST COULDN'T SIT THERE AND TAKE IT.
IT'S OKAY. I HATE BEING AROUND PEOPLE ANYWAY.
YOU MAY BE DULL AND UNREFINED, BUT...
YOU'RE DEFINITELY NOT BORING.
THE KING GAVE ME TO YOU, AND THAT MEANS THAT YOU'RE SOMEBODY.
BELIEVE ME, GOING IN THERE IS THE LAST THING I WANT TO DO...
BUT IT'S THE ONLY WAY WE CAN HAND OVER THOSE BEAN CAKES.
キラキラ
SPARKLE SPARKLE
わくわくわく
EXCITED
ころん。。。
PLOP
A-ARE WE GOING IN?
キラキラキラキラーッ
SPARKLE SPARKLE

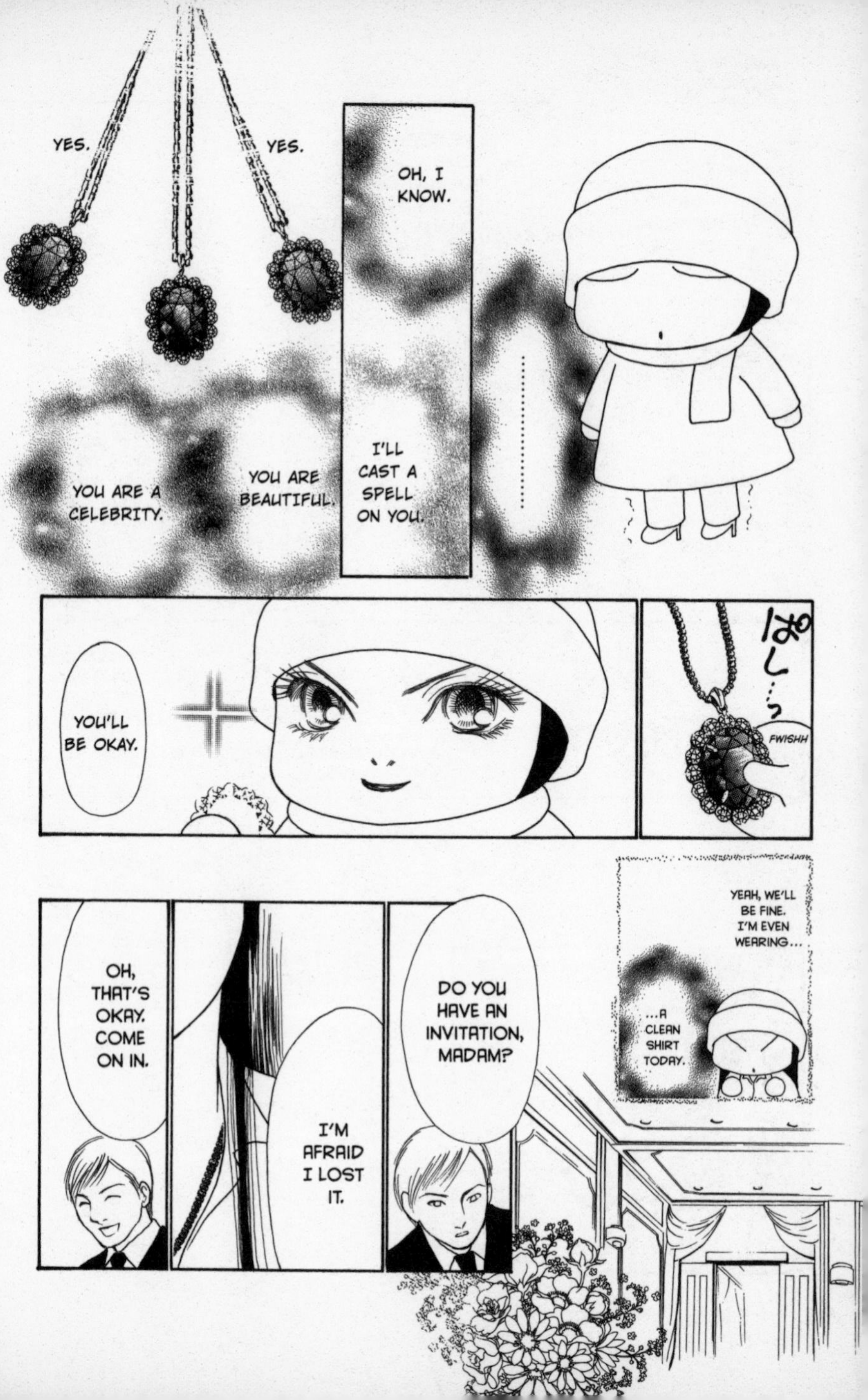
......
OH, I KNOW.
I'LL CAST A SPELL ON YOU.
YES.
YES.
YOU ARE BEAUTIFUL.
YOU ARE A CELEBRITY.
ぱしっ
FWISHH
YOU'LL BE OKAY.
YEAH, WE'LL BE FINE. I'M EVEN WEARING...
...A CLEAN SHIRT TODAY.
DO YOU HAVE AN INVITATION, MADAM?
I'M AFRAID I LOST IT.
OH, THAT'S OKAY. COME ON IN.

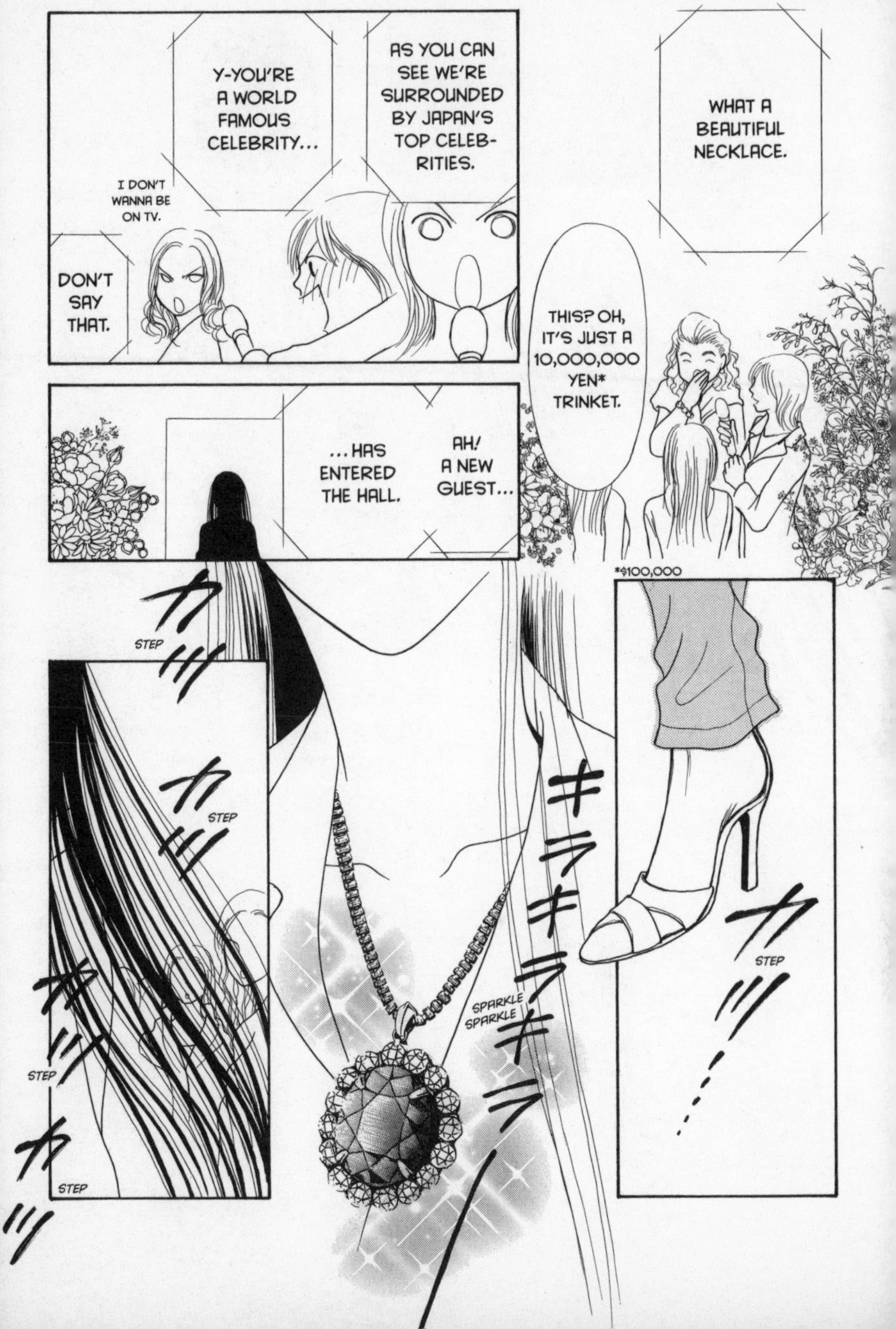
WHAT A BEAUTIFUL NECKLACE.
THIS? OH, IT'S JUST A 10,000,000 YEN* TRINKET.
AS YOU CAN SEE WE'RE SURROUNDED BY JAPAN'S TOP CELEB-RITIES.
Y-YOU'RE A WORLD FAMOUS CELEBRITY...
I DON'T WANNA BE ON TV.
DON'T SAY THAT.
AH! A NEW GUEST...
...HAS ENTERED THE HALL.
*$100,000
STEP
SPARKLE SPARKLE
STEP
STEP
STEP
STEP

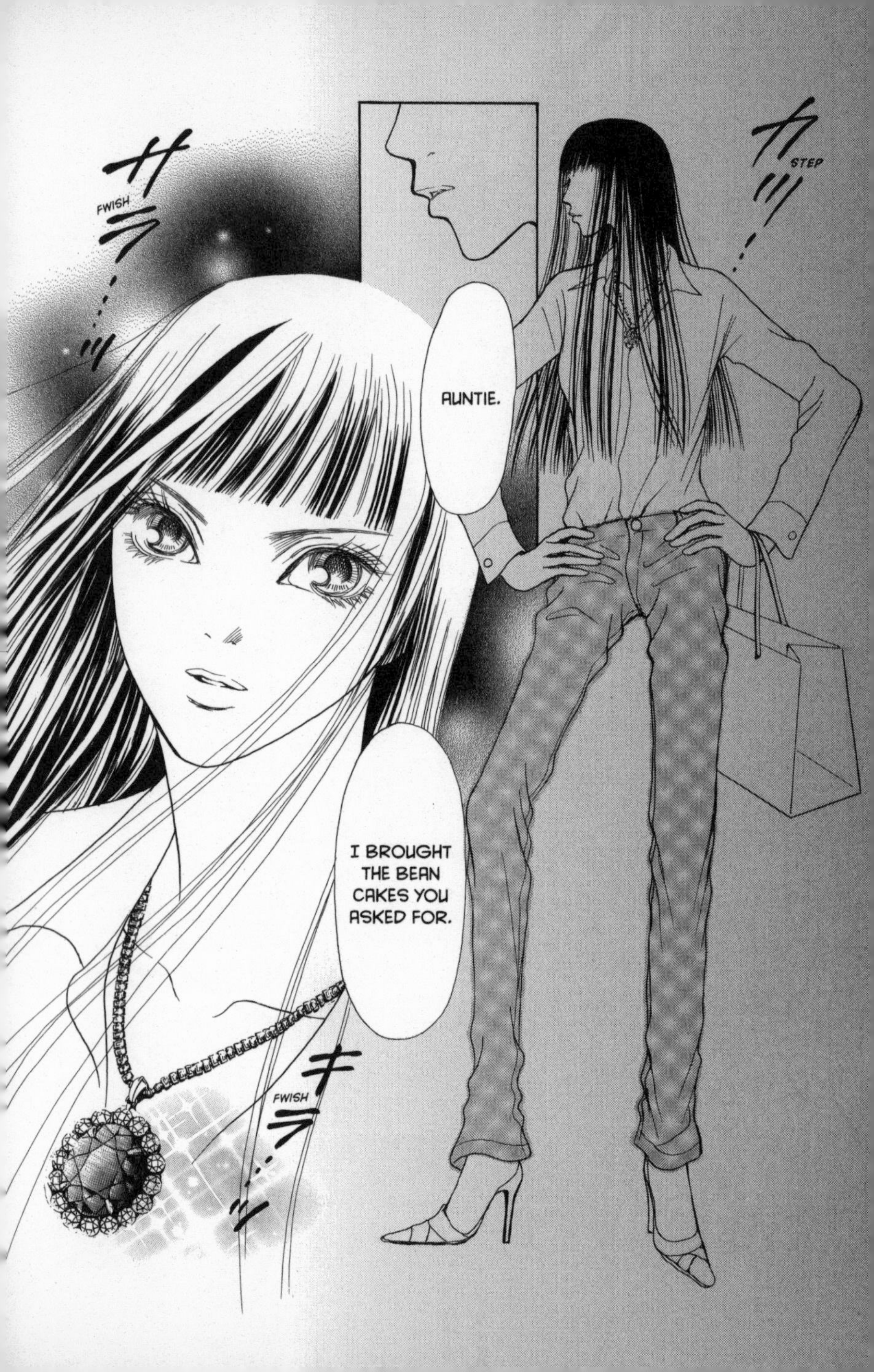
STEP
AUNTIE.
I BROUGHT THE BEAN CAKES YOU ASKED FOR.
FWISH
FWISH

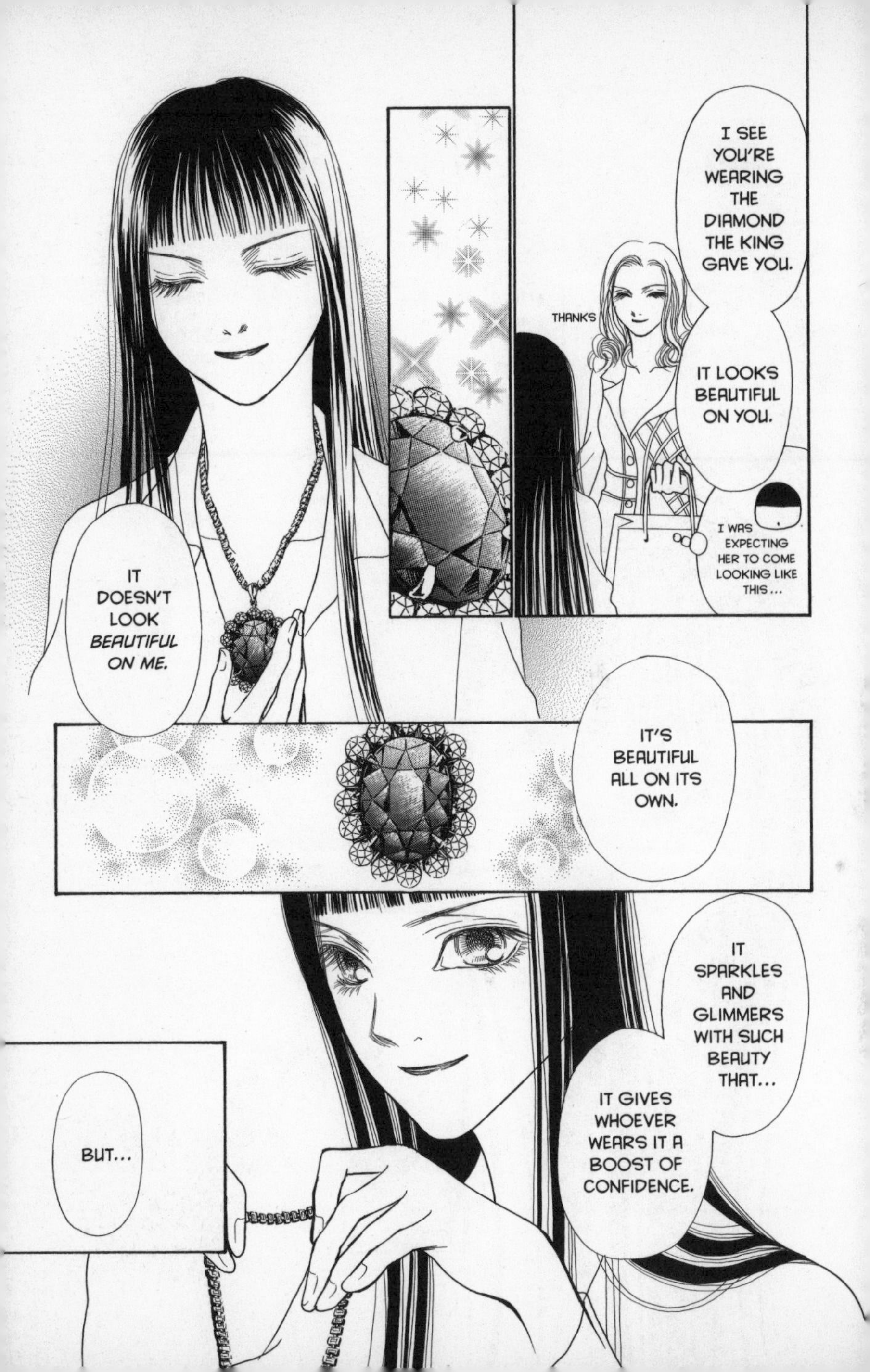
I SEE YOU'RE WEARING THE DIAMOND THE KING GAVE YOU.
THANKS
IT LOOKS BEAUTIFUL ON YOU.
I WAS EXPECTING HER TO COME LOOKING LIKE THIS...
IT DOESN'T LOOK *BEAUTIFUL* ON ME.
IT'S BEAUTIFUL ALL ON ITS OWN.
IT SPARKLES AND GLIMMERS WITH SUCH BEAUTY THAT...
IT GIVES WHOEVER WEARS IT A BOOST OF CONFIDENCE.
BUT...

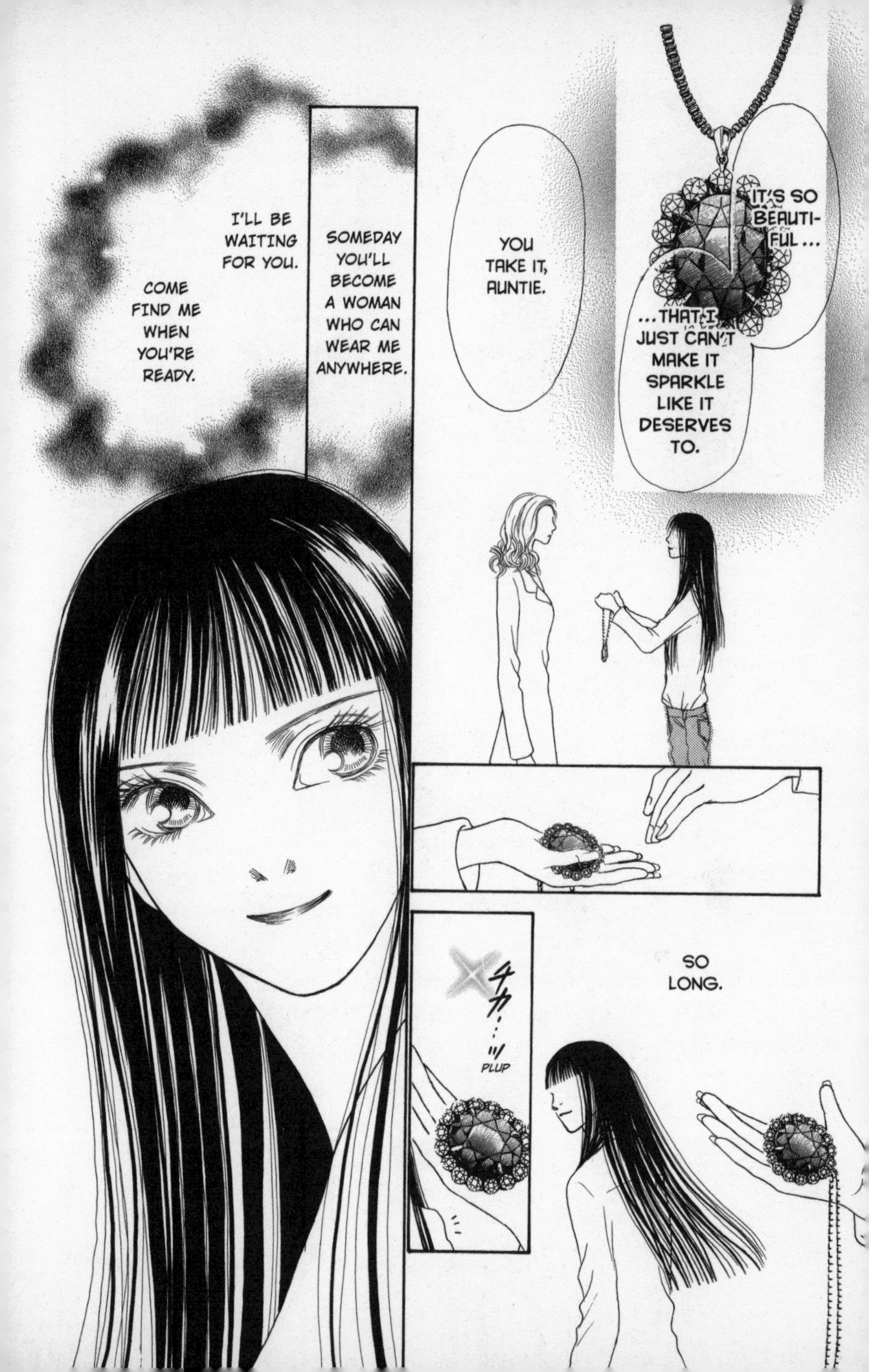
IT'S SO BEAUTIFUL...
...THAT I JUST CAN'T MAKE IT SPARKLE LIKE IT DESERVES TO.
YOU TAKE IT, AUNTIE.
SO LONG.
チカ…ッ
PLUP
SOMEDAY YOU'LL BECOME A WOMAN WHO CAN WEAR ME ANYWHERE.
I'LL BE WAITING FOR YOU.
COME FIND ME WHEN YOU'RE READY.

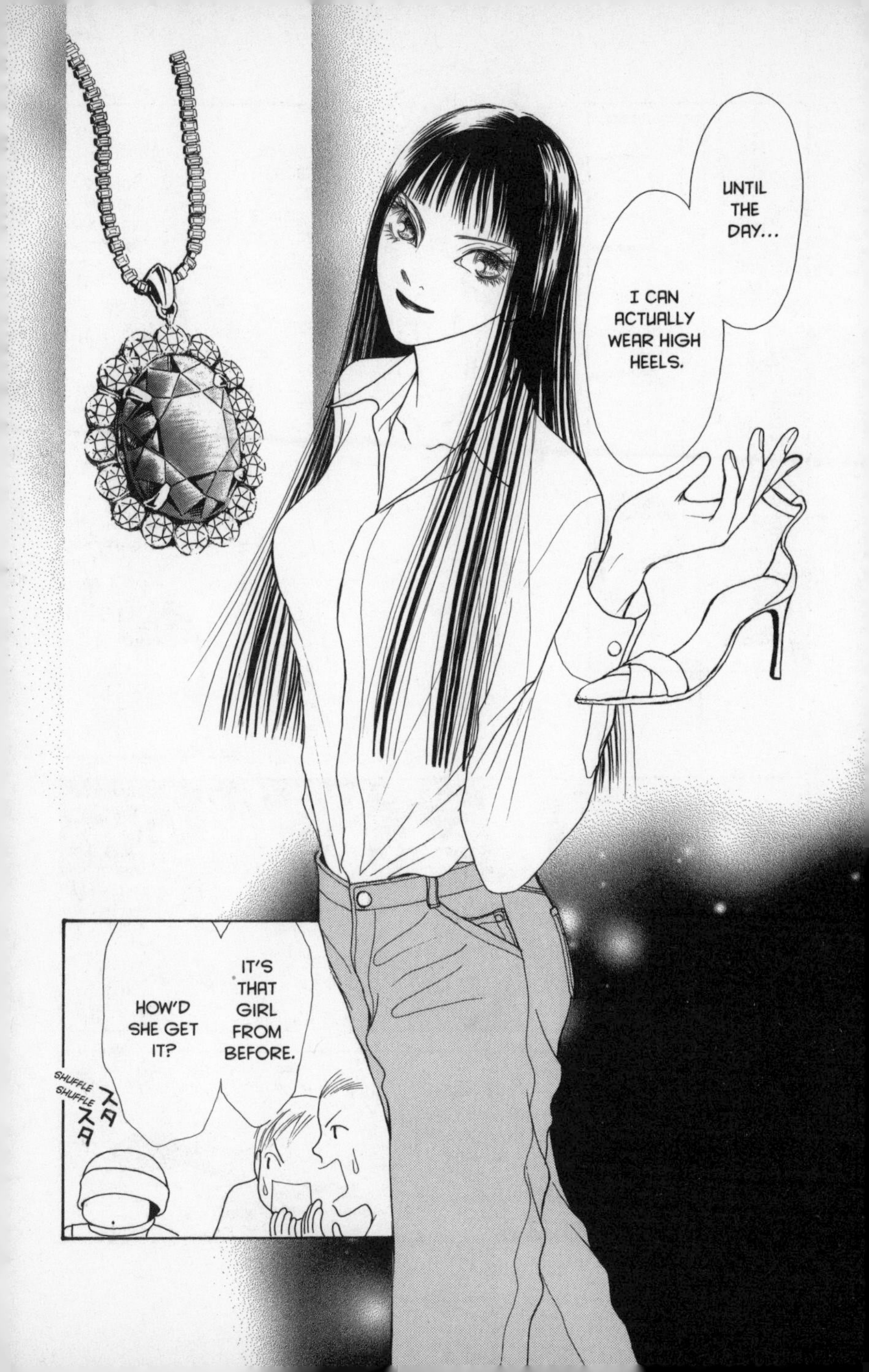
UNTIL THE DAY...
I CAN ACTUALLY WEAR HIGH HEELS.
IT'S THAT GIRL FROM BEFORE.
HOW'D SHE GET IT?
SHUFFLE SHUFFLE
スタスタ

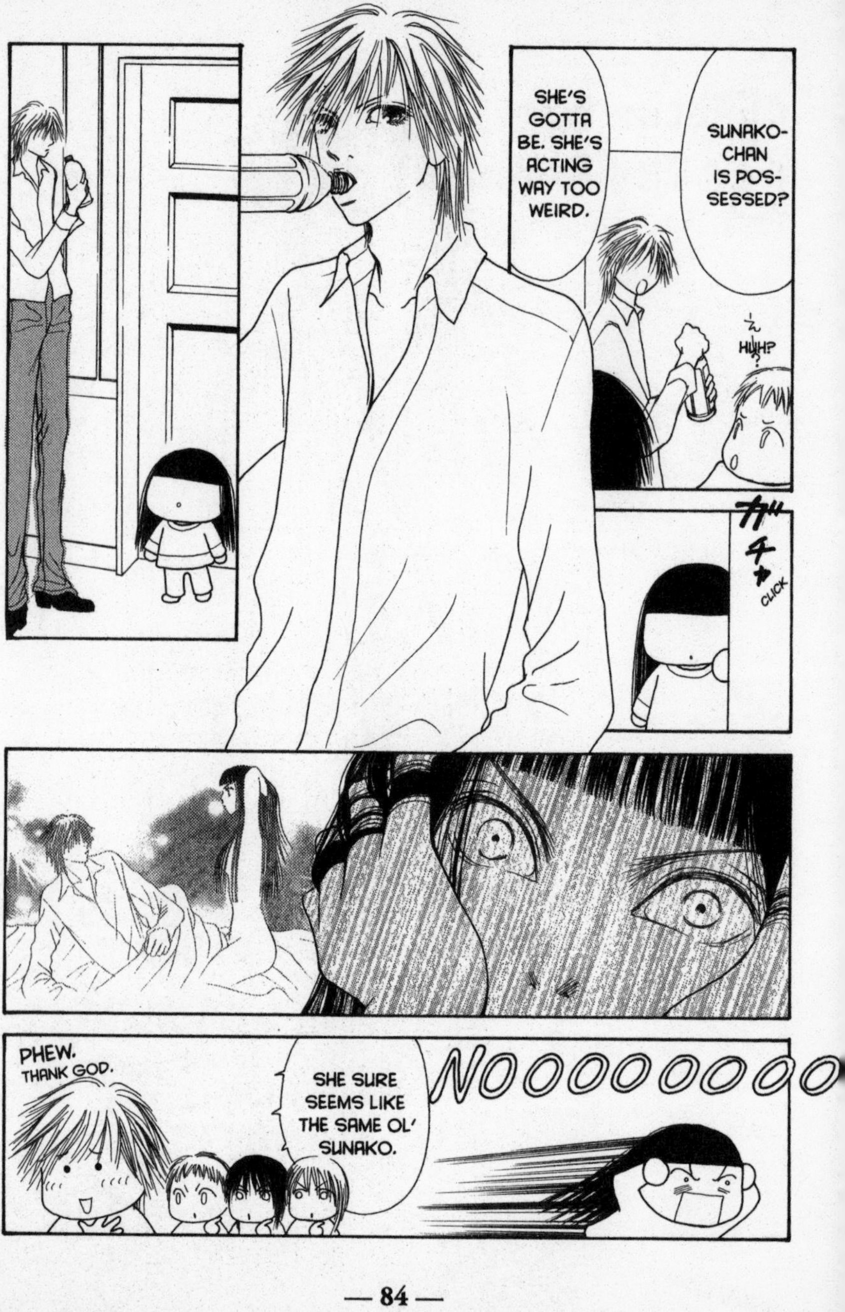
SUNAKO-CHAN IS POS-SESSED?
SHE'S GOTTA BE. SHE'S ACTING WAY TOO WEIRD.
え
HUH?
ガチャ
CLICK
NOOOOOOOOO
SHE SURE SEEMS LIKE THE SAME OL' SUNAKO.
PHEW. THANK GOD.

Chapter 53

The Brilliant Accident Part 2

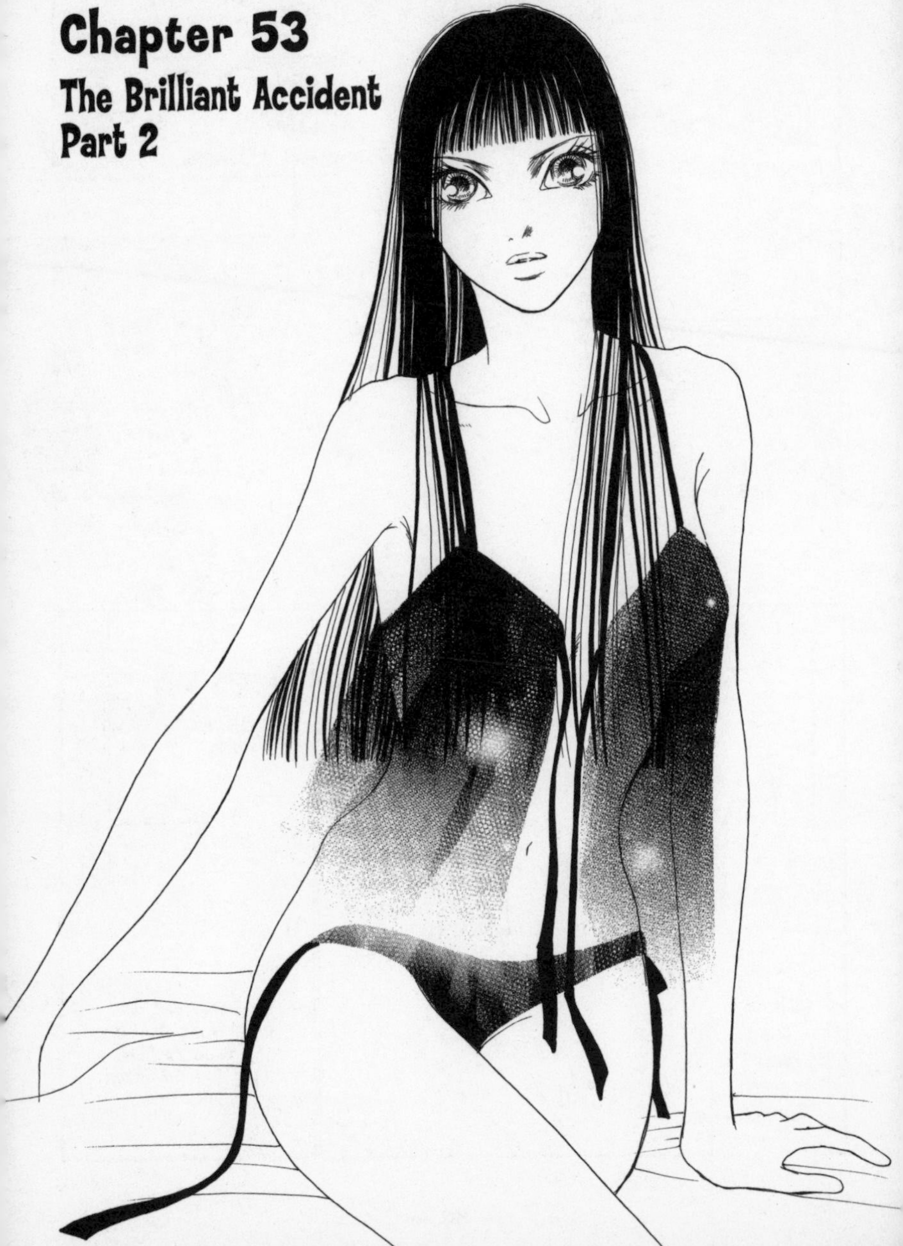

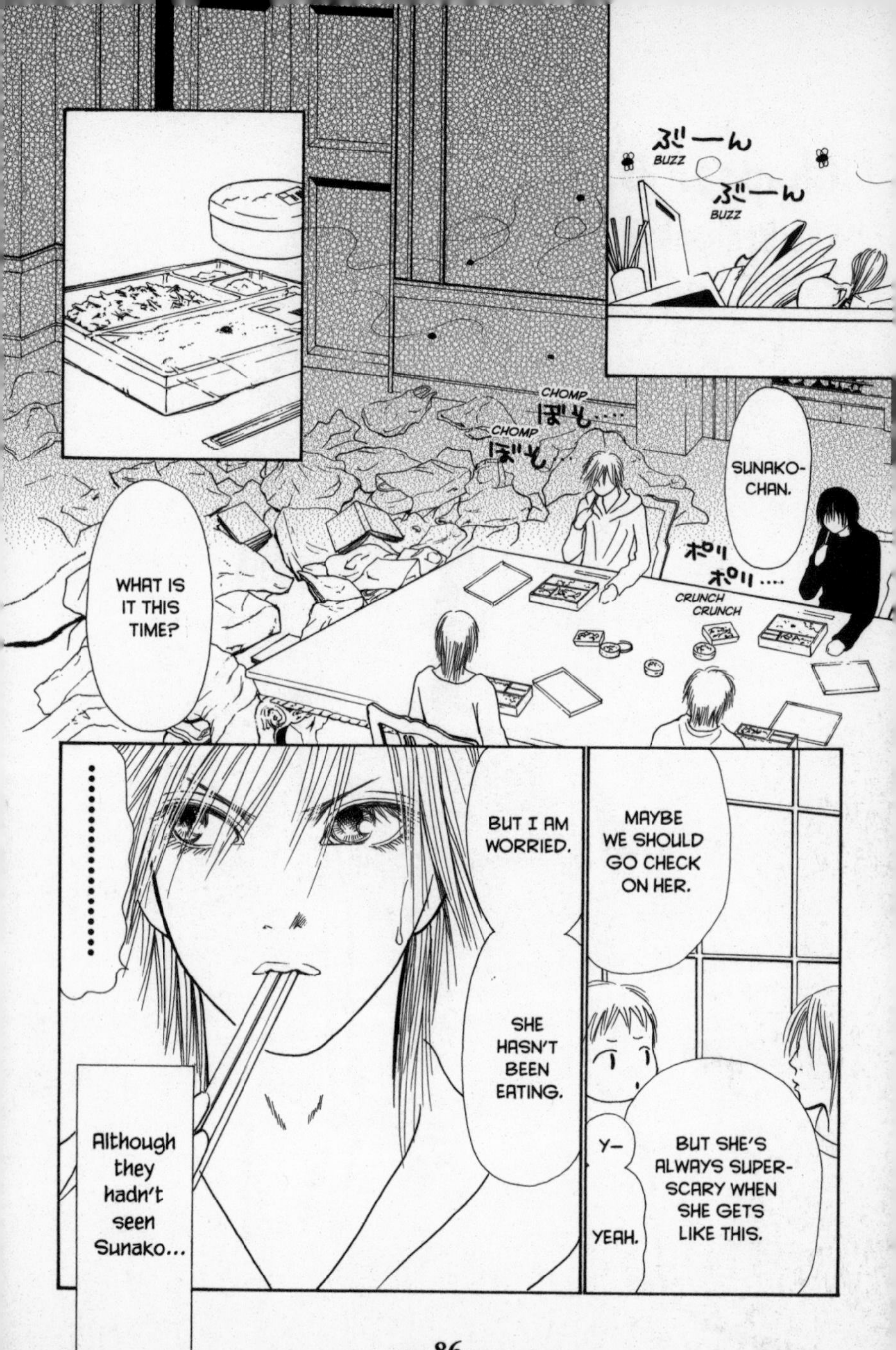

ぶーん
BUZZ
ぶーん
BUZZ
SUNAKO-CHAN.
CHOMP
ぼそ....
CHOMP
ぼそ...
ポリ
ポリ....
CRUNCH
CRUNCH
WHAT IS IT THIS TIME?
MAYBE WE SHOULD GO CHECK ON HER.
BUT SHE'S ALWAYS SUPER-SCARY WHEN SHE GETS LIKE THIS.
Y—
YEAH.
BUT I AM WORRIED.
SHE HASN'T BEEN EATING.
....
Although they hadn't seen Sunako...

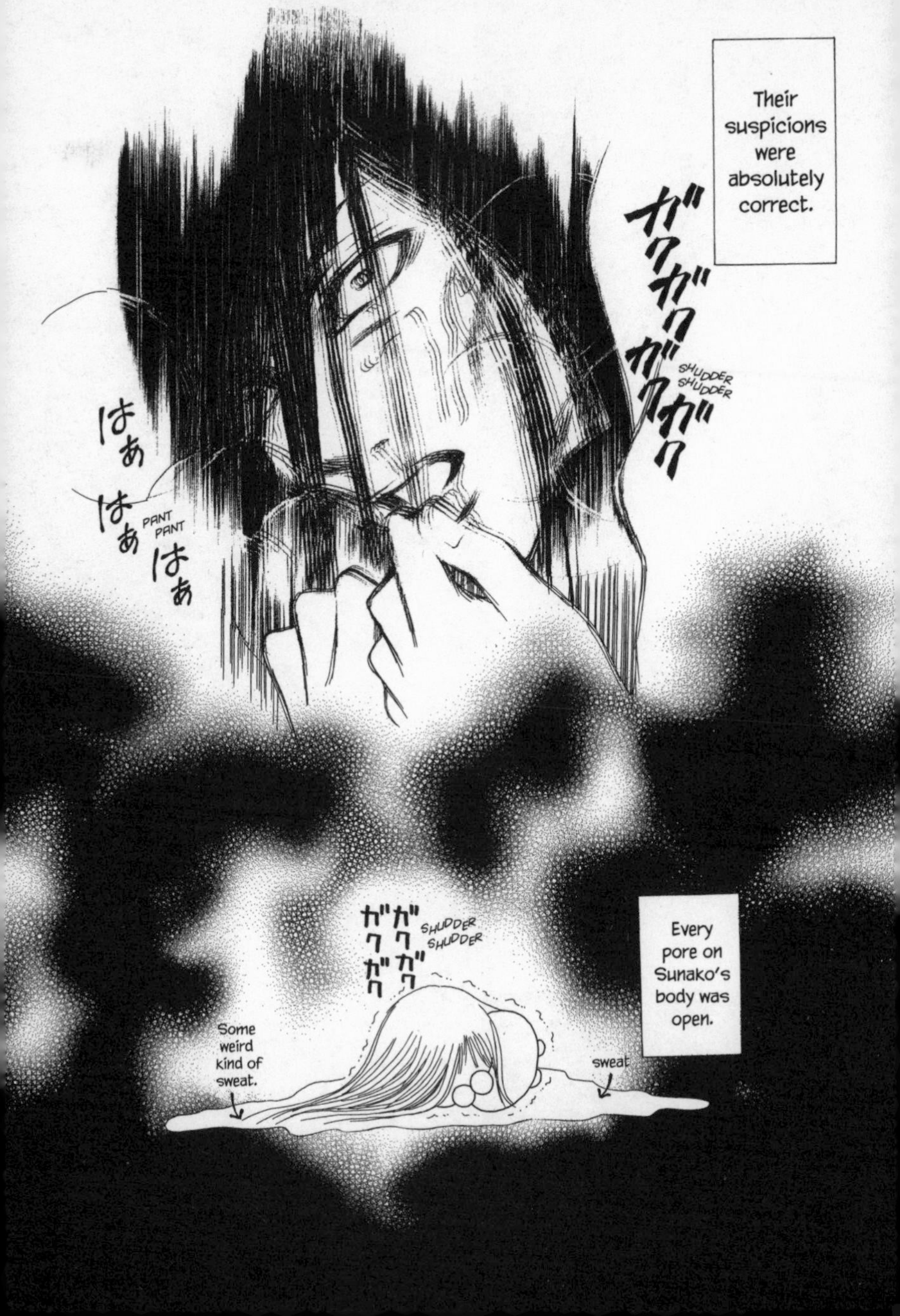
Their suspicions were absolutely correct.
ガクガクガクガク
SHUDDER SHUDDER
はぁはぁはぁ
PANT PANT
Every pore on Sunako's body was open.
ガクガクガクガク
SHUDDER SHUDDER
sweat
Some weird kind of sweat.

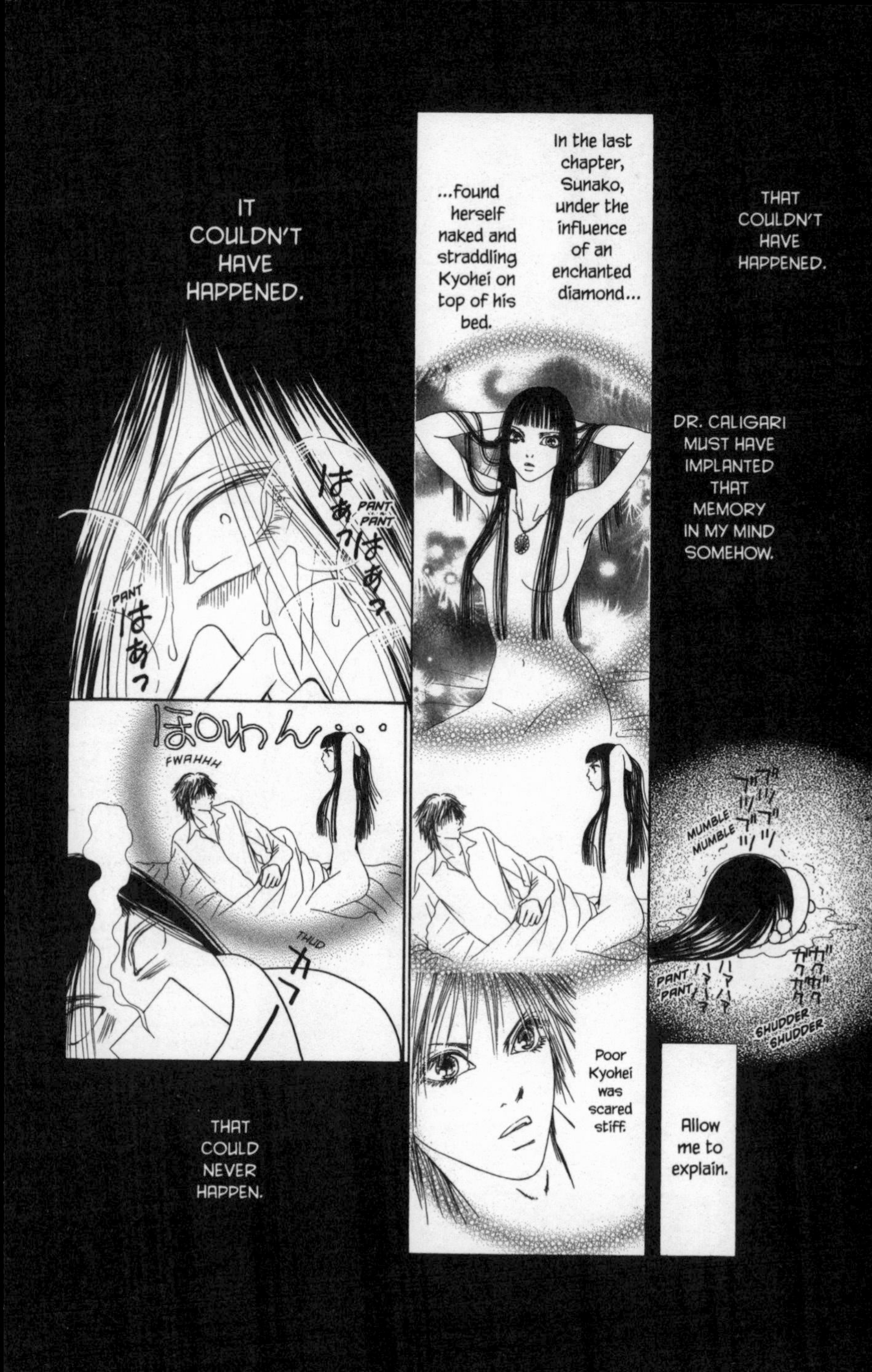
THAT COULDN'T HAVE HAPPENED.
In the last chapter, Sunako, under the influence of an enchanted diamond...
...found herself naked and straddling Kyohei on top of his bed.
IT COULDN'T HAVE HAPPENED.
DR. CALIGARI MUST HAVE IMPLANTED THAT MEMORY IN MY MIND SOMEHOW.
はあっはあっ PANT PANT
はあっ PANT
MUMBLE MUMBLE
PANT PANT
SHUDDER SHUDDER
ほわん… FWAHHH
THUD
Poor Kyohei was scared stiff.
Allow me to explain.
THAT COULD NEVER HAPPEN.

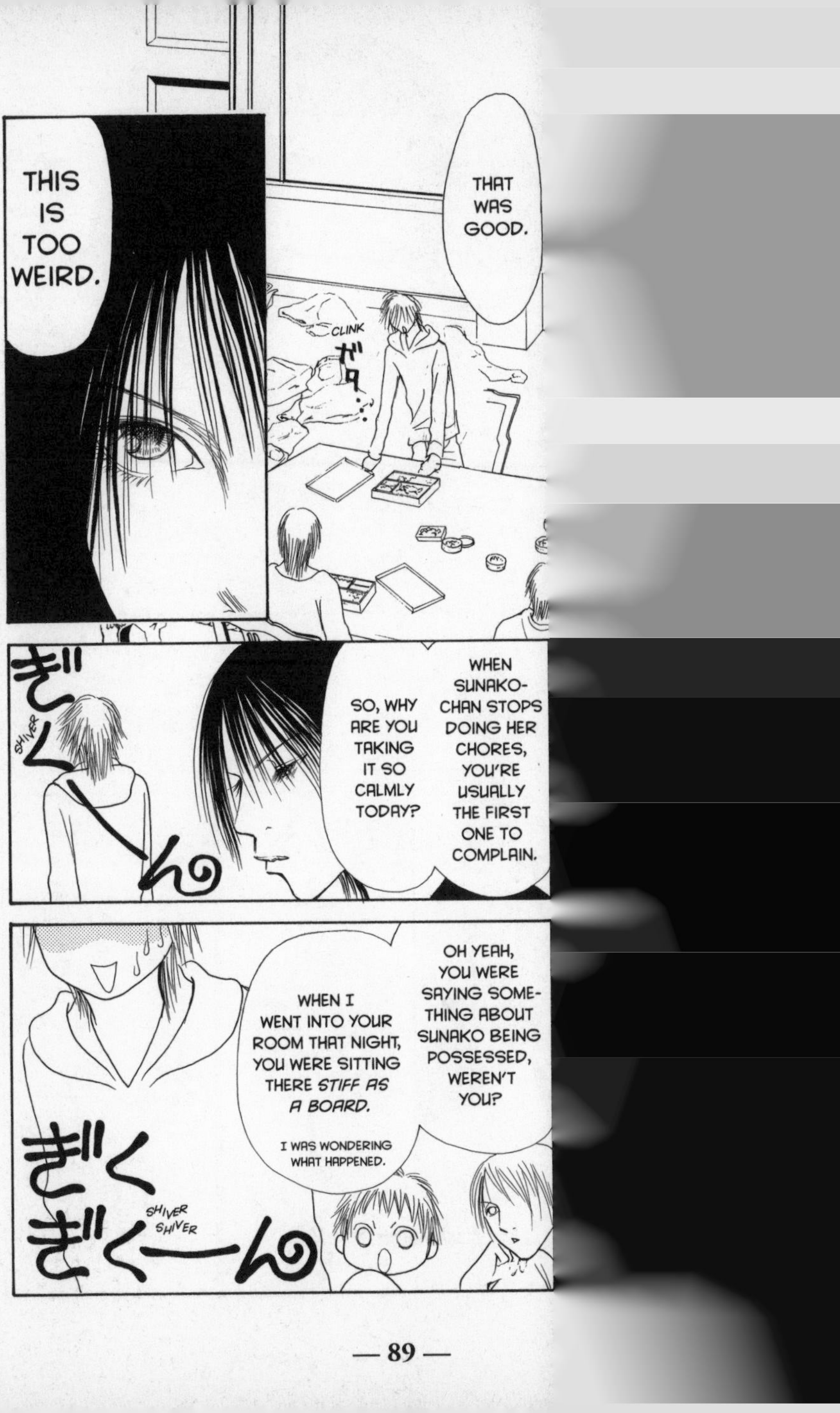
THAT WAS GOOD.
ガタ
CLINK
THIS IS TOO WEIRD.
WHEN SUNAKO-CHAN STOPS DOING HER CHORES, YOU'RE USUALLY THE FIRST ONE TO COMPLAIN.
SO, WHY ARE YOU TAKING IT SO CALMLY TODAY?
ぎくん
SHIVER
OH YEAH, YOU WERE SAYING SOME-THING ABOUT SUNAKO BEING POSSESSED, WEREN'T YOU?
WHEN I WENT INTO YOUR ROOM THAT NIGHT, YOU WERE SITTING THERE *STIFF AS A BOARD.*
I WAS WONDERING WHAT HAPPENED.
ぎくぎくーん
SHIVER SHIVER

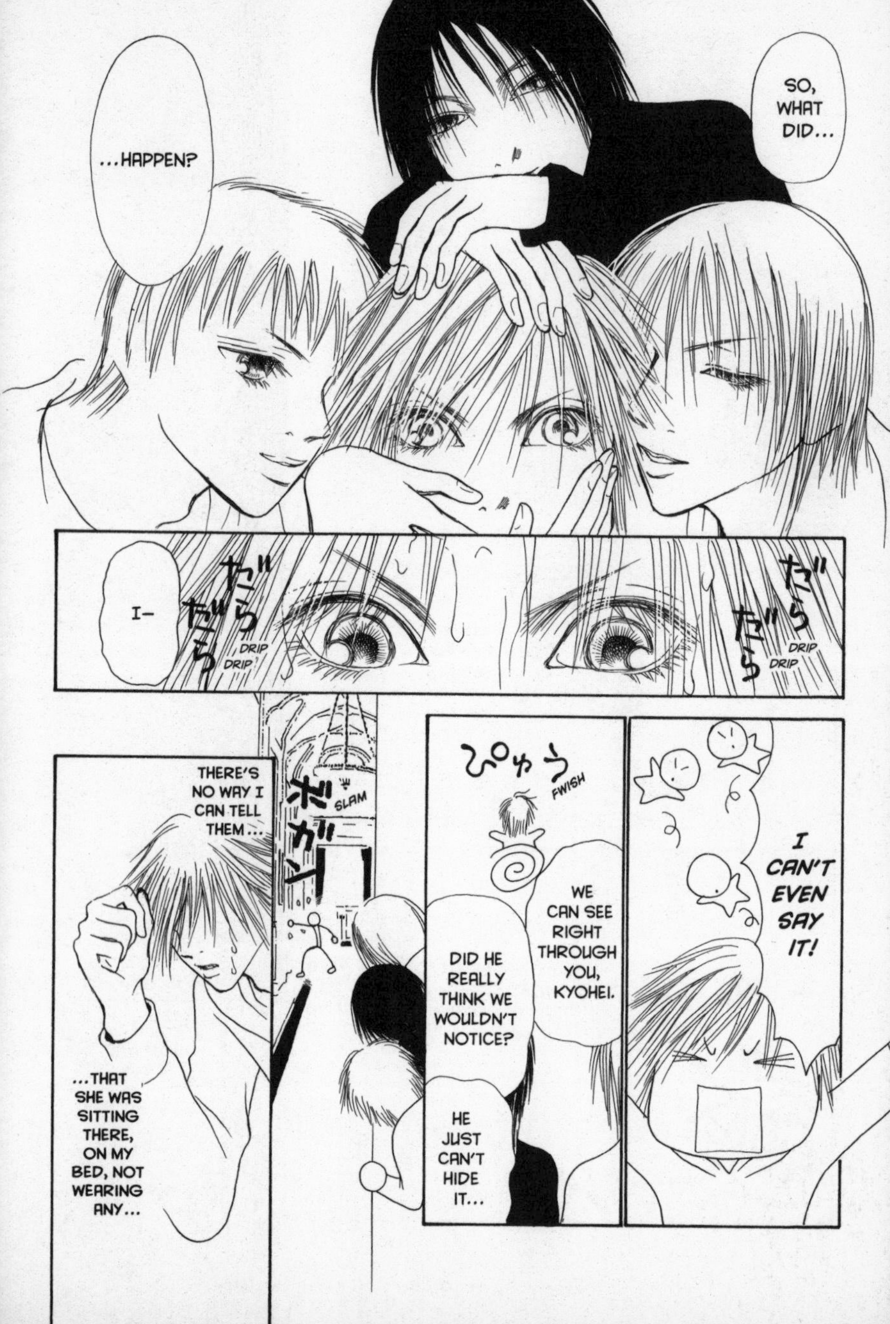
SO, WHAT DID...
...HAPPEN?
I-
だらだら DRIP DRIP
だらだら DRIP DRIP
I CAN'T EVEN SAY IT!
ぴゅう FWISH
WE CAN SEE RIGHT THROUGH YOU, KYOHEI.
DID HE REALLY THINK WE WOULDN'T NOTICE?
HE JUST CAN'T HIDE IT...
THERE'S NO WAY I CAN TELL THEM...
ボガン SLAM
...THAT SHE WAS SITTING THERE, ON MY BED, NOT WEARING ANY...

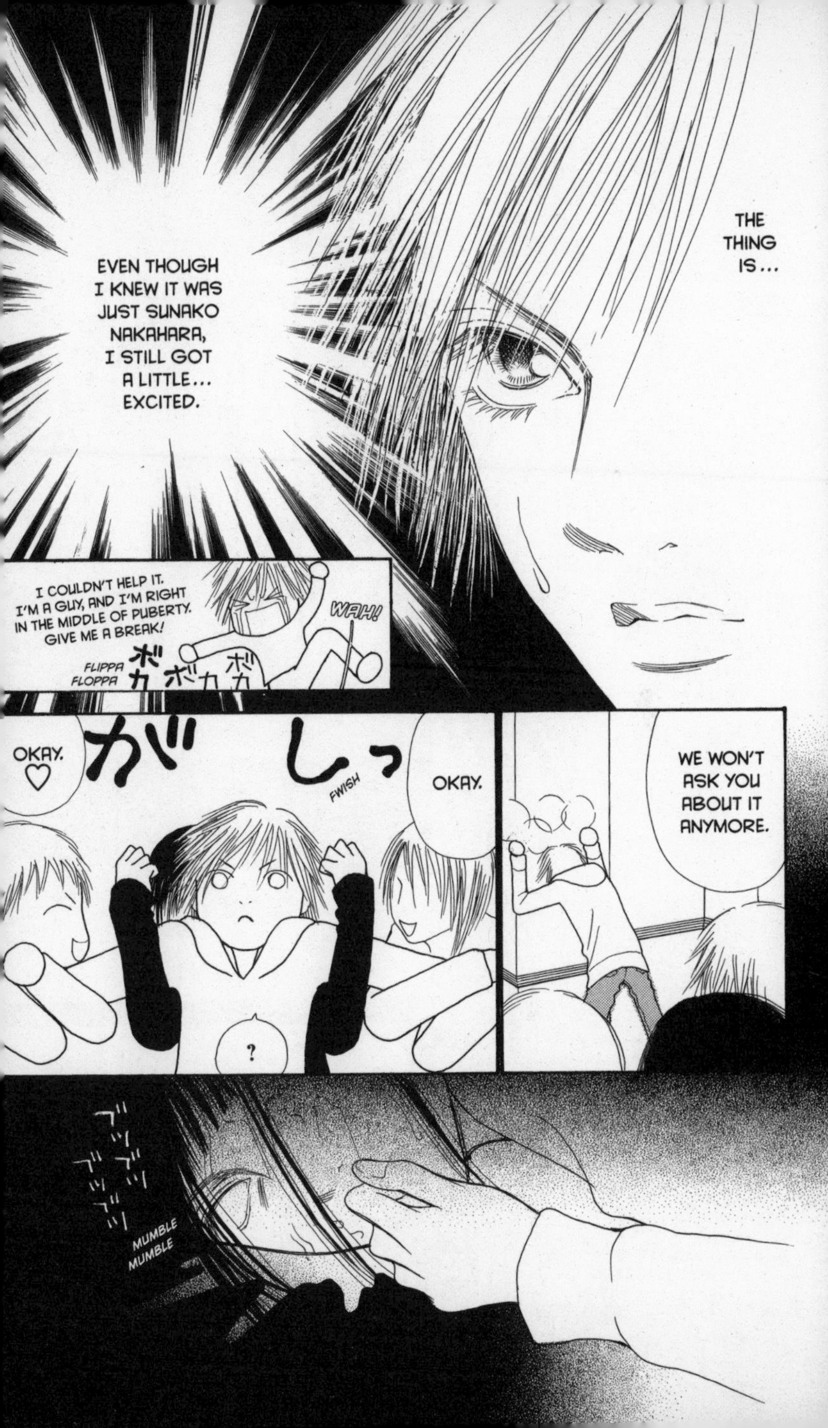
THE THING IS...
EVEN THOUGH I KNEW IT WAS JUST SUNAKO NAKAHARA, I STILL GOT A LITTLE... EXCITED.
I COULDN'T HELP IT. I'M A GUY, AND I'M RIGHT IN THE MIDDLE OF PUBERTY. GIVE ME A BREAK!
WAH!
ボカボカボカ
FLIPPA FLOPPA
WE WON'T ASK YOU ABOUT IT ANYMORE.
OKAY.
がしっ
FWISH
OKAY. ♡
?
ブツブツブツブツ
MUMBLE MUMBLE

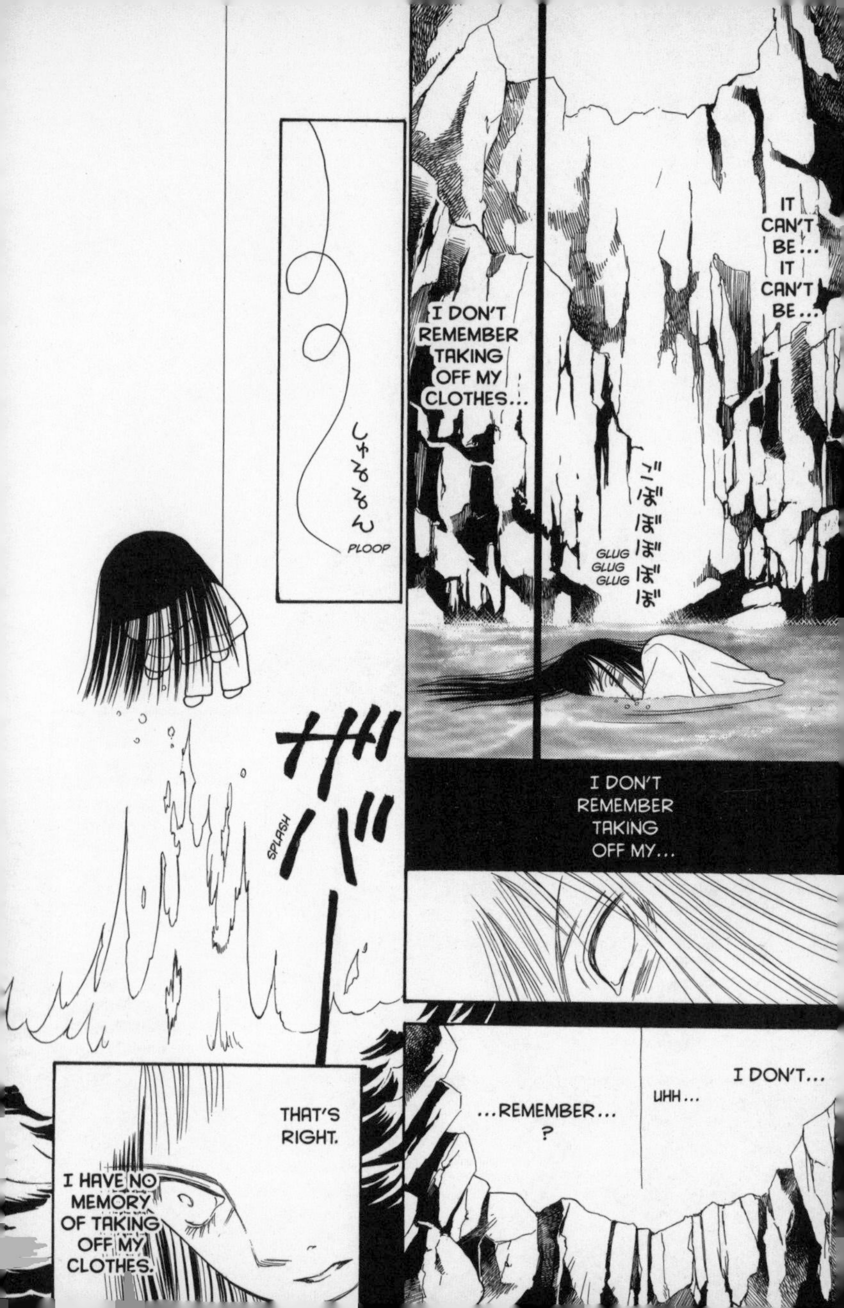
IT CAN'T BE... IT CAN'T BE...
ごぼぼぼぼ
GLUG GLUG GLUG
I DON'T REMEMBER TAKING OFF MY CLOTHES...
I DON'T REMEMBER TAKING OFF MY...
I DON'T...
UHH...
...REMEMBER... ?
しゅるるん
PLOOP
ザバー
SPLASH
THAT'S RIGHT.
I HAVE NO MEMORY OF TAKING OFF MY CLOTHES.

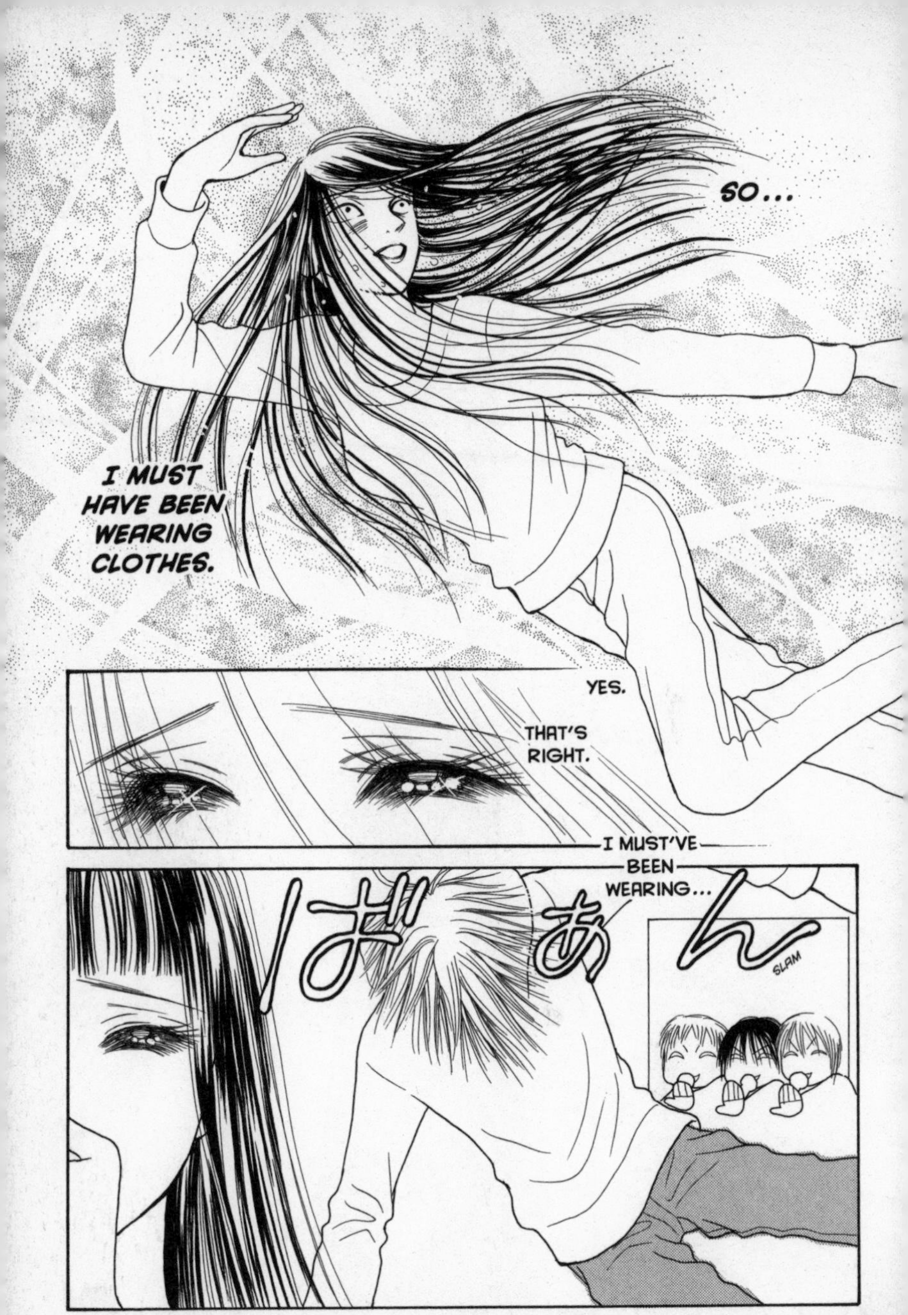
SO...
I MUST HAVE BEEN WEARING CLOTHES.
YES.
THAT'S RIGHT.
I MUST'VE BEEN WEARING...
ばあん
SLAM

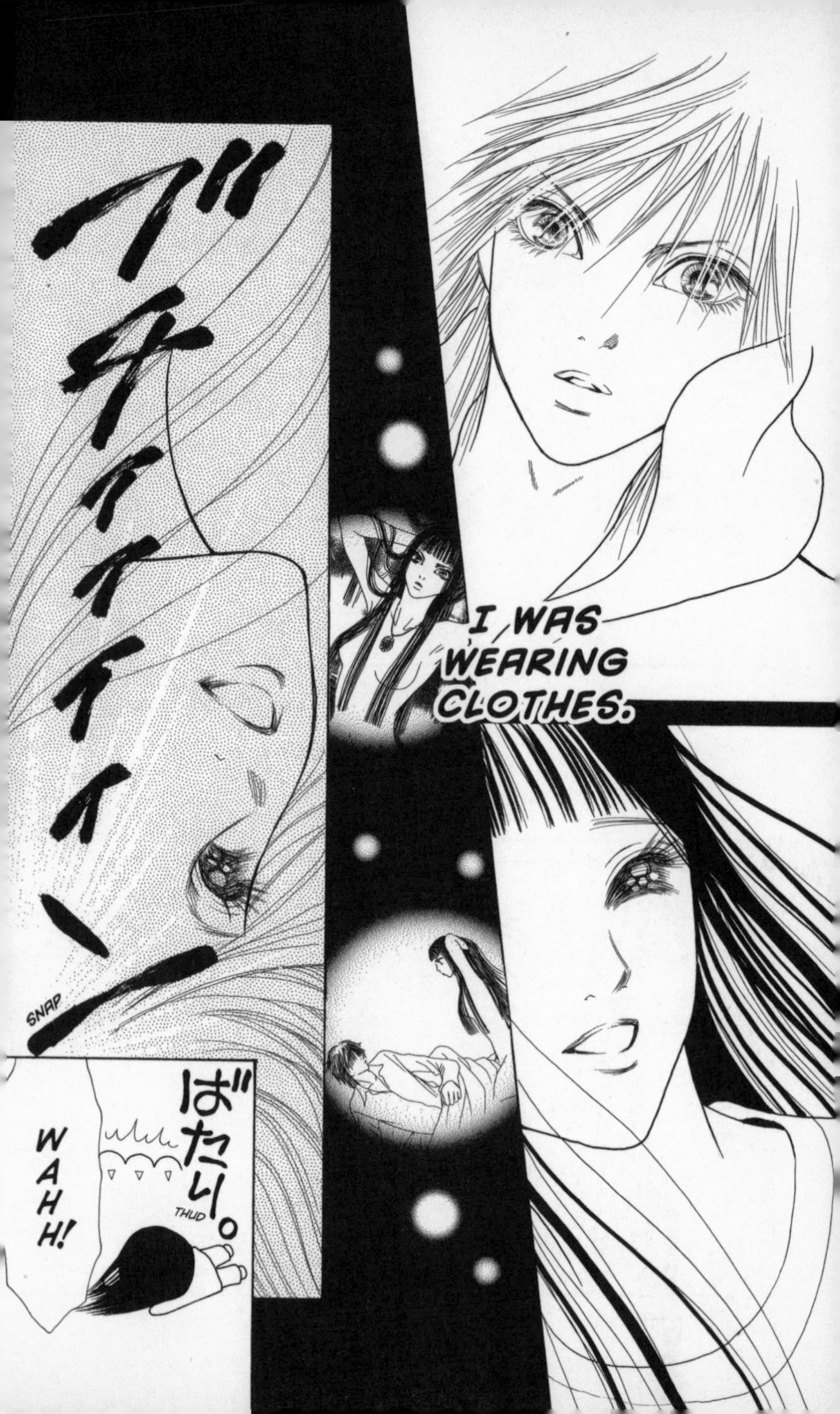
I WAS WEARING CLOTHES.
ブチイイイー
SNAP
ばたり。
THUD
WAHH!

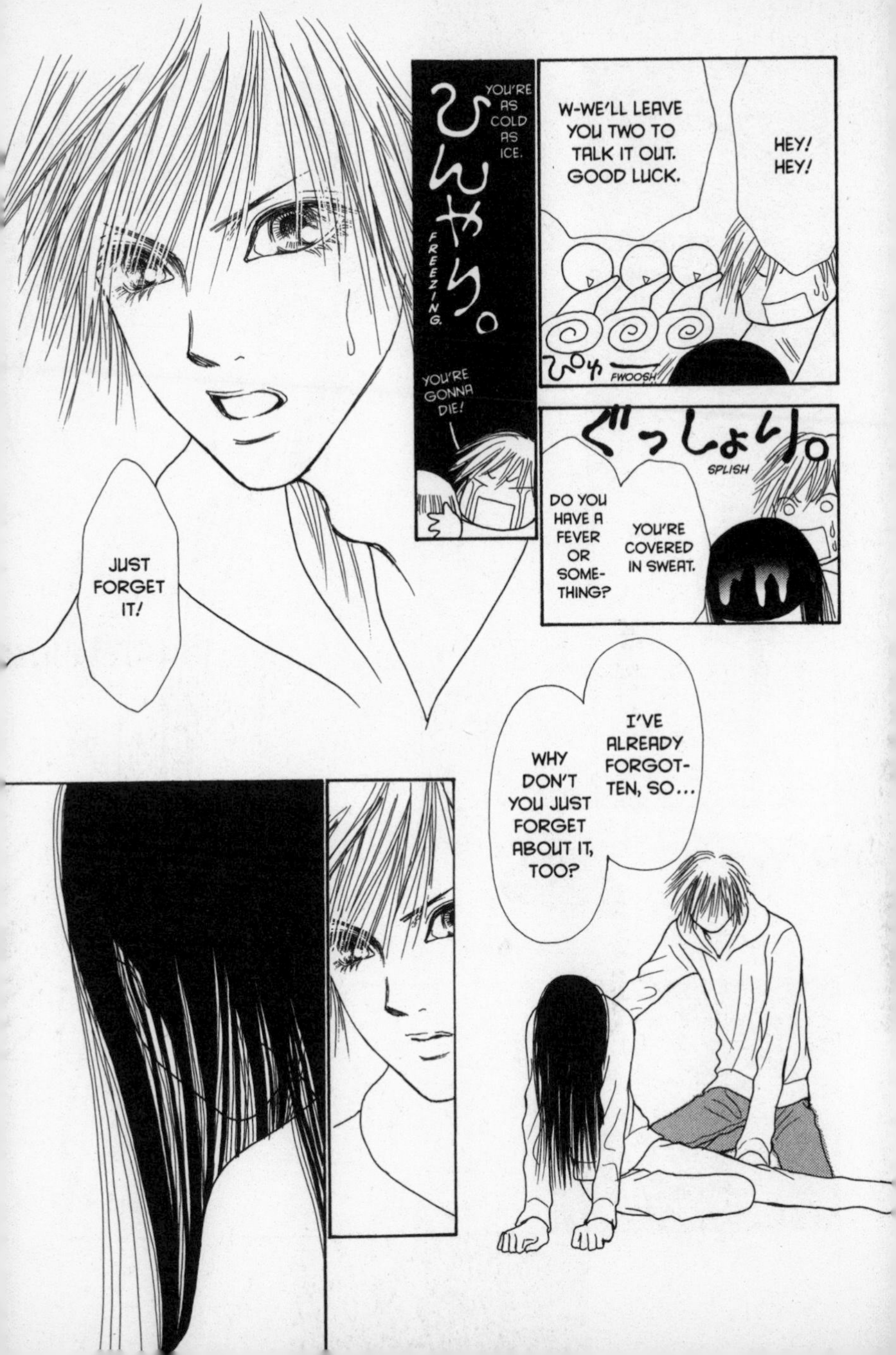
HEY! HEY!
W-WE'LL LEAVE YOU TWO TO TALK IT OUT. GOOD LUCK.
ぴゅー
FWOOSH
ぐっしょり。
SPLISH
YOU'RE COVERED IN SWEAT.
DO YOU HAVE A FEVER OR SOMETHING?
ひんやり。
FREEZING.
YOU'RE AS COLD AS ICE.
YOU'RE GONNA DIE!
JUST FORGET IT!
I'VE ALREADY FORGOTTEN, SO...
WHY DON'T YOU JUST FORGET ABOUT IT, TOO?

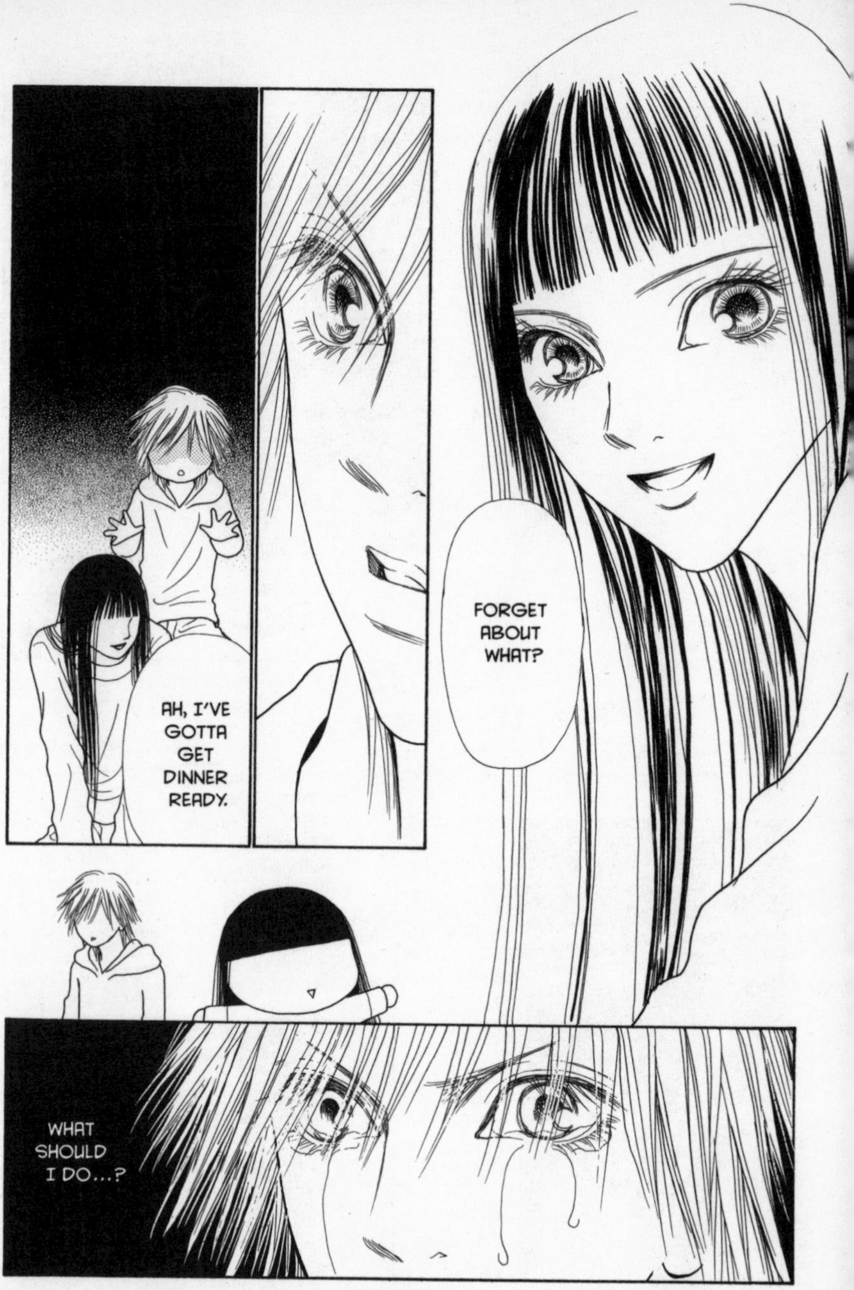
FORGET ABOUT WHAT?
AH, I'VE GOTTA GET DINNER READY.
WHAT SHOULD I DO...?

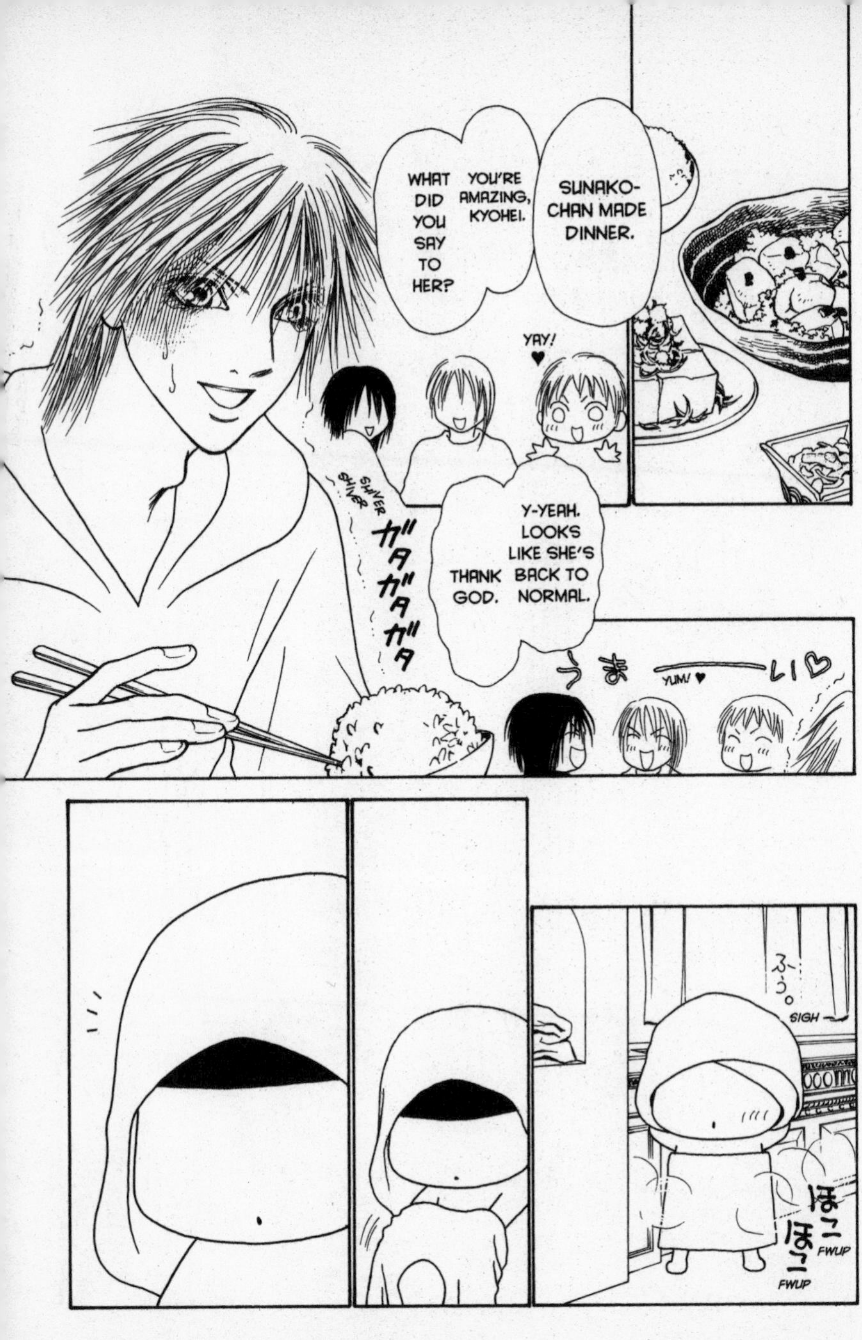
SUNAKO-CHAN MADE DINNER.
YOU'RE AMAZING, KYOHEI.
WHAT DID YOU SAY TO HER?
YAY! ♥
Y-YEAH. LOOKS LIKE SHE'S BACK TO NORMAL.
THANK GOD.
ガタガタガタ
SHIVER SHIVER
うま——い♡
YUM! ♥
ふう。
SIGH
ほこほこ
FWUP FWUP

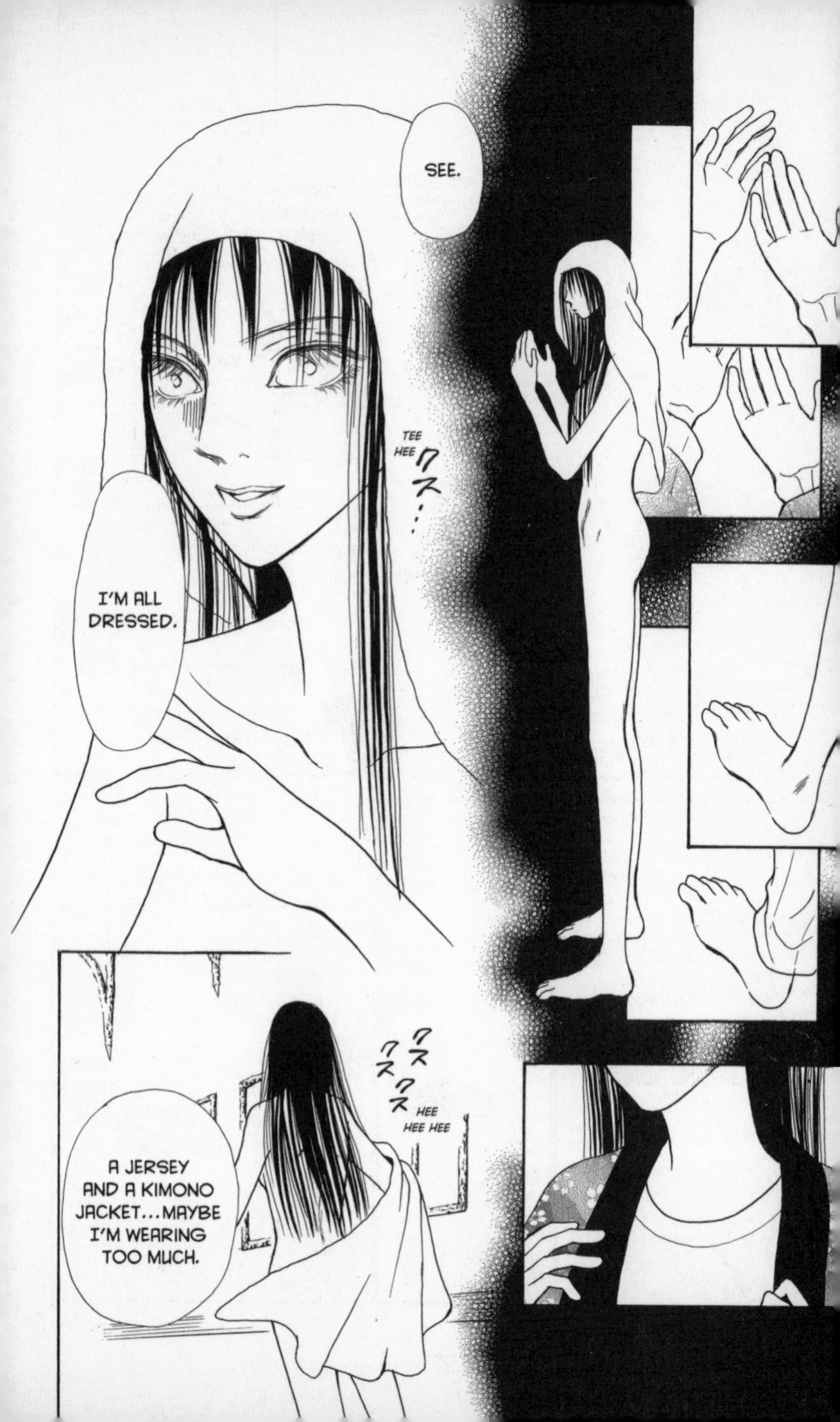
SEE.
TEE HEE
クス・・
I'M ALL DRESSED.
クスクスクス
HEE HEE HEE
A JERSEY AND A KIMONO JACKET...MAYBE I'M WEARING TOO MUCH.

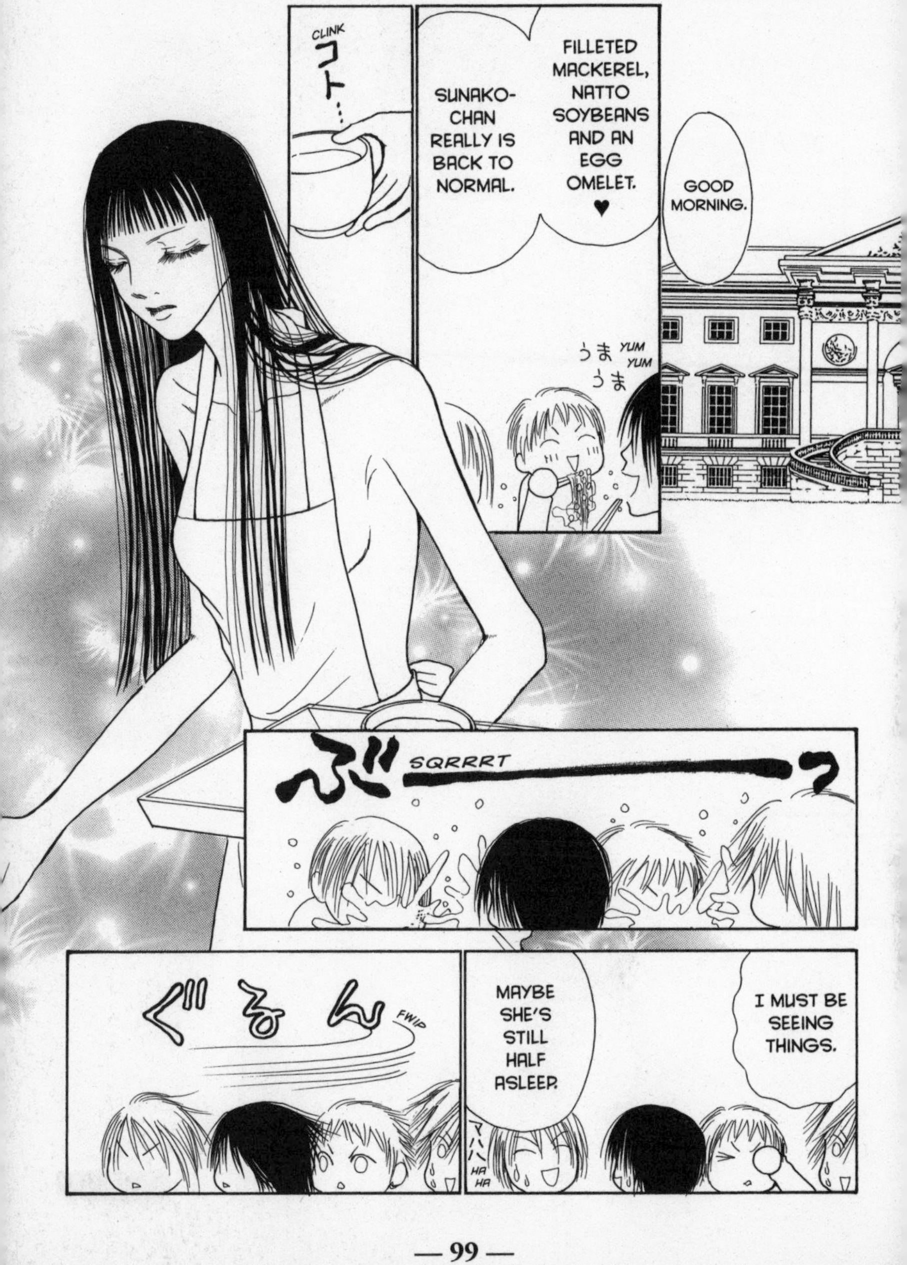
GOOD MORNING.
FILLETED MACKEREL, NATTO SOYBEANS AND AN EGG OMELET. ♥
SUNAKO-CHAN REALLY IS BACK TO NORMAL.
うま YUM
うま YUM
CLINK
コト…
ぶ——っ SQRRRT
I MUST BE SEEING THINGS.
MAYBE SHE'S STILL HALF ASLEEP.
アハハ HA HA
ぐるん FWIP

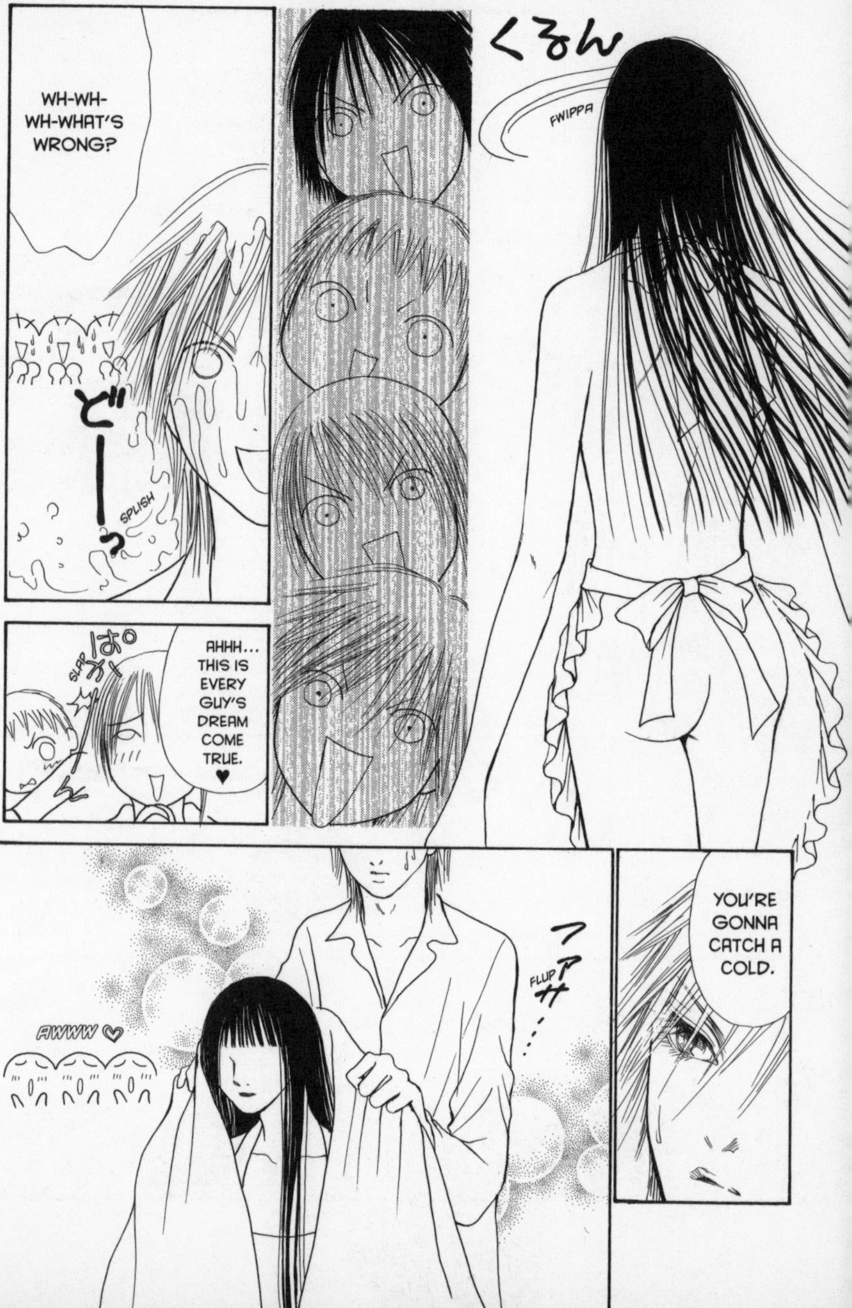
くるん
FWIPPA
WH-WH-WH-WHAT'S WRONG?
どーっ
SPLISH
SLAP
AHHH... THIS IS EVERY GUY'S DREAM COME TRUE. ♥
YOU'RE GONNA CATCH A COLD.
ファサ…
FLUP
AWWW ♡

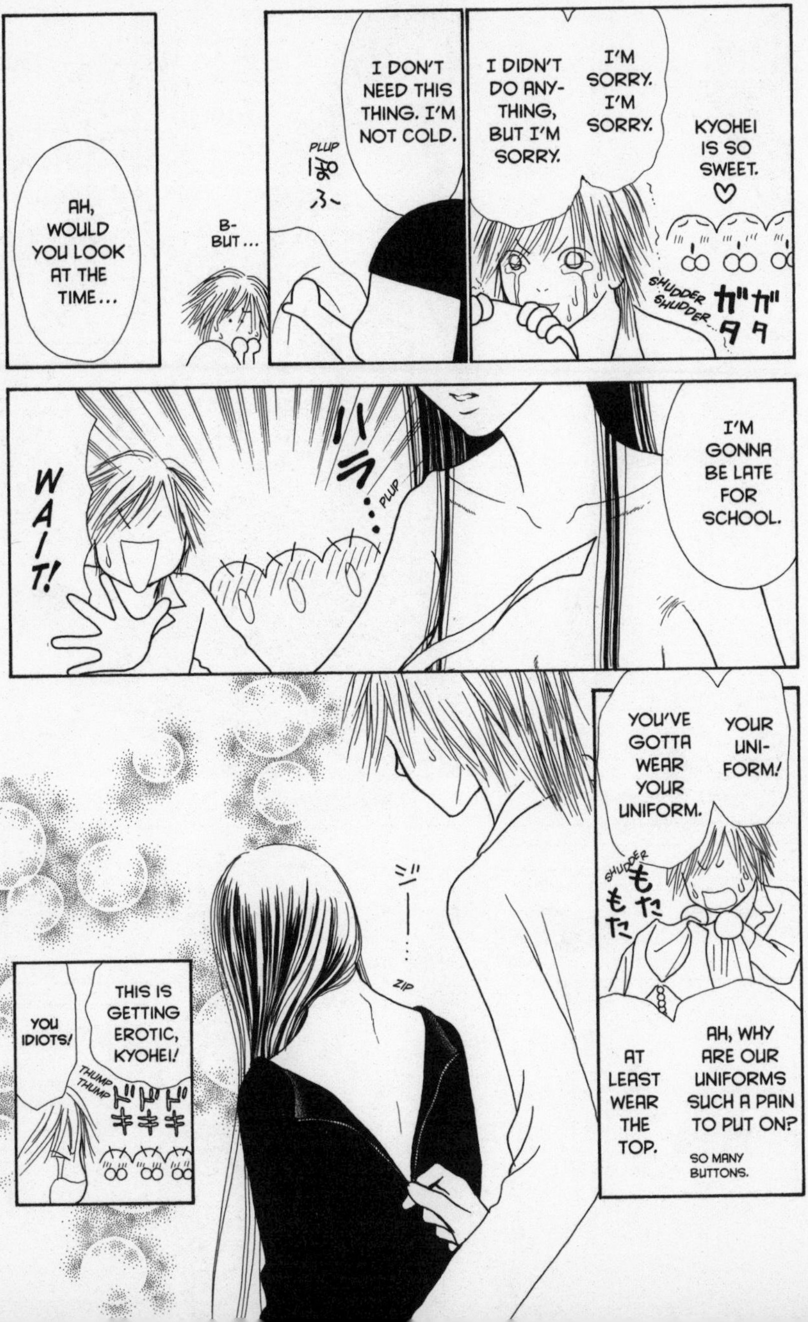
I'M SORRY. I'M SORRY.
I DIDN'T DO ANY-THING, BUT I'M SORRY.
KYOHEI IS SO SWEET. ♡
SHUDDER SHUDDER
ガガタタ
I DON'T NEED THIS THING. I'M NOT COLD.
PLUP
ぽふ~
B-BUT…
AH, WOULD YOU LOOK AT THE TIME…
I'M GONNA BE LATE FOR SCHOOL.
ハラ…
PLUP
WAIT!
YOUR UNI-FORM!
YOU'VE GOTTA WEAR YOUR UNIFORM.
SHUDDER
もたもた
AH, WHY ARE OUR UNIFORMS SUCH A PAIN TO PUT ON?
SO MANY BUTTONS.
AT LEAST WEAR THE TOP.
ジー…
ZIP
THIS IS GETTING EROTIC, KYOHEI!
YOU IDIOTS!
THUMP THUMP
ドドドキキキ

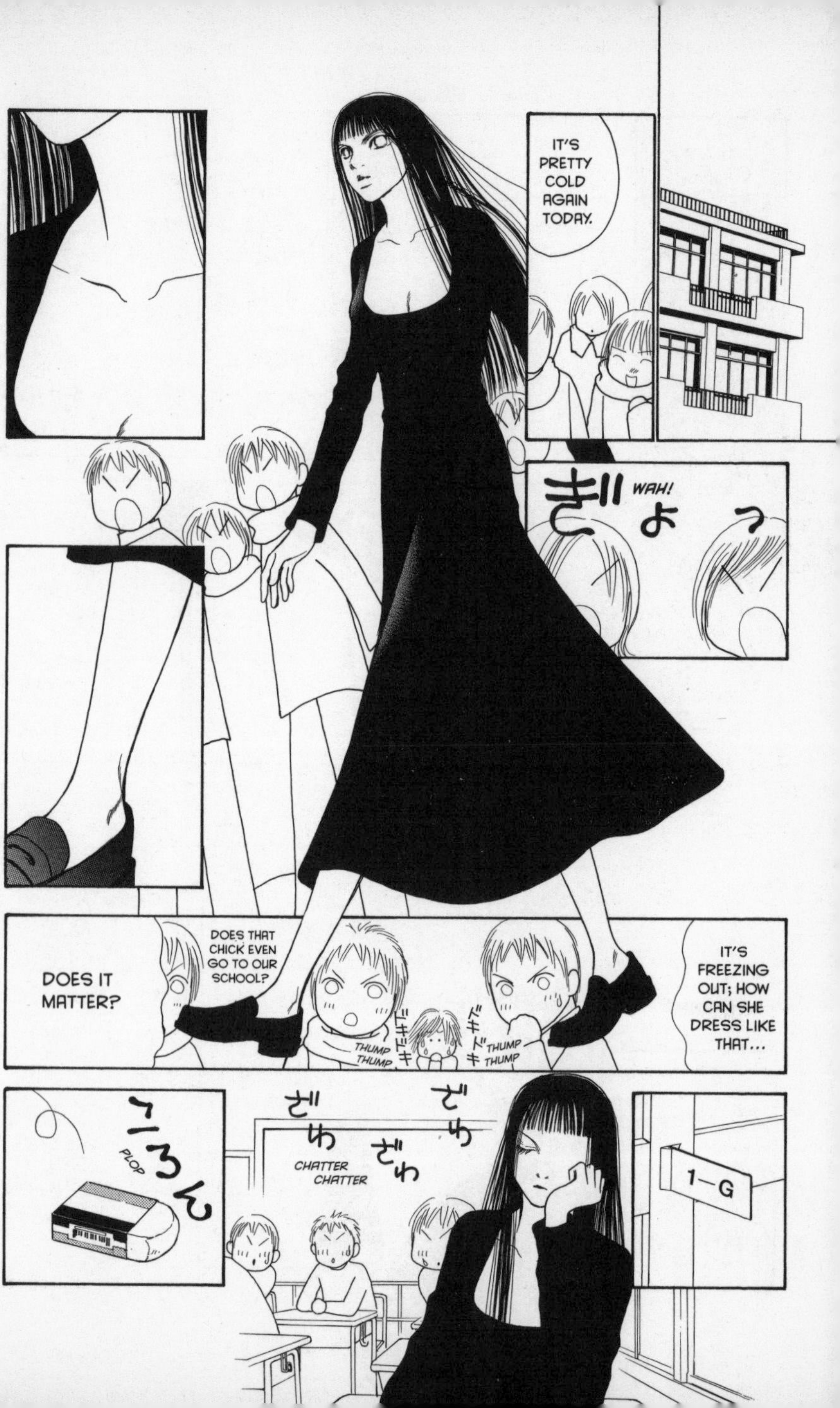
IT'S PRETTY COLD AGAIN TODAY.
ぎょっ
WAH!
IT'S FREEZING OUT; HOW CAN SHE DRESS LIKE THAT...
ドキドキ
THUMP THUMP
ドキドキ
THUMP THUMP
DOES THAT CHICK EVEN GO TO OUR SCHOOL?
DOES IT MATTER?
1—G
ざわ ざわ
ざわ ざわ
CHATTER CHATTER
ころん
PLOP

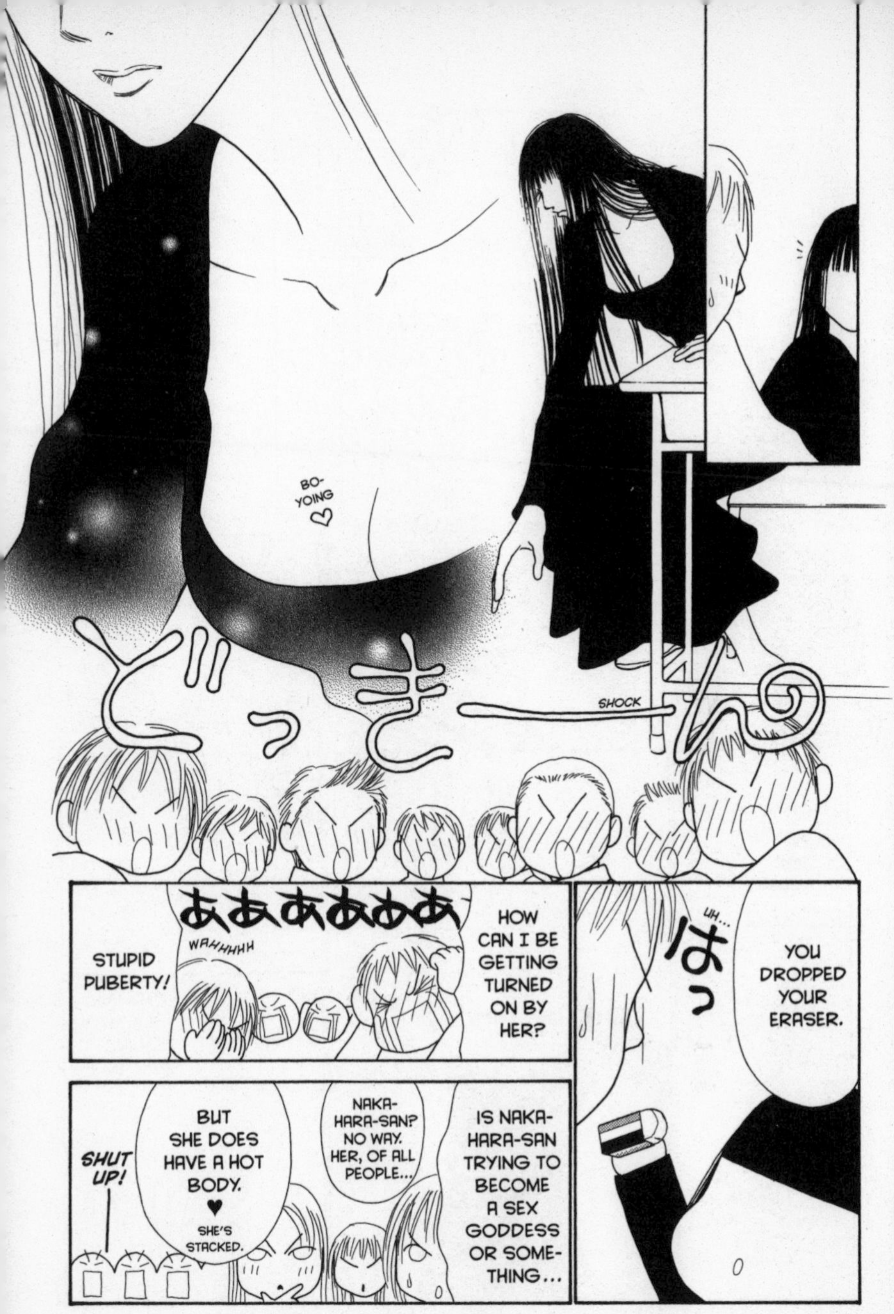
BO-YOING ♡
どっきーん
SHOCK
UH...
ばっ
YOU DROPPED YOUR ERASER.
ああああああ
WAHHHHH
HOW CAN I BE GETTING TURNED ON BY HER?
STUPID PUBERTY!
IS NAKA-HARA-SAN TRYING TO BECOME A SEX GODDESS OR SOME-THING...
NAKA-HARA-SAN? NO WAY. HER, OF ALL PEOPLE...
BUT SHE DOES HAVE A HOT BODY. ♥
SHE'S STACKED.
SHUT UP!

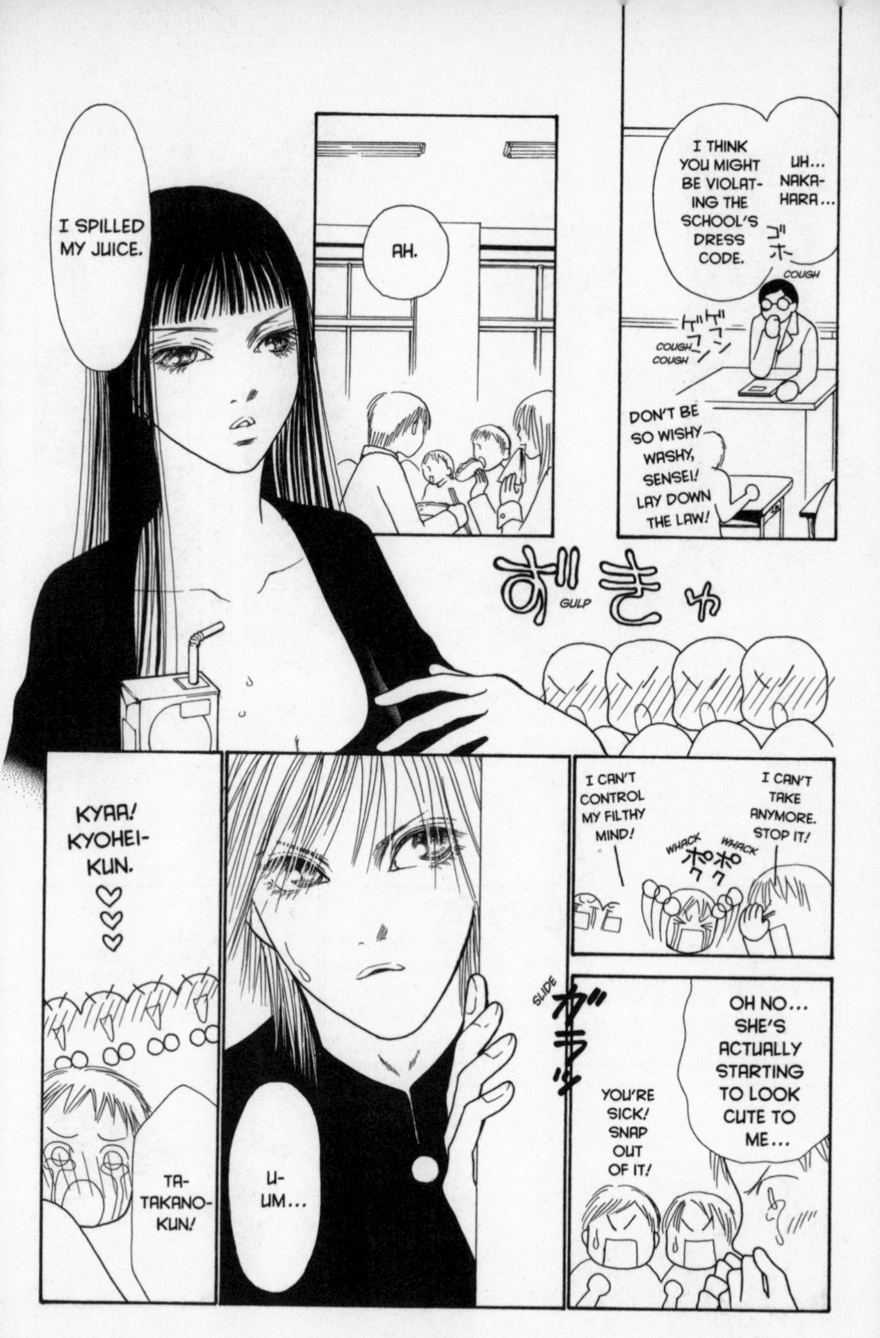
UH... NAKA-HARA...
I THINK YOU MIGHT BE VIOLAT-ING THE SCHOOL'S DRESS CODE.
COUGH
COUGH COUGH
DON'T BE SO WISHY WASHY, SENSEI! LAY DOWN THE LAW!
AH.
I SPILLED MY JUICE.
GULP
I CAN'T TAKE ANYMORE. STOP IT!
WHACK WHACK
I CAN'T CONTROL MY FILTHY MIND!
OH NO... SHE'S ACTUALLY STARTING TO LOOK CUTE TO ME...
YOU'RE SICK! SNAP OUT OF IT!
SLIDE
U-UM...
KYAA! KYOHEI-KUN. ♡♡♡
TA-TAKANO-KUN!

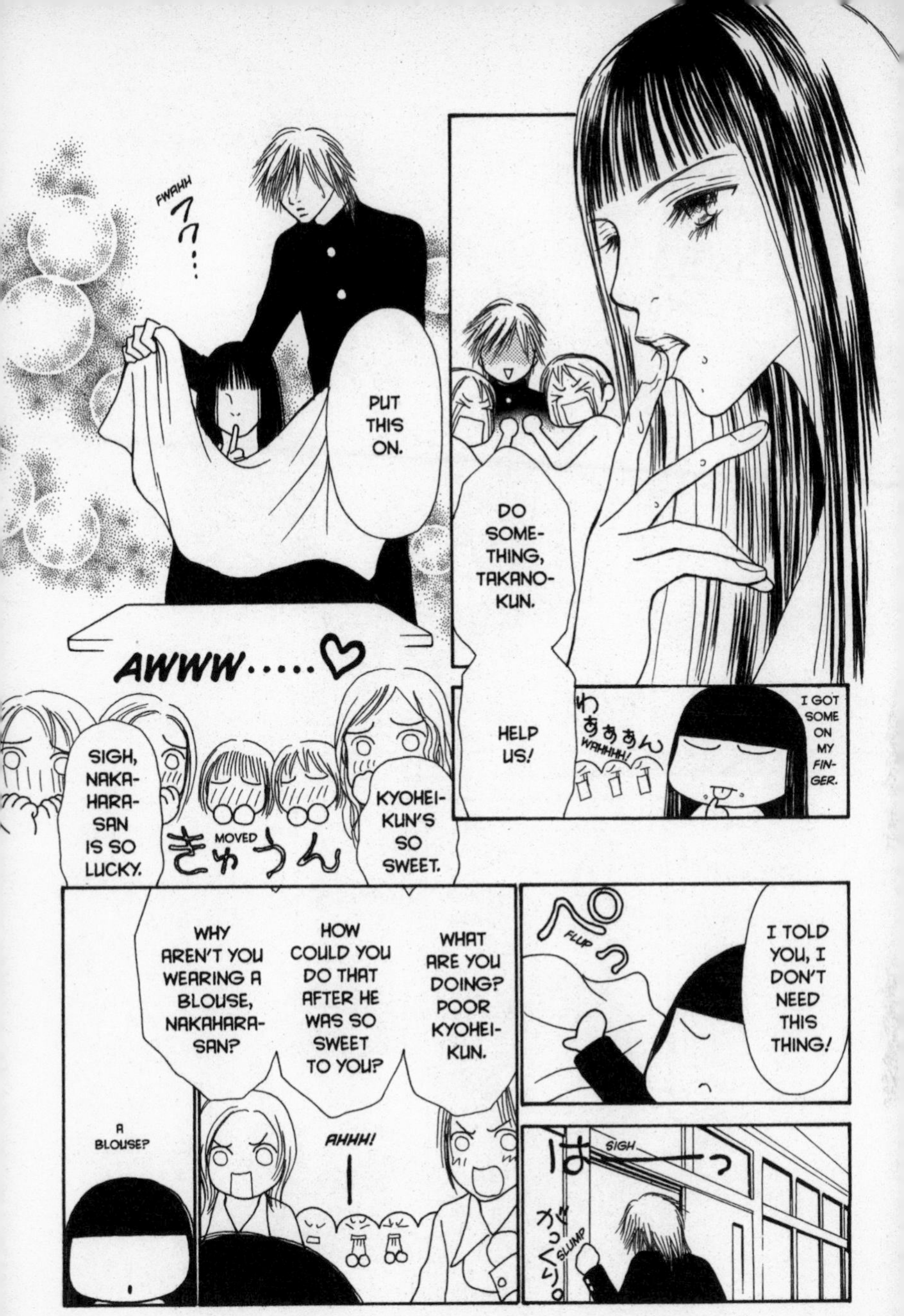
DO SOME-THING, TAKANO-KUN.
HELP US!
WAHHHH!
I GOT SOME ON MY FIN-GER.
FWAHH
PUT THIS ON.
AWWW.....♡
KYOHEI-KUN'S SO SWEET.
MOVED
きゅうん
SIGH, NAKA-HARA-SAN IS SO LUCKY.
FLUP
I TOLD YOU, I DON'T NEED THIS THING!
SIGH
SLUMP
WHAT ARE YOU DOING? POOR KYOHEI-KUN.
HOW COULD YOU DO THAT AFTER HE WAS SO SWEET TO YOU?
WHY AREN'T YOU WEARING A BLOUSE, NAKAHARA-SAN?
AHHH!
A BLOUSE?

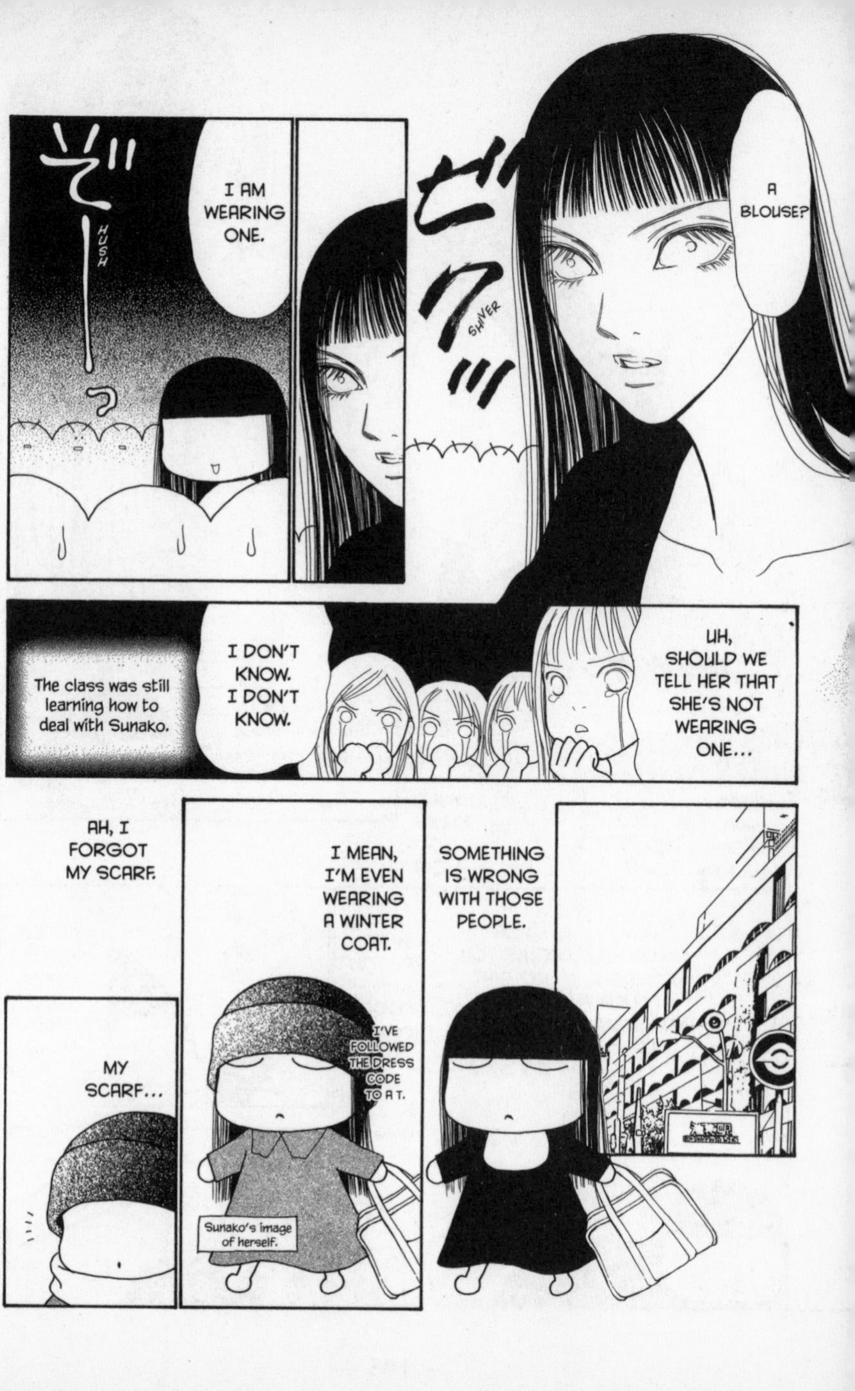
A BLOUSE?
SHIVER
I AM WEARING ONE.
HUSH
UH, SHOULD WE TELL HER THAT SHE'S NOT WEARING ONE...
I DON'T KNOW. I DON'T KNOW.
The class was still learning how to deal with Sunako.
SOMETHING IS WRONG WITH THOSE PEOPLE.
I MEAN, I'M EVEN WEARING A WINTER COAT.
I'VE FOLLOWED THE DRESS CODE TO A T.
Sunako's image of herself.
AH, I FORGOT MY SCARF.
MY SCARF...

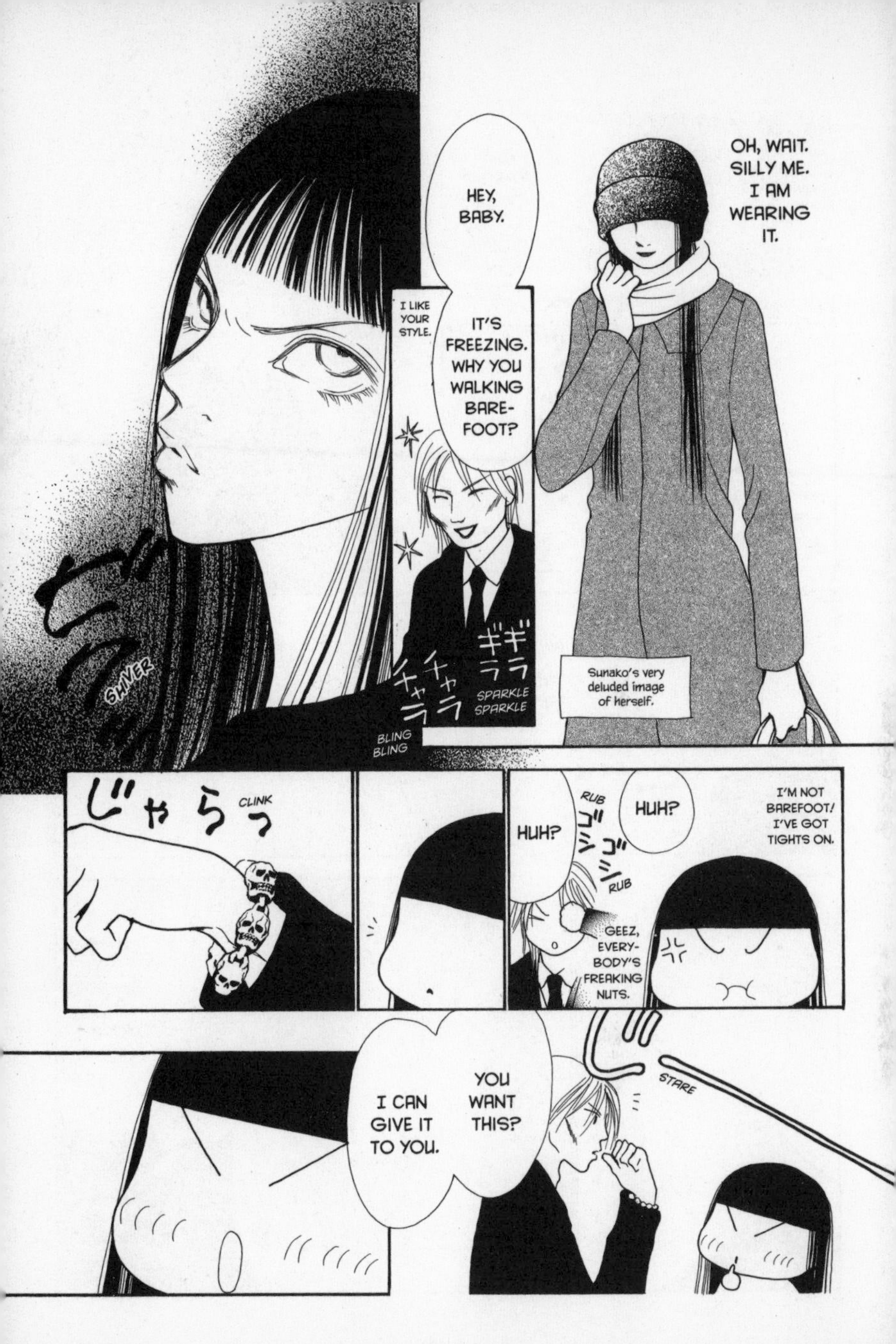
OH, WAIT. SILLY ME. I AM WEARING IT.
Sunako's very deluded image of herself.
HEY, BABY.
I LIKE YOUR STYLE.
IT'S FREEZING. WHY YOU WALKING BARE-FOOT?
ギギララ
SPARKLE SPARKLE
チャチャララ
BLING BLING
SHIVER
HUH?
HUH?
ゴシゴシ
RUB
RUB
I'M NOT BAREFOOT! I'VE GOT TIGHTS ON.
GEEZ, EVERY-BODY'S FREAKING NUTS.
じゃらっ
CLINK
STARE
YOU WANT THIS?
I CAN GIVE IT TO YOU.

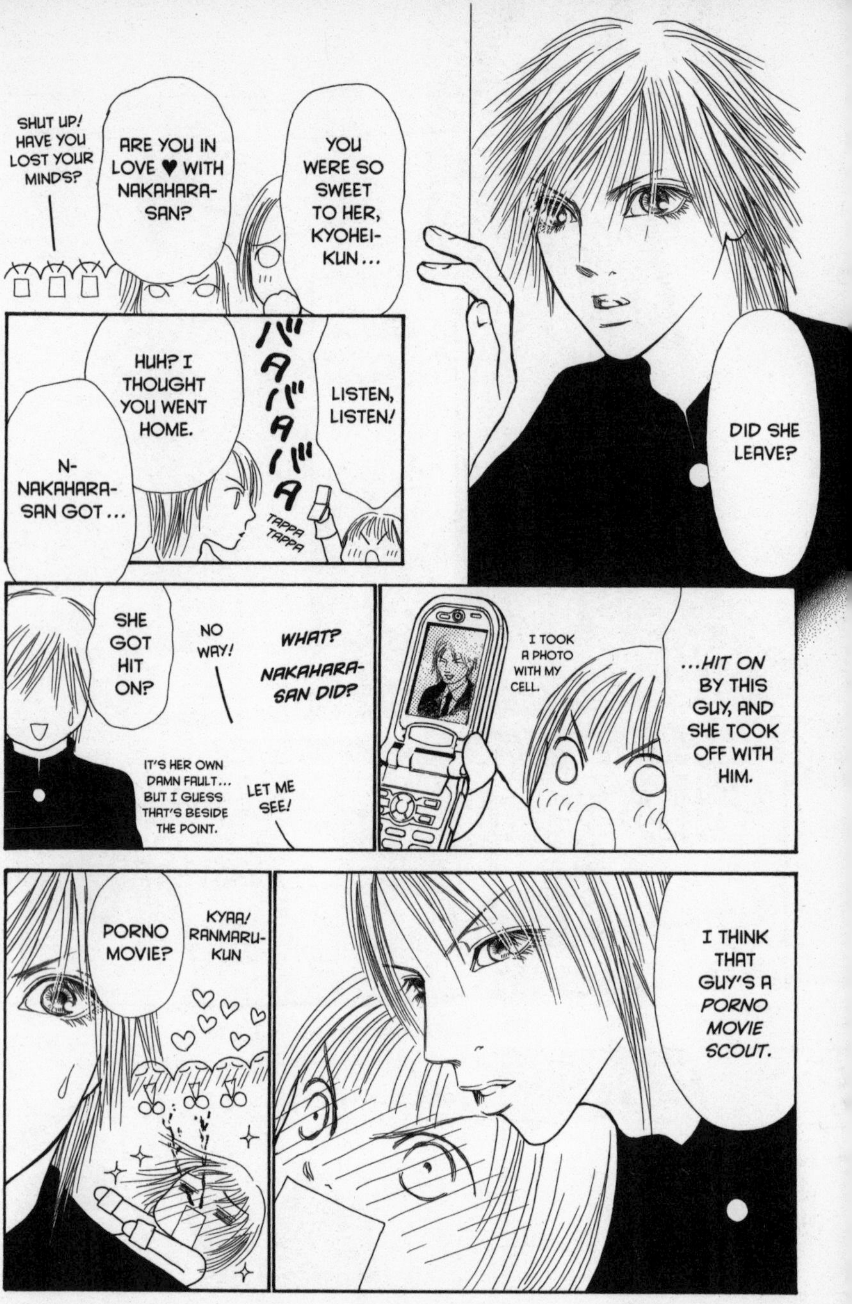
DID SHE LEAVE?
YOU WERE SO SWEET TO HER, KYOHEI-KUN...
ARE YOU IN LOVE ♥ WITH NAKAHARA-SAN?
SHUT UP! HAVE YOU LOST YOUR MINDS?
バタバタバタ
TAPPA TAPPA
LISTEN, LISTEN!
HUH? I THOUGHT YOU WENT HOME.
N-NAKAHARA-SAN GOT...
...*HIT ON* BY THIS GUY, AND SHE TOOK OFF WITH HIM.
I TOOK A PHOTO WITH MY CELL.
WHAT? NAKAHARA-SAN DID?
NO WAY!
SHE GOT HIT ON?
LET ME SEE!
IT'S HER OWN DAMN FAULT... BUT I GUESS THAT'S BESIDE THE POINT.
I THINK THAT GUY'S A *PORNO MOVIE SCOUT.*
KYAA! RANMARU-KUN
PORNO MOVIE?

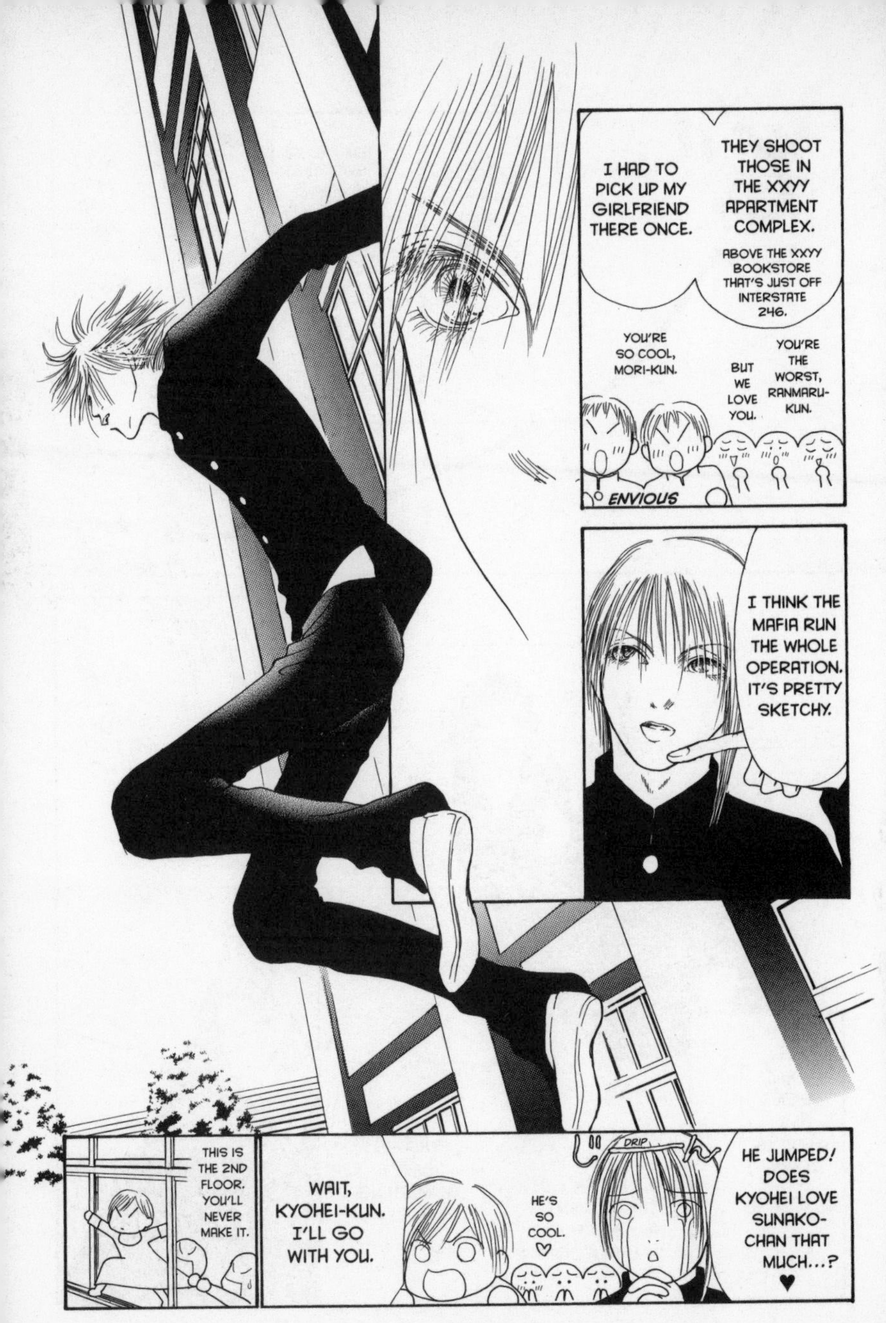

THEY SHOOT THOSE IN THE XXYY APARTMENT COMPLEX.
ABOVE THE XXYY BOOKSTORE THAT'S JUST OFF INTERSTATE 246.
I HAD TO PICK UP MY GIRLFRIEND THERE ONCE.
YOU'RE THE WORST, RANMARU-KUN.
BUT WE LOVE YOU.
YOU'RE SO COOL, MORI-KUN.
ENVIOUS
I THINK THE MAFIA RUN THE WHOLE OPERATION. IT'S PRETTY SKETCHY.
DRIP
HE JUMPED! DOES KYOHEI LOVE SUNAKO-CHAN THAT MUCH...? ♥
HE'S SO COOL. ♡
WAIT, KYOHEI-KUN. I'LL GO WITH YOU.
THIS IS THE 2ND FLOOR. YOU'LL NEVER MAKE IT.

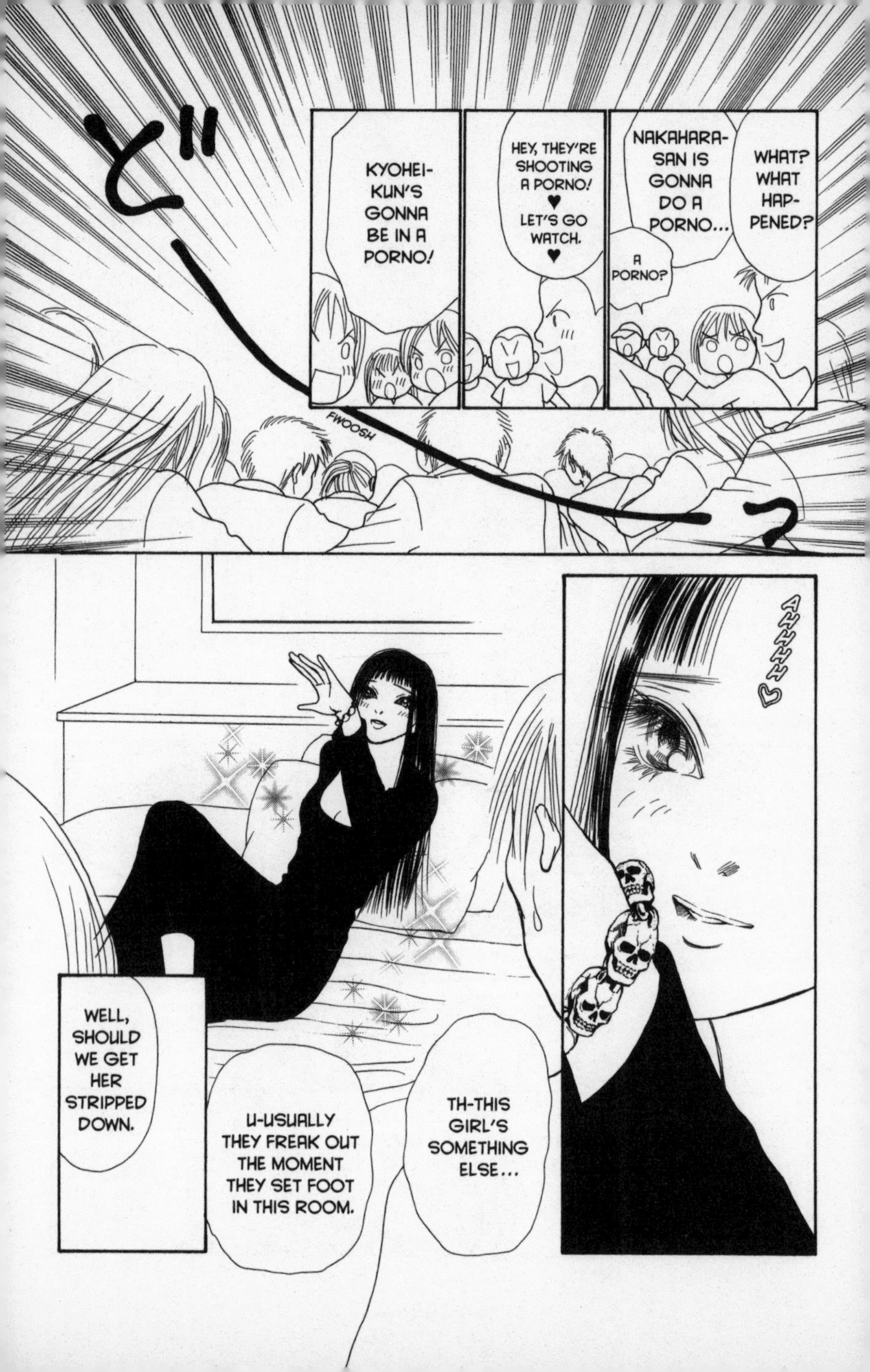
WHAT? WHAT HAP-PENED?
NAKAHARA-SAN IS GONNA DO A PORNO...
A PORNO?
HEY, THEY'RE SHOOTING A PORNO! ♥ LET'S GO WATCH. ♥
KYOHEI-KUN'S GONNA BE IN A PORNO!
どーっ
FWOOSH
AHHHHH ♥
TH-THIS GIRL'S SOMETHING ELSE...
U-USUALLY THEY FREAK OUT THE MOMENT THEY SET FOOT IN THIS ROOM.
WELL, SHOULD WE GET HER STRIPPED DOWN.

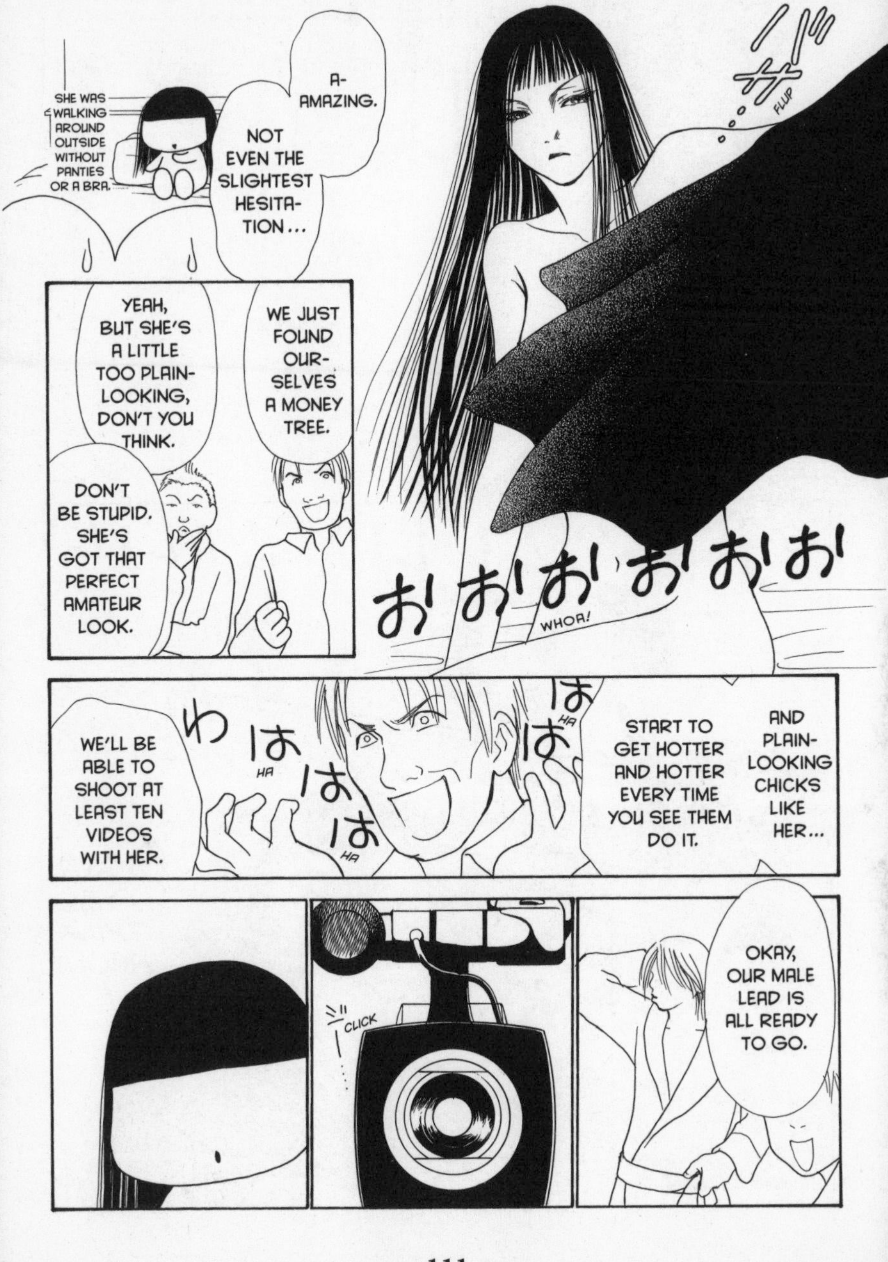
FLUP
WHOA!
A-AMAZING.
NOT EVEN THE SLIGHTEST HESITATION...
SHE WAS WALKING AROUND OUTSIDE WITHOUT PANTIES OR A BRA.
WE JUST FOUND OURSELVES A MONEY TREE.
YEAH, BUT SHE'S A LITTLE TOO PLAIN-LOOKING, DON'T YOU THINK.
DON'T BE STUPID. SHE'S GOT THAT PERFECT AMATEUR LOOK.
AND PLAIN-LOOKING CHICKS LIKE HER...
START TO GET HOTTER AND HOTTER EVERY TIME YOU SEE THEM DO IT.
HA HA HA
WE'LL BE ABLE TO SHOOT AT LEAST TEN VIDEOS WITH HER.
OKAY, OUR MALE LEAD IS ALL READY TO GO.
CLICK

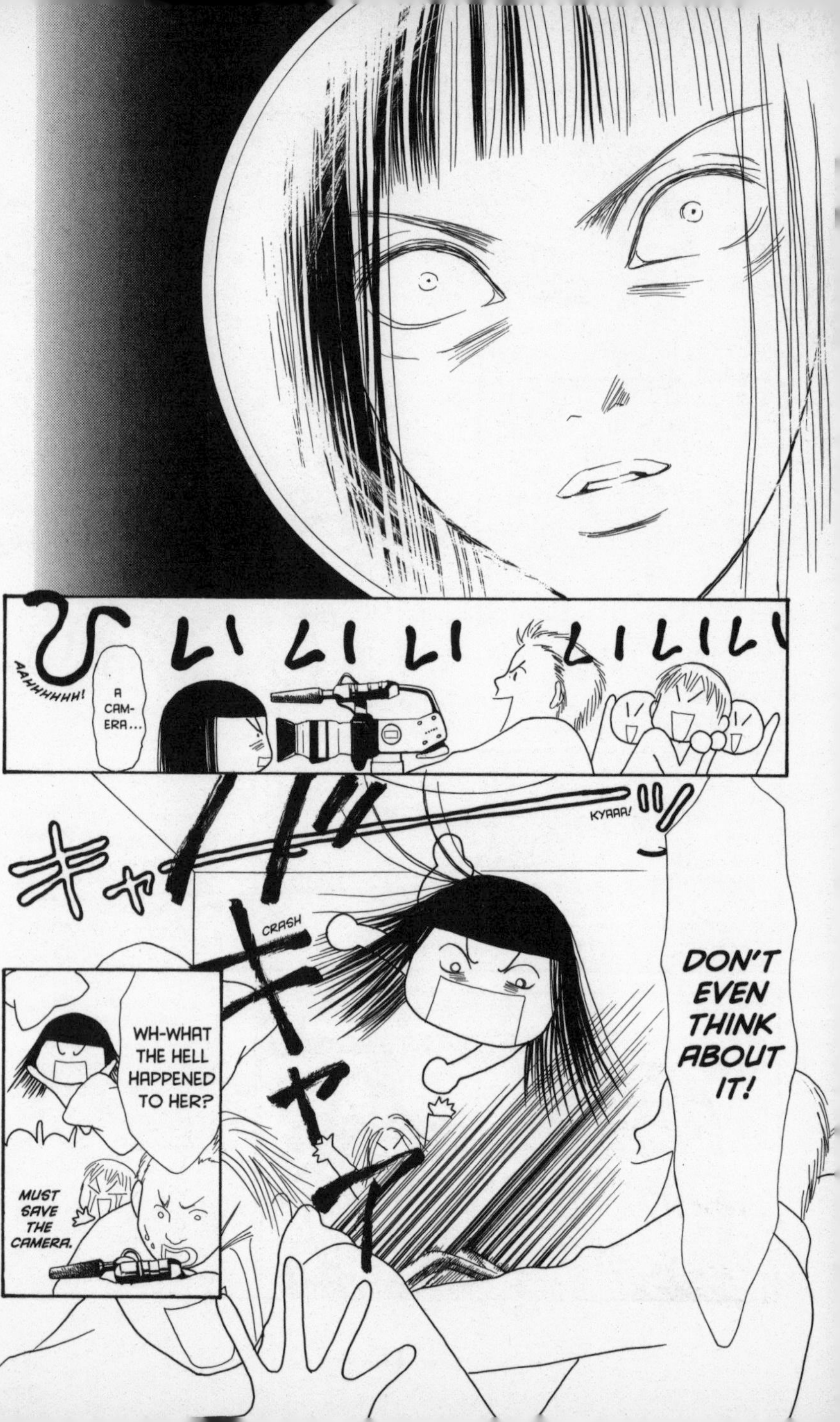

AAHHHHHH!
A CAM-ERA...
KYAAA!
DON'T EVEN THINK ABOUT IT!
CRASH
WH-WHAT THE HELL HAPPENED TO HER?
MUST SAVE THE CAMERA.

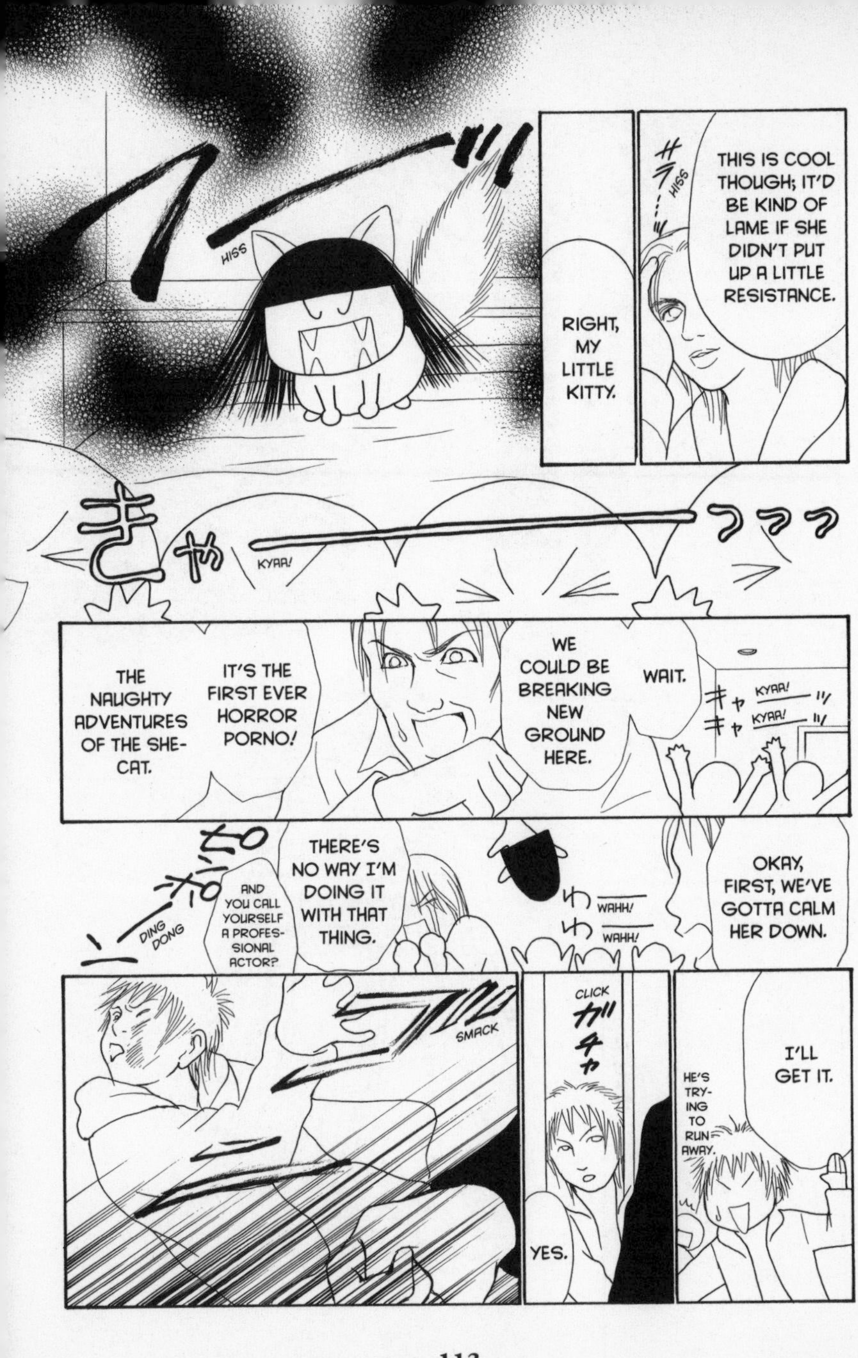
HISS
THIS IS COOL THOUGH; IT'D BE KIND OF LAME IF SHE DIDN'T PUT UP A LITTLE RESISTANCE.
RIGHT, MY LITTLE KITTY.
HISS
KYAA!
WAIT.
KYAA!
KYAA!
WE COULD BE BREAKING NEW GROUND HERE.
IT'S THE FIRST EVER HORROR PORNO!
THE NAUGHTY ADVENTURES OF THE SHE-CAT.
OKAY, FIRST, WE'VE GOTTA CALM HER DOWN.
WAHH!
WAHH!
THERE'S NO WAY I'M DOING IT WITH THAT THING.
AND YOU CALL YOURSELF A PROFESSIONAL ACTOR?
DING DONG
I'LL GET IT.
HE'S TRYING TO RUN AWAY.
CLICK
YES.
SMACK

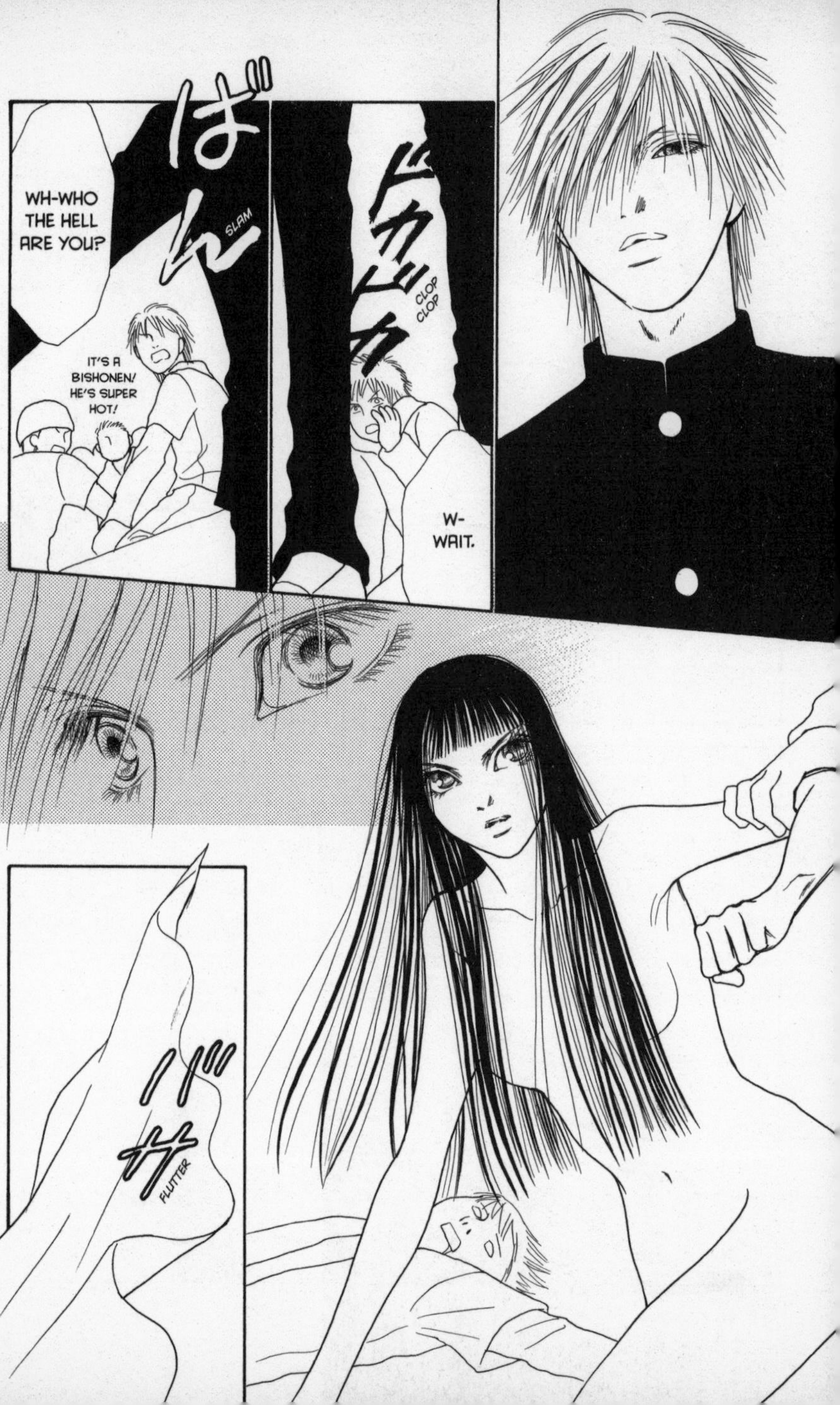
ドカドカ
CLOP CLOP
W- WAIT.
ばん
SLAM
WH-WHO THE HELL ARE YOU?
IT'S A BISHONEN! HE'S SUPER HOT!
バサ
FLUTTER

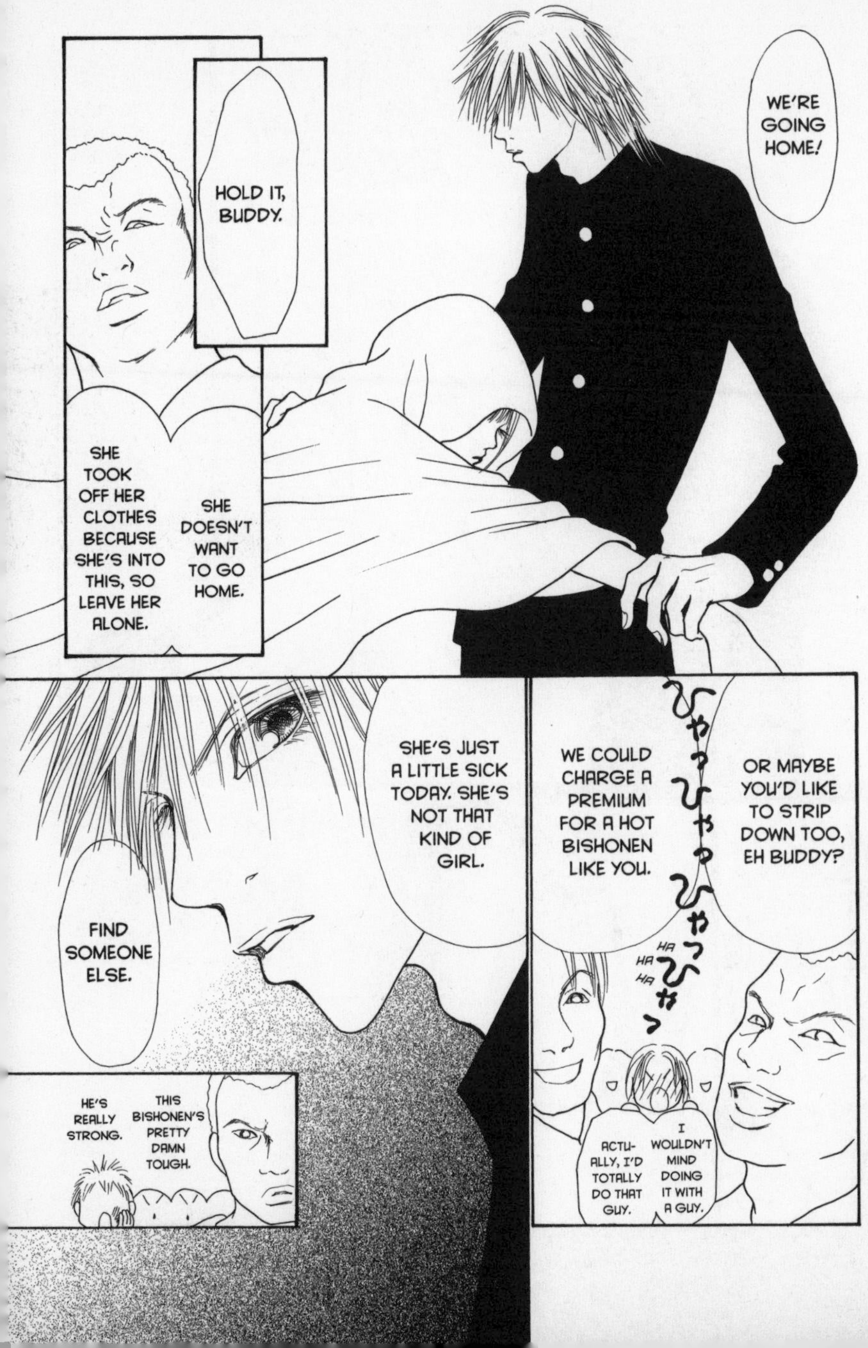
WE'RE GOING HOME!
HOLD IT, BUDDY.
SHE DOESN'T WANT TO GO HOME.
SHE TOOK OFF HER CLOTHES BECAUSE SHE'S INTO THIS, SO LEAVE HER ALONE.
OR MAYBE YOU'D LIKE TO STRIP DOWN TOO, EH BUDDY?
ひゃっひゃっひゃっひゃっひゃっ
WE COULD CHARGE A PREMIUM FOR A HOT BISHONEN LIKE YOU.
HA HA HA
I WOULDN'T MIND DOING IT WITH A GUY.
ACTU-ALLY, I'D TOTALLY DO THAT GUY.
SHE'S JUST A LITTLE SICK TODAY. SHE'S NOT THAT KIND OF GIRL.
FIND SOMEONE ELSE.
THIS BISHONEN'S PRETTY DAMN TOUGH.
HE'S REALLY STRONG.

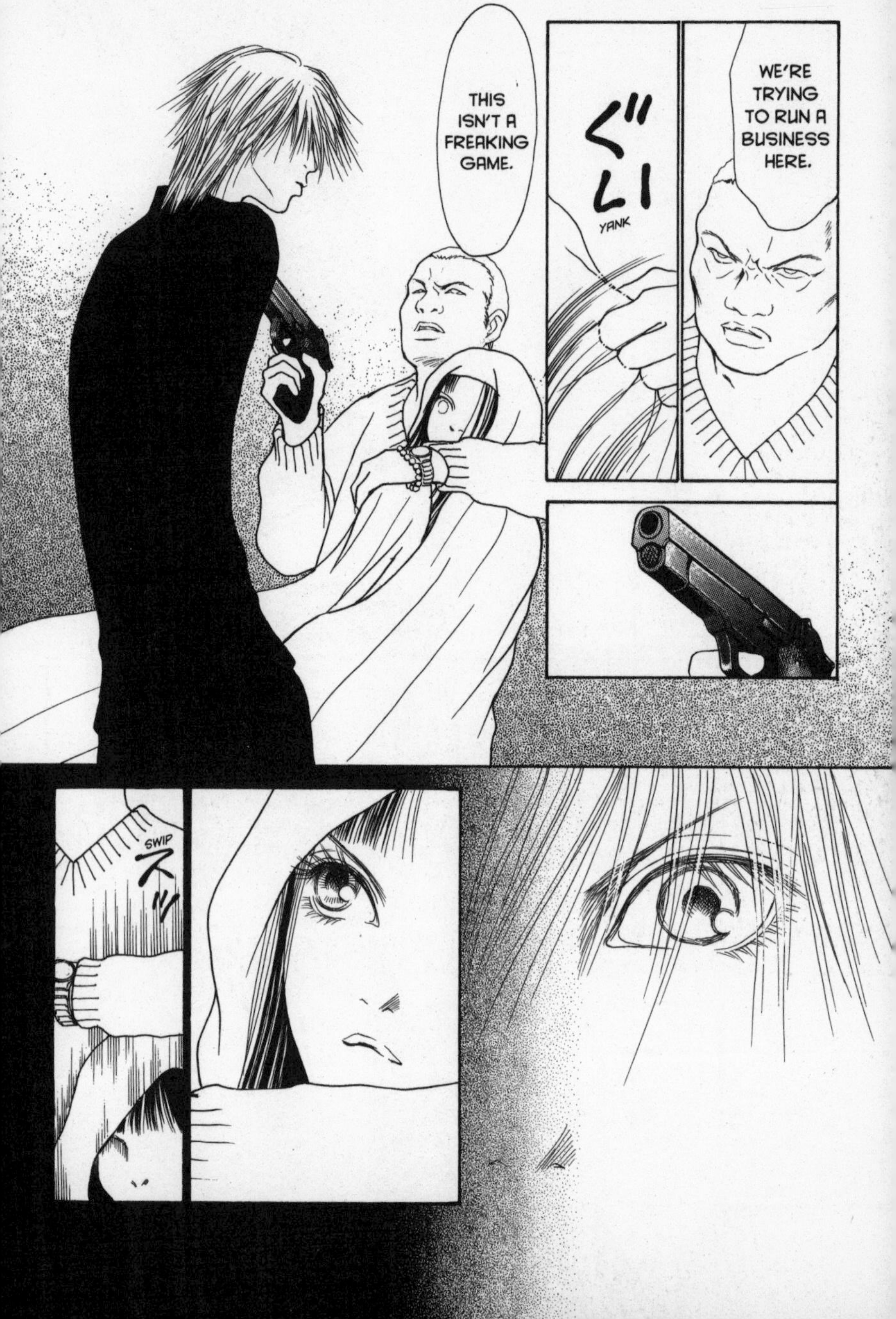
WE'RE TRYING TO RUN A BUSINESS HERE.
ぐい
YANK
THIS ISN'T A FREAKING GAME.
SWIP
スッ

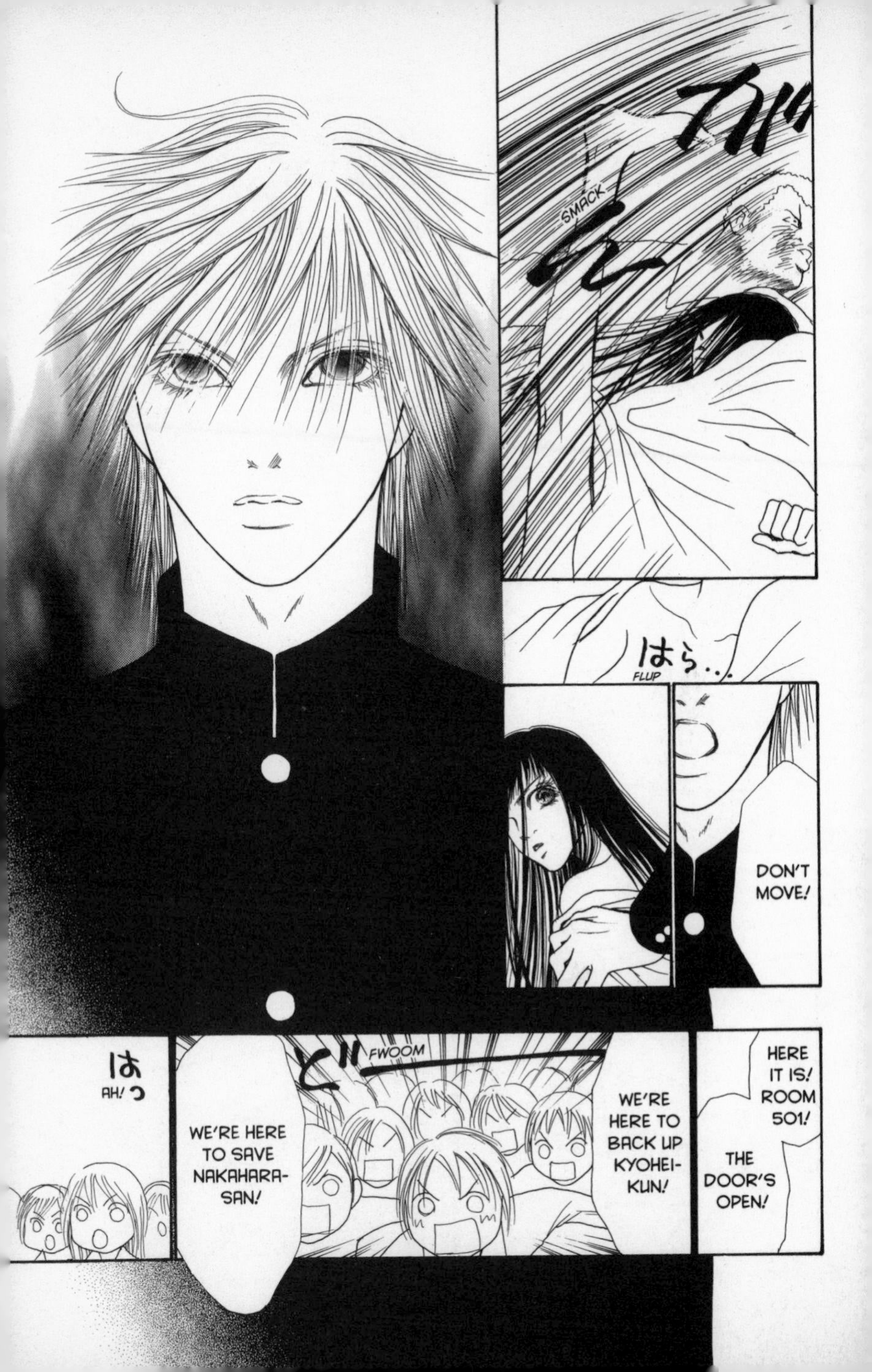
SMACK
はら...
FLUP
DON'T MOVE!
HERE IT IS! ROOM 501!
THE DOOR'S OPEN!
WE'RE HERE TO BACK UP KYOHEI-KUN!
ど
FWOOM
WE'RE HERE TO SAVE NAKAHARA-SAN!
はっ
AH!

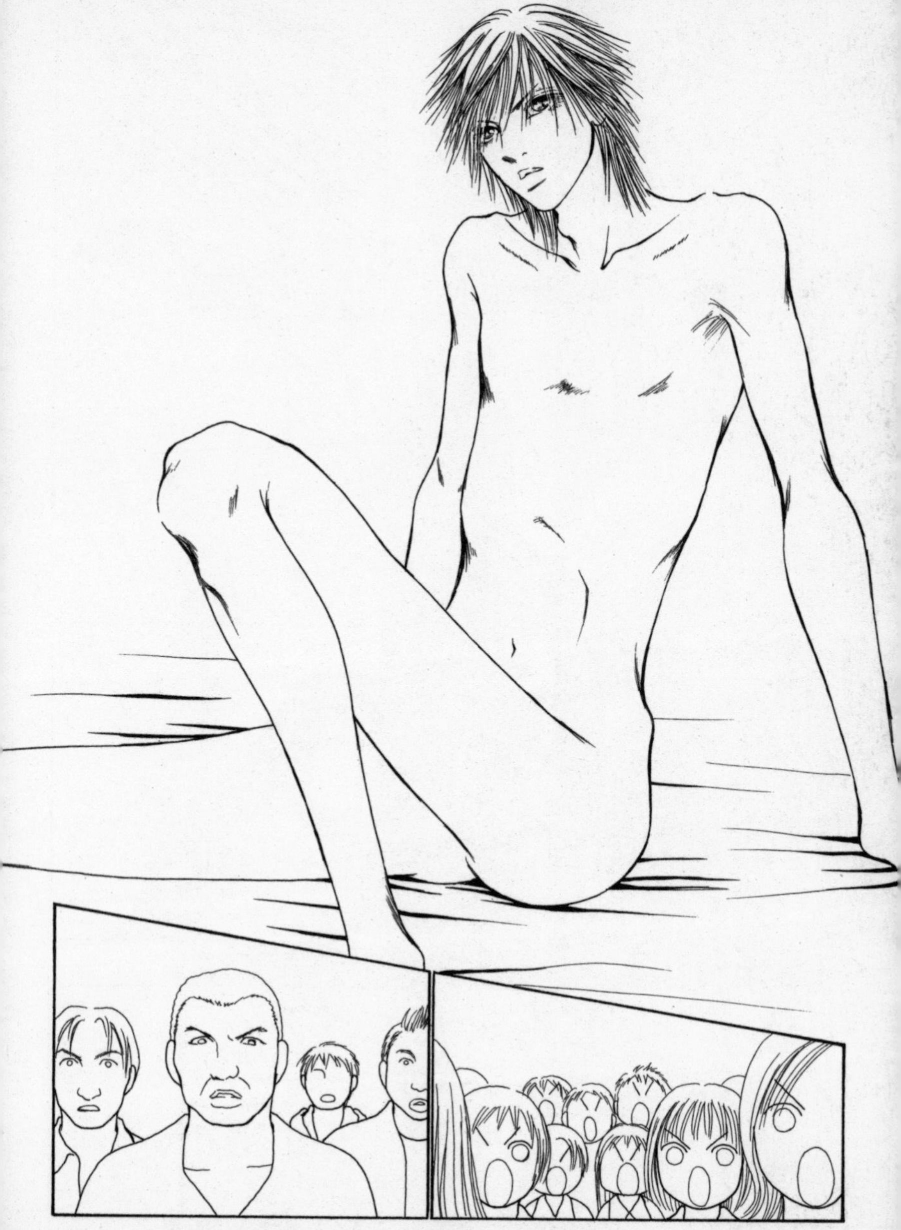

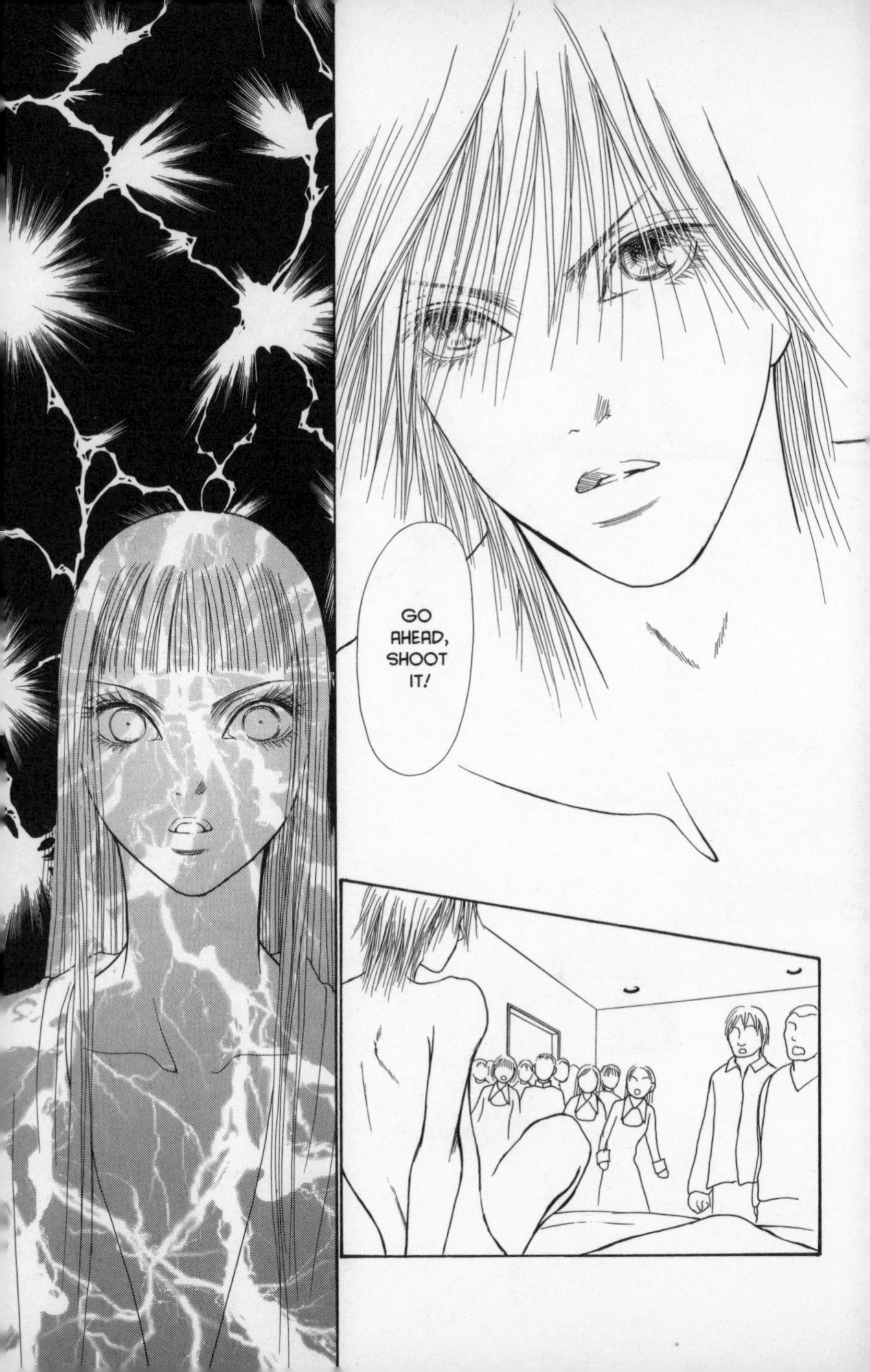
GO AHEAD, SHOOT IT!

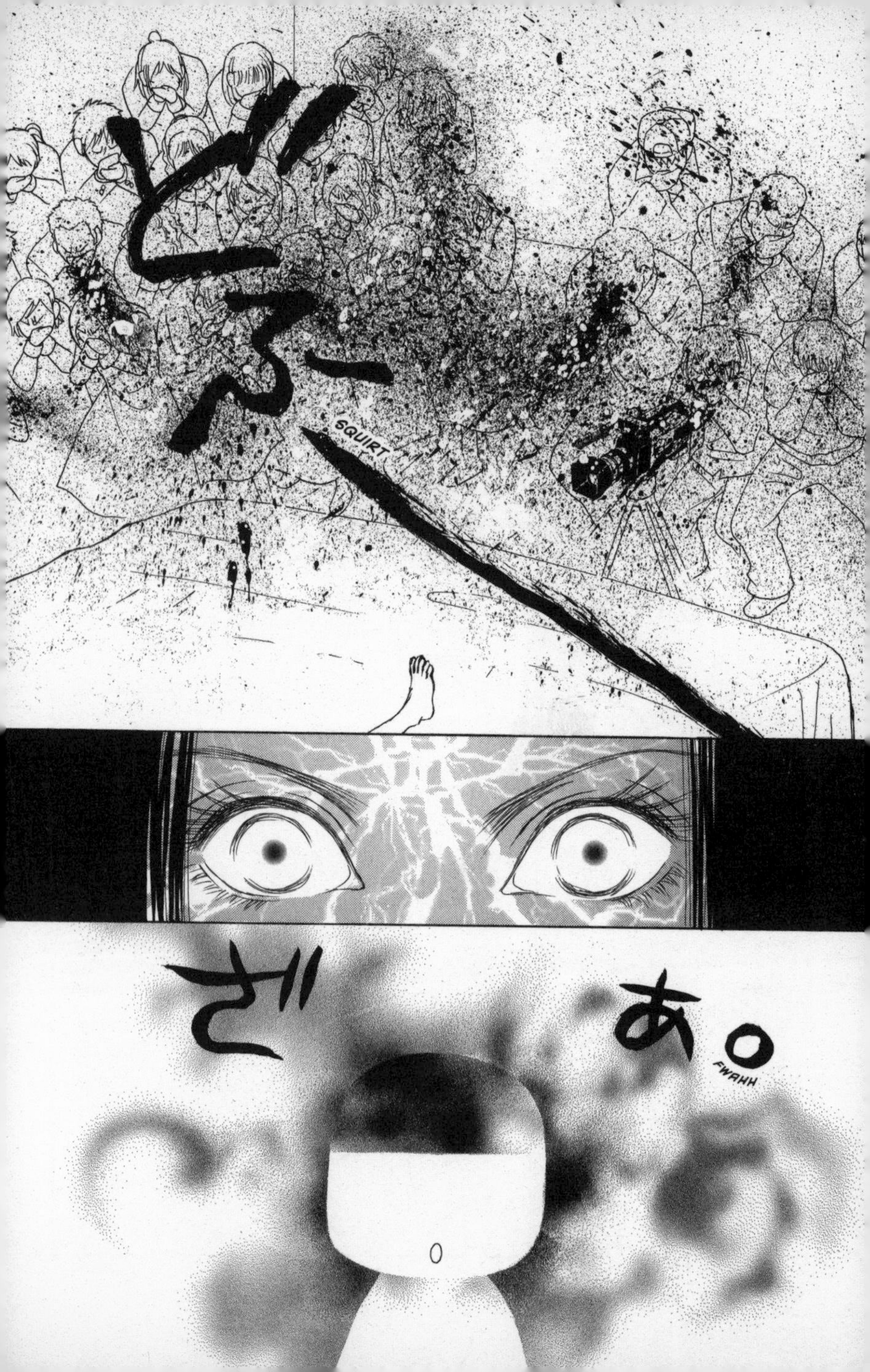
SQUIRT
FWAHH

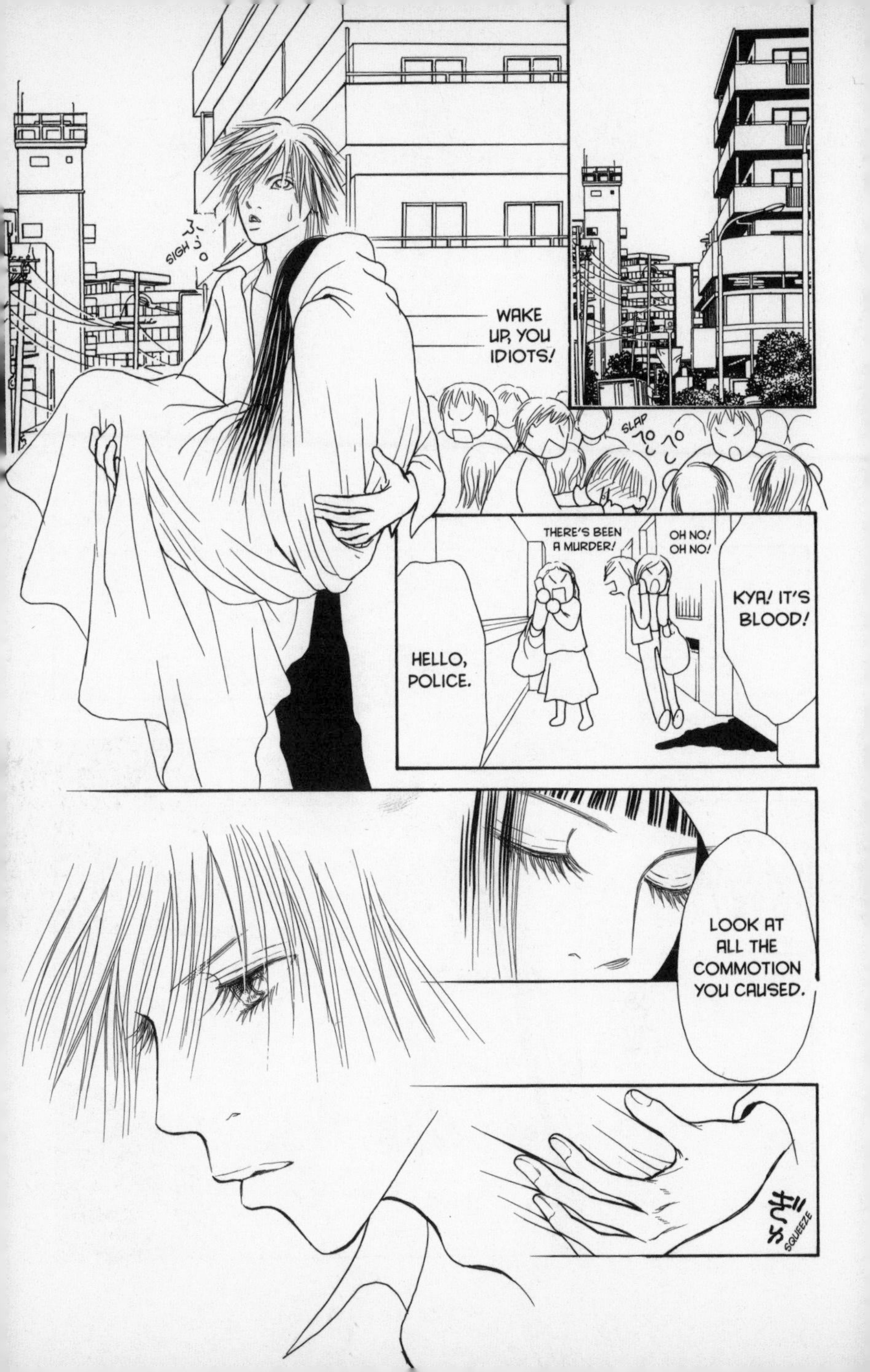
WAKE UP, YOU IDIOTS!
SLAP
KYA! IT'S BLOOD!
OH NO! OH NO!
THERE'S BEEN A MURDER!
HELLO, POLICE.
SIGH
LOOK AT ALL THE COMMOTION YOU CAUSED.
SQUEEZE

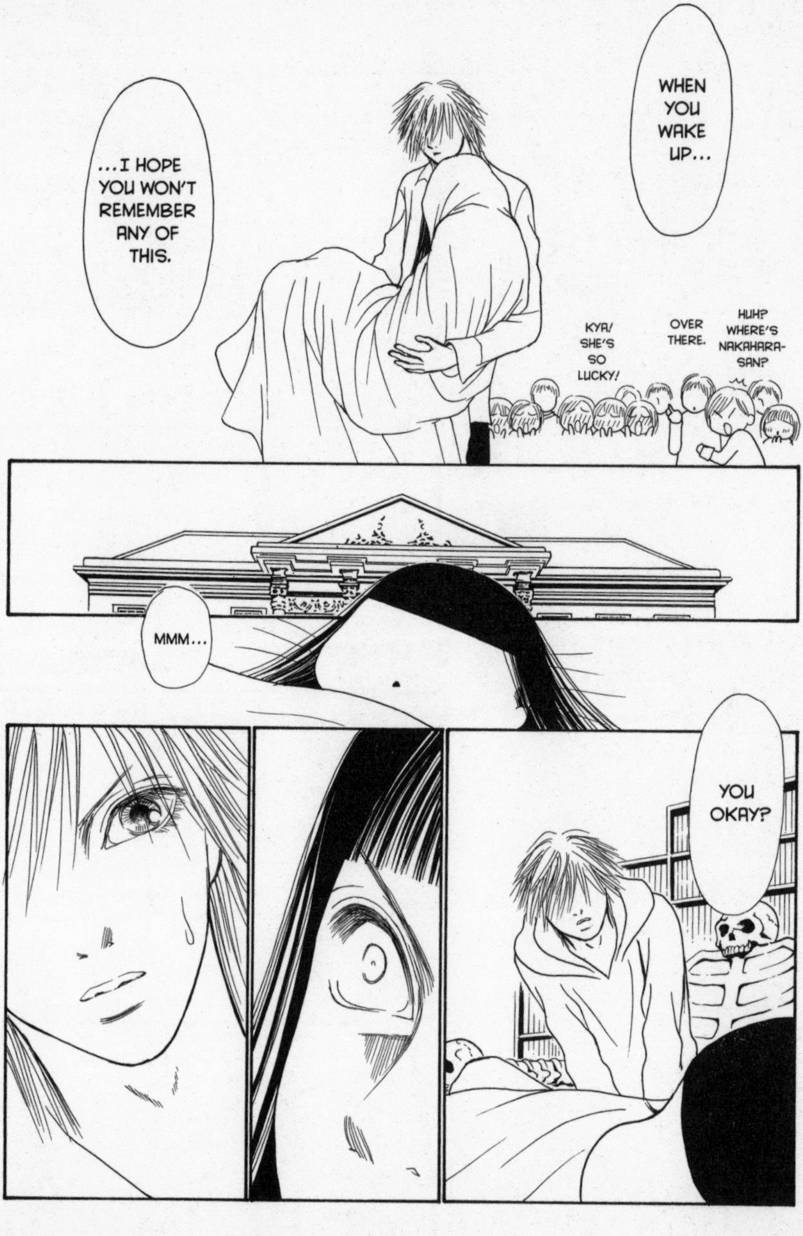
WHEN YOU WAKE UP...
...I HOPE YOU WON'T REMEMBER ANY OF THIS.
HUH? WHERE'S NAKAHARA-SAN?
OVER THERE.
KYA! SHE'S SO LUCKY!
MMM...
YOU OKAY?

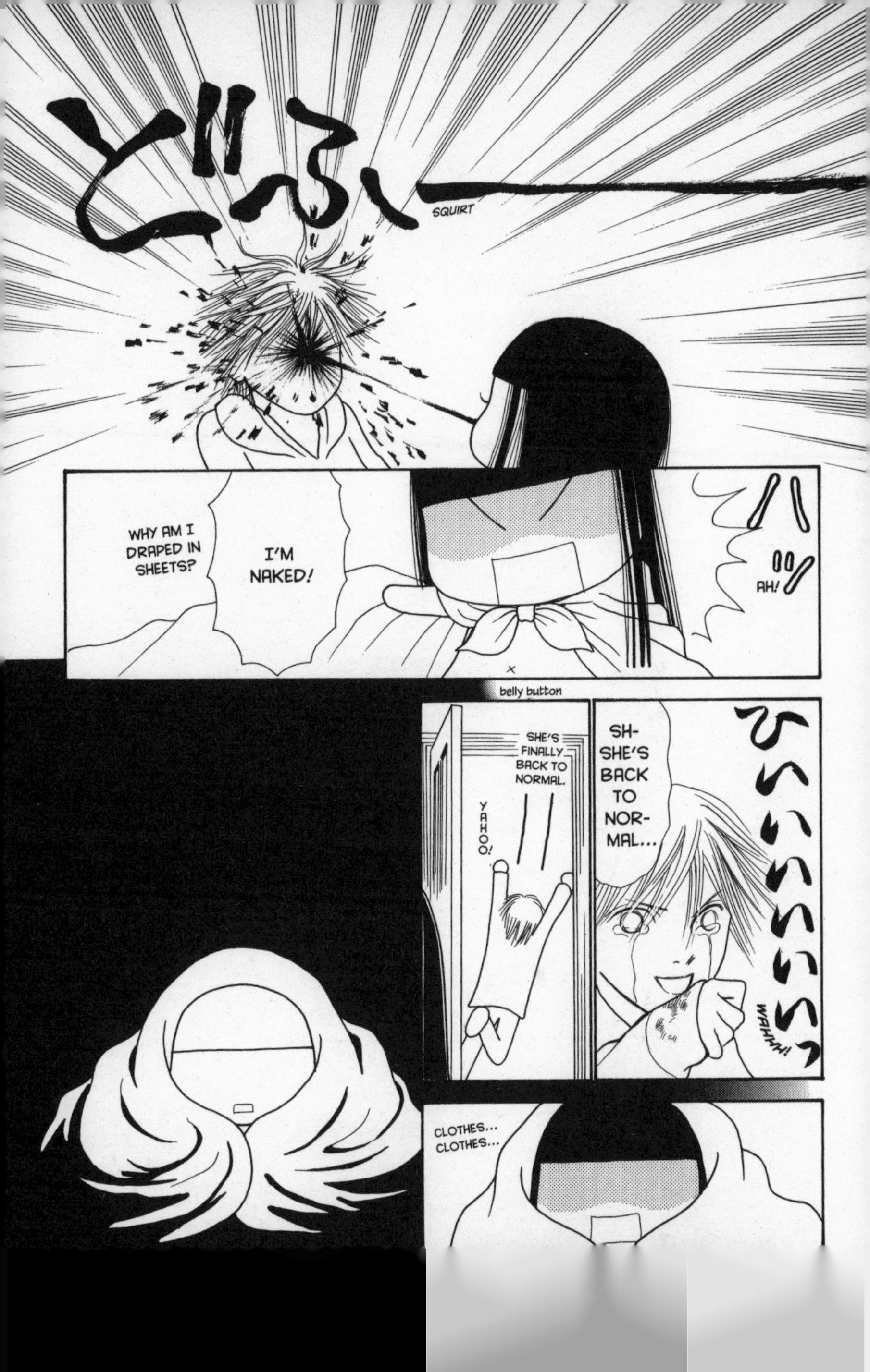
SQUIRT
AH!
I'M NAKED!
WHY AM I DRAPED IN SHEETS?
belly button
SH-SHE'S BACK TO NOR-MAL...
WAHH!
SHE'S FINALLY BACK TO NORMAL.
YAHOO!
CLOTHES... CLOTHES...

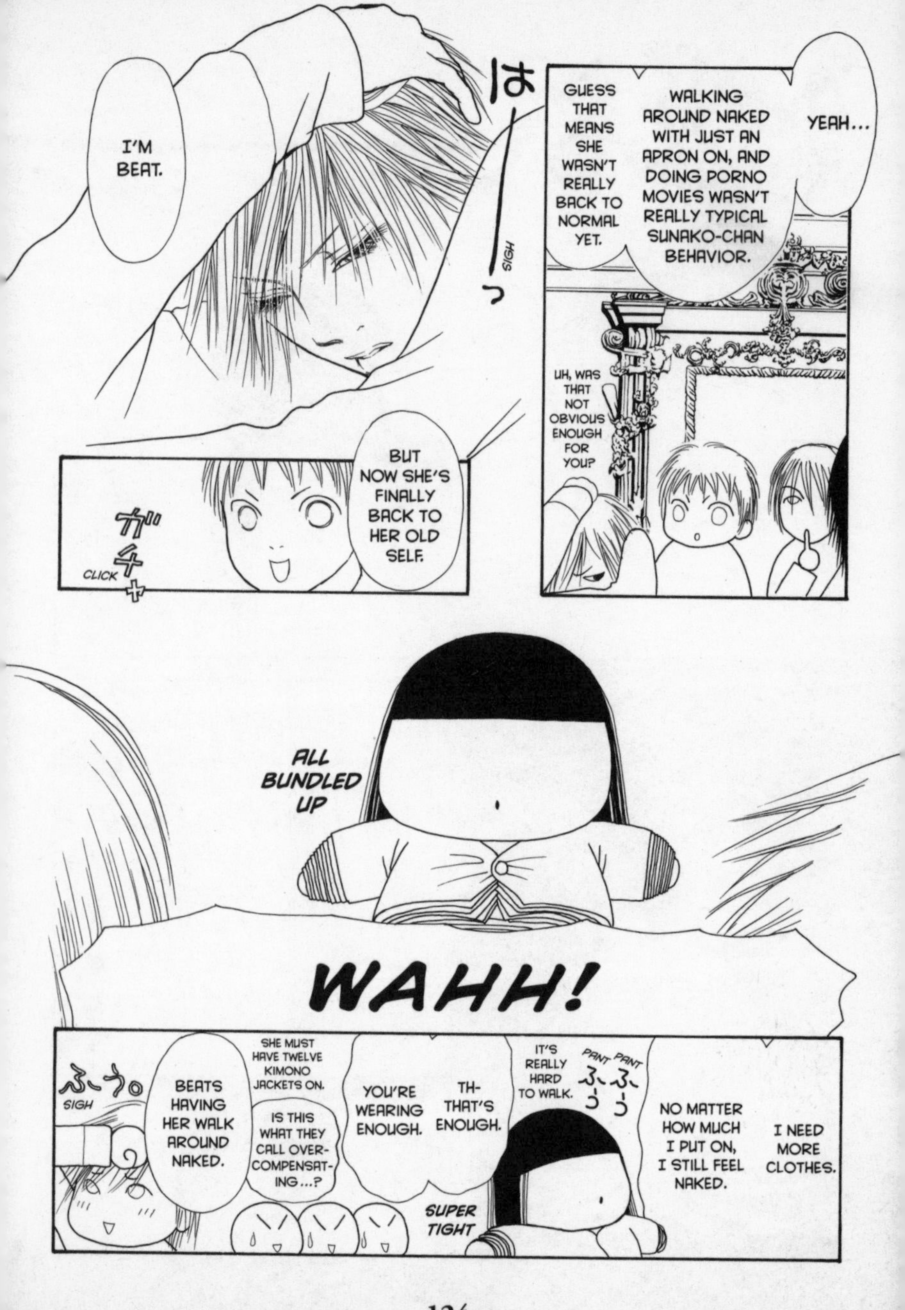
YEAH...
WALKING AROUND NAKED WITH JUST AN APRON ON, AND DOING PORNO MOVIES WASN'T REALLY TYPICAL SUNAKO-CHAN BEHAVIOR.
GUESS THAT MEANS SHE WASN'T REALLY BACK TO NORMAL YET.
UH, WAS THAT NOT OBVIOUS ENOUGH FOR YOU?
はーっ
SIGH
I'M BEAT.
BUT NOW SHE'S FINALLY BACK TO HER OLD SELF.
ガチャ
CLICK
ALL BUNDLED UP
WAHH!
I NEED MORE CLOTHES.
NO MATTER HOW MUCH I PUT ON, I STILL FEEL NAKED.
PANT PANT
ふーっ ふーっ
IT'S REALLY HARD TO WALK.
TH- THAT'S ENOUGH.
YOU'RE WEARING ENOUGH.
SUPER TIGHT
SHE MUST HAVE TWELVE KIMONO JACKETS ON.
IS THIS WHAT THEY CALL OVER-COMPENSATING...?
BEATS HAVING HER WALK AROUND NAKED.
ふーっ。
SIGH

Chapter 54
Gourmet Love

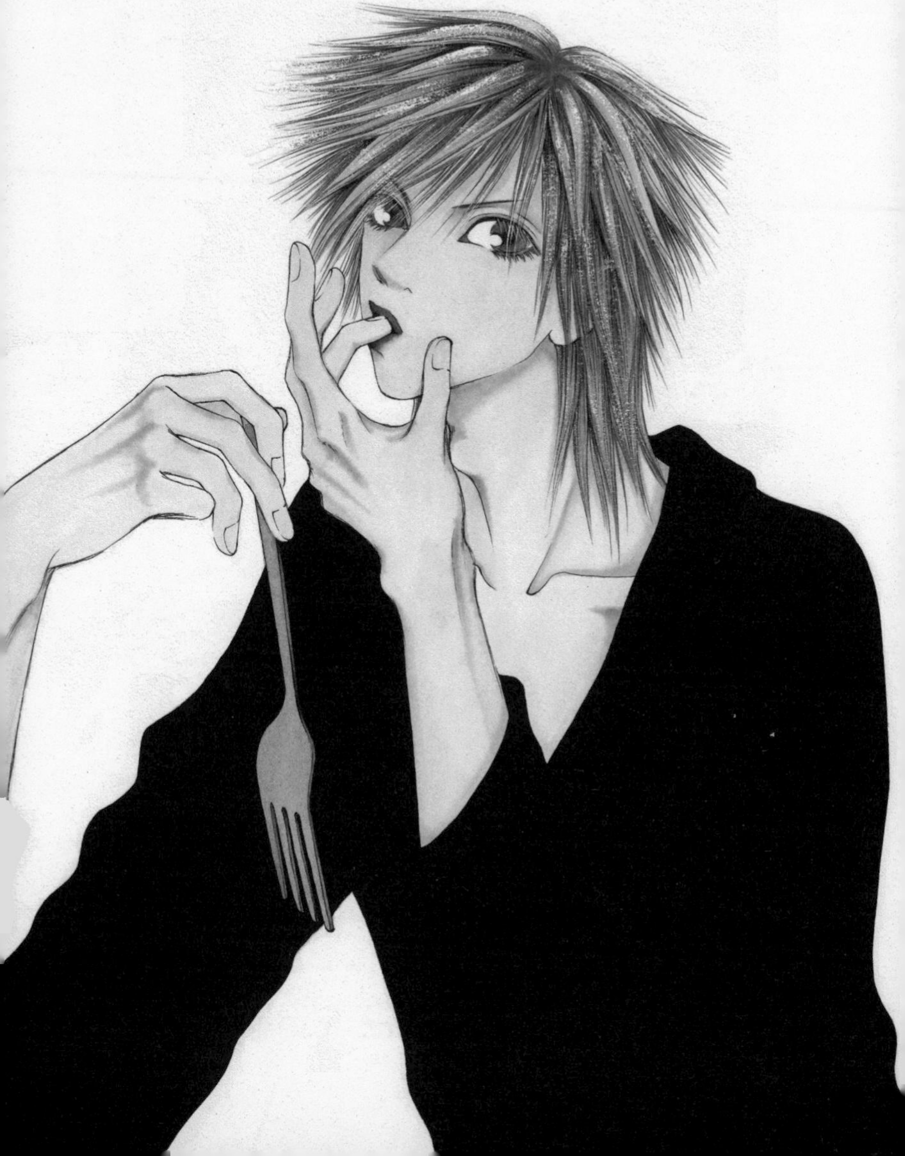

I'm Tennosuke Hayakawa.

Nice to meet you. ♥

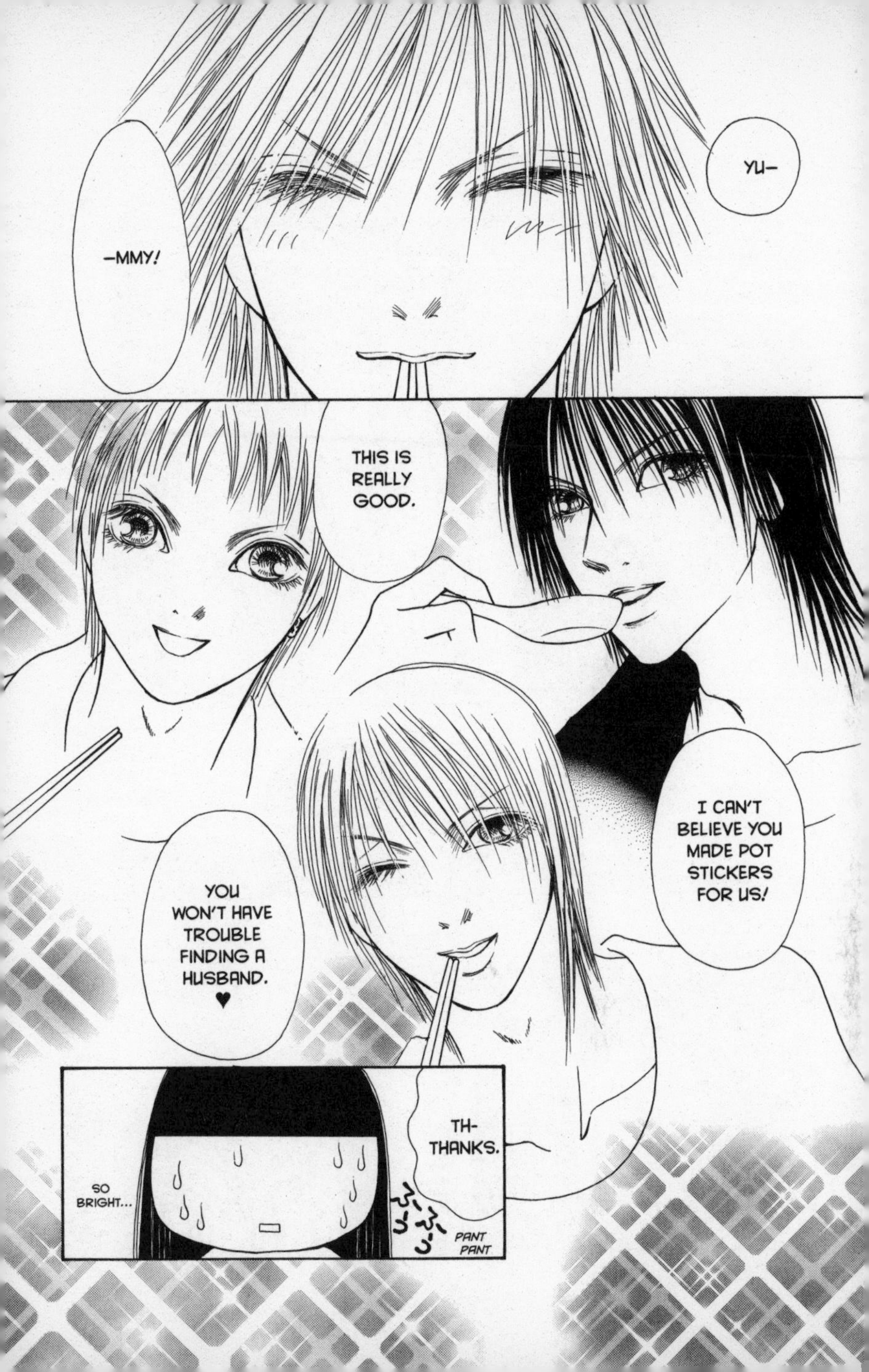
YU-
-MMY!
THIS IS REALLY GOOD.
I CAN'T BELIEVE YOU MADE POT STICKERS FOR US!
YOU WON'T HAVE TROUBLE FINDING A HUSBAND. ♥
TH- THANKS.
PANT PANT
SO BRIGHT...

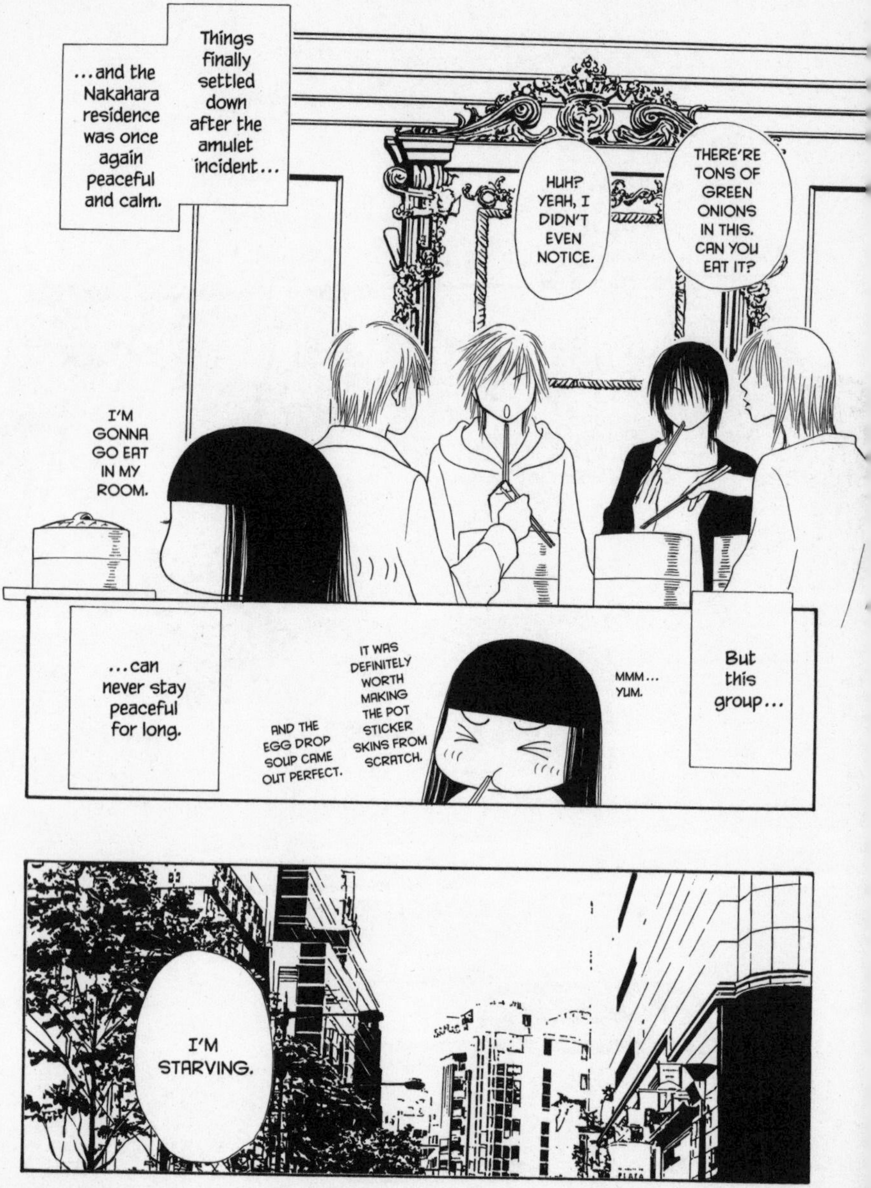

Things finally settled down after the amulet incident...
...and the Nakahara residence was once again peaceful and calm.
THERE'RE TONS OF GREEN ONIONS IN THIS. CAN YOU EAT IT?
HUH? YEAH, I DIDN'T EVEN NOTICE.
I'M GONNA GO EAT IN MY ROOM.
But this group...
MMM... YUM.
IT WAS DEFINITELY WORTH MAKING THE POT STICKER SKINS FROM SCRATCH.
AND THE EGG DROP SOUP CAME OUT PERFECT.
...can never stay peaceful for long.
I'M STARVING.

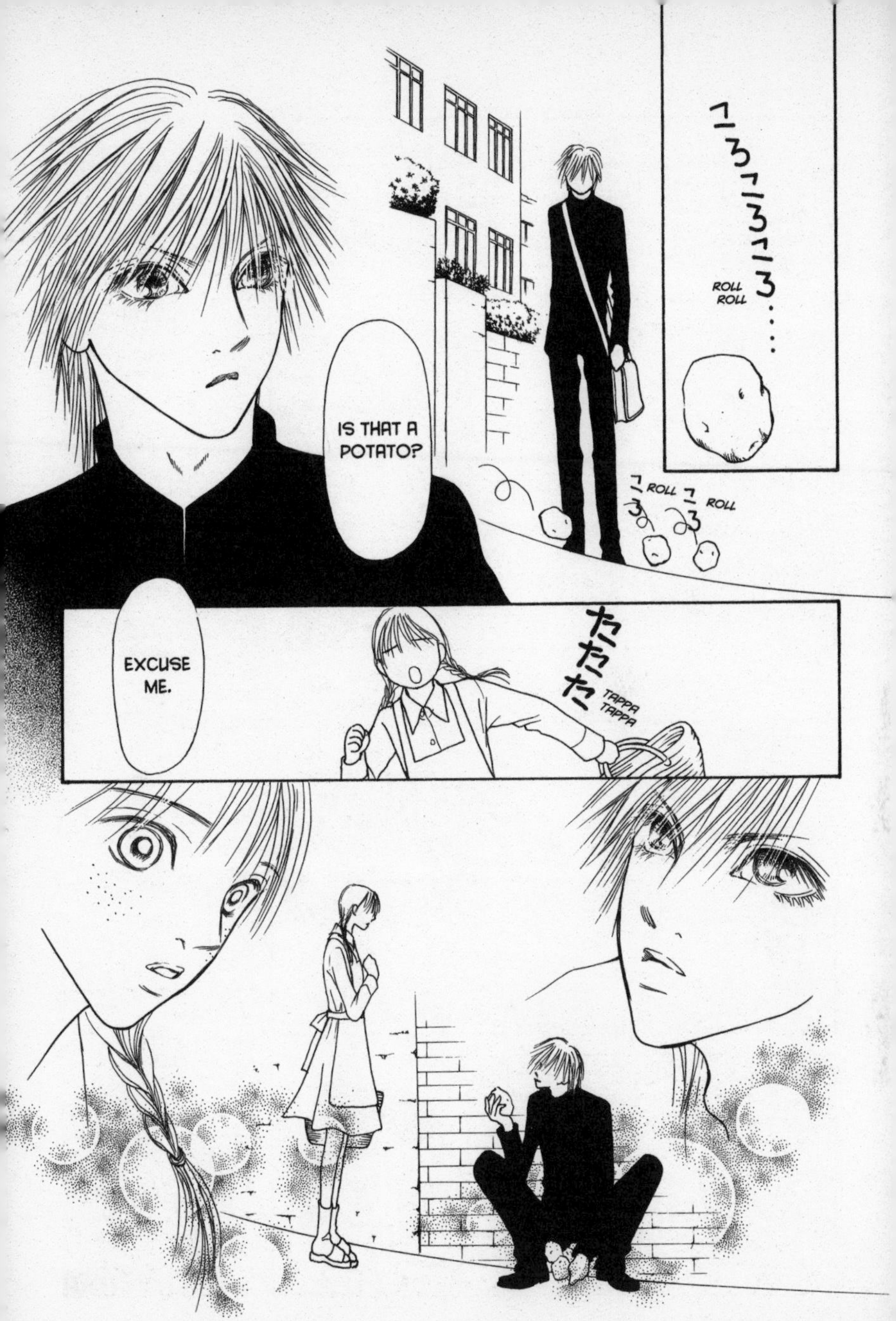
ころころころ…
ROLL ROLL
ころ ROLL ころ ROLL
IS THAT A POTATO?
たたた
TAPPA TAPPA
EXCUSE ME.

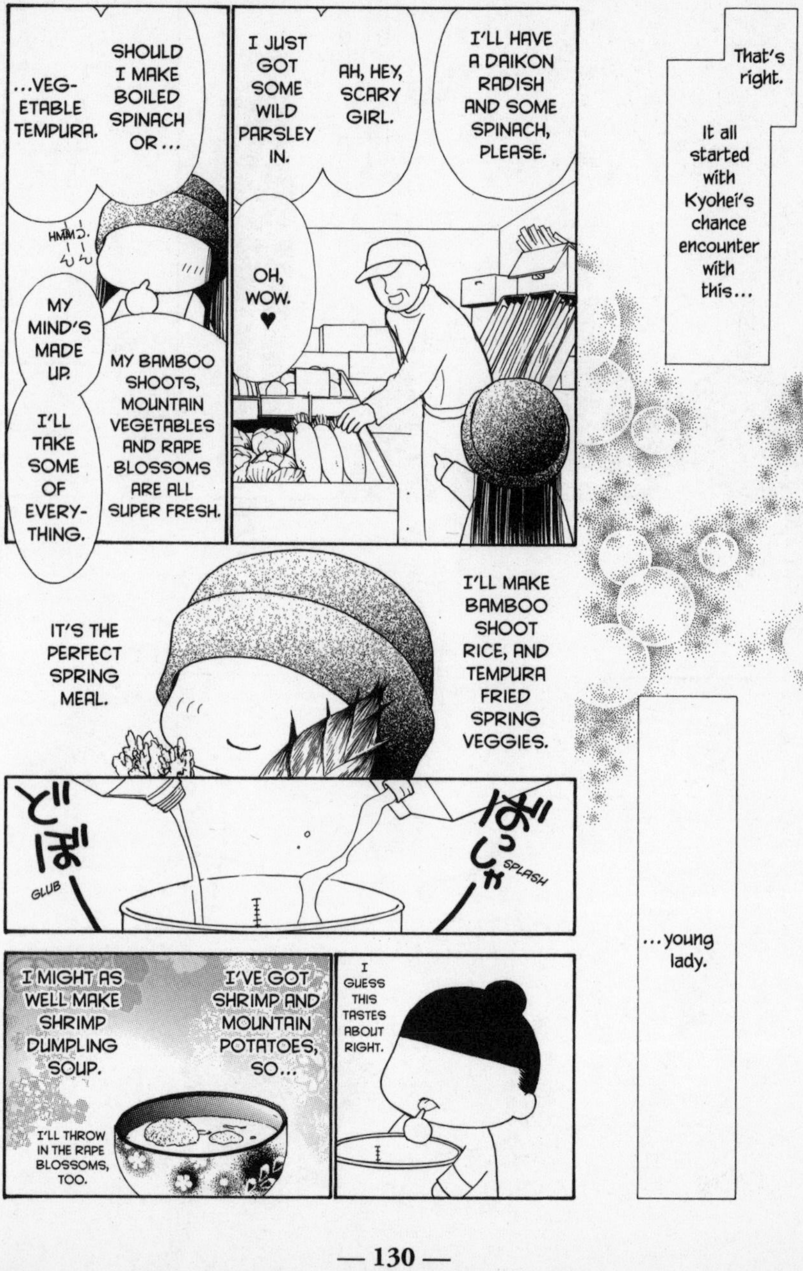
That's right.
It all started with Kyohei's chance encounter with this...
...young lady.
I'LL HAVE A DAIKON RADISH AND SOME SPINACH, PLEASE.
AH, HEY, SCARY GIRL.
I JUST GOT SOME WILD PARSLEY IN.
OH, WOW. ♥
SHOULD I MAKE BOILED SPINACH OR...
...VEG-ETABLE TEMPURA.
HMM
MY BAMBOO SHOOTS, MOUNTAIN VEGETABLES AND RAPE BLOSSOMS ARE ALL SUPER FRESH.
MY MIND'S MADE UP.
I'LL TAKE SOME OF EVERY-THING.
I'LL MAKE BAMBOO SHOOT RICE, AND TEMPURA FRIED SPRING VEGGIES.
IT'S THE PERFECT SPRING MEAL.
ばしゃ
SPLASH
どぼ
GLUB
I GUESS THIS TASTES ABOUT RIGHT.
I'VE GOT SHRIMP AND MOUNTAIN POTATOES, SO...
I MIGHT AS WELL MAKE SHRIMP DUMPLING SOUP.
I'LL THROW IN THE RAPE BLOSSOMS, TOO.

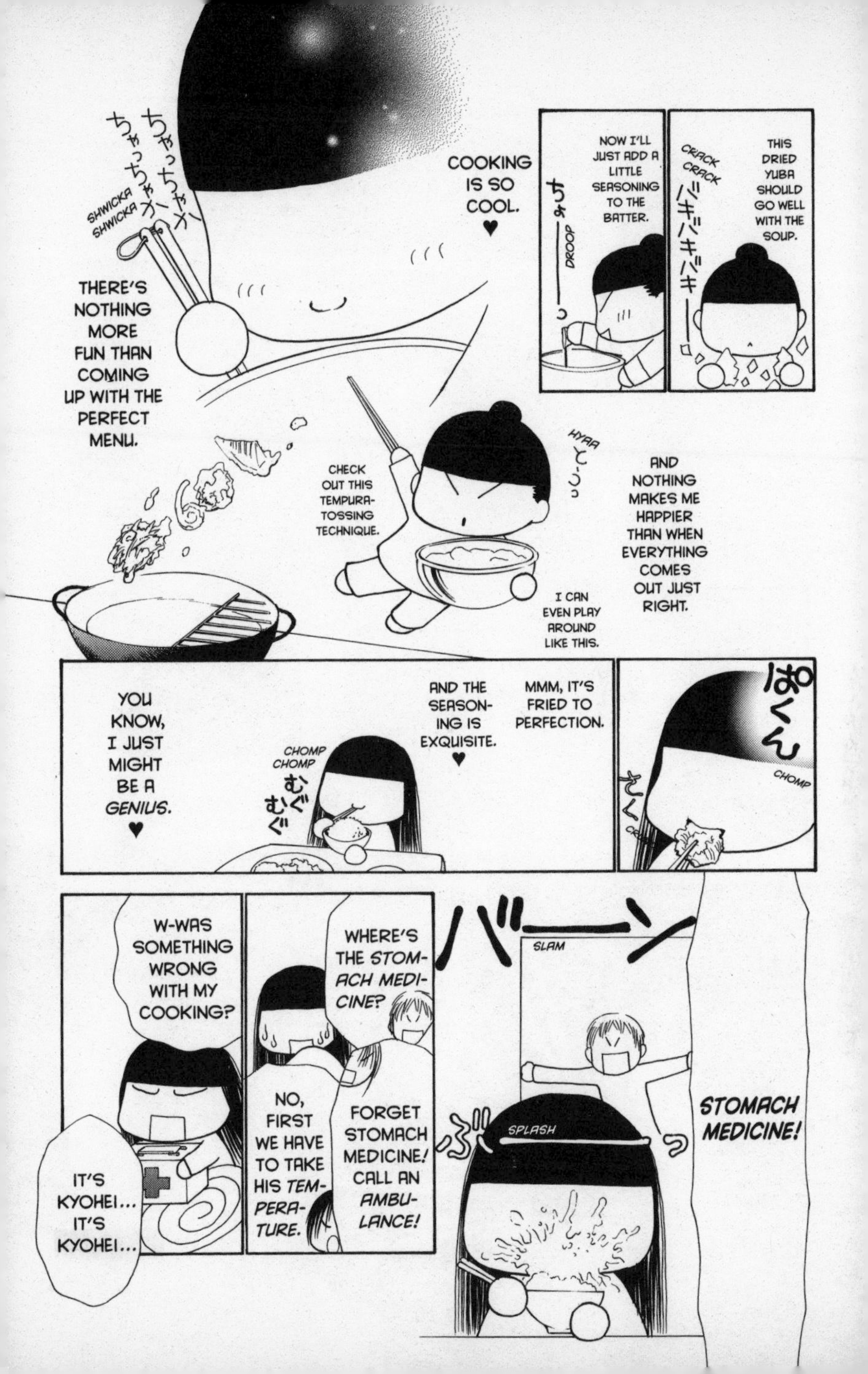
THIS DRIED YUBA SHOULD GO WELL WITH THE SOUP.
CRACK CRACK
バキバキー
NOW I'LL JUST ADD A LITTLE SEASONING TO THE BATTER.
ちょ
DROOP
COOKING IS SO COOL. ♥
SHWICKA SHWICKA
THERE'S NOTHING MORE FUN THAN COMING UP WITH THE PERFECT MENU.
AND NOTHING MAKES ME HAPPIER THAN WHEN EVERYTHING COMES OUT JUST RIGHT.
I CAN EVEN PLAY AROUND LIKE THIS.
HYAA
とーっ
CHECK OUT THIS TEMPURA-TOSSING TECHNIQUE.
ぱくん
CHOMP
さく
MMM, IT'S FRIED TO PERFECTION.
AND THE SEASON-ING IS EXQUISITE. ♥
CHOMP CHOMP
むぐむぐ
YOU KNOW, I JUST MIGHT BE A *GENIUS.* ♥
STOMACH MEDICINE!
バーン
SLAM
ぶっ
SPLASH
WHERE'S THE *STOMACH MEDICINE?*
FORGET STOMACH MEDICINE! CALL AN *AMBULANCE!*
NO, FIRST WE HAVE TO TAKE HIS *TEMPERATURE.*
W-WAS SOMETHING WRONG WITH MY COOKING?
IT'S KYOHEI... IT'S KYOHEI...

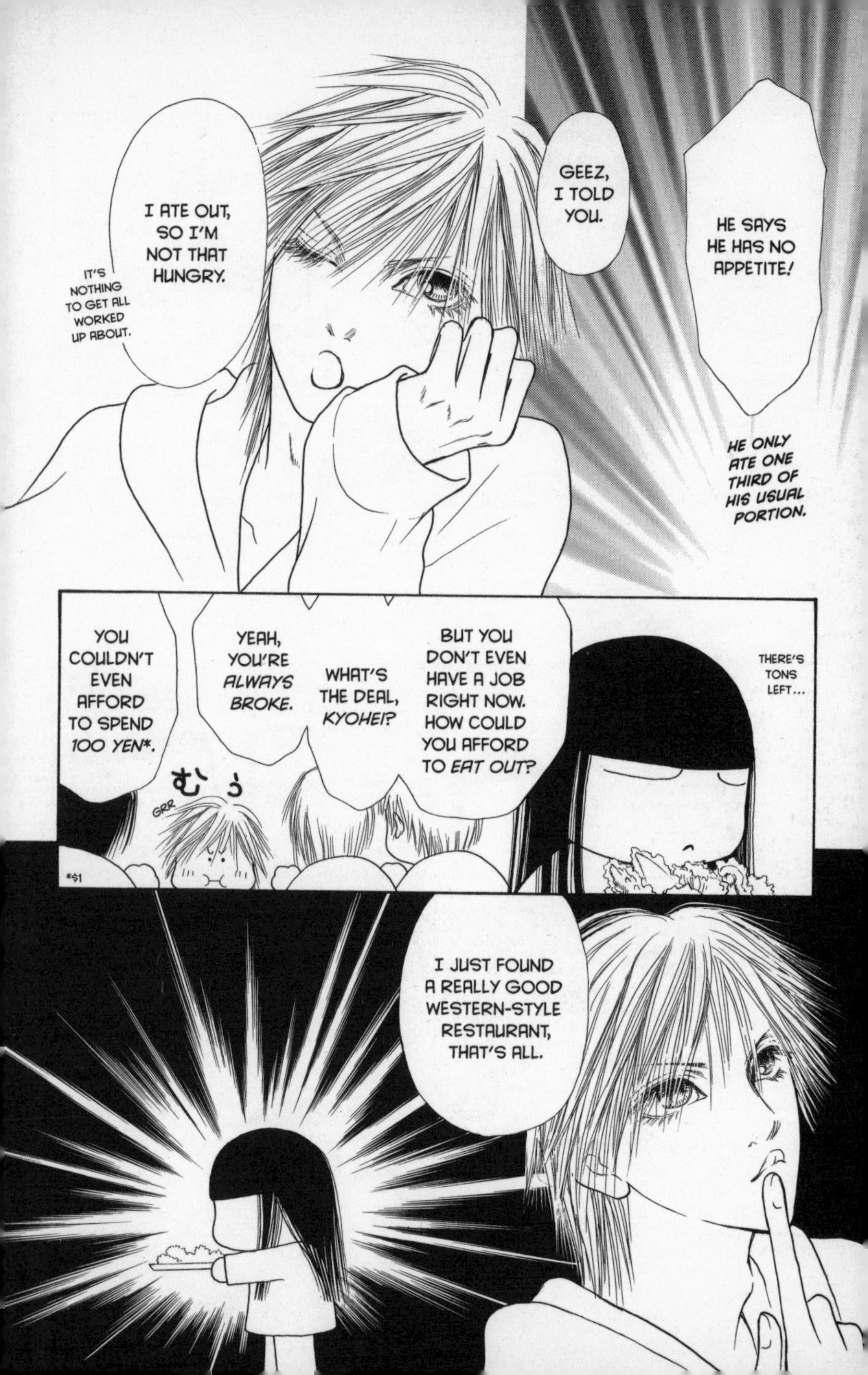
HE SAYS HE HAS NO APPETITE!
HE ONLY ATE ONE THIRD OF HIS USUAL PORTION.
GEEZ, I TOLD YOU.
I ATE OUT, SO I'M NOT THAT HUNGRY.
IT'S NOTHING TO GET ALL WORKED UP ABOUT.
THERE'S TONS LEFT...
BUT YOU DON'T EVEN HAVE A JOB RIGHT NOW. HOW COULD YOU AFFORD TO EAT OUT?
WHAT'S THE DEAL, KYOHEI!?
YEAH, YOU'RE ALWAYS BROKE.
YOU COULDN'T EVEN AFFORD TO SPEND 100 YEN*.
むぅ
GRR
*$1
I JUST FOUND A REALLY GOOD WESTERN-STYLE RESTAURANT, THAT'S ALL.

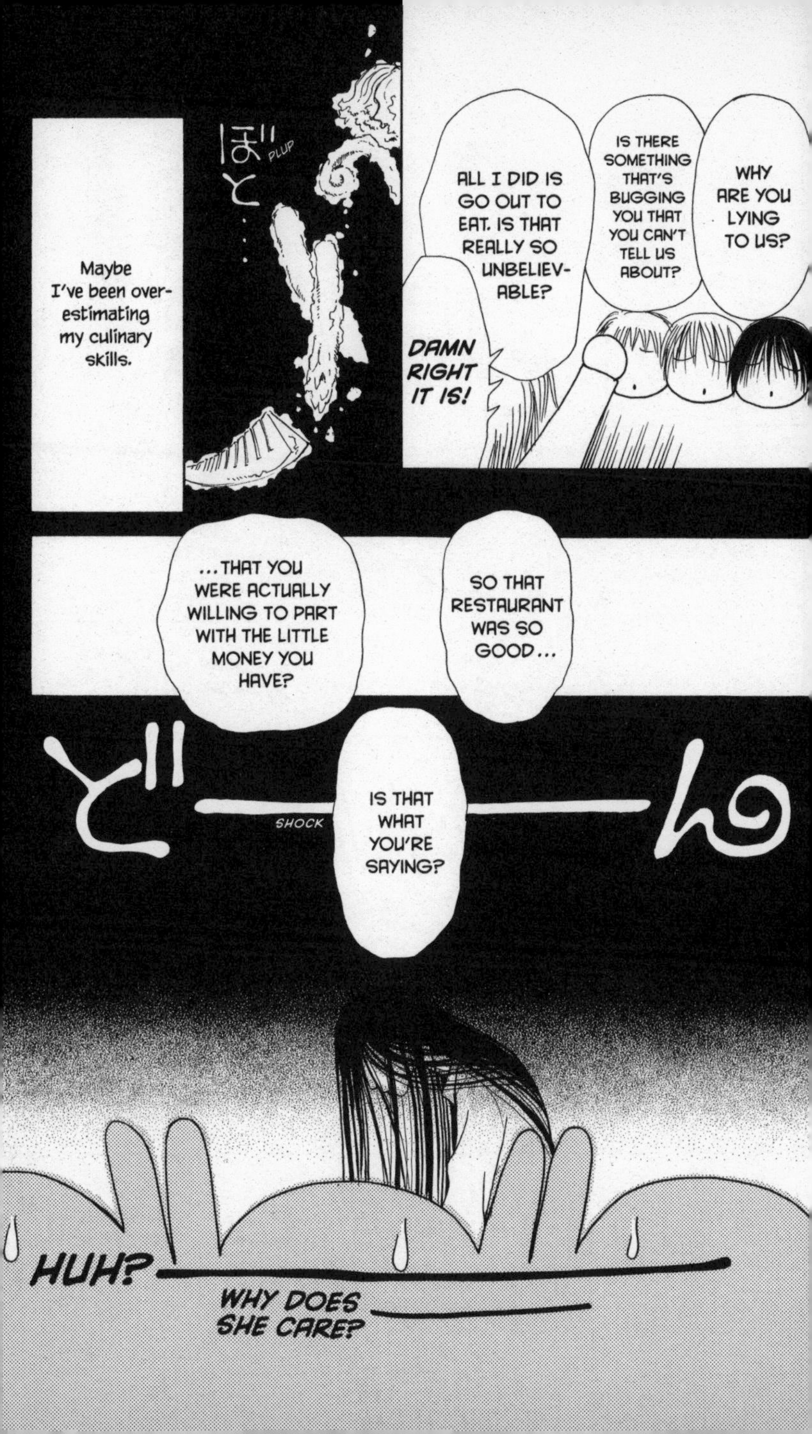
WHY ARE YOU LYING TO US?
IS THERE SOMETHING THAT'S BUGGING YOU THAT YOU CAN'T TELL US ABOUT?
ALL I DID IS GO OUT TO EAT. IS THAT REALLY SO UNBELIEV-ABLE?
DAMN RIGHT IT IS!
ぽと
PLUP
Maybe I've been over-estimating my culinary skills.
SO THAT RESTAURANT WAS SO GOOD...
...THAT YOU WERE ACTUALLY WILLING TO PART WITH THE LITTLE MONEY YOU HAVE?
どーーん
SHOCK
IS THAT WHAT YOU'RE SAYING?
HUH?
WHY DOES SHE CARE?

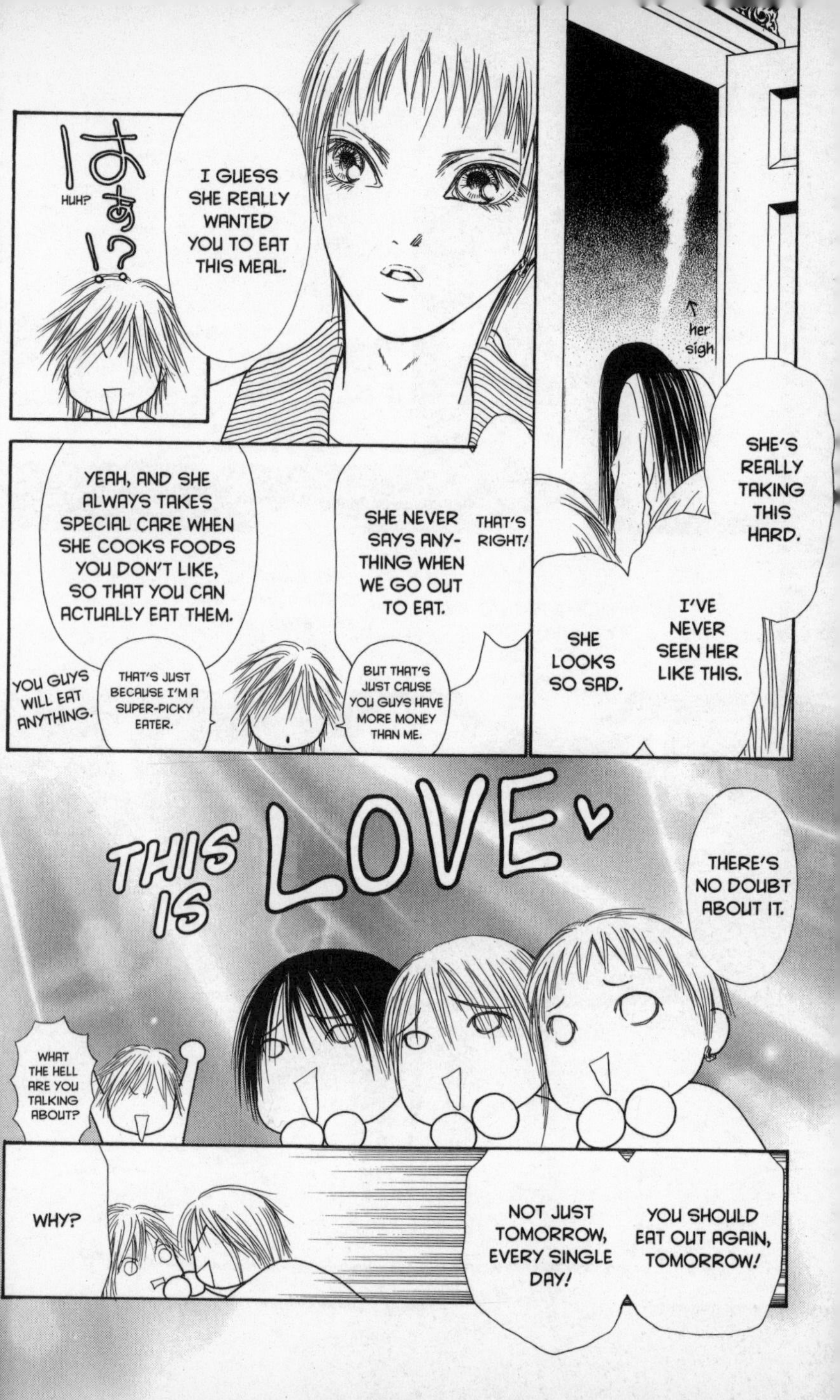
her sigh
SHE'S REALLY TAKING THIS HARD.
I'VE NEVER SEEN HER LIKE THIS.
SHE LOOKS SO SAD.
I GUESS SHE REALLY WANTED YOU TO EAT THIS MEAL.
はぁ!?
HUH?
THAT'S RIGHT!
SHE NEVER SAYS ANY-THING WHEN WE GO OUT TO EAT.
YEAH, AND SHE ALWAYS TAKES SPECIAL CARE WHEN SHE COOKS FOODS YOU DON'T LIKE, SO THAT YOU CAN ACTUALLY EAT THEM.
BUT THAT'S JUST CAUSE YOU GUYS HAVE MORE MONEY THAN ME.
THAT'S JUST BECAUSE I'M A SUPER-PICKY EATER.
YOU GUYS WILL EAT ANYTHING.
THERE'S NO DOUBT ABOUT IT.
THIS IS LOVE
WHAT THE HELL ARE YOU TALKING ABOUT?
YOU SHOULD EAT OUT AGAIN, TOMORROW!
NOT JUST TOMORROW, EVERY SINGLE DAY!
WHY?

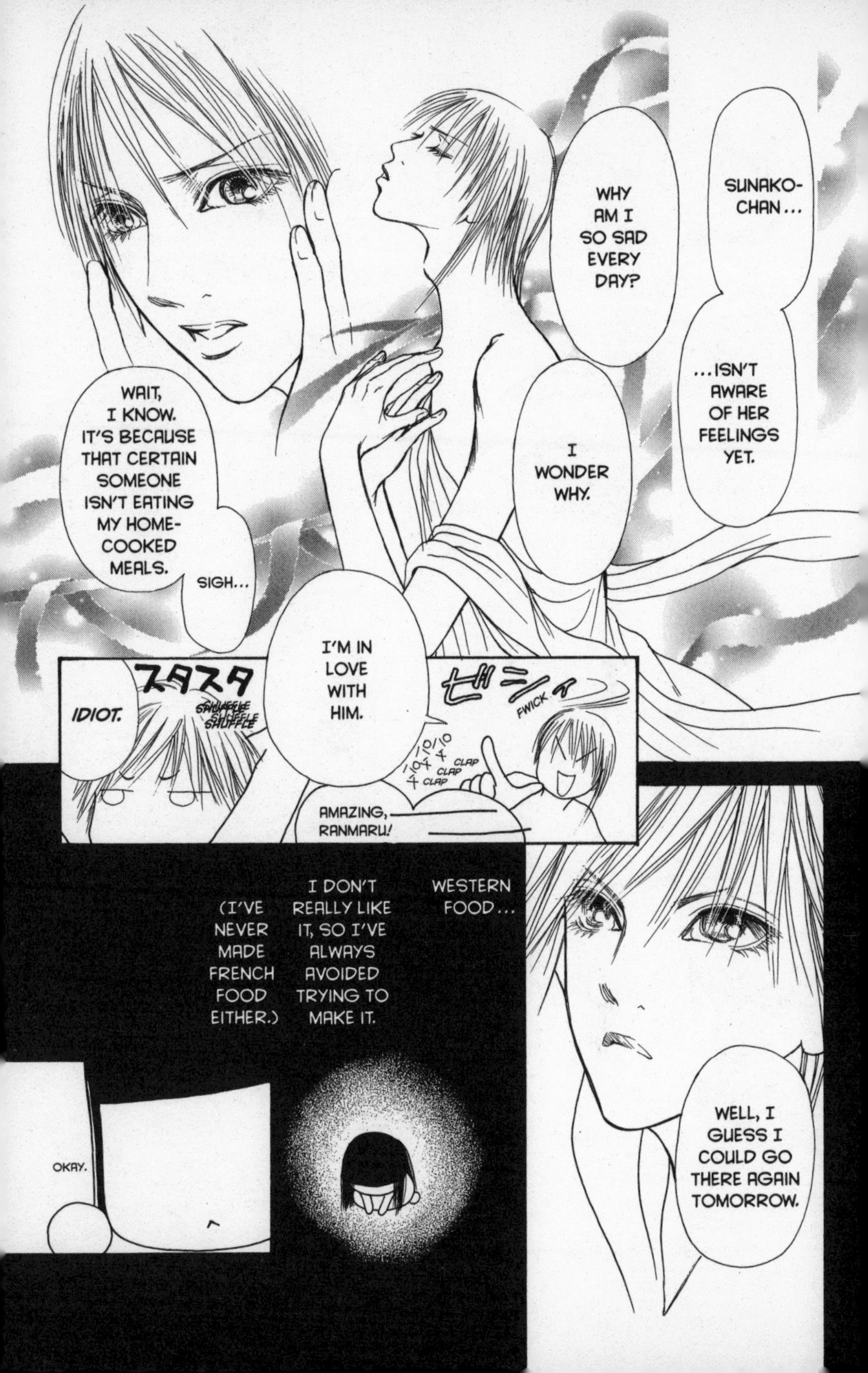
SUNAKO-CHAN...
...ISN'T AWARE OF HER FEELINGS YET.
WHY AM I SO SAD EVERY DAY?
I WONDER WHY.
WAIT, I KNOW. IT'S BECAUSE THAT CERTAIN SOMEONE ISN'T EATING MY HOME-COOKED MEALS.
SIGH...
I'M IN LOVE WITH HIM.
FWICK
CLAP CLAP CLAP
AMAZING, RANMARU!
スタスタ
SHUFFLE SHUFFLE SHUFFLE
IDIOT.
WESTERN FOOD...
I DON'T REALLY LIKE IT, SO I'VE ALWAYS AVOIDED TRYING TO MAKE IT.
(I'VE NEVER MADE FRENCH FOOD EITHER.)
WELL, I GUESS I COULD GO THERE AGAIN TOMORROW.
OKAY.

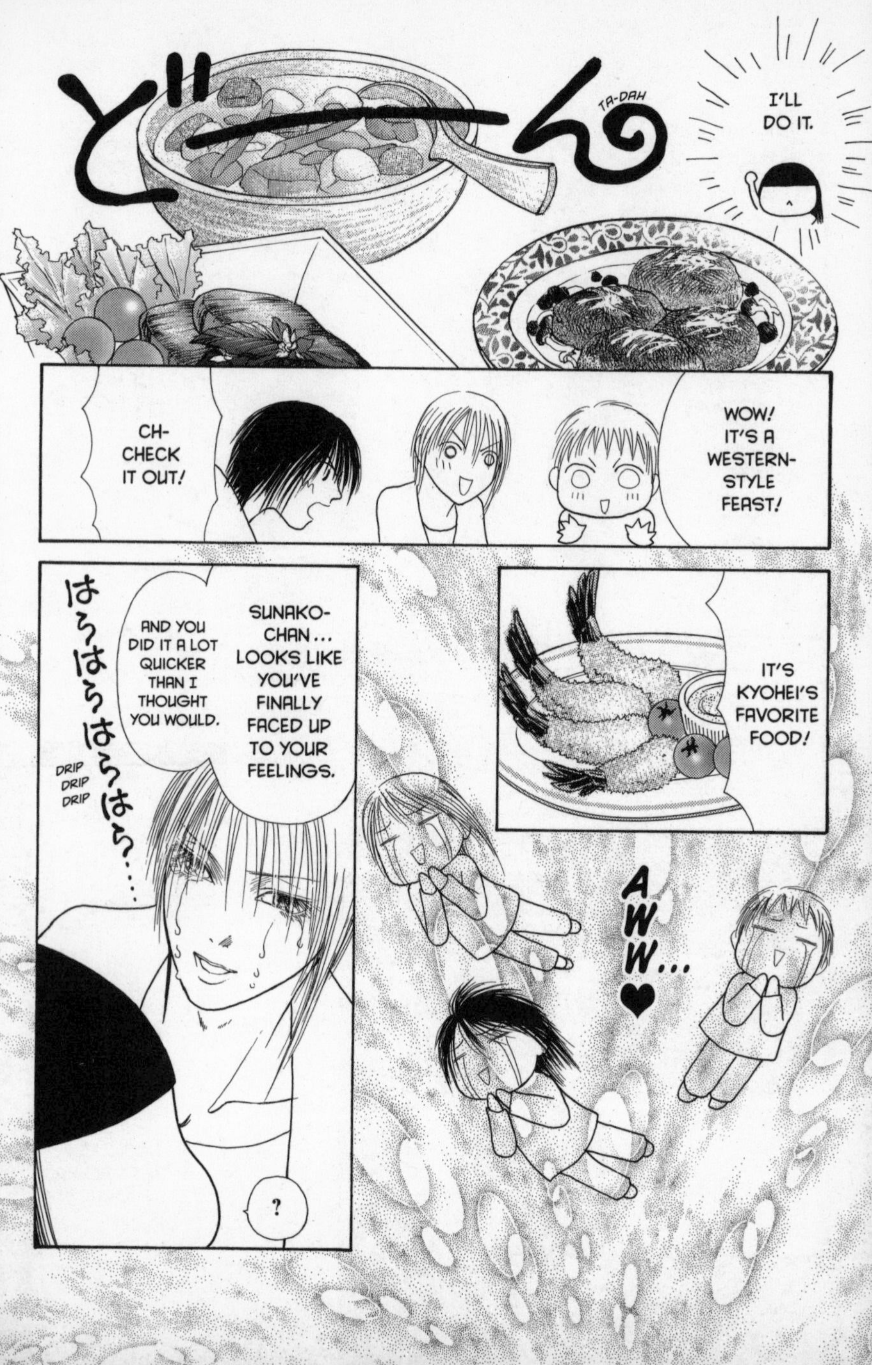
I'LL DO IT.
どーん
TA-DAH
WOW! IT'S A WESTERN-STYLE FEAST!
CH-CHECK IT OUT!
IT'S KYOHEI'S FAVORITE FOOD!
AWW...♥
SUNAKO-CHAN... LOOKS LIKE YOU'VE FINALLY FACED UP TO YOUR FEELINGS.
AND YOU DID IT A LOT QUICKER THAN I THOUGHT YOU WOULD.
はらはらはらはら…
DRIP DRIP DRIP
?

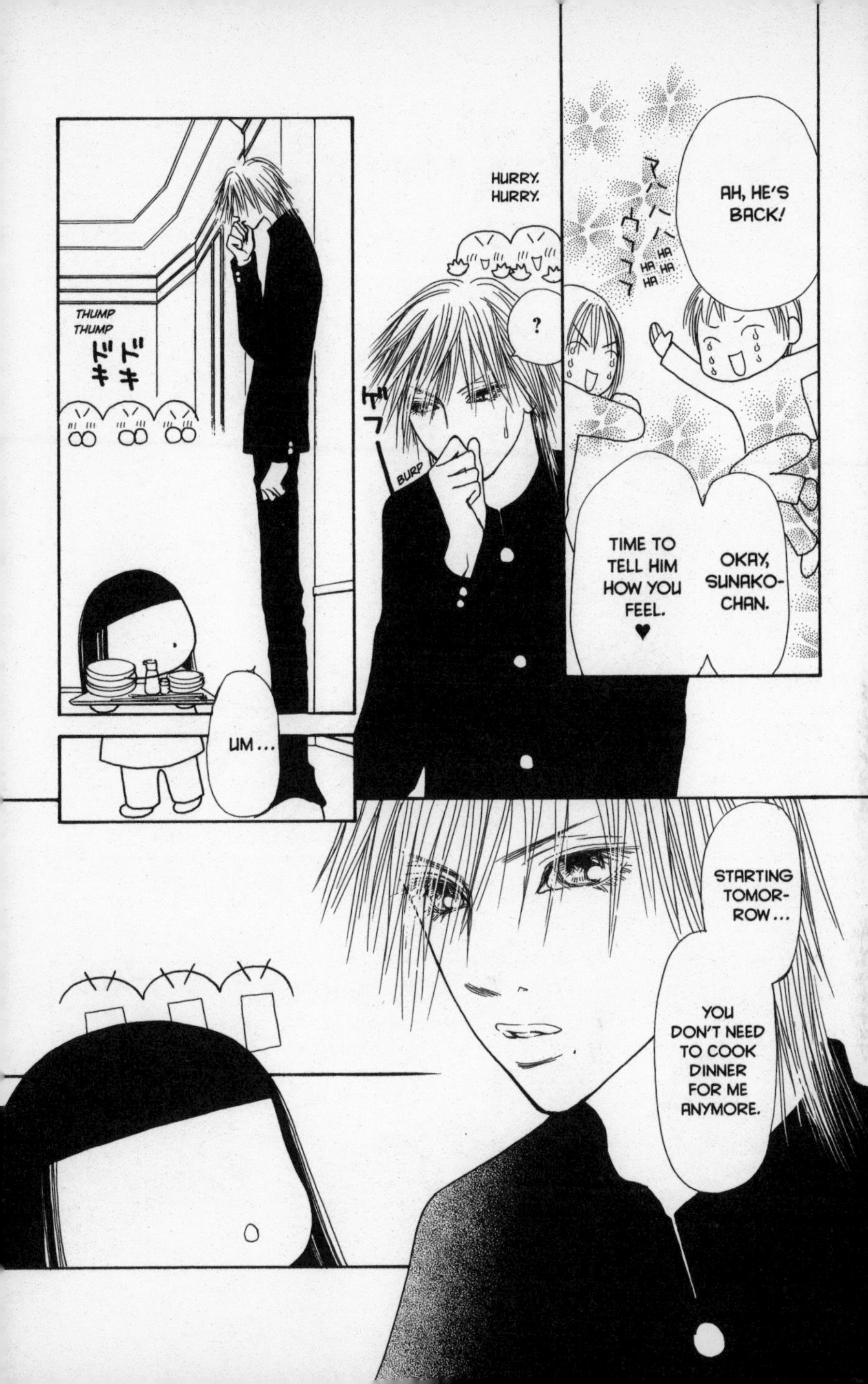
AH, HE'S BACK!
アハハハ ウフフフ
HA HA HA HA
OKAY, SUNAKO-CHAN.
TIME TO TELL HIM HOW YOU FEEL. ♥
HURRY. HURRY.
?
ゲフ
BURP
THUMP THUMP
ドキドキ
UM...
STARTING TOMORROW...
YOU DON'T NEED TO COOK DINNER FOR ME ANYMORE.

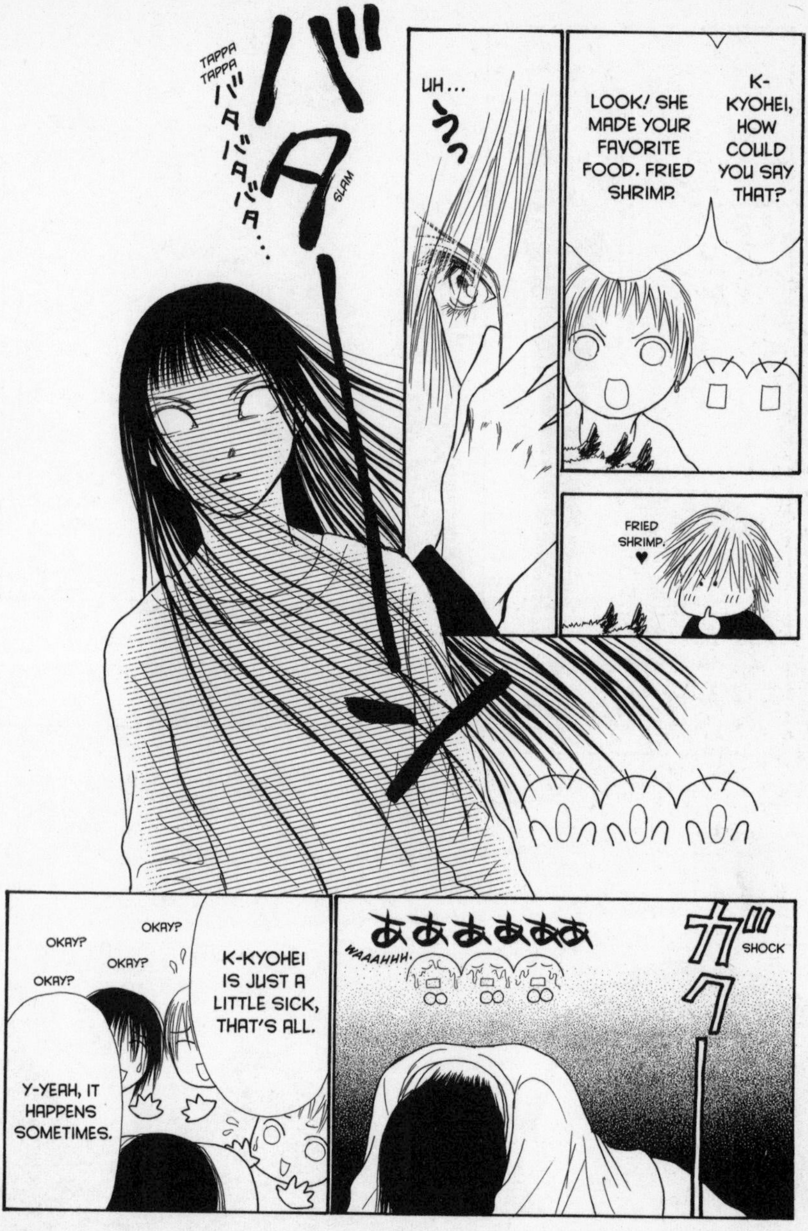
K-KYOHEI, HOW COULD YOU SAY THAT?
LOOK! SHE MADE YOUR FAVORITE FOOD. FRIED SHRIMP.
FRIED SHRIMP. ♥
UH...
うっ
バターン
SLAM
TAPPA TAPPA
バタバタバタ...
ガク
SHOCK
ああああああ
WAAAHHH.
K-KYOHEI IS JUST A LITTLE SICK, THAT'S ALL.
OKAY?
OKAY?
OKAY?
OKAY?
Y-YEAH, IT HAPPENS SOMETIMES.

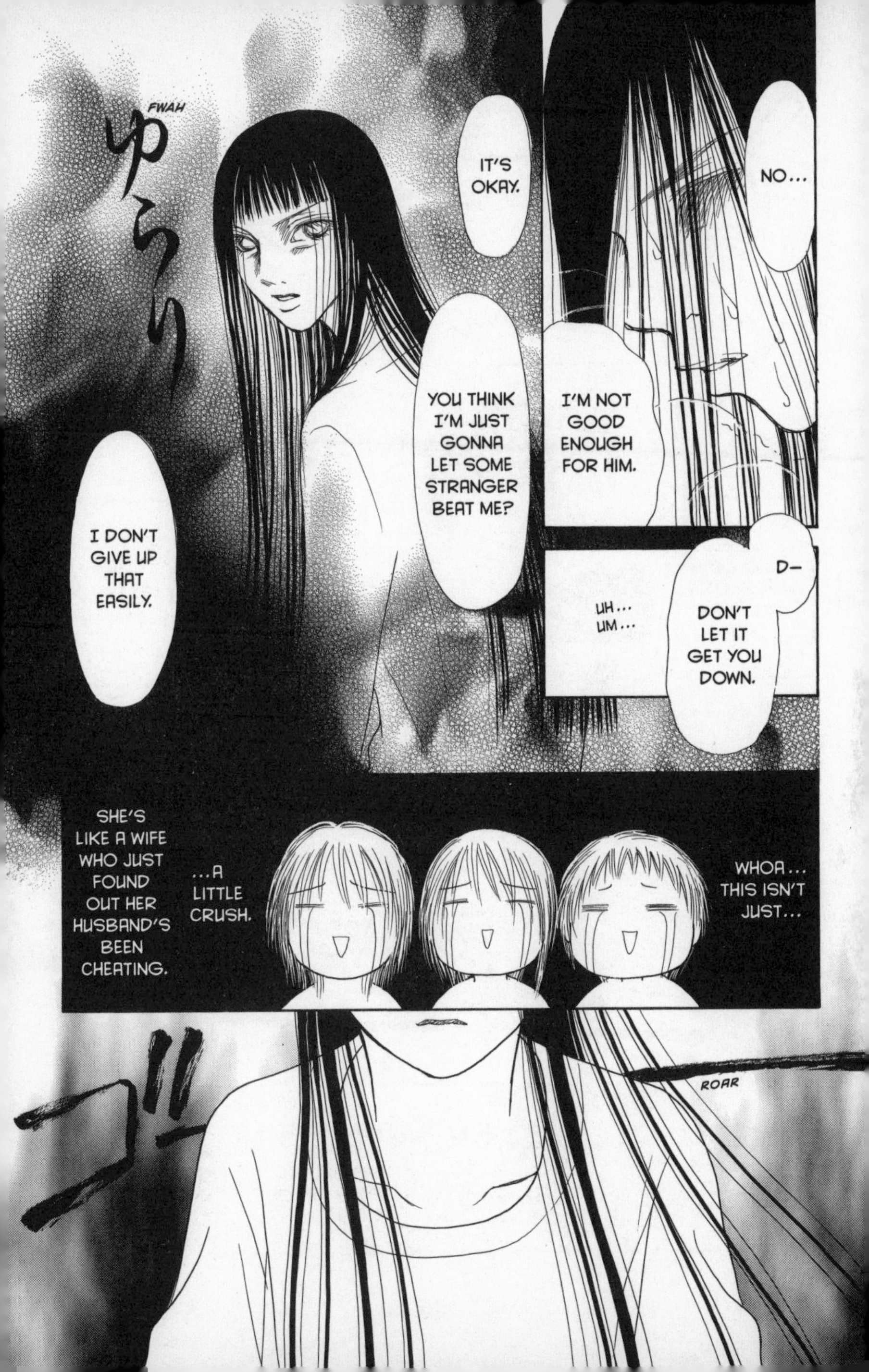
NO...
I'M NOT GOOD ENOUGH FOR HIM.
D—
DON'T LET IT GET YOU DOWN.
UH... UM...
IT'S OKAY.
YOU THINK I'M JUST GONNA LET SOME STRANGER BEAT ME?
FWAH
I DON'T GIVE UP THAT EASILY.
WHOA... THIS ISN'T JUST...
...A LITTLE CRUSH.
SHE'S LIKE A WIFE WHO JUST FOUND OUT HER HUSBAND'S BEEN CHEATING.
ROAR

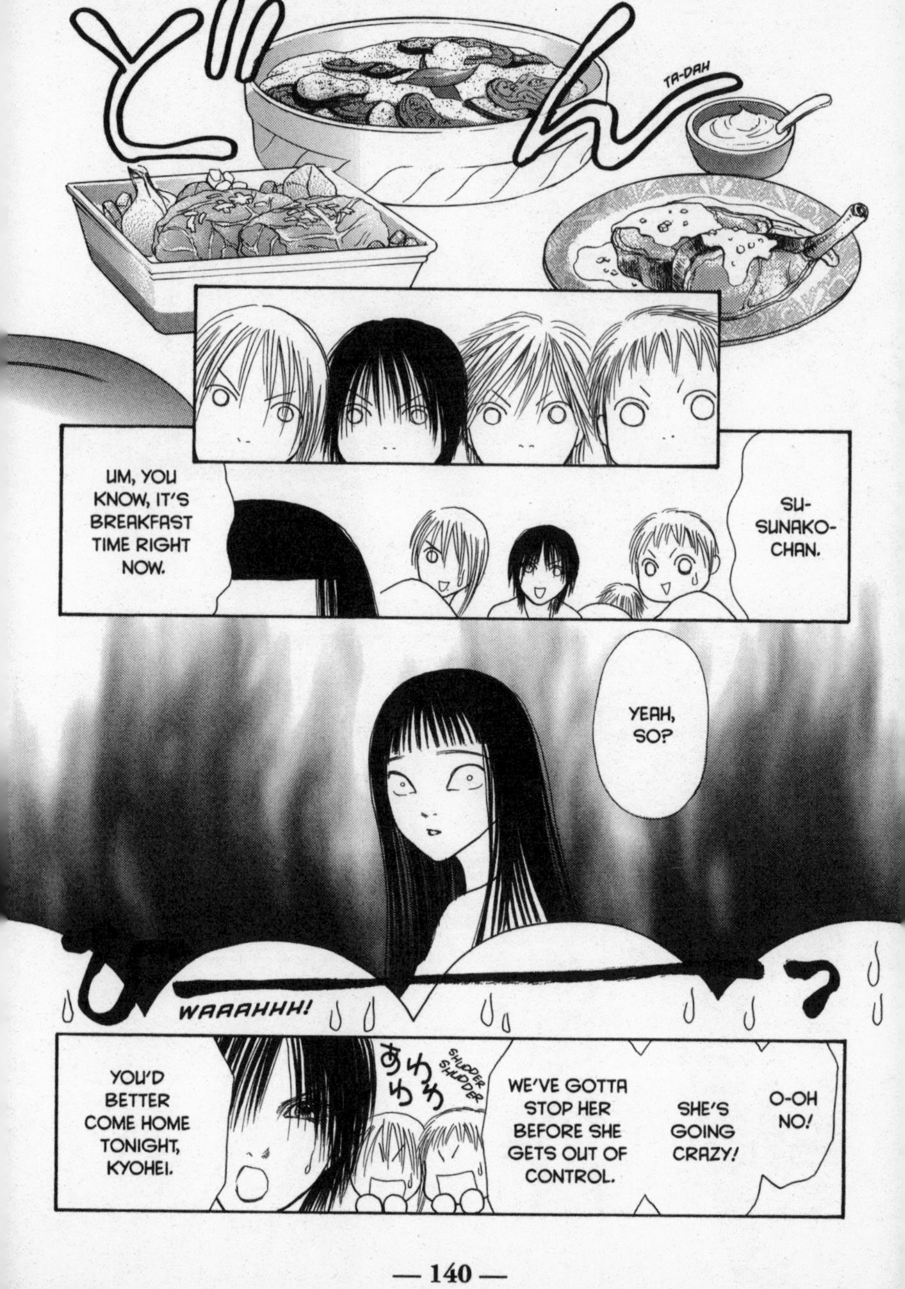
TA-DAH
SU-SUNAKO-CHAN.
UM, YOU KNOW, IT'S BREAKFAST TIME RIGHT NOW.
YEAH, SO?
WAAAHHH!
O-OH NO!
SHE'S GOING CRAZY!
WE'VE GOTTA STOP HER BEFORE SHE GETS OUT OF CONTROL.
SHUDDER SHUDDER
YOU'D BETTER COME HOME TONIGHT, KYOHEI.

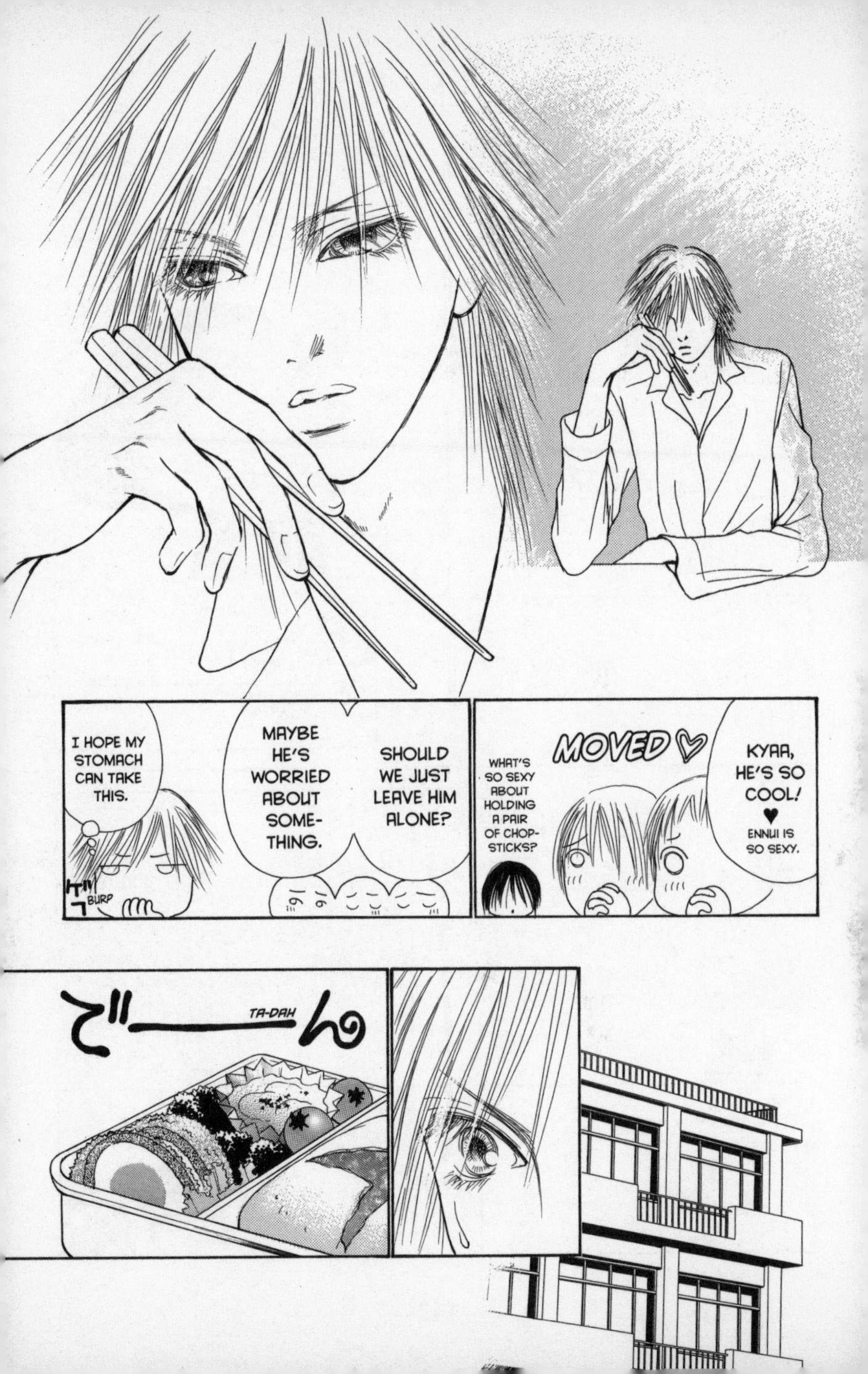
KYAA, HE'S SO COOL! ♥
ENNUI IS SO SEXY.
MOVED ♡
WHAT'S SO SEXY ABOUT HOLDING A PAIR OF CHOP-STICKS?
SHOULD WE JUST LEAVE HIM ALONE?
MAYBE HE'S WORRIED ABOUT SOME-THING.
I HOPE MY STOMACH CAN TAKE THIS.
BURP
でーーん
TA-DAH

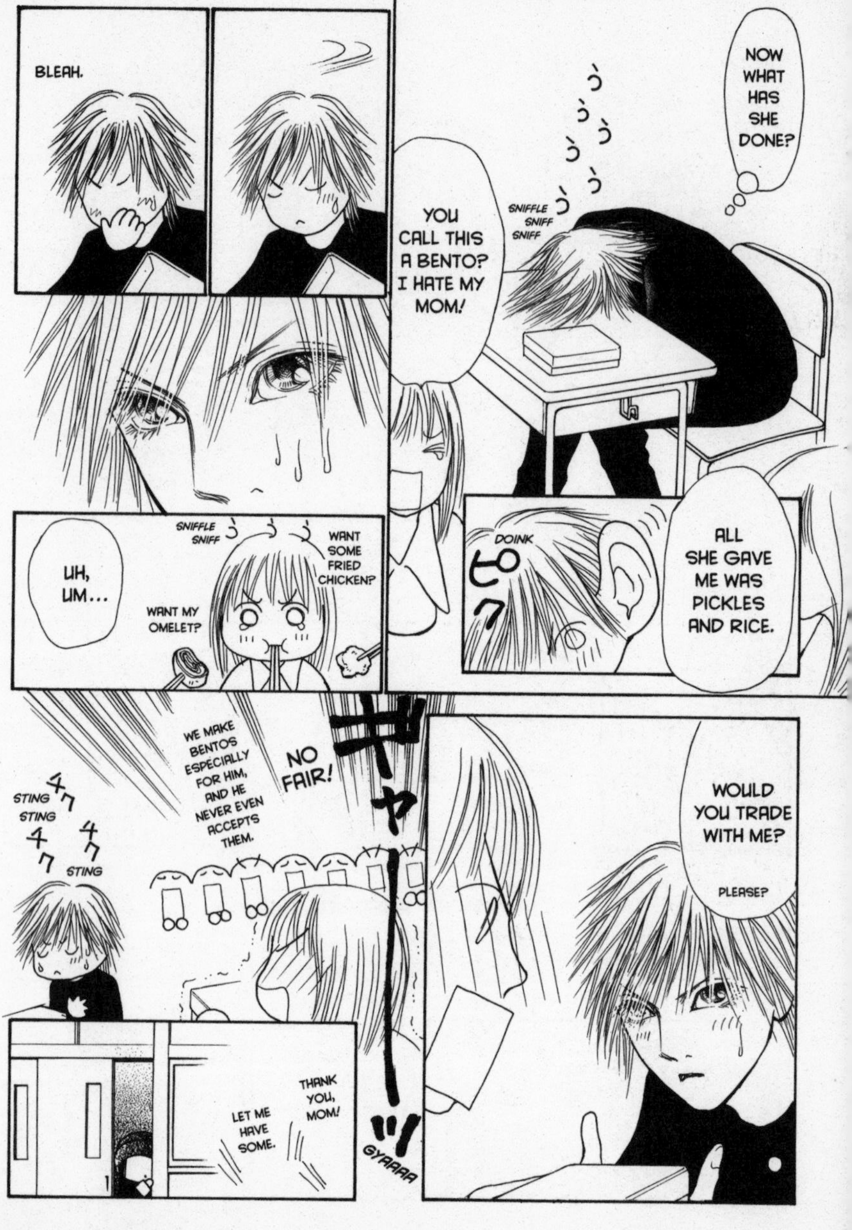
NOW WHAT HAS SHE DONE?
SNIFFLE SNIFF SNIFF
YOU CALL THIS A BENTO? I HATE MY MOM!
DOINK
ALL SHE GAVE ME WAS PICKLES AND RICE.
BLEAH.
WANT SOME FRIED CHICKEN?
SNIFFLE SNIFF
WANT MY OMELET?
UH, UM...
WOULD YOU TRADE WITH ME?
PLEASE?
GYAAAA
NO FAIR!
WE MAKE BENTOS ESPECIALLY FOR HIM, AND HE NEVER EVEN ACCEPTS THEM.
STING STING STING
THANK YOU, MOM!
LET ME HAVE SOME.

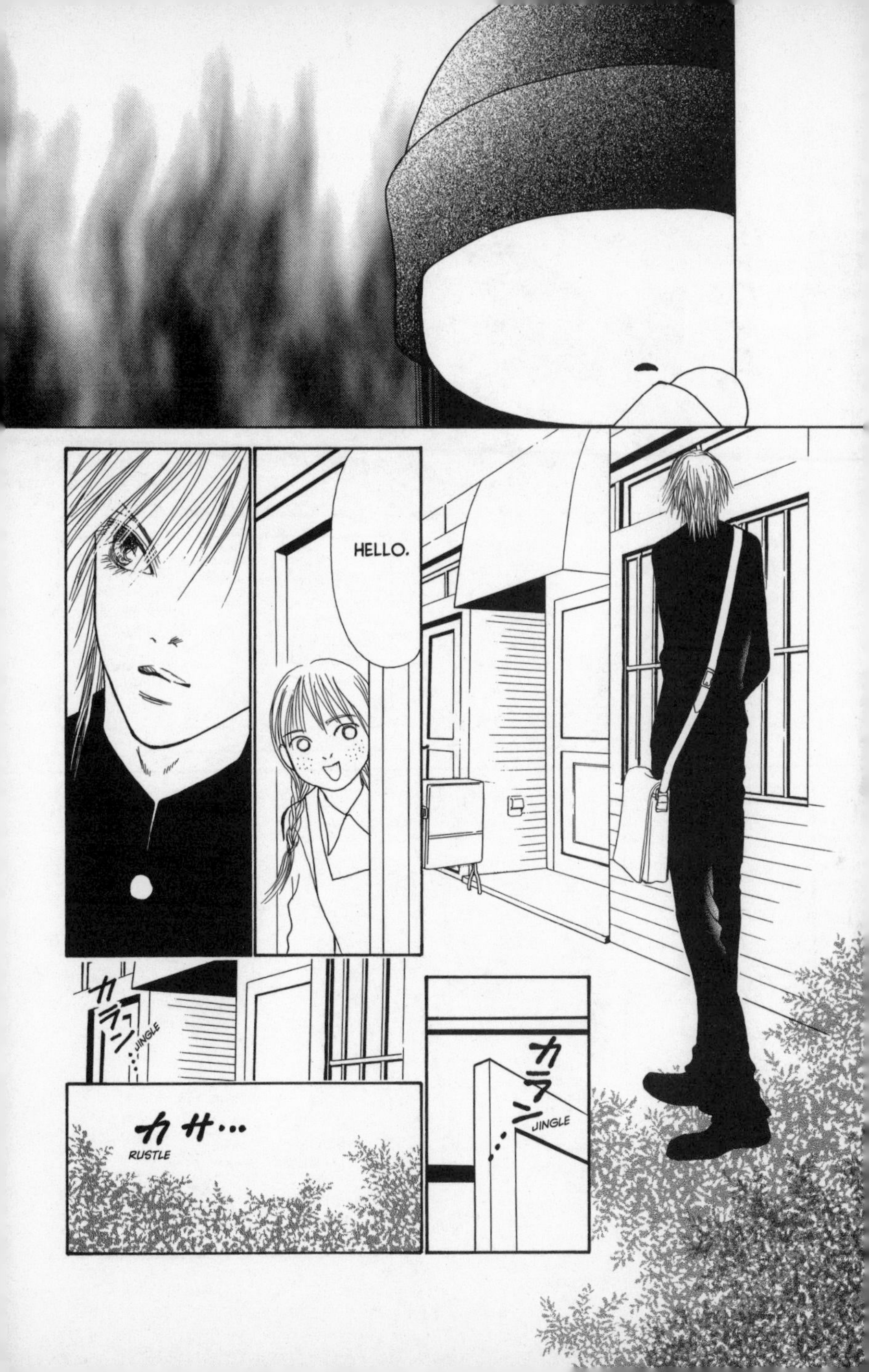
HELLO.
カラン… JINGLE
カラン… JINGLE
カサ… RUSTLE

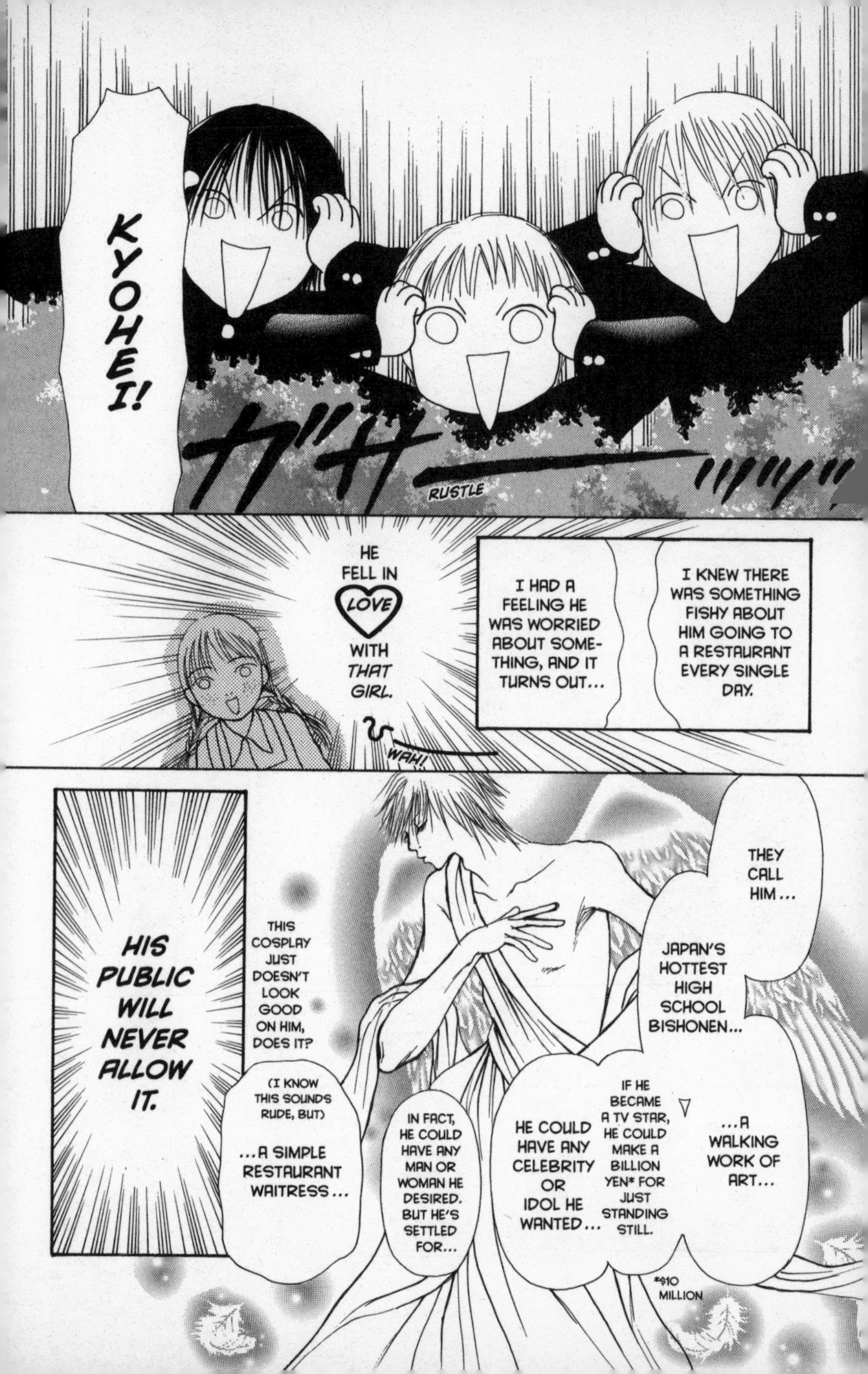
KYOHEI!
ガサー
RUSTLE
I KNEW THERE WAS SOMETHING FISHY ABOUT HIM GOING TO A RESTAURANT EVERY SINGLE DAY.
I HAD A FEELING HE WAS WORRIED ABOUT SOME-THING, AND IT TURNS OUT...
HE FELL IN LOVE WITH THAT GIRL.
WAH!
THEY CALL HIM...
JAPAN'S HOTTEST HIGH SCHOOL BISHONEN...
...A WALKING WORK OF ART...
IF HE BECAME A TV STAR, HE COULD MAKE A BILLION YEN* FOR JUST STANDING STILL.
HE COULD HAVE ANY CELEBRITY OR IDOL HE WANTED...
IN FACT, HE COULD HAVE ANY MAN OR WOMAN HE DESIRED. BUT HE'S SETTLED FOR...
(I KNOW THIS SOUNDS RUDE, BUT)
...A SIMPLE RESTAURANT WAITRESS...
THIS COSPLAY JUST DOESN'T LOOK GOOD ON HIM, DOES IT?
HIS PUBLIC WILL NEVER ALLOW IT.
*$10 MILLION

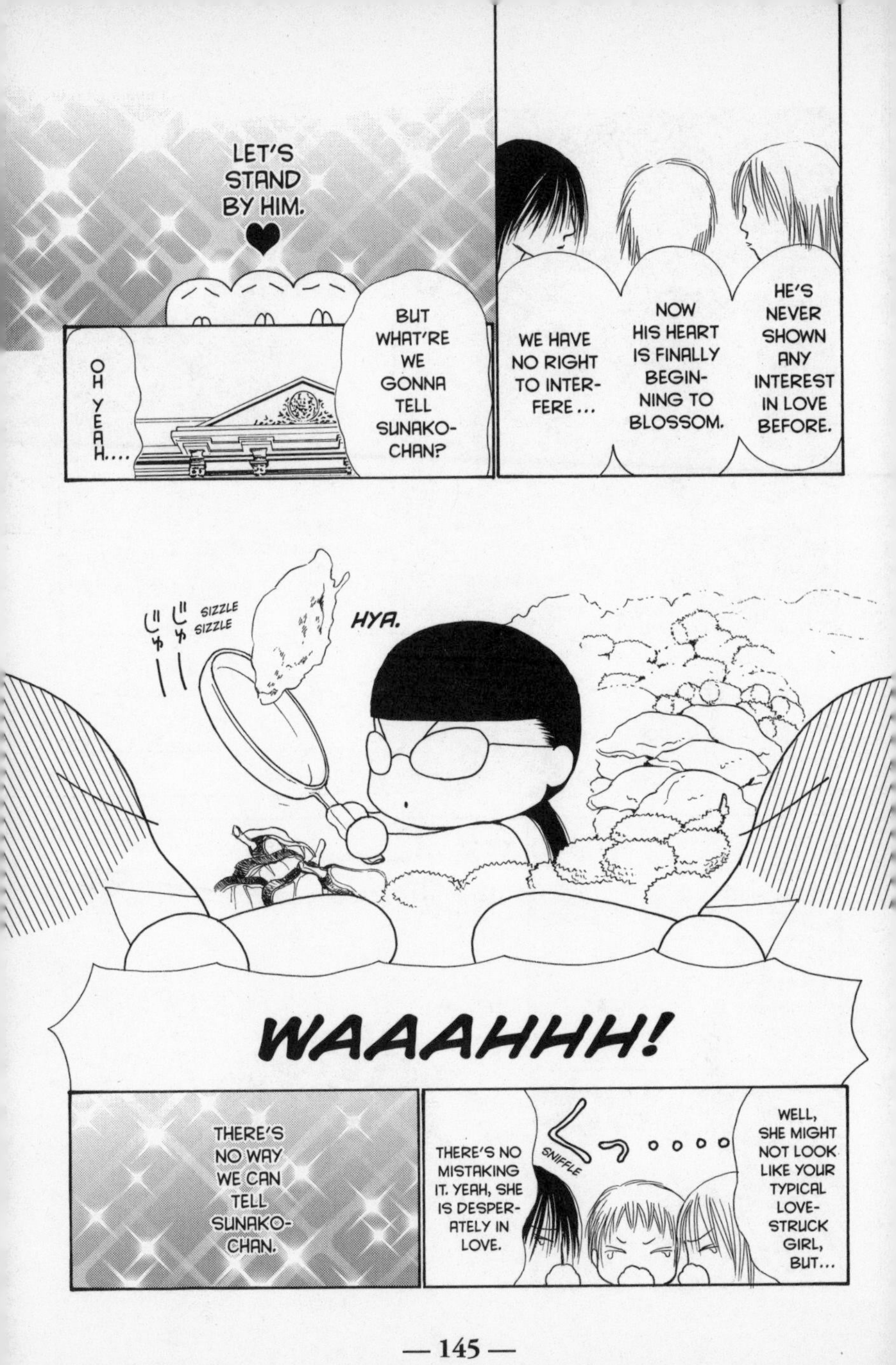
HE'S NEVER SHOWN ANY INTEREST IN LOVE BEFORE.
NOW HIS HEART IS FINALLY BEGINNING TO BLOSSOM.
WE HAVE NO RIGHT TO INTERFERE...
BUT WHAT'RE WE GONNA TELL SUNAKO-CHAN?
OH YEAH....
LET'S STAND BY HIM. ♥
HYA.
じゅーじゅー
SIZZLE SIZZLE
WAAAHHH!
WELL, SHE MIGHT NOT LOOK LIKE YOUR TYPICAL LOVE-STRUCK GIRL, BUT...
くっ....
SNIFFLE
THERE'S NO MISTAKING IT. YEAH, SHE IS DESPERATELY IN LOVE.
THERE'S NO WAY WE CAN TELL SUNAKO-CHAN.

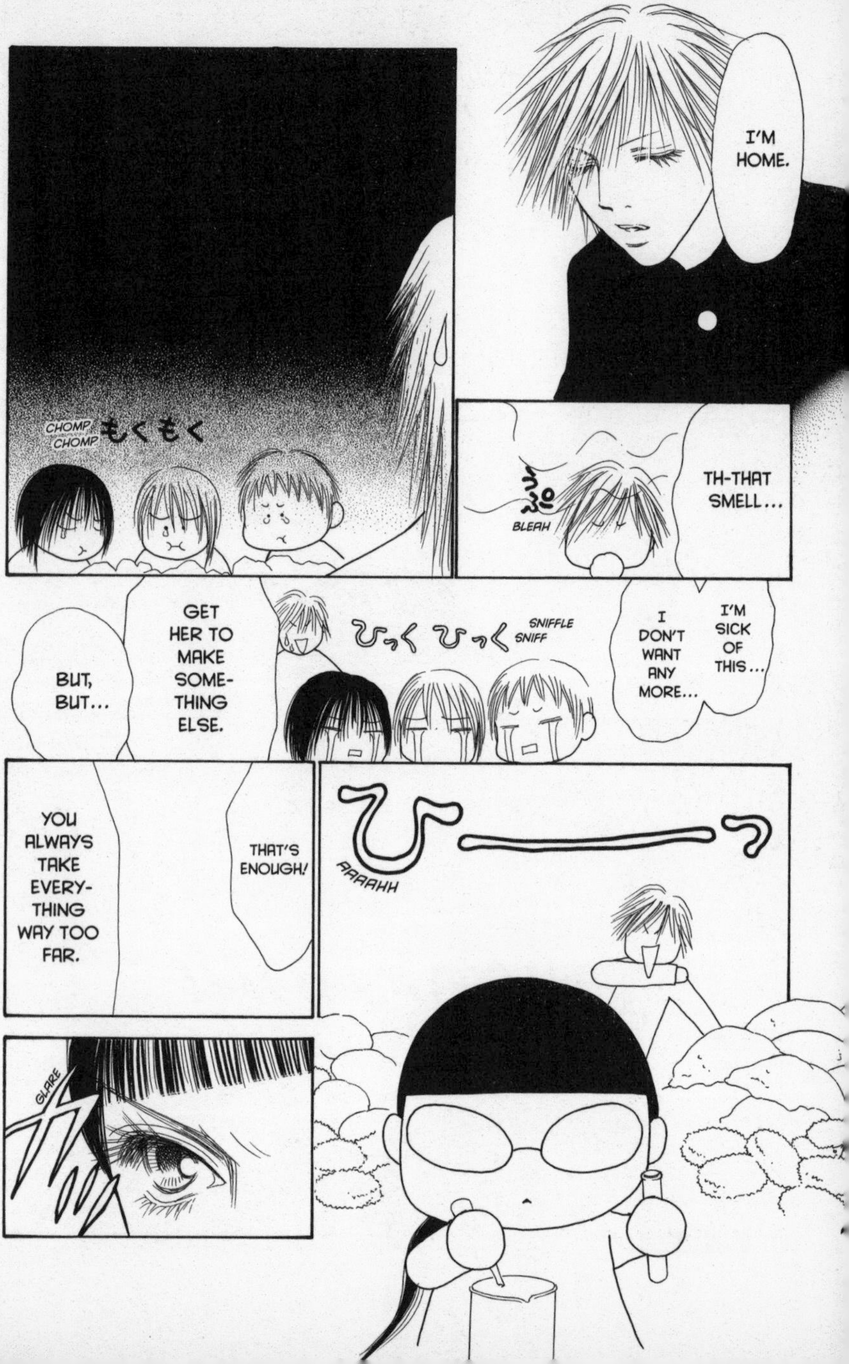
I'M HOME.
BLEAH
TH-THAT SMELL...
CHOMP CHOMP もくもく
I'M SICK OF THIS...
I DON'T WANT ANY MORE...
ひっく ひっく
SNIFFLE SNIFF
GET HER TO MAKE SOMETHING ELSE.
BUT, BUT...
ひーっ
AAAAHH
THAT'S ENOUGH!
YOU ALWAYS TAKE EVERYTHING WAY TOO FAR.
GLARE

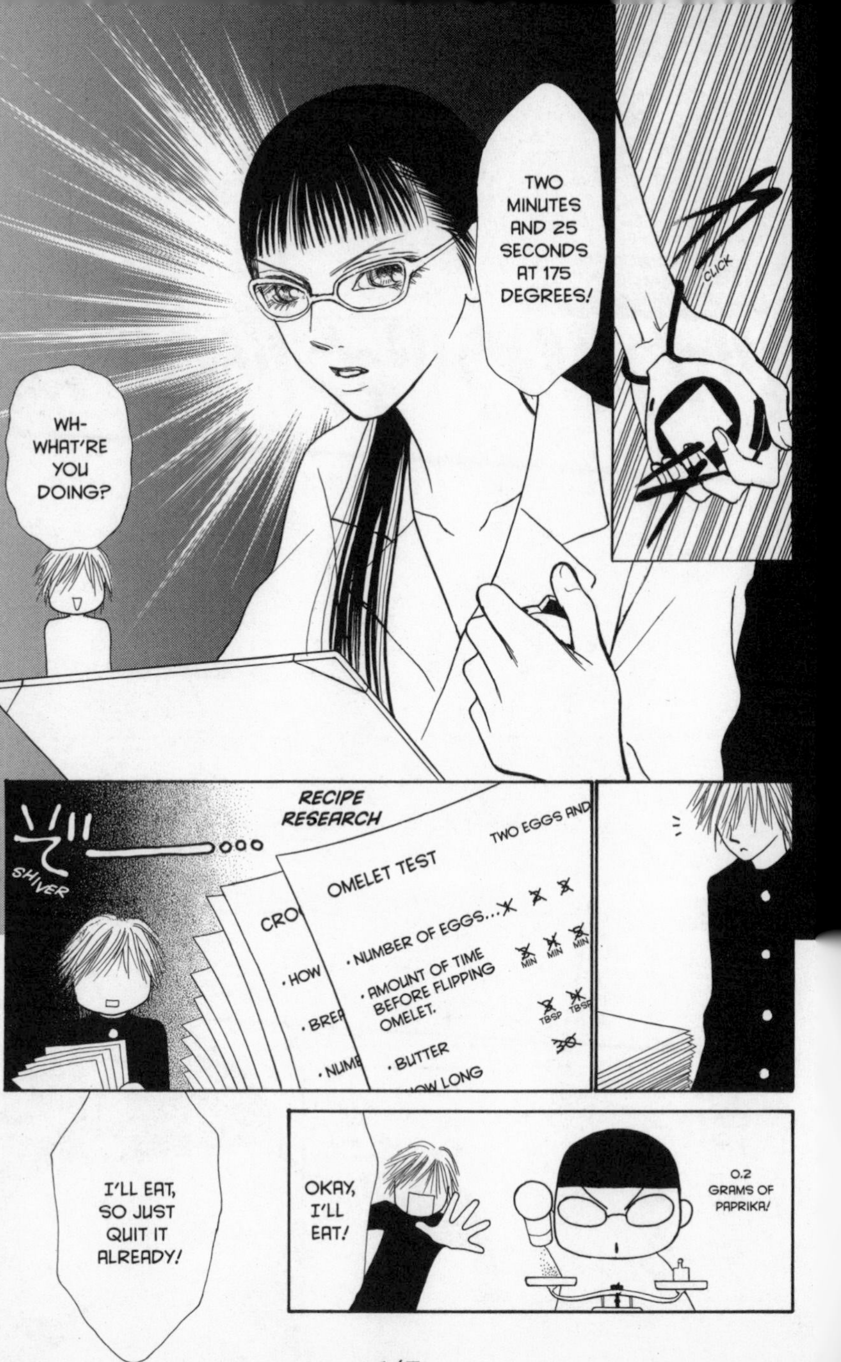
CLICK
TWO MINUTES AND 25 SECONDS AT 175 DEGREES!
WH-WHAT'RE YOU DOING?
RECIPE RESEARCH
TWO EGGS AND
OMELET TEST
· NUMBER OF EGGS...
· AMOUNT OF TIME BEFORE FLIPPING OMELET.
MIN MIN MIN
TBSP TBSP
· BUTTER
HOW LONG
CRO
· HOW
· BREA
· NUMB
SHIVER
0.2 GRAMS OF PAPRIKA!
OKAY, I'LL EAT!
I'LL EAT, SO JUST QUIT IT ALREADY!

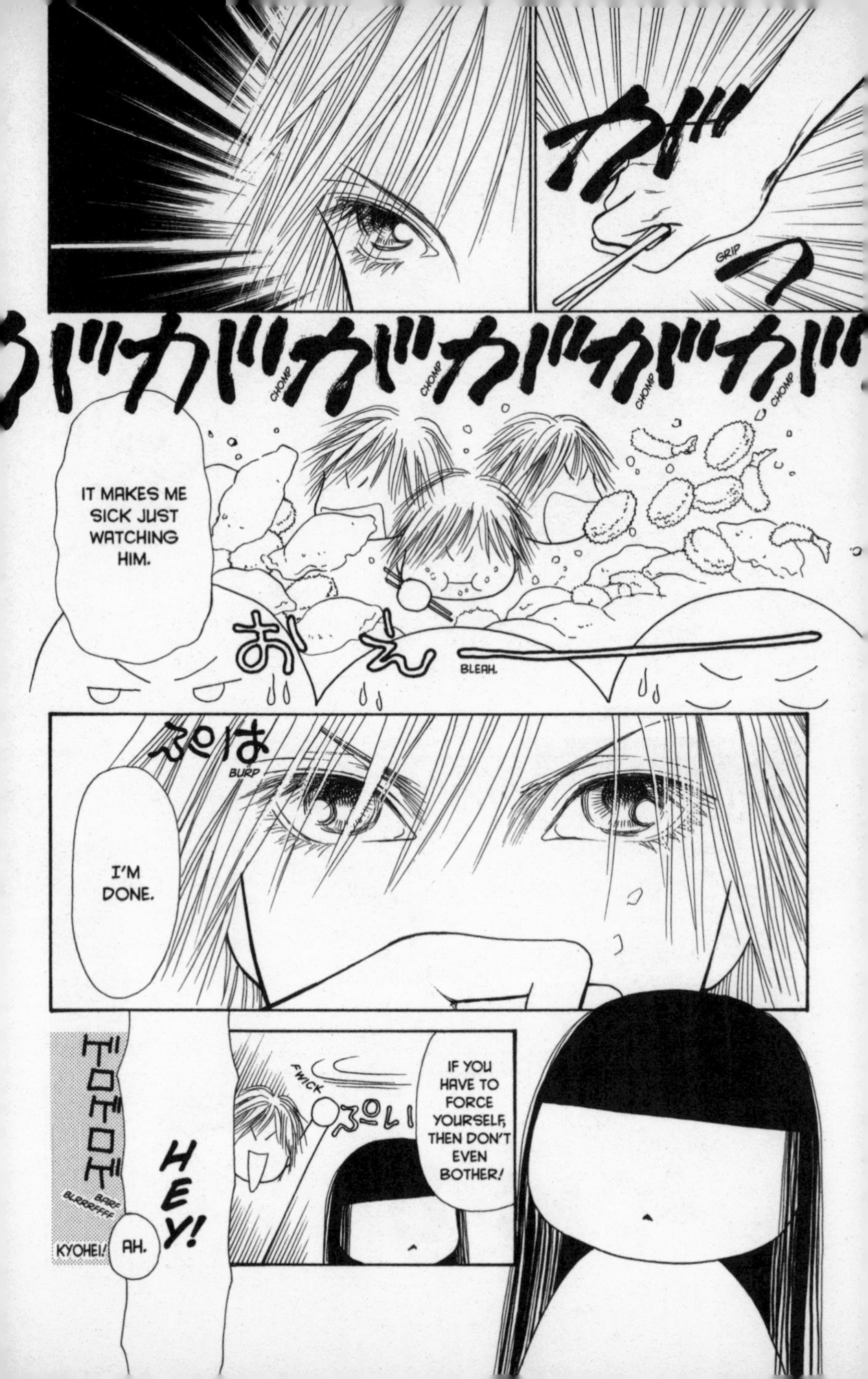
GRIP
CHOMP
CHOMP
CHOMP
CHOMP
IT MAKES ME SICK JUST WATCHING HIM.
BLEAH.
BURP
I'M DONE.
IF YOU HAVE TO FORCE YOURSELF, THEN DON'T EVEN BOTHER!
FWICK
HEY!
AH.
BARF BLRRRFFFF
KYOHEI!

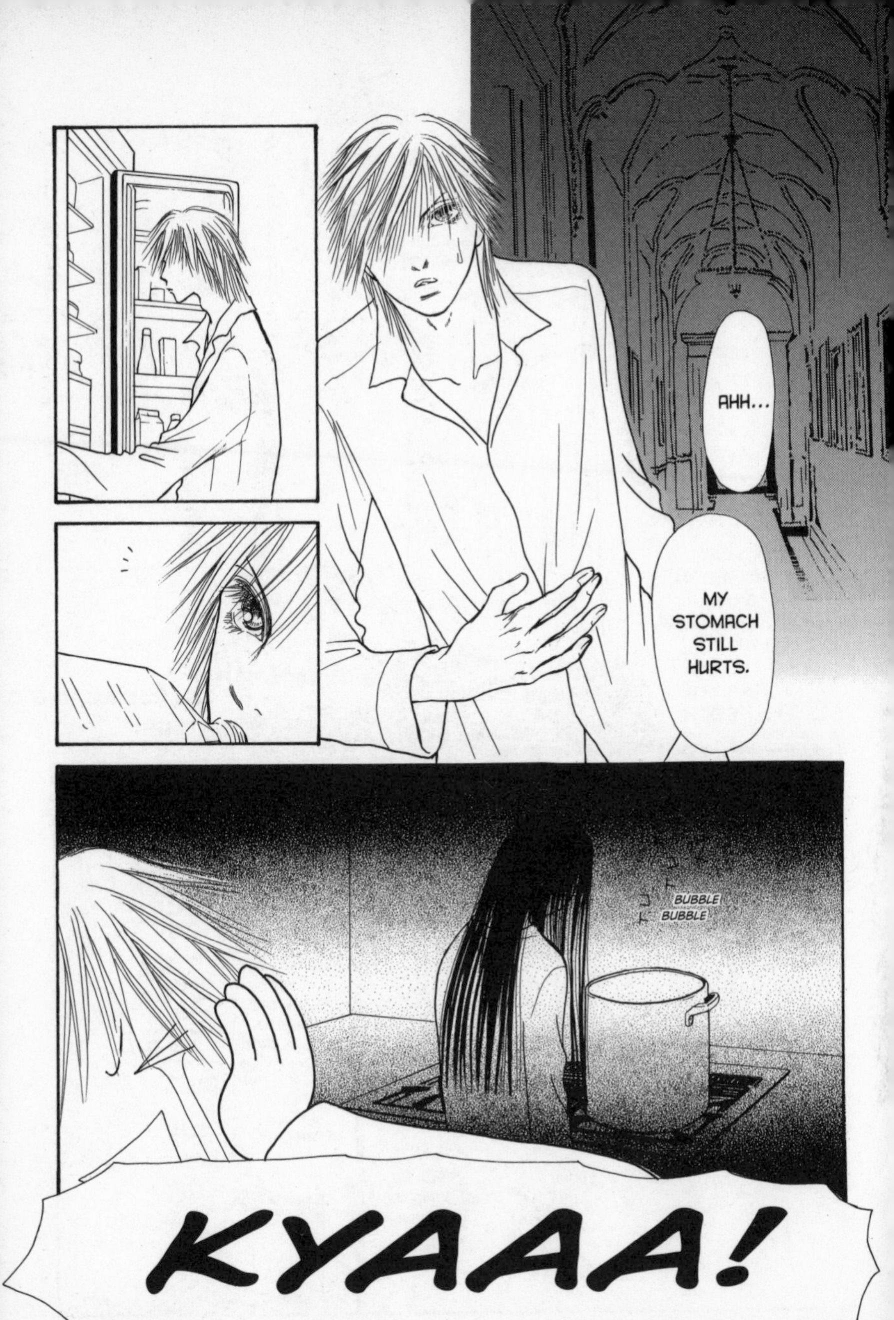
AHH...
MY STOMACH STILL HURTS.
BUBBLE BUBBLE
KYAAA!

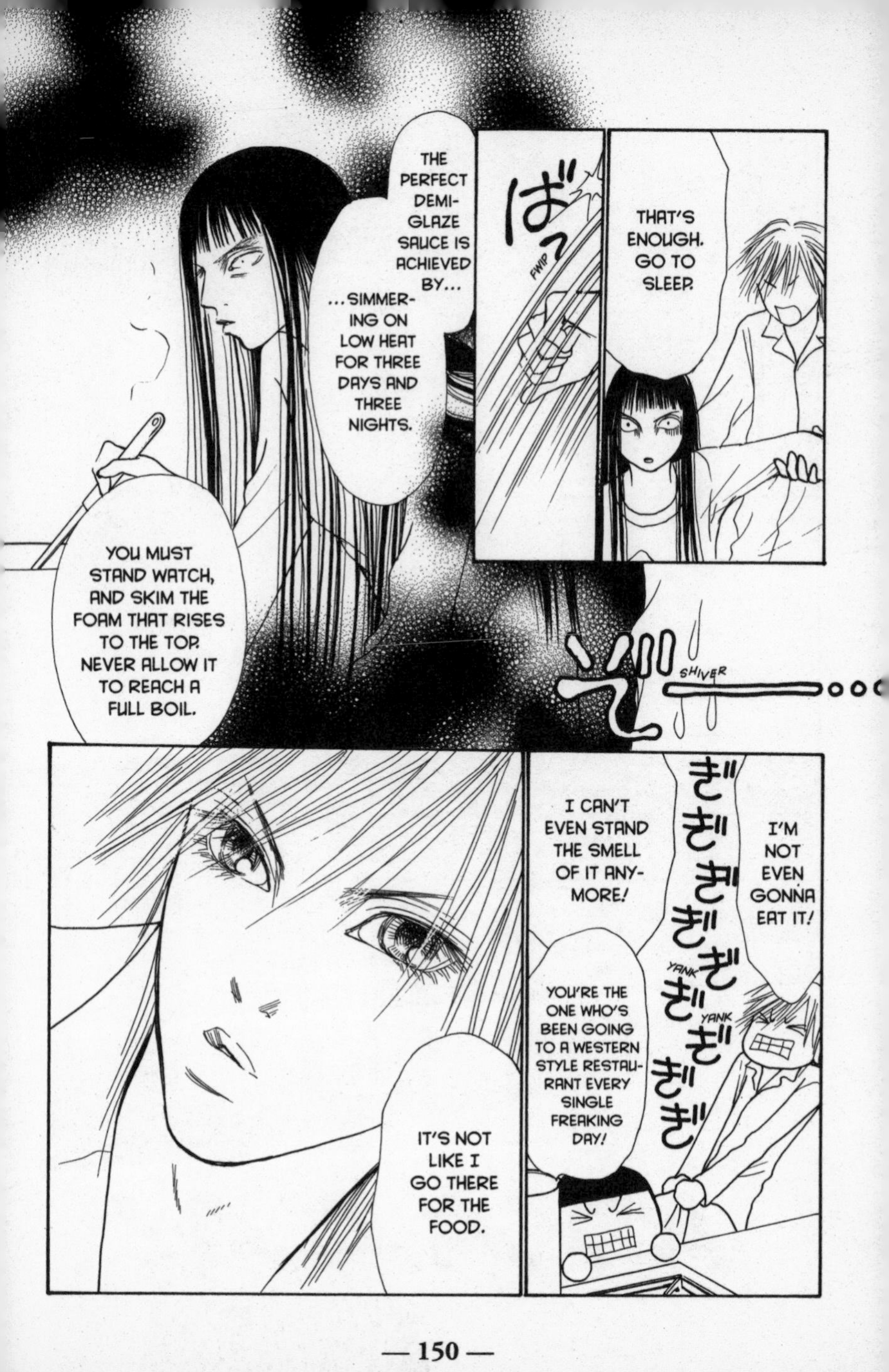
THE PERFECT DEMI-GLAZE SAUCE IS ACHIEVED BY...
...SIMMERING ON LOW HEAT FOR THREE DAYS AND THREE NIGHTS.
YOU MUST STAND WATCH, AND SKIM THE FOAM THAT RISES TO THE TOP. NEVER ALLOW IT TO REACH A FULL BOIL.
ばっ
FWIP
THAT'S ENOUGH. GO TO SLEEP.
ぞっ
SHIVER
I'M NOT EVEN GONNA EAT IT!
I CAN'T EVEN STAND THE SMELL OF IT ANY-MORE!
YANK
YANK
YOU'RE THE ONE WHO'S BEEN GOING TO A WESTERN STYLE RESTAU-RANT EVERY SINGLE FREAKING DAY!
IT'S NOT LIKE I GO THERE FOR THE FOOD.

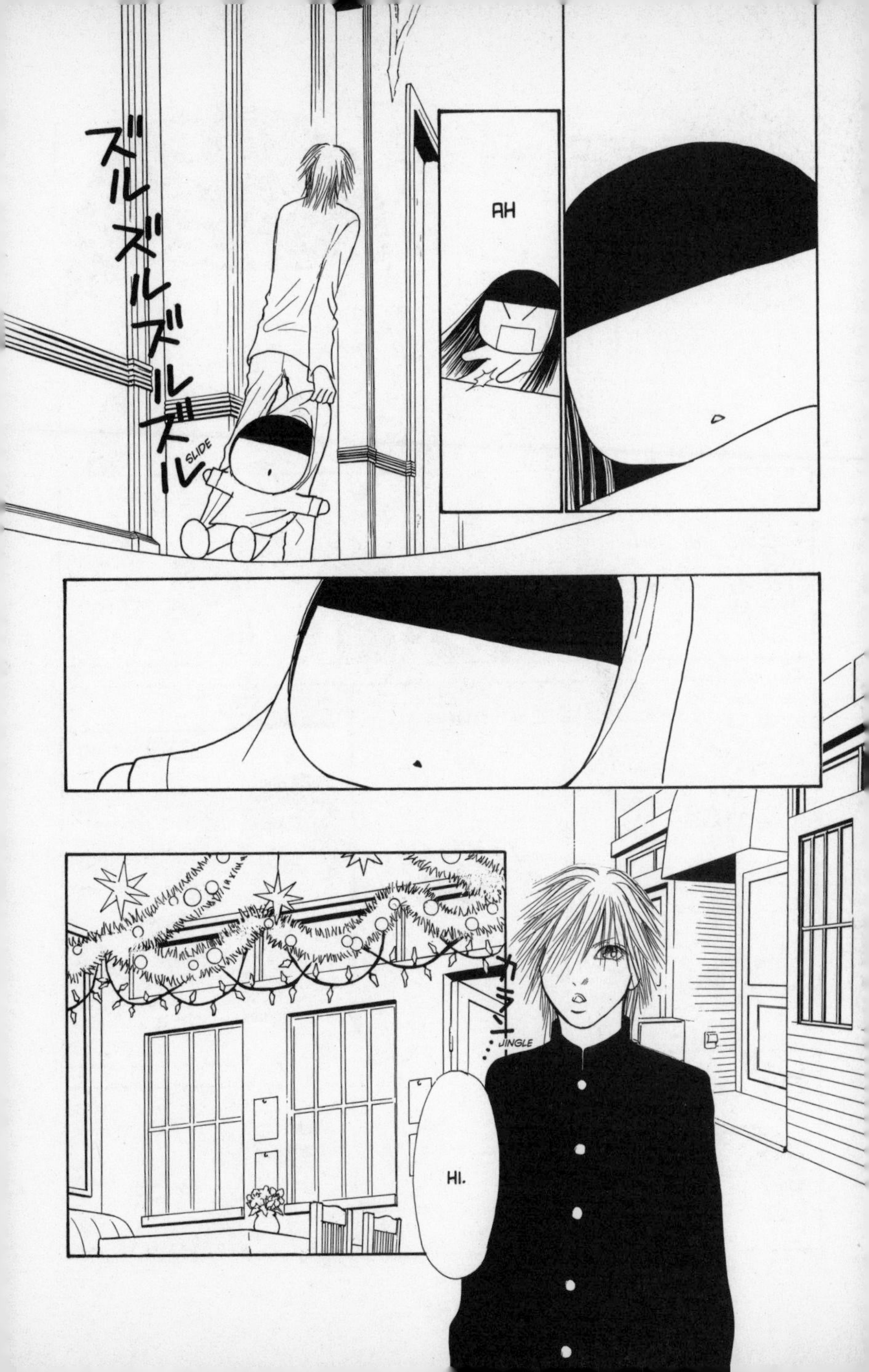
AH
ズルズルズルズル
SLIDE
JINGLE
HI.

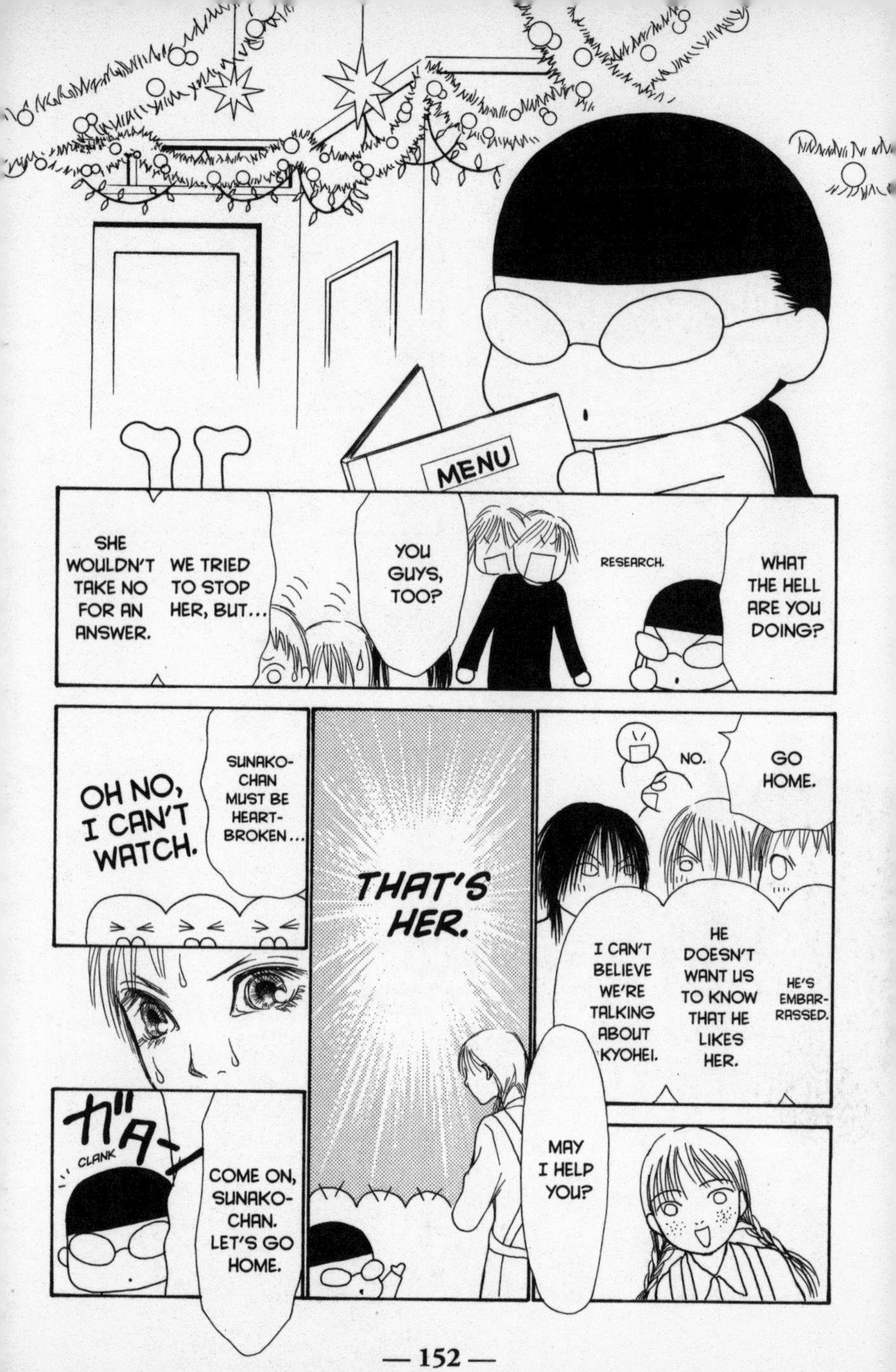
MENU
WHAT THE HELL ARE YOU DOING?
RESEARCH.
YOU GUYS, TOO?
WE TRIED TO STOP HER, BUT...
SHE WOULDN'T TAKE NO FOR AN ANSWER.
GO HOME.
NO.
HE'S EMBARRASSED.
HE DOESN'T WANT US TO KNOW THAT HE LIKES HER.
I CAN'T BELIEVE WE'RE TALKING ABOUT KYOHEI.
MAY I HELP YOU?
THAT'S HER.
SUNAKO-CHAN MUST BE HEART-BROKEN...
OH NO, I CAN'T WATCH.
COME ON, SUNAKO-CHAN. LET'S GO HOME.
ガターン
CLANK

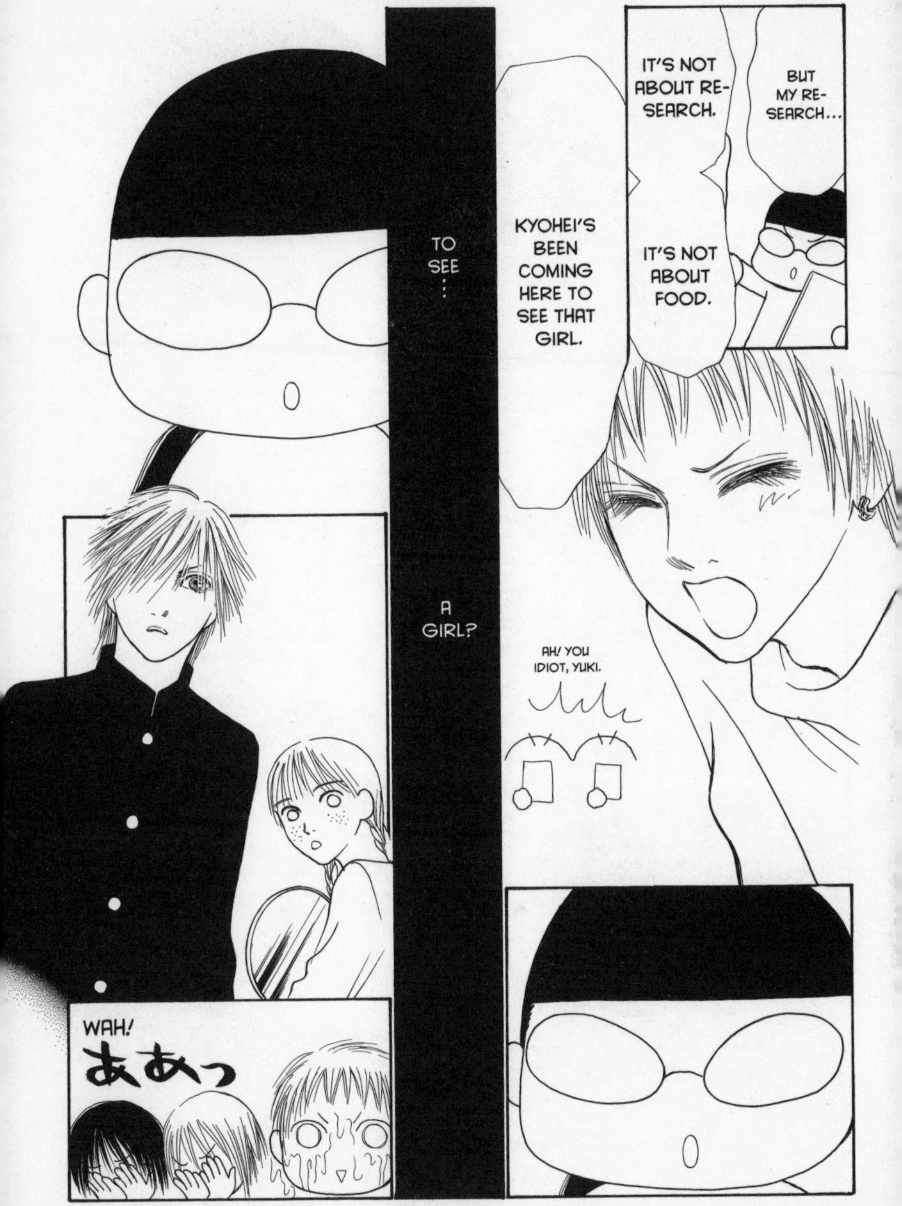
BUT MY RE-SEARCH...
IT'S NOT ABOUT RE-SEARCH.
IT'S NOT ABOUT FOOD.
KYOHEI'S BEEN COMING HERE TO SEE THAT GIRL.
AH! YOU IDIOT, YUKI.
TO SEE...
A GIRL?
WAH!
ああっ

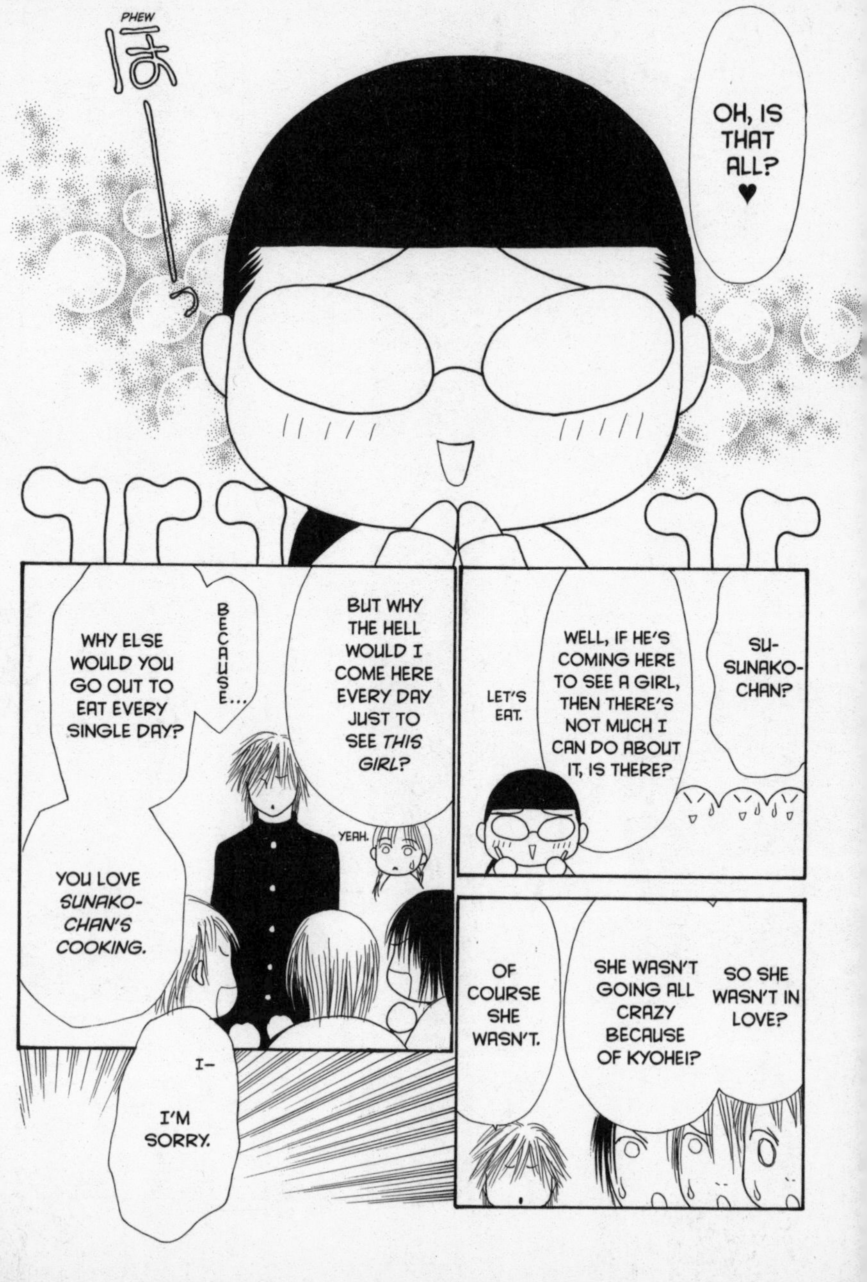
OH, IS THAT ALL? ♥
PHEW
ほーっ
SU-SUNAKO-CHAN?
WELL, IF HE'S COMING HERE TO SEE A GIRL, THEN THERE'S NOT MUCH I CAN DO ABOUT IT, IS THERE?
LET'S EAT.
SO SHE WASN'T IN LOVE?
SHE WASN'T GOING ALL CRAZY BECAUSE OF KYOHEI?
OF COURSE SHE WASN'T.
BUT WHY THE HELL WOULD I COME HERE EVERY DAY JUST TO SEE *THIS GIRL*?
YEAH.
BECAUSE...
WHY ELSE WOULD YOU GO OUT TO EAT EVERY SINGLE DAY?
YOU LOVE *SUNAKO-CHAN'S COOKING*.
I— I'M SORRY.

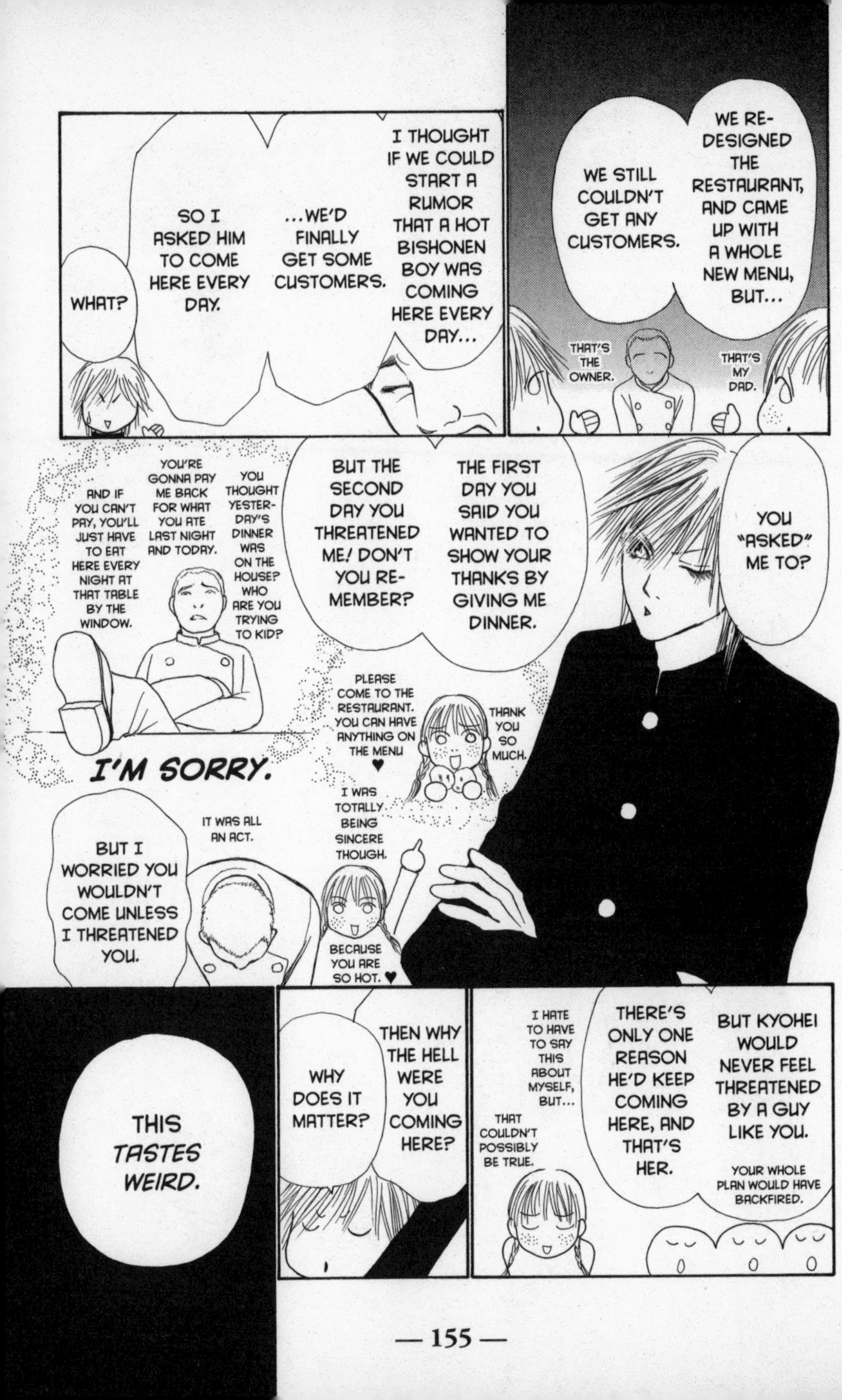
WE RE-DESIGNED THE RESTAURANT, AND CAME UP WITH A WHOLE NEW MENU, BUT...
WE STILL COULDN'T GET ANY CUSTOMERS.
THAT'S MY DAD.
THAT'S THE OWNER.
I THOUGHT IF WE COULD START A RUMOR THAT A HOT BISHONEN BOY WAS COMING HERE EVERY DAY...
...WE'D FINALLY GET SOME CUSTOMERS.
SO I ASKED HIM TO COME HERE EVERY DAY.
WHAT?
YOU "ASKED" ME TO?
THE FIRST DAY YOU SAID YOU WANTED TO SHOW YOUR THANKS BY GIVING ME DINNER.
BUT THE SECOND DAY YOU THREATENED ME! DON'T YOU RE-MEMBER?
YOU THOUGHT YESTER-DAY'S DINNER WAS ON THE HOUSE? WHO ARE YOU TRYING TO KID?
YOU'RE GONNA PAY ME BACK FOR WHAT YOU ATE LAST NIGHT AND TODAY.
AND IF YOU CAN'T PAY, YOU'LL JUST HAVE TO EAT HERE EVERY NIGHT AT THAT TABLE BY THE WINDOW.
THANK YOU SO MUCH.
PLEASE COME TO THE RESTAURANT. YOU CAN HAVE ANYTHING ON THE MENU ♥
I'M SORRY.
I WAS TOTALLY BEING SINCERE THOUGH.
BECAUSE YOU ARE SO HOT. ♥
IT WAS ALL AN ACT.
BUT I WORRIED YOU WOULDN'T COME UNLESS I THREATENED YOU.
BUT KYOHEI WOULD NEVER FEEL THREATENED BY A GUY LIKE YOU.
YOUR WHOLE PLAN WOULD HAVE BACKFIRED.
THERE'S ONLY ONE REASON HE'D KEEP COMING HERE, AND THAT'S HER.
I HATE TO HAVE TO SAY THIS ABOUT MYSELF, BUT...
THAT COULDN'T POSSIBLY BE TRUE.
THEN WHY THE HELL WERE YOU COMING HERE?
WHY DOES IT MATTER?
THIS TASTES WEIRD.

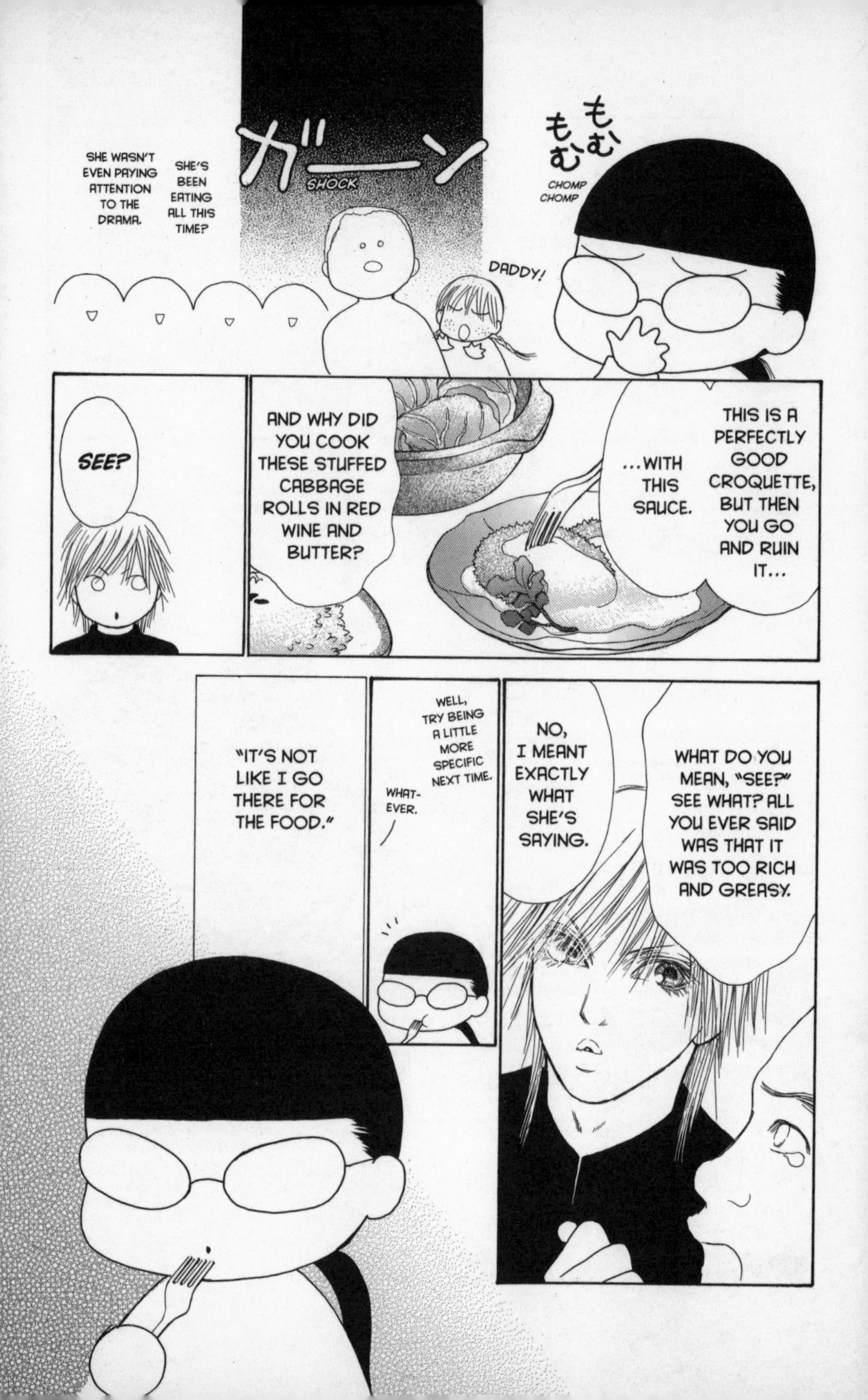
もむ もむ
CHOMP CHOMP
DADDY!
ガーン
SHOCK
SHE'S BEEN EATING ALL THIS TIME?
SHE WASN'T EVEN PAYING ATTENTION TO THE DRAMA.
THIS IS A PERFECTLY GOOD CROQUETTE, BUT THEN YOU GO AND RUIN IT...
...WITH THIS SAUCE.
AND WHY DID YOU COOK THESE STUFFED CABBAGE ROLLS IN RED WINE AND BUTTER?
SEE?
WHAT DO YOU MEAN, "SEE?" SEE WHAT? ALL YOU EVER SAID WAS THAT IT WAS TOO RICH AND GREASY.
NO, I MEANT EXACTLY WHAT SHE'S SAYING.
WELL, TRY BEING A LITTLE MORE SPECIFIC NEXT TIME.
WHAT-EVER.
"IT'S NOT LIKE I GO THERE FOR THE FOOD."

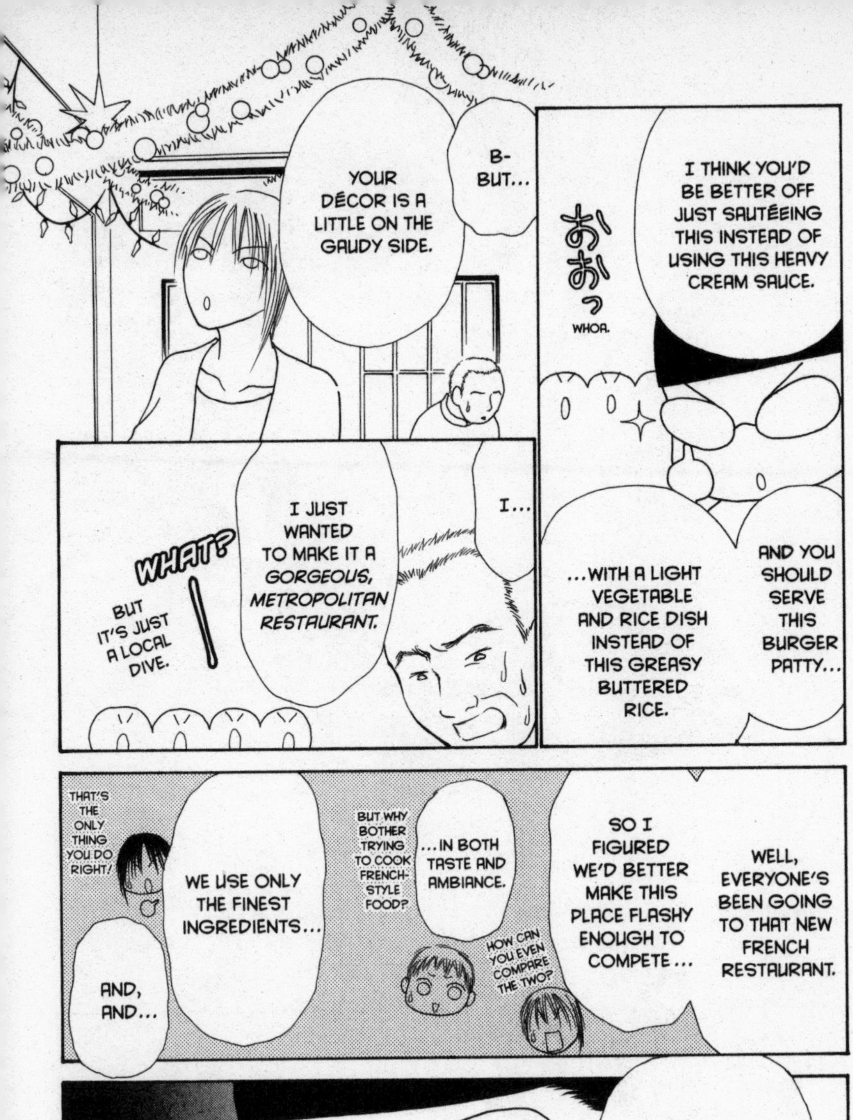
I THINK YOU'D BE BETTER OFF JUST SAUTÉEING THIS INSTEAD OF USING THIS HEAVY CREAM SAUCE.
おおっ
WHOA.
AND YOU SHOULD SERVE THIS BURGER PATTY...
...WITH A LIGHT VEGETABLE AND RICE DISH INSTEAD OF THIS GREASY BUTTERED RICE.
YOUR DÉCOR IS A LITTLE ON THE GAUDY SIDE.
B-BUT...
I...
I JUST WANTED TO MAKE IT A *GORGEOUS, METROPOLITAN RESTAURANT.*
WHAT?
BUT IT'S JUST A LOCAL DIVE.
WELL, EVERYONE'S BEEN GOING TO THAT NEW FRENCH RESTAURANT.
SO I FIGURED WE'D BETTER MAKE THIS PLACE FLASHY ENOUGH TO COMPETE...
HOW CAN YOU EVEN COMPARE THE TWO?
...IN BOTH TASTE AND AMBIANCE.
BUT WHY BOTHER TRYING TO COOK FRENCH-STYLE FOOD?
WE USE ONLY THE FINEST INGREDIENTS...
THAT'S THE ONLY THING YOU DO RIGHT!
AND, AND...
YOU GUYS WORKED AT THAT RESTAURANT, AND HELPED MAKE A NAME FOR IT, SO...

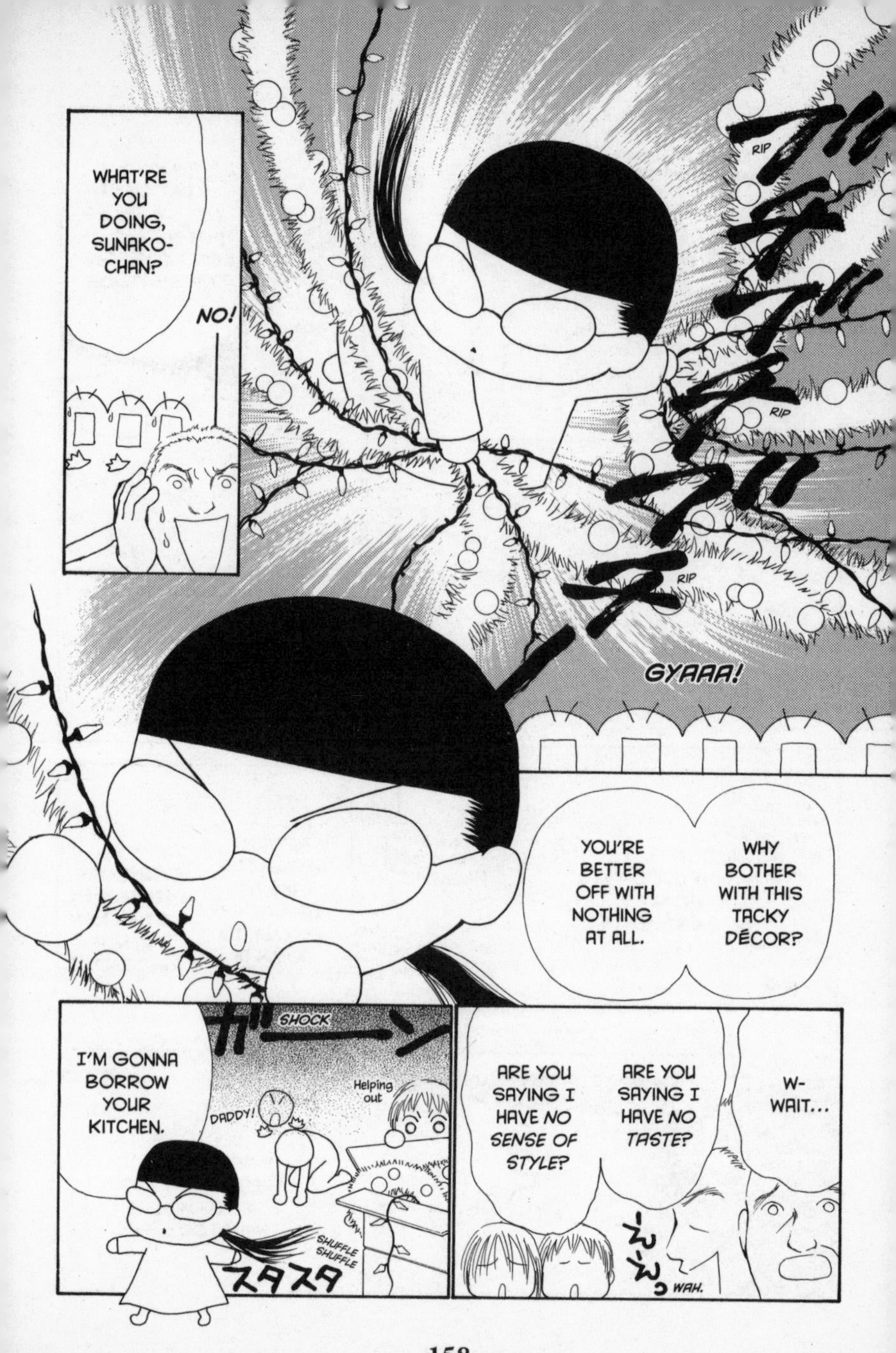
RIP
RIP
RIP
GYAAA!
WHAT'RE YOU DOING, SUNAKO-CHAN?
NO!
WHY BOTHER WITH THIS TACKY DÉCOR?
YOU'RE BETTER OFF WITH NOTHING AT ALL.
W-WAIT...
ARE YOU SAYING I HAVE NO TASTE?
ARE YOU SAYING I HAVE NO SENSE OF STYLE?
WAH.
SHOCK
I'M GONNA BORROW YOUR KITCHEN.
Helping out
DADDY!
SHUFFLE SHUFFLE
スタスタ

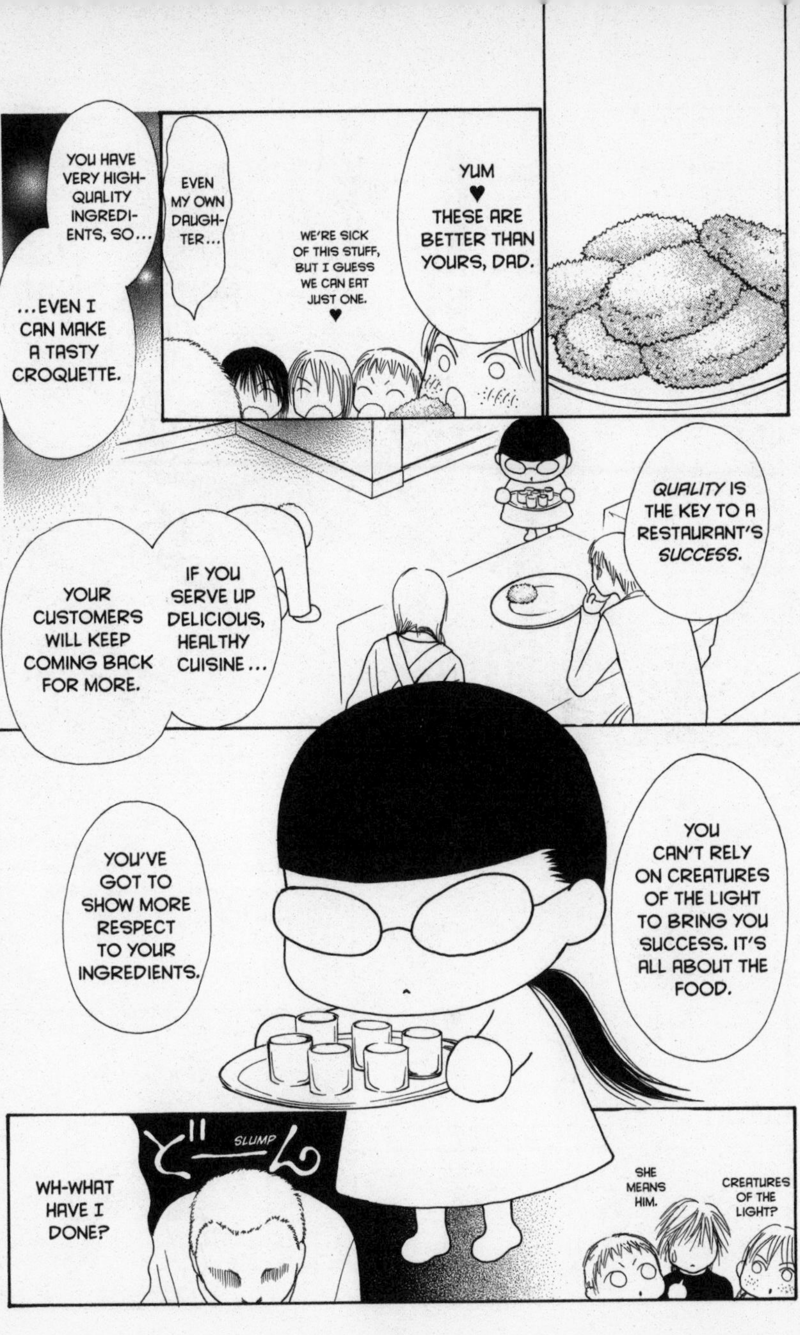
YUM ♥ THESE ARE BETTER THAN YOURS, DAD.
WE'RE SICK OF THIS STUFF, BUT I GUESS WE CAN EAT JUST ONE. ♥
EVEN MY OWN DAUGH-TER...
YOU HAVE VERY HIGH-QUALITY INGREDI-ENTS, SO...
...EVEN I CAN MAKE A TASTY CROQUETTE.
QUALITY IS THE KEY TO A RESTAURANT'S *SUCCESS*.
IF YOU SERVE UP DELICIOUS, HEALTHY CUISINE...
YOUR CUSTOMERS WILL KEEP COMING BACK FOR MORE.
YOU CAN'T RELY ON CREATURES OF THE LIGHT TO BRING YOU SUCCESS. IT'S ALL ABOUT THE FOOD.
YOU'VE GOT TO SHOW MORE RESPECT TO YOUR INGREDIENTS.
CREATURES OF THE LIGHT?
SHE MEANS HIM.
SLUMP
WH-WHAT HAVE I DONE?

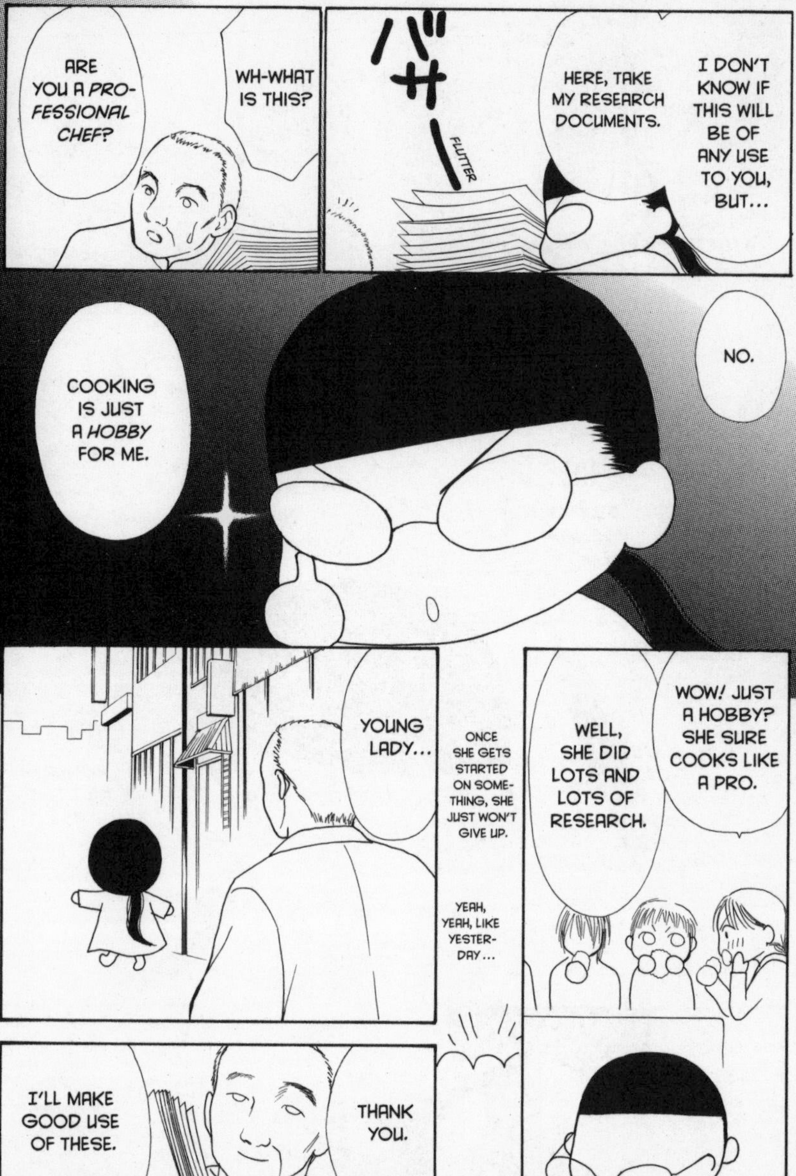
バサー
FLUTTER
I DON'T KNOW IF THIS WILL BE OF ANY USE TO YOU, BUT...
HERE, TAKE MY RESEARCH DOCUMENTS.
WH-WHAT IS THIS?
ARE YOU A *PROFESSIONAL CHEF*?
NO.
COOKING IS JUST A *HOBBY* FOR ME.
WOW! JUST A HOBBY? SHE SURE COOKS LIKE A PRO.
WELL, SHE DID LOTS AND LOTS OF RESEARCH.
ONCE SHE GETS STARTED ON SOMETHING, SHE JUST WON'T GIVE UP.
YEAH, YEAH, LIKE YESTERDAY...
YOUNG LADY...
THANK YOU.
I'LL MAKE GOOD USE OF THESE.

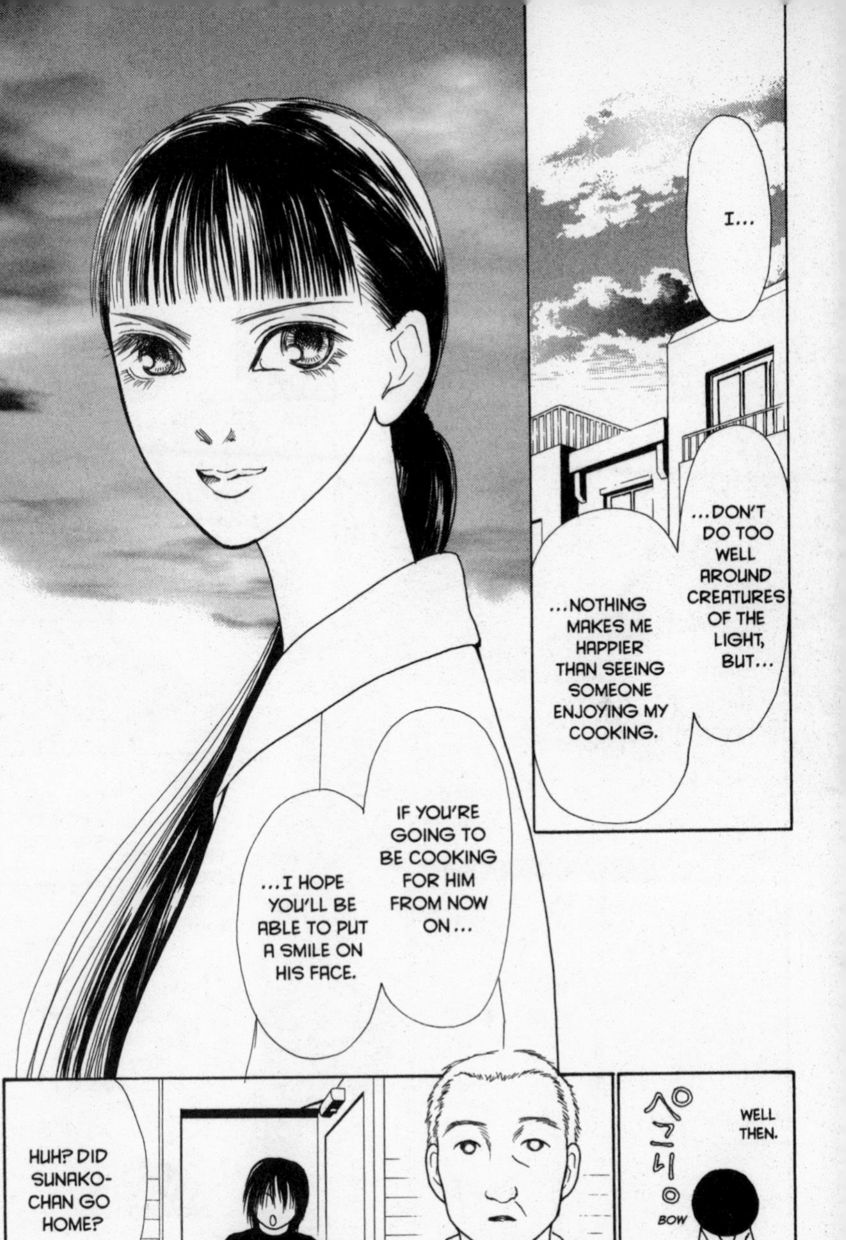
I...
...DON'T DO TOO WELL AROUND CREATURES OF THE LIGHT, BUT...
...NOTHING MAKES ME HAPPIER THAN SEEING SOMEONE ENJOYING MY COOKING.
IF YOU'RE GOING TO BE COOKING FOR HIM FROM NOW ON...
...I HOPE YOU'LL BE ABLE TO PUT A SMILE ON HIS FACE.
WELL THEN.
BOW
HUH? DID SUNAKO-CHAN GO HOME?

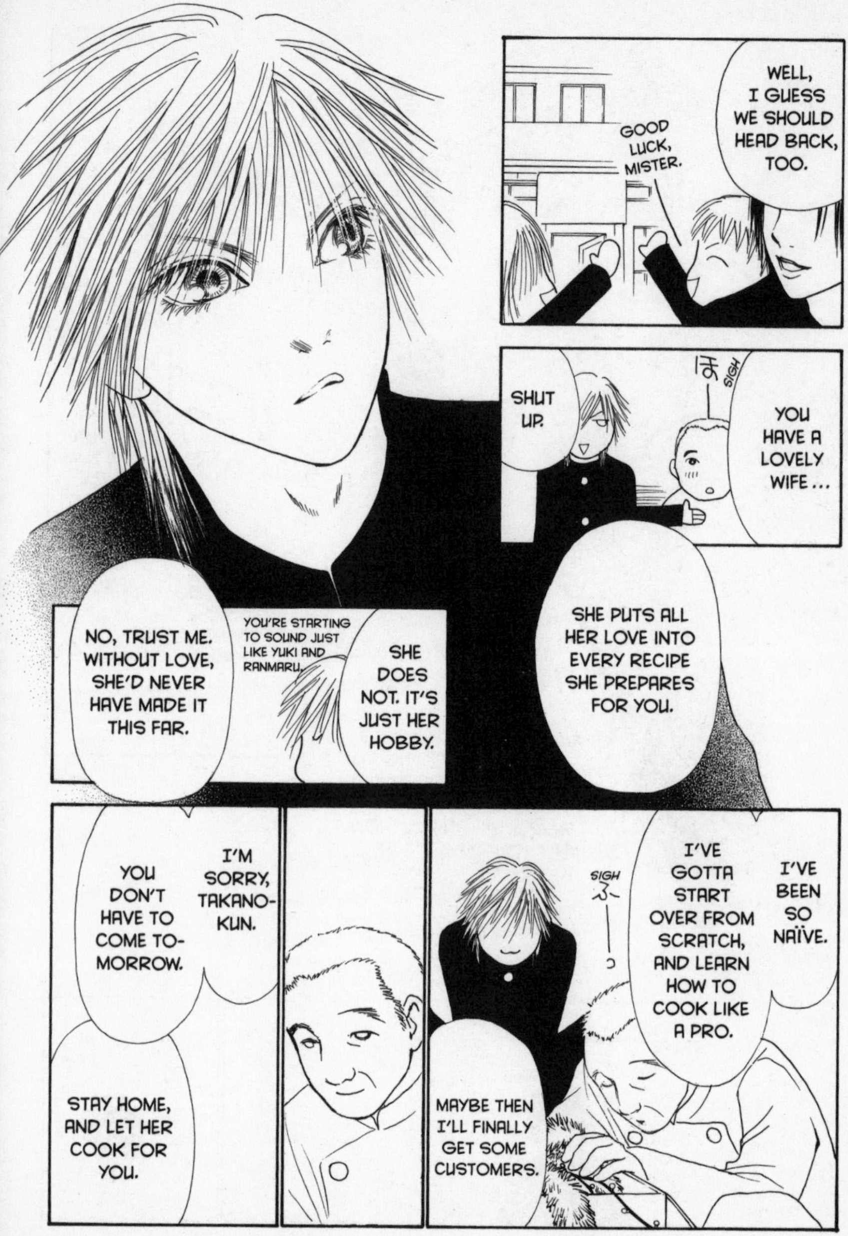
WELL, I GUESS WE SHOULD HEAD BACK, TOO.
GOOD LUCK, MISTER.
YOU HAVE A LOVELY WIFE...
ほ SIGH
SHUT UP.
SHE PUTS ALL HER LOVE INTO EVERY RECIPE SHE PREPARES FOR YOU.
SHE DOES NOT. IT'S JUST HER HOBBY.
YOU'RE STARTING TO SOUND JUST LIKE YUKI AND RANMARU.
NO, TRUST ME. WITHOUT LOVE, SHE'D NEVER HAVE MADE IT THIS FAR.
I'VE BEEN SO NAÏVE.
I'VE GOTTA START OVER FROM SCRATCH, AND LEARN HOW TO COOK LIKE A PRO.
SIGH ふ～っ
MAYBE THEN I'LL FINALLY GET SOME CUSTOMERS.
I'M SORRY, TAKANO-KUN.
YOU DON'T HAVE TO COME TO-MORROW.
STAY HOME, AND LET HER COOK FOR YOU.

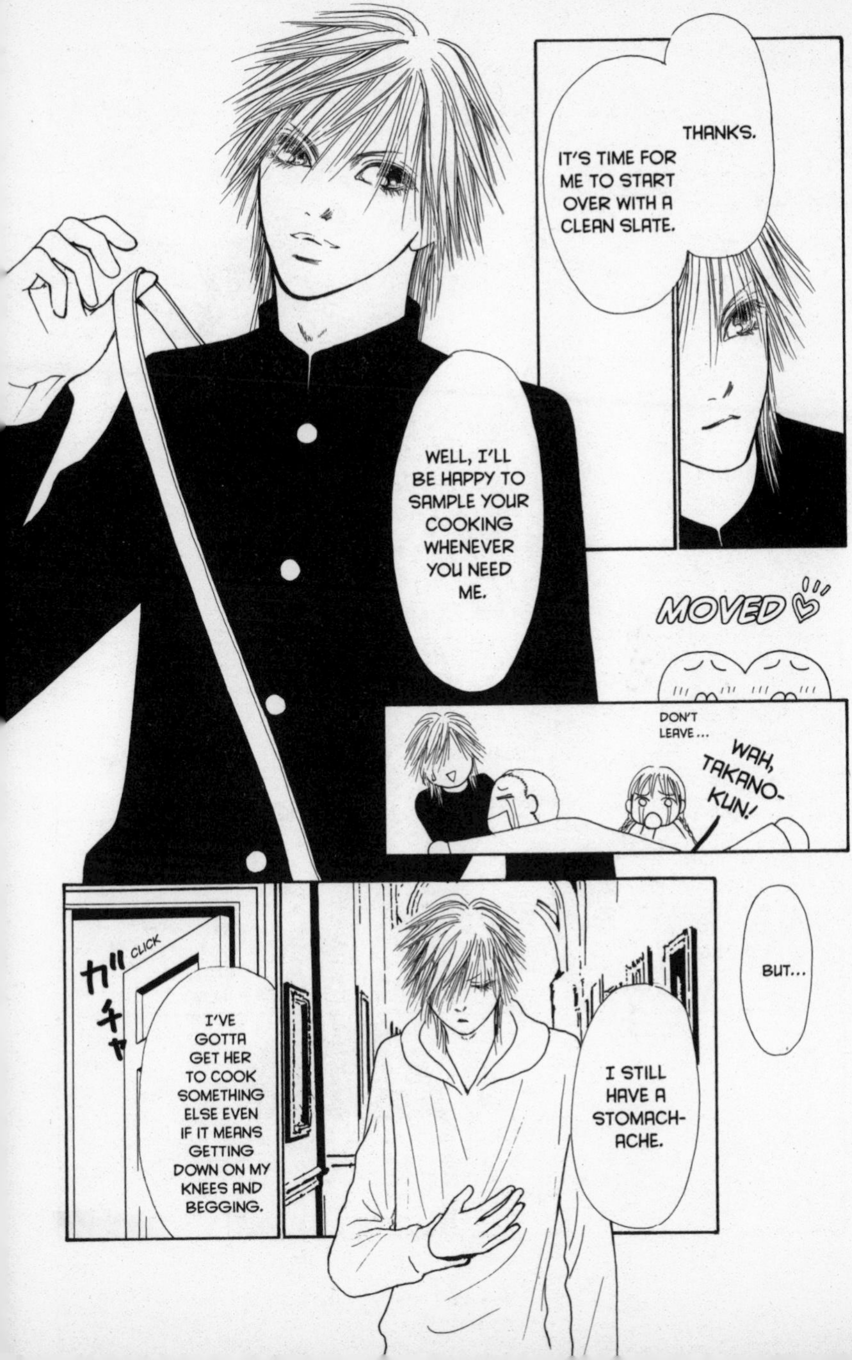
THANKS.
IT'S TIME FOR ME TO START OVER WITH A CLEAN SLATE.
WELL, I'LL BE HAPPY TO SAMPLE YOUR COOKING WHENEVER YOU NEED ME.
MOVED
DON'T LEAVE...
WAH, TAKANO-KUN!
BUT...
I STILL HAVE A STOMACH-ACHE.
ガチャ
CLICK
I'VE GOTTA GET HER TO COOK SOMETHING ELSE EVEN IF IT MEANS GETTING DOWN ON MY KNEES AND BEGGING.

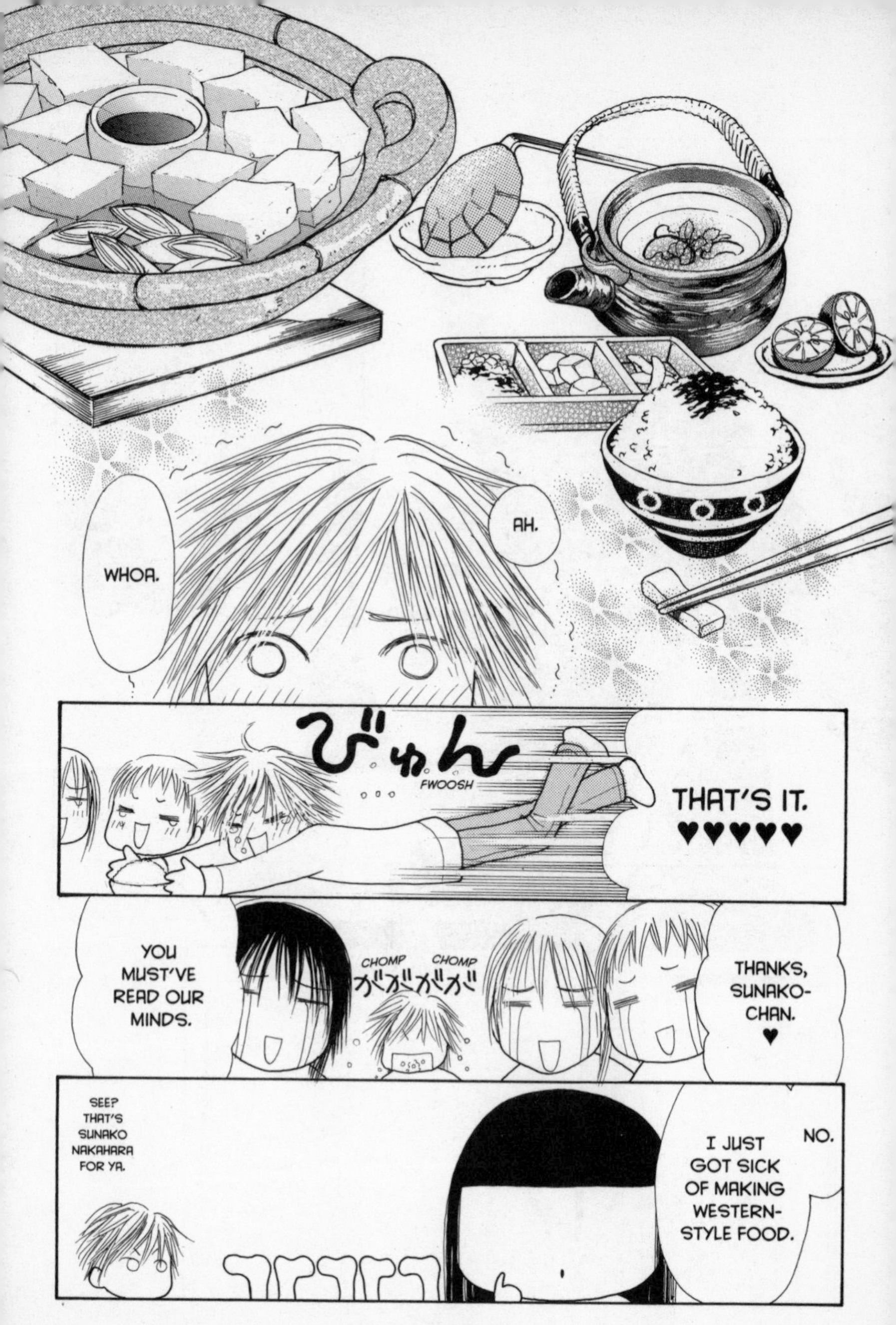
AH.
WHOA.
THAT'S IT. ♥♥♥♥♥
びゅん
FWOOSH
THANKS, SUNAKO-CHAN. ♥
CHOMP CHOMP
がががが
YOU MUST'VE READ OUR MINDS.
NO.
I JUST GOT SICK OF MAKING WESTERN-STYLE FOOD.
SEE? THAT'S SUNAKO NAKAHARA FOR YA.

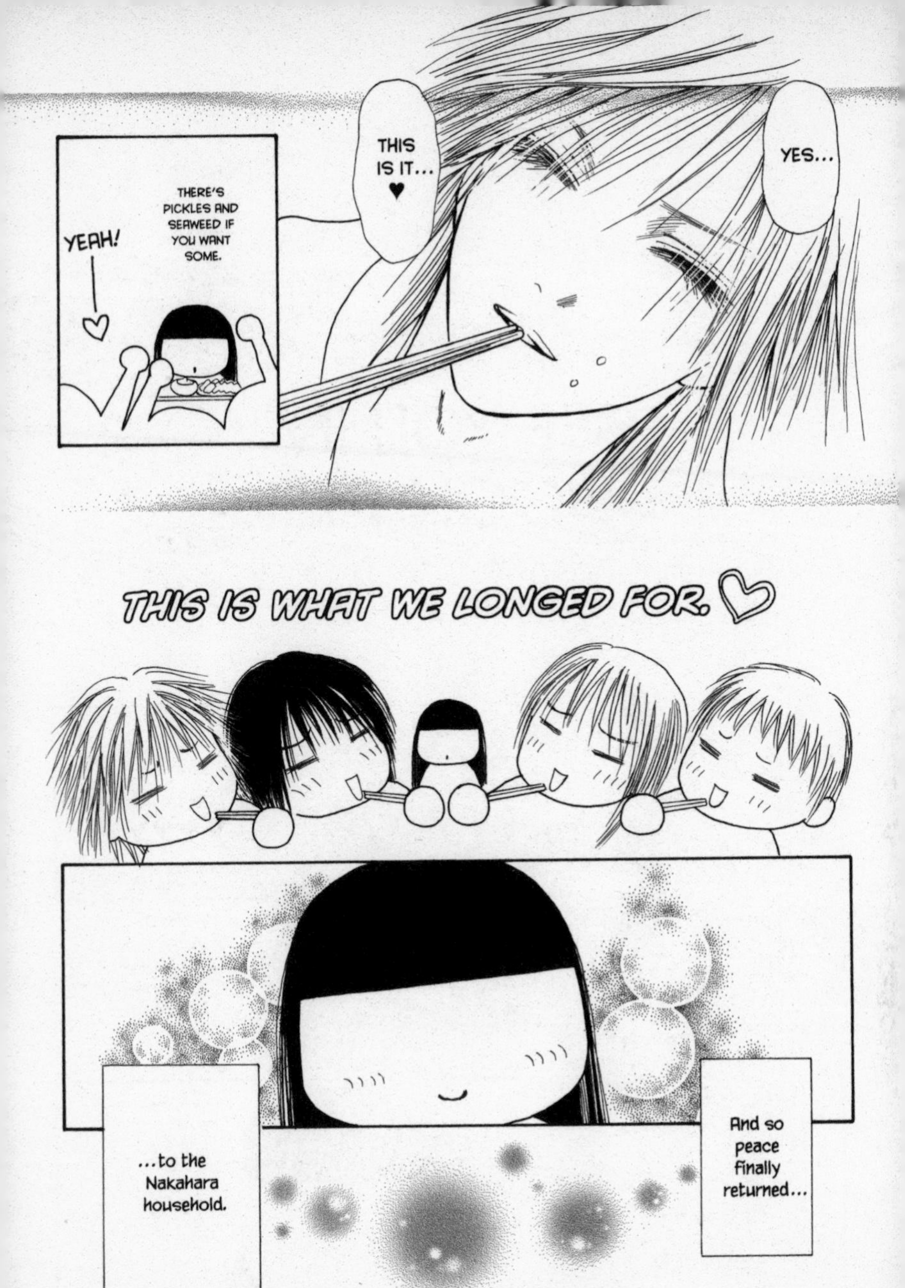
YES...
THIS IS IT... ♥
THERE'S PICKLES AND SEAWEED IF YOU WANT SOME.
YEAH! ♥
THIS IS WHAT WE LONGED FOR. ♡
And so peace finally returned...
...to the Nakahara household.

CONTINUED IN THE WALLFLOWER BOOK 14

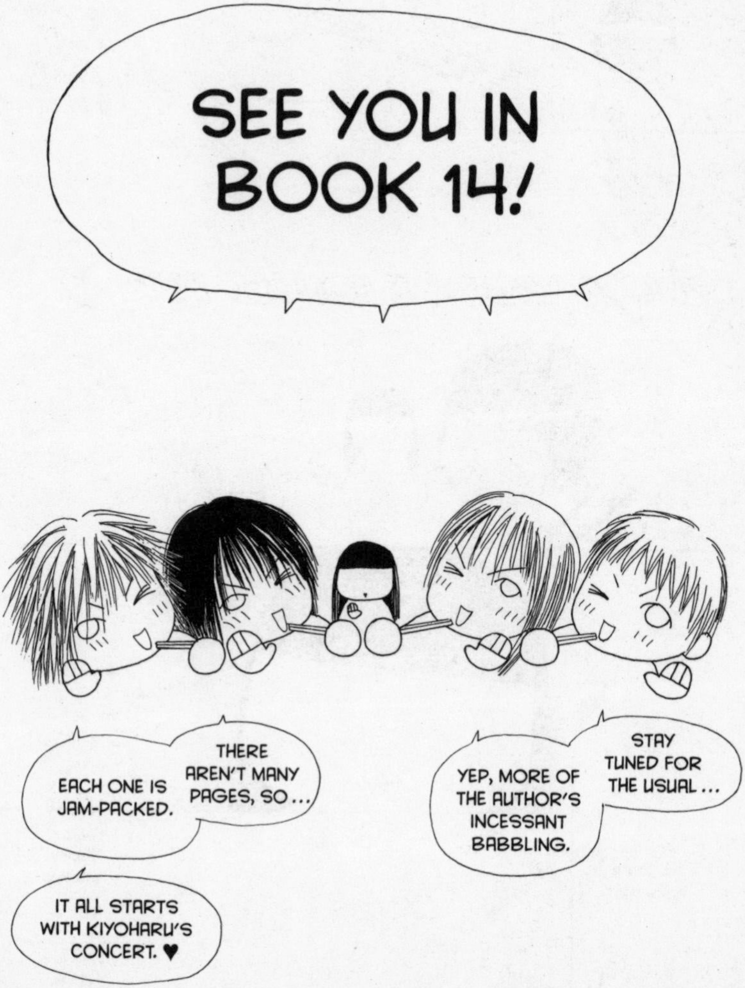
SEE YOU IN BOOK 14!
STAY TUNED FOR THE USUAL...
YEP, MORE OF THE AUTHOR'S INCESSANT BABBLING.
THERE AREN'T MANY PAGES, SO...
EACH ONE IS JAM-PACKED.
IT ALL STARTS WITH KIYOHARU'S CONCERT. ♥

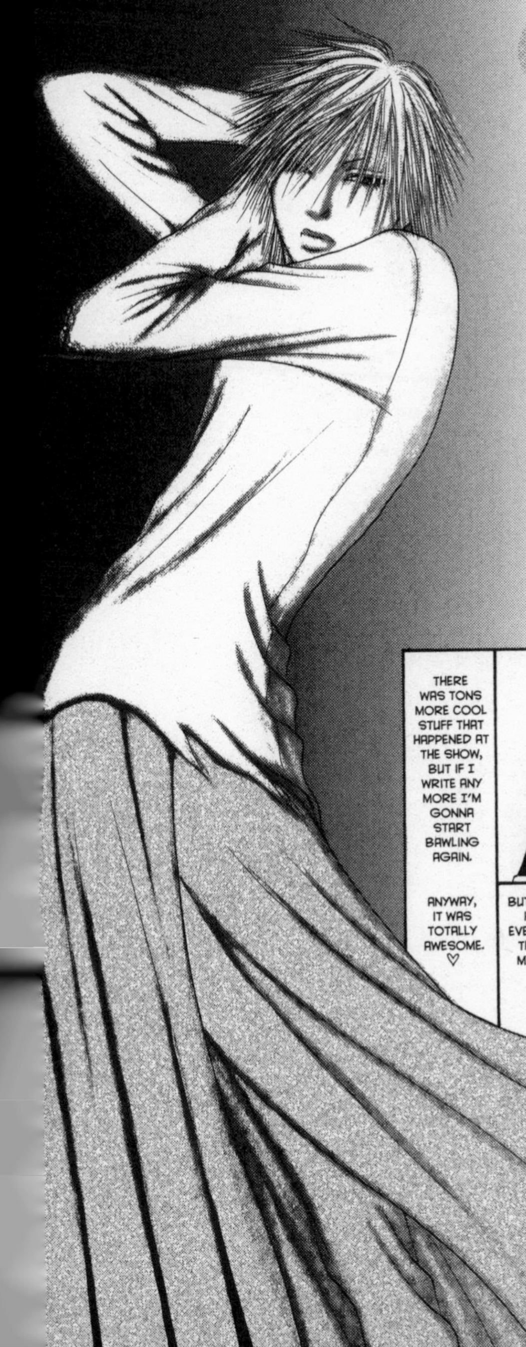

KIYOHARU

TOUR 2005
ANGEL'S SONGS

APRIL 29TH
AT SHINAGAWA
PRINCE HOTEL'S
STELLAR BALL

IT WAS A TWO-DAY CONCERT, BUT I ONLY GOT TO GO ONE DAY BECAUSE I HAD A DEADLINE... AHH...(I CRIED ALL DAY.)

ALTHOUGH I ONLY GOT TO SEE HIM ONCE, IT WAS STILL AN *AWESOME* SHOW!

I COULDN'T STOP *CRYING.* I USUALLY CRY WHEN I SEE HIS SHOWS, BUT THIS TIME I WAS TOTALLY SOBBING. I GOT GOOSE BUMPS WHEN HE CAME OUT ONSTAGE. ♡♡♡♡♡ I MEAN, HE WAS SOOOOO GORGEOUS. (MY EYES FILLED WITH TEARS THE MOMENT I SAW HIM.) I CRIED WHEN HE TALKED ONSTAGE, AND SOBBED WHEN HE PLAYED ONE OF HIS CLASSIC SONGS. I ENDED UP CRYING THROUGH THE WHOLE SHOW.

HE WAS SOOOO FREAKING COOL.

I THINK HIS LATEST TOUR WAS AWESOME. (AS USUAL) I LOVE THE NEW ALBUM "MELLOW." ♡

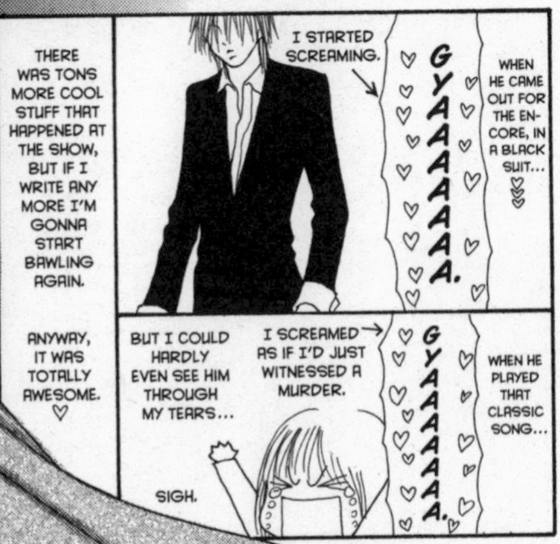

WHEN HE CAME OUT FOR THE ENCORE, IN A BLACK SUIT... ♡♡♡
GYAAAAAAA.
I STARTED SCREAMING.
THERE WAS TONS MORE COOL STUFF THAT HAPPENED AT THE SHOW, BUT IF I WRITE ANY MORE I'M GONNA START BAWLING AGAIN.
WHEN HE PLAYED THAT CLASSIC SONG...
GYAAAAAAA.
I SCREAMED AS IF I'D JUST WITNESSED A MURDER.
BUT I COULD HARDLY EVEN SEE HIM THROUGH MY TEARS...
SIGH.
ANYWAY, IT WAS TOTALLY AWESOME. ♡

HE LOOKED SO CUTE IN THAT SKIRT. ♡♡♡

WHEN I WENT TO SEE HIS SHOW IN SENDAI, I CRIED THE MOST WHEN HE PLAYED "LAST SONG" AND "ALSTROEMERIA."

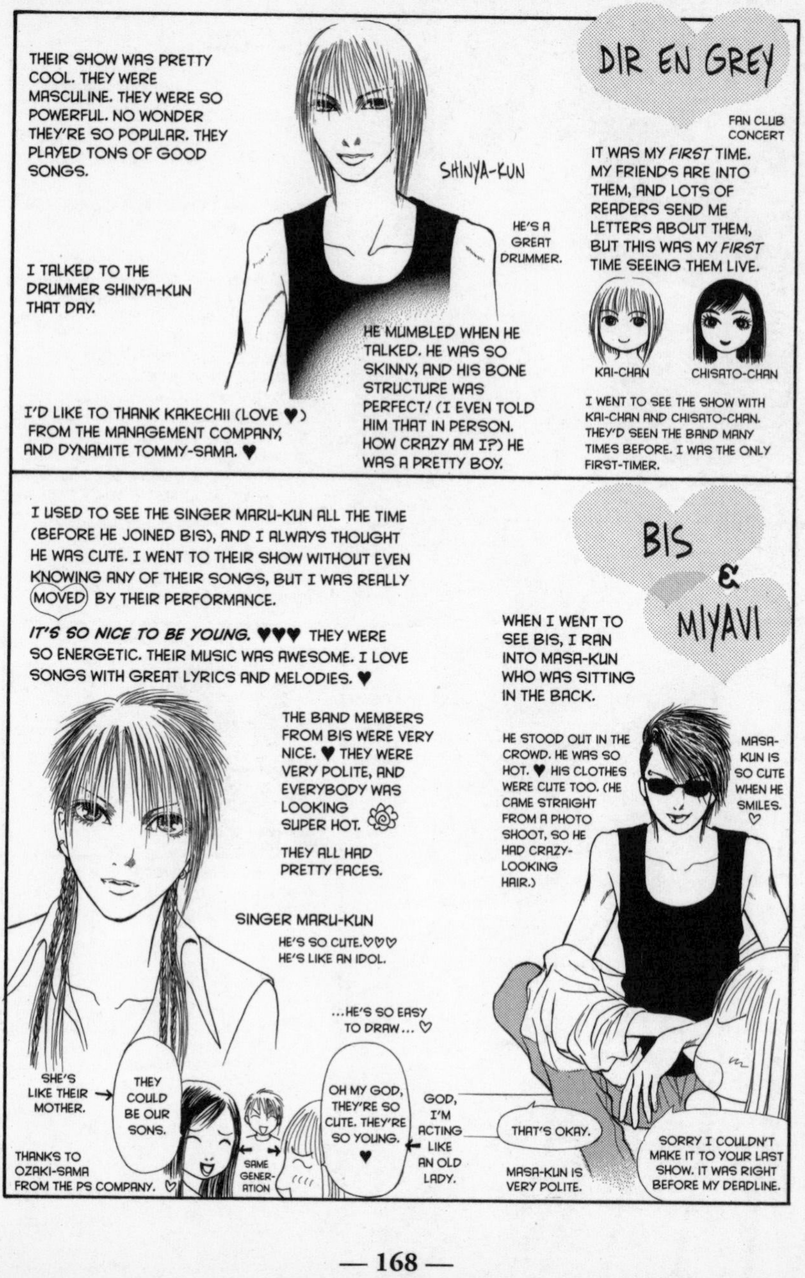

DIR EN GREY
FAN CLUB CONCERT
IT WAS MY *FIRST* TIME. MY FRIENDS ARE INTO THEM, AND LOTS OF READERS SEND ME LETTERS ABOUT THEM, BUT THIS WAS MY *FIRST* TIME SEEING THEM LIVE.
KAI-CHAN
CHISATO-CHAN
I WENT TO SEE THE SHOW WITH KAI-CHAN AND CHISATO-CHAN. THEY'D SEEN THE BAND MANY TIMES BEFORE. I WAS THE ONLY FIRST-TIMER.
SHINYA-KUN
HE'S A GREAT DRUMMER.
HE MUMBLED WHEN HE TALKED. HE WAS SO SKINNY, AND HIS BONE STRUCTURE WAS PERFECT! (I EVEN TOLD HIM THAT IN PERSON. HOW CRAZY AM I?) HE WAS A PRETTY BOY.
THEIR SHOW WAS PRETTY COOL. THEY WERE MASCULINE. THEY WERE SO POWERFUL. NO WONDER THEY'RE SO POPULAR. THEY PLAYED TONS OF GOOD SONGS.
I TALKED TO THE DRUMMER SHINYA-KUN THAT DAY.
I'D LIKE TO THANK KAKECHII (LOVE ♥) FROM THE MANAGEMENT COMPANY, AND DYNAMITE TOMMY-SAMA. ♥
BIS & MIYAVI
WHEN I WENT TO SEE BIS, I RAN INTO MASA-KUN WHO WAS SITTING IN THE BACK.
MASA-KUN IS SO CUTE WHEN HE SMILES. ♡
HE STOOD OUT IN THE CROWD. HE WAS SO HOT. ♥ HIS CLOTHES WERE CUTE TOO. (HE CAME STRAIGHT FROM A PHOTO SHOOT, SO HE HAD CRAZY-LOOKING HAIR.)
SORRY I COULDN'T MAKE IT TO YOUR LAST SHOW. IT WAS RIGHT BEFORE MY DEADLINE.
THAT'S OKAY.
MASA-KUN IS VERY POLITE.
I USED TO SEE THE SINGER MARU-KUN ALL THE TIME (BEFORE HE JOINED BIS), AND I ALWAYS THOUGHT HE WAS CUTE. I WENT TO THEIR SHOW WITHOUT EVEN KNOWING ANY OF THEIR SONGS, BUT I WAS REALLY MOVED BY THEIR PERFORMANCE.
IT'S SO NICE TO BE YOUNG. ♥♥♥ THEY WERE SO ENERGETIC. THEIR MUSIC WAS AWESOME. I LOVE SONGS WITH GREAT LYRICS AND MELODIES. ♥
THE BAND MEMBERS FROM BIS WERE VERY NICE. ♥ THEY WERE VERY POLITE, AND EVERYBODY WAS LOOKING SUPER HOT.
THEY ALL HAD PRETTY FACES.
SINGER MARU-KUN
HE'S SO CUTE. ♡♡♡ HE'S LIKE AN IDOL.
...HE'S SO EASY TO DRAW... ♡
GOD, I'M ACTING LIKE AN OLD LADY.
OH MY GOD, THEY'RE SO CUTE. THEY'RE SO YOUNG. ♥
SAME GENER-ATION
THEY COULD BE OUR SONS.
SHE'S LIKE THEIR MOTHER.
THANKS TO OZAKI-SAMA FROM THE PS COMPANY. ♡

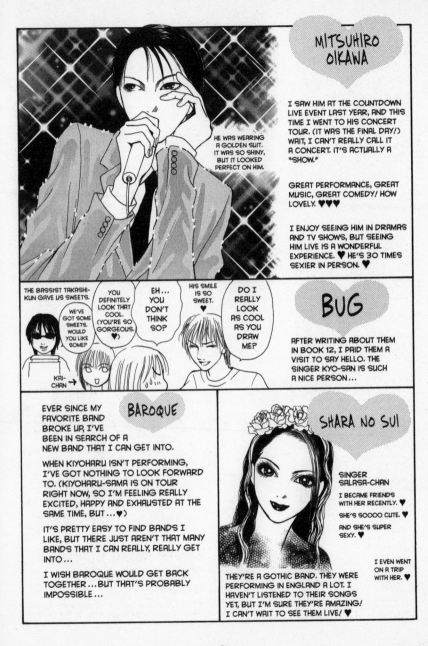

MITSUHIRO OIKAWA

I SAW HIM AT THE COUNTDOWN LIVE EVENT LAST YEAR, AND THIS TIME I WENT TO HIS CONCERT TOUR. (IT WAS THE FINAL DAY!) WAIT, I CAN'T REALLY CALL IT A CONCERT. IT'S ACTUALLY A "SHOW."

GREAT PERFORMANCE, GREAT MUSIC, GREAT COMEDY! HOW LOVELY. ♥♥♥

I ENJOY SEEING HIM IN DRAMAS AND TV SHOWS, BUT SEEING HIM LIVE IS A WONDERFUL EXPERIENCE. ♥ HE'S 30 TIMES SEXIER IN PERSON. ♥

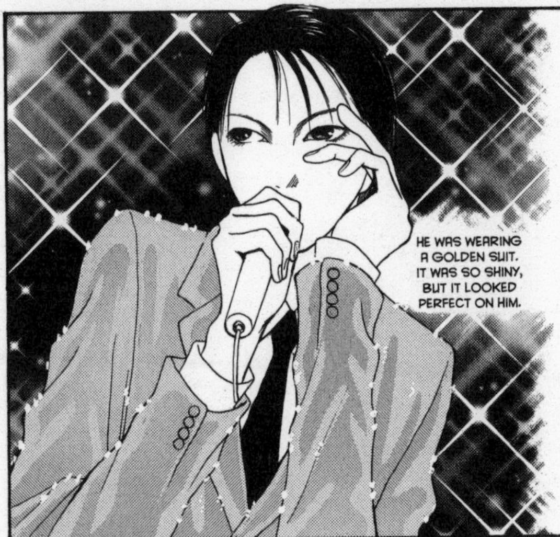
HE WAS WEARING A GOLDEN SUIT. IT WAS SO SHINY, BUT IT LOOKED PERFECT ON HIM.

BUG

AFTER WRITING ABOUT THEM IN BOOK 12, I PAID THEM A VISIT TO SAY HELLO. THE SINGER KYO-SAN IS SUCH A NICE PERSON...

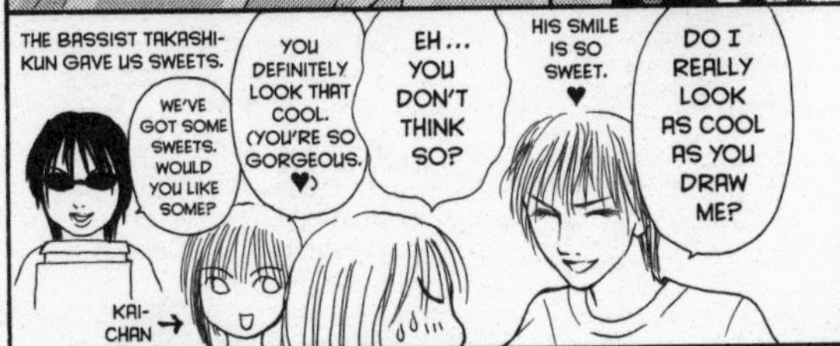
DO I REALLY LOOK AS COOL AS YOU DRAW ME?
HIS SMILE IS SO SWEET. ♥
EH... YOU DON'T THINK SO?
YOU DEFINITELY LOOK THAT COOL. (YOU'RE SO GORGEOUS. ♥)
THE BASSIST TAKASHI-KUN GAVE US SWEETS.
WE'VE GOT SOME SWEETS. WOULD YOU LIKE SOME?
KAI-CHAN →

SHARA NO SUI

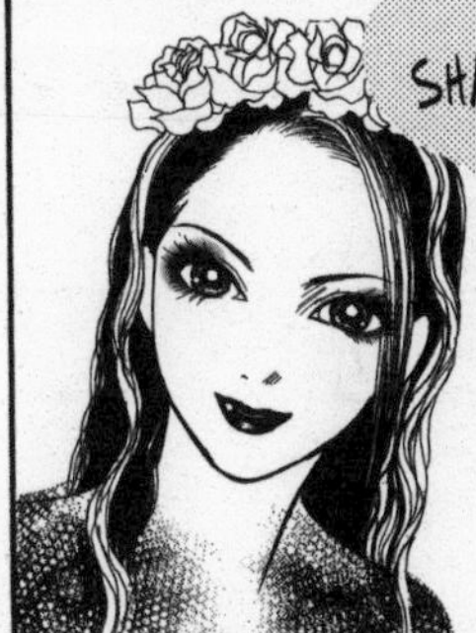

SINGER SALASA-CHAN

I BECAME FRIENDS WITH HER RECENTLY. ♥

SHE'S SOOOO CUTE. ♥

AND SHE'S SUPER SEXY. ♥

I EVEN WENT ON A TRIP WITH HER. ♥

THEY'RE A GOTHIC BAND. THEY WERE PERFORMING IN ENGLAND A LOT. I HAVEN'T LISTENED TO THEIR SONGS YET, BUT I'M SURE THEY'RE AMAZING! I CAN'T WAIT TO SEE THEM LIVE! ♥

BAROQUE

EVER SINCE MY FAVORITE BAND BROKE UP, I'VE BEEN IN SEARCH OF A NEW BAND THAT I CAN GET INTO.

WHEN KIYOHARU ISN'T PERFORMING, I'VE GOT NOTHING TO LOOK FORWARD TO. (KIYOHARU-SAMA IS ON TOUR RIGHT NOW, SO I'M FEELING REALLY EXCITED, HAPPY AND EXHAUSTED AT THE SAME TIME, BUT ... ♥)

IT'S PRETTY EASY TO FIND BANDS I LIKE, BUT THERE JUST AREN'T THAT MANY BANDS THAT I CAN REALLY, REALLY GET INTO...

I WISH BAROQUE WOULD GET BACK TOGETHER... BUT THAT'S PROBABLY IMPOSSIBLE...

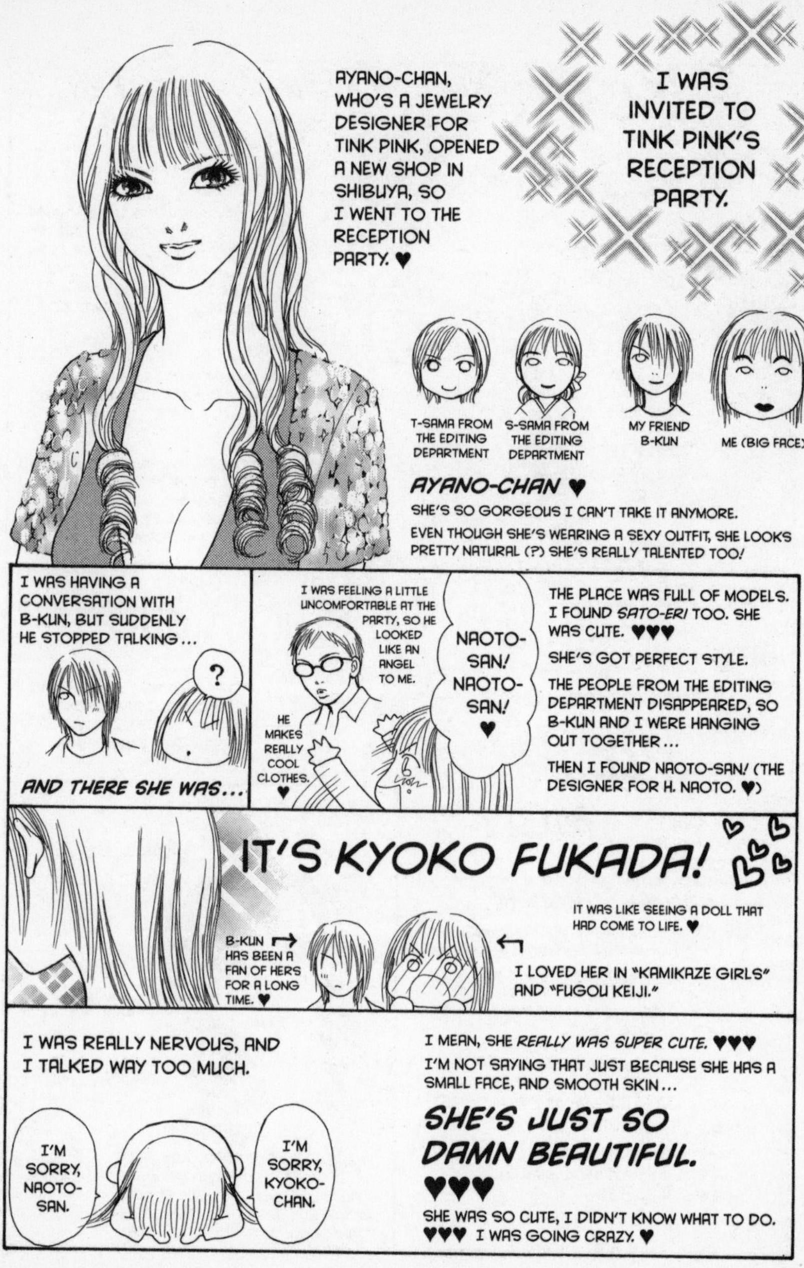
I WAS INVITED TO TINK PINK'S RECEPTION PARTY.
AYANO-CHAN, WHO'S A JEWELRY DESIGNER FOR TINK PINK, OPENED A NEW SHOP IN SHIBUYA, SO I WENT TO THE RECEPTION PARTY. ♥
ME (BIG FACE)
MY FRIEND B-KUN
S-SAMA FROM THE EDITING DEPARTMENT
T-SAMA FROM THE EDITING DEPARTMENT
AYANO-CHAN ♥
SHE'S SO GORGEOUS I CAN'T TAKE IT ANYMORE.
EVEN THOUGH SHE'S WEARING A SEXY OUTFIT, SHE LOOKS PRETTY NATURAL (?) SHE'S REALLY TALENTED TOO!
THE PLACE WAS FULL OF MODELS. I FOUND SATO-ERI TOO. SHE WAS CUTE. ♥♥♥
SHE'S GOT PERFECT STYLE.
THE PEOPLE FROM THE EDITING DEPARTMENT DISAPPEARED, SO B-KUN AND I WERE HANGING OUT TOGETHER...
THEN I FOUND NAOTO-SAN! (THE DESIGNER FOR H. NAOTO. ♥)
NAOTO-SAN! NAOTO-SAN! ♥
I WAS FEELING A LITTLE UNCOMFORTABLE AT THE PARTY, SO HE LOOKED LIKE AN ANGEL TO ME.
HE MAKES REALLY COOL CLOTHES. ♥
I WAS HAVING A CONVERSATION WITH B-KUN, BUT SUDDENLY HE STOPPED TALKING...
?
AND THERE SHE WAS...
IT'S KYOKO FUKADA!
IT WAS LIKE SEEING A DOLL THAT HAD COME TO LIFE. ♥
I LOVED HER IN "KAMIKAZE GIRLS" AND "FUGOU KEIJI."
B-KUN HAS BEEN A FAN OF HERS FOR A LONG TIME. ♥
I MEAN, SHE REALLY WAS SUPER CUTE. ♥♥♥
I'M NOT SAYING THAT JUST BECAUSE SHE HAS A SMALL FACE, AND SMOOTH SKIN...
SHE'S JUST SO DAMN BEAUTIFUL. ♥♥♥
SHE WAS SO CUTE, I DIDN'T KNOW WHAT TO DO. ♥♥♥ I WAS GOING CRAZY. ♥
I'M SORRY, KYOKO-CHAN.
I'M SORRY, NAOTO-SAN.
I WAS REALLY NERVOUS, AND I TALKED WAY TOO MUCH.

THANKS FOR BUYING KODANSHA COMICS.

I JUST GOT BACK FROM KIYOHARU'S TWO-DAY CONCERT IN SENDAI, SO I'M PRETTY EXCITED. (I REALLY ENJOYED THE CONCERT IN SHINAGAWA, BUT I COULDN'T RESIST GOING TO THE SENDAI CONCERT.)

I'M SO GLAD I WENT. HE WAS SO COOL! ♥♥♥

I WONDER WHY HE'S SO COOL? ♥♥♥

I MEAN YOU COULD SNAP A PHOTO OF HIM ANY TIME OF DAY 24/7 AND HE'LL ALWAYS LOOK HOT. ♥
HIS EVERY SINGLE MOVEMENT IS COOL. ♥♥♥

IF THERE'S A GUY ON THIS EARTH WHO'S EVEN MORE GORGEOUS THAN KIYOHARU, I WANNA SEE HIM. BUT, NO ONE COULD POSSIBLY BE HOTTER THAN HE IS.

AAAAAHHH.

I LOOKED LIKE THIS. →

THANK YOU SO MUCH FOR YOUR LETTERS. ♥♥♥

I DON'T HAVE ANY PLANS TO START A WEBSITE. (I HARDLY EVER USE MY PC.) THE ONLY WAY I CAN COMMUNICATE WITH YOU IS VIA LETTERS.

WRITING MANGA IS ALWAYS A STRUGGLE FOR ME, AND I GET BUMMED OUT EVERY TIME I SEE THE FINAL PRINT, BUT I ALWAYS FEEL MUCH BETTER AFTER READING YOUR LETTERS. THEY'RE REALLY ENCOURAGING. (I'M REALLY HAPPY WHEN MY FRIENDS ENCOURAGE ME TOO. ♥)

SOME DAY I'D LIKE TO WRITE A MANGA THAT GIVES ME COMPLETE SATISFACTION...I WONDER IF THAT'LL EVER HAPPEN...

I'LL BECOME A BETTER MANGA ARTIST.

I'LL WORK EVEN HARDER.

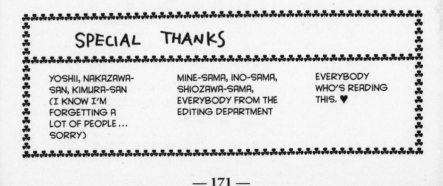

SPECIAL THANKS

YOSHII, NAKAZAWA-SAN, KIMURA-SAN (I KNOW I'M FORGETTING A LOT OF PEOPLE... SORRY)

MINE-SAMA, INO-SAMA, SHIOZAWA-SAMA, EVERYBODY FROM THE EDITING DEPARTMENT

EVERYBODY WHO'S READING THIS. ♥

About the Creator

Tomoko Hayakawa was born on March 4.

Since her debut as a manga creator, Tomoko Hayakawa has worked on many shojo titles with the theme of romantic love—only to realize that she could write about other subjects as well. She decided to pack her newest story with the things she likes most, which led to her current, enormously popular series, *The Wallflower*.

Her favorite things are: Tim Burton's *The Nightmare Before Christmas*, Jean-Paul Gaultier, and samurai dramas on TV. Her hobbies are collecting items with skull designs and watching *bishonen* (beautiful boys). Her dream is to build a mansion like the one the Addams family lives in. Her favorite pastime is to lie around at home with her cat, Ten (whose full name is Tennosuke).

Her zodiac sign is Pisces, and her blood group is AB.

Translation Notes

Japanese is a tricky language for most Westerners, and translation is often more art than science. For your edification and reading pleasure, here are notes on some of the places where we could have gone in a different direction in our translation of the work, or where a Japanese cultural reference is used.

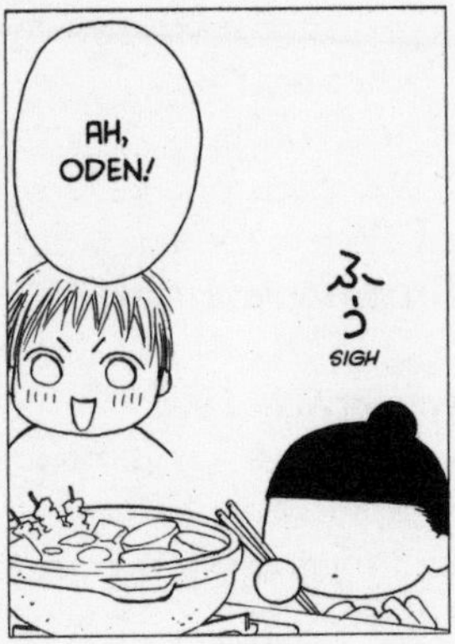

AH, ODEN!
ふ～っ
SIGH

Oden, page 20

Oden is a tasty dish made up of various ingredients boiled in soup stock. Common ingredients include daikon radish, hard-boiled eggs, *konyaku* (yam cake), and various types of fish cake.

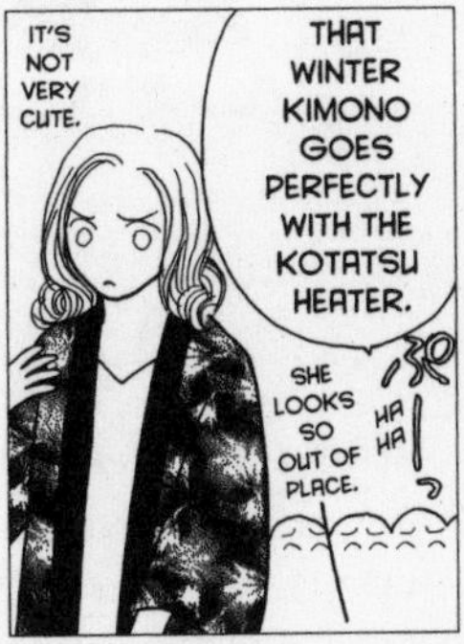

THAT WINTER KIMONO GOES PERFECTLY WITH THE KOTATSU HEATER.
IT'S NOT VERY CUTE.
HA HA
SHE LOOKS SO OUT OF PLACE.

Kotatsu, page 21

A *kotatsu* is a sort of table with a heater underneath it. It's a common fixture in most Japanese households. To the Japanese, the *kotatsu* is a quintessential symbol of winter.

Yon, page 50

Yon is a Korean actor who stars in the series *Fuyu no Sonata*. This Korean drama became wildly popular in Japan, and helped start Japan's Korean drama boom.

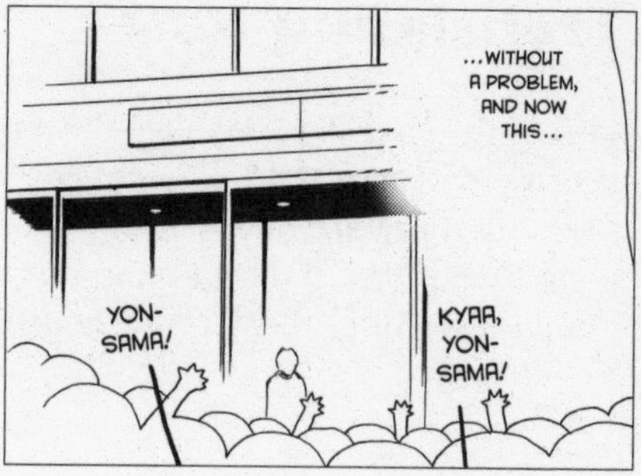
...WITHOUT A PROBLEM, AND NOW THIS...
KYAA, YON-SAMA!
YON-SAMA!

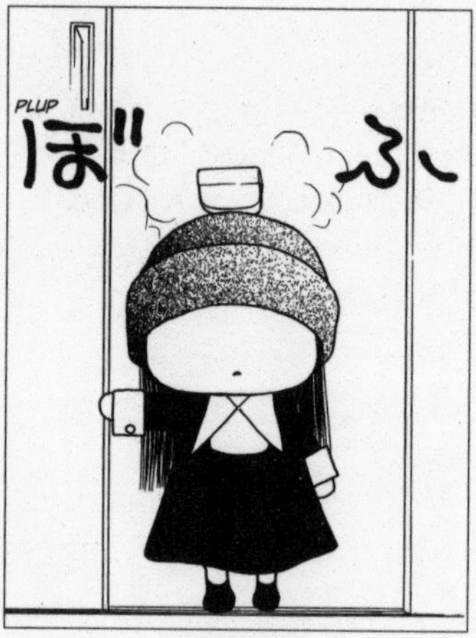
PLUP
ぼ゛ふ

What's on Sunako's head? page 58

That thing on Sunako's head is a chalkboard eraser. This is a common school prank in Japan. People lodge an eraser in a sliding door so that it will fall on top of the first person who opens the door.

Beginning of class, page 59

This is the standard way that Japanese students begin and end every class.

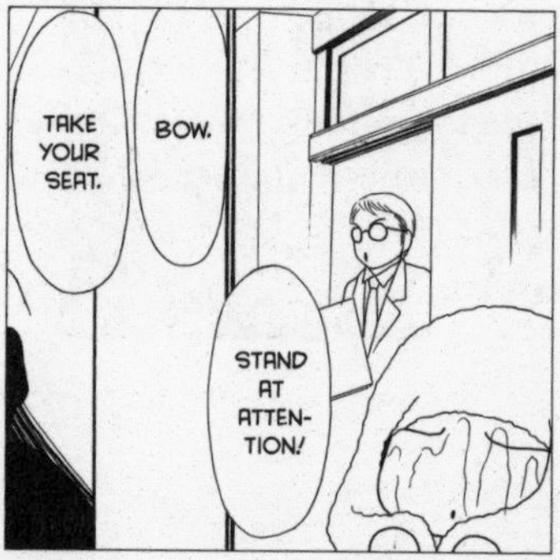
BOW.
TAKE YOUR SEAT.
STAND AT ATTEN-TION!

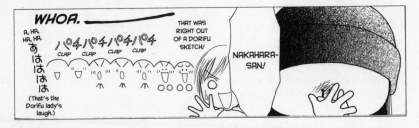

NAKAHARA-SAN!
THAT WAS RIGHT OUT OF A DORIFU SKETCH!
WHOA.
パチパチパチパチ
CLAP CLAP CLAP CLAP
A, HA, HA, HA.
あはははは
(That's the Dorifu lady's laugh.)

Dorifu, page 59

Dorifu, short for Drifters, is a Japanese sketch comedy group known for its slapstick style. In their television sketches they constantly use a sound effect of a woman laughing uproariously.

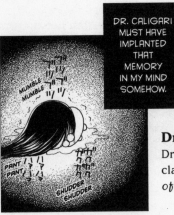

DR. CALIGARI MUST HAVE IMPLANTED THAT MEMORY IN MY MIND SOMEHOW.
MUMBLE MUMBLE
SHUDDER SHUDDER
PANT PANT

Dr. Caligari, page 88

Dr. Caligari is the mad scientist from the classic German silent film *The Cabinet of Dr. Caligari.*

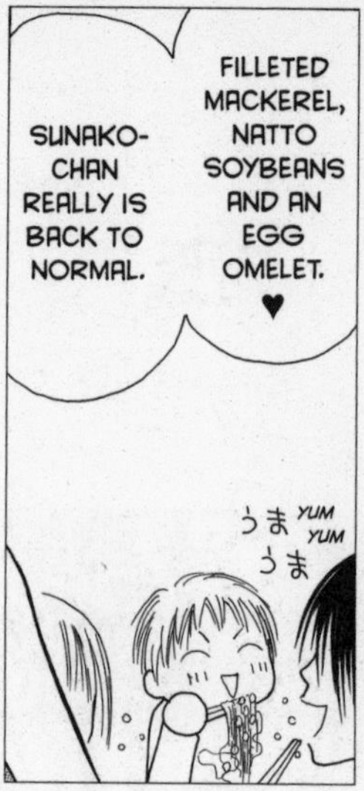
FILLETED MACKEREL, NATTO SOYBEANS AND AN EGG OMELET. ♥
SUNAKO-CHAN REALLY IS BACK TO NORMAL.
うま YUM YUM うま

Natto, page 99

Natto is a popular breakfast dish made from fermented soy beans. It's famous for its pungent aroma and sticky consistency.

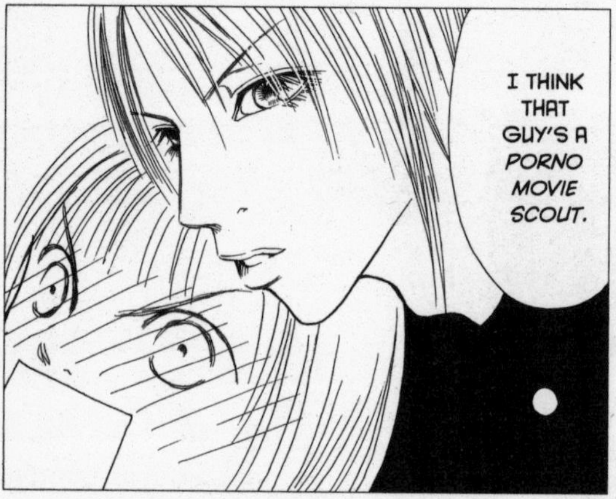
I THINK THAT GUY'S A *PORNO MOVIE SCOUT*.

Porno movie scout, page 108

In Japan, seedy-looking guys often accost attractive women and try to convince them to work in the porn industry. Porn scouts sometimes stand in front of large train stations and popular shopping areas looking for their next victim.

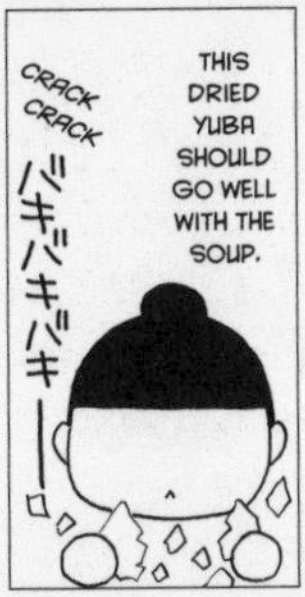
THIS DRIED YUBA SHOULD GO WELL WITH THE SOUP.
CRACK CRACK
バキバキバキー！！

Yuba, page 131

Yuba is a type of tofu made from collecting the skin from boiled soy milk.

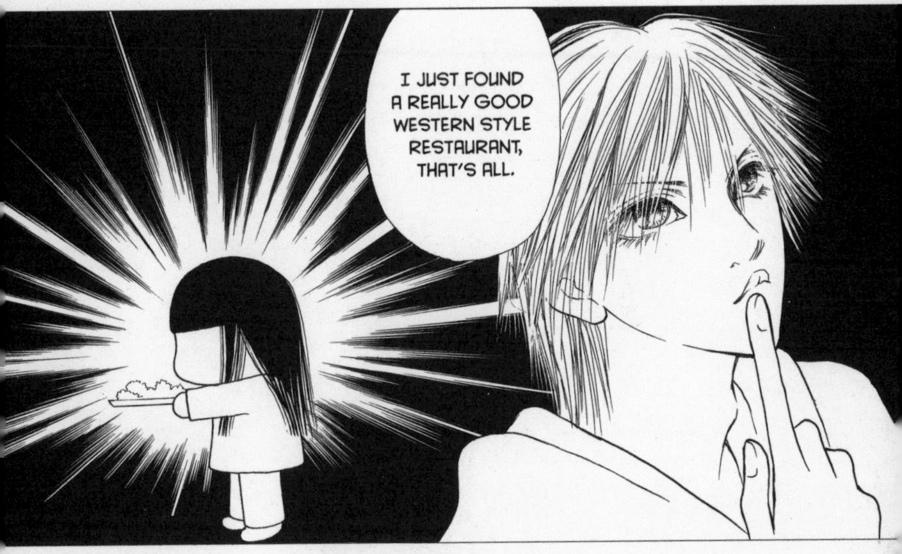
I JUST FOUND A REALLY GOOD WESTERN STYLE RESTAURANT, THAT'S ALL.

Western-style restaurant, page 132

Kyohei is referring to a *yoshokuya*-style restaurant. *Yoshokuya* restaurants serve what the Japanese perceive to be Western/European-style food. Common *yoshokuya* foods are fried shrimp, rice-filled omelets, stuffed cabbage, hamburger steaks with gravy, potatoes au gratin, croquettes, and spaghetti. *Yoshokuya* foods are generally heavy on greasy, creamy, deep-fried goodness. They are the antithesis of the traditional Japanese cooking that is Sunako's specialty.

Preview of volume 14

We're pleased to present you with a preview from volume 14. Be sure to check our website (www.delreymanga.com) to see when this volume will be available in English. For now you'll have to make do with Japanese!

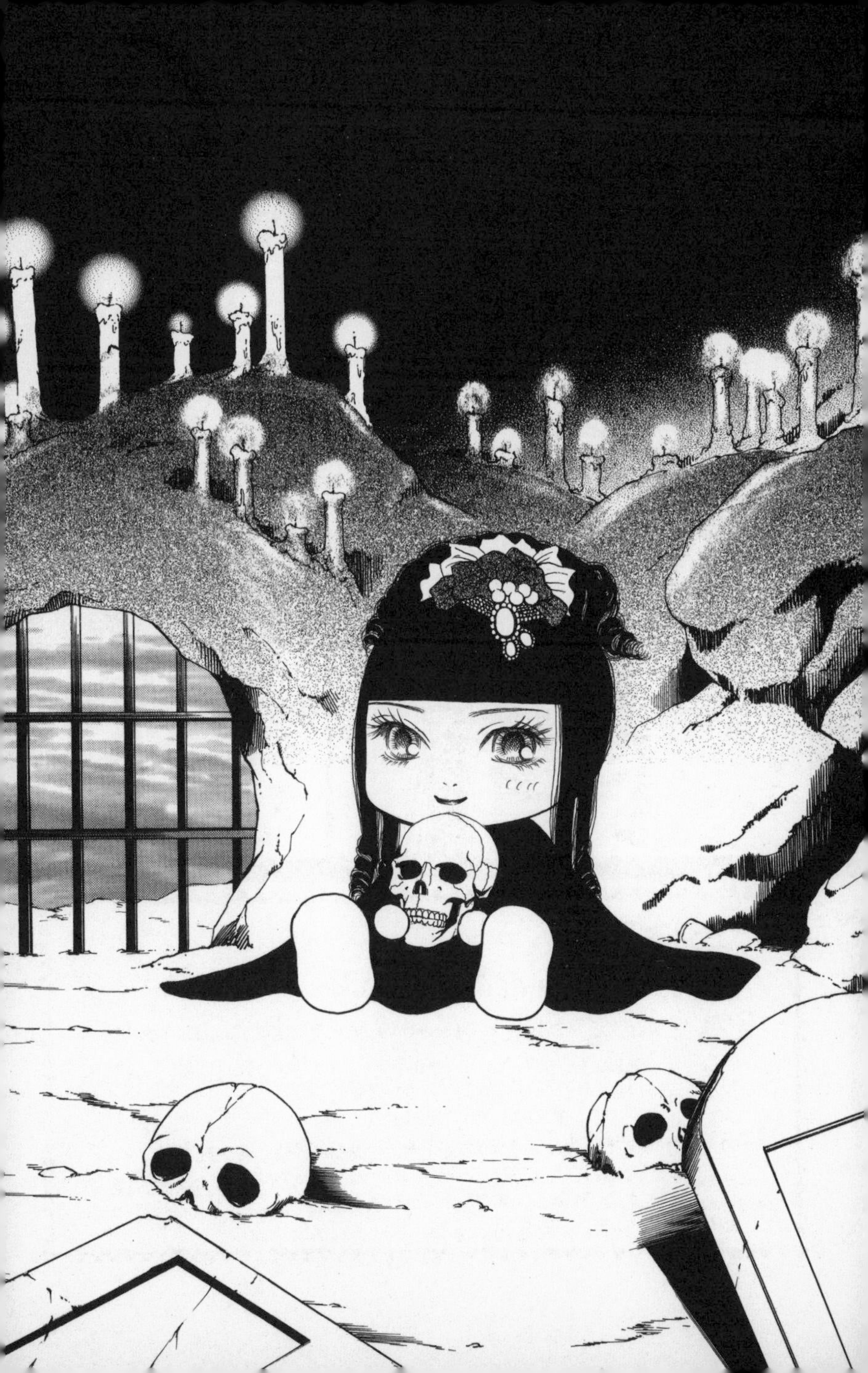

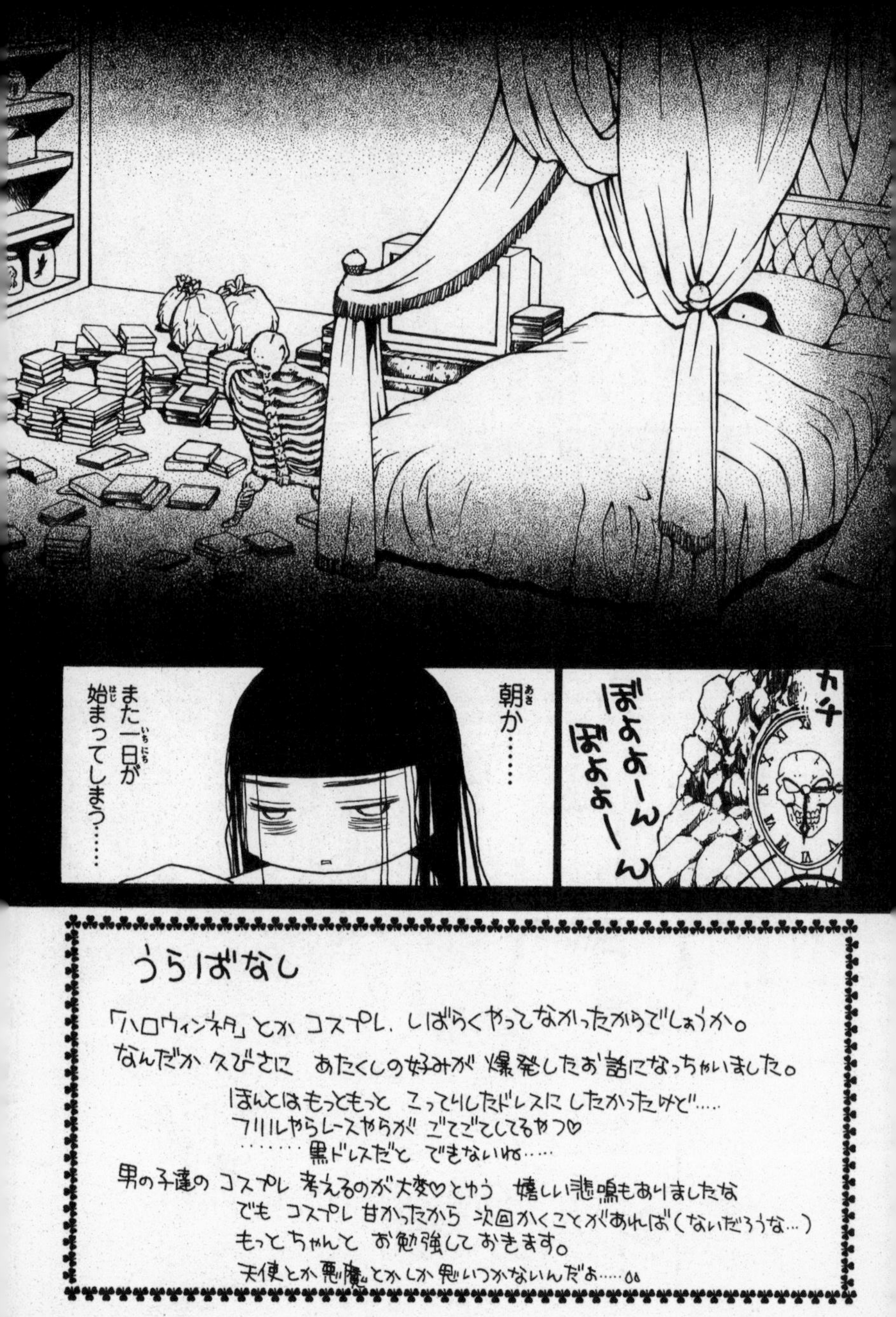
カチ
ぼよよーん
ぼよよーん
朝か……
また一日が始まってしまう……

うらばなし

「ハロウィンネタ」とか コスプレ、しばらくやってなかったからでしょうか。
なんだか 久びさに あたくしの好みが 爆発したお話になっちゃいました。
ほんとはもっともっと こってりしたドレスにしたかったけど……
フリルやらレースやらが ごてごてしてるやつ♡
………黒ドレスだと できないね……
男の子達の コスプレ 考えるのが大変♡とゆう 嬉しい悲鳴もありましたな
でも コスプレ 甘かったから 次回かくことがあれば（ないだろうな…）
もっとちゃんと お勉強しておきます。
天使とか悪魔とかしか 思いつかないんだよ……

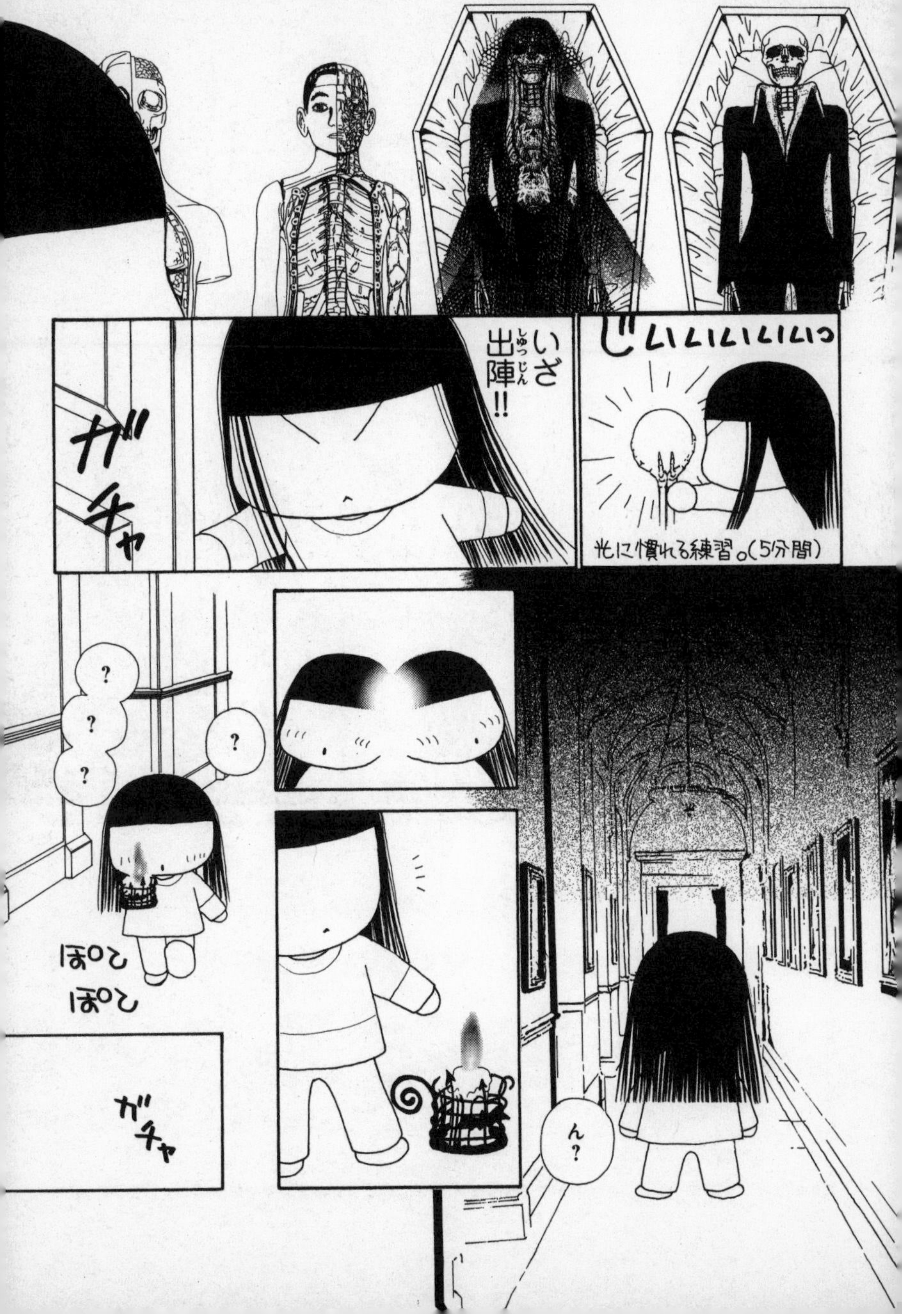
じぃぃぃぃぃっ
光に慣れる練習。(5分間)
いざ出陣(しゅつじん)!!
ガチャ
ん?
?
?
?
?
ぽてぽて
ガチャ

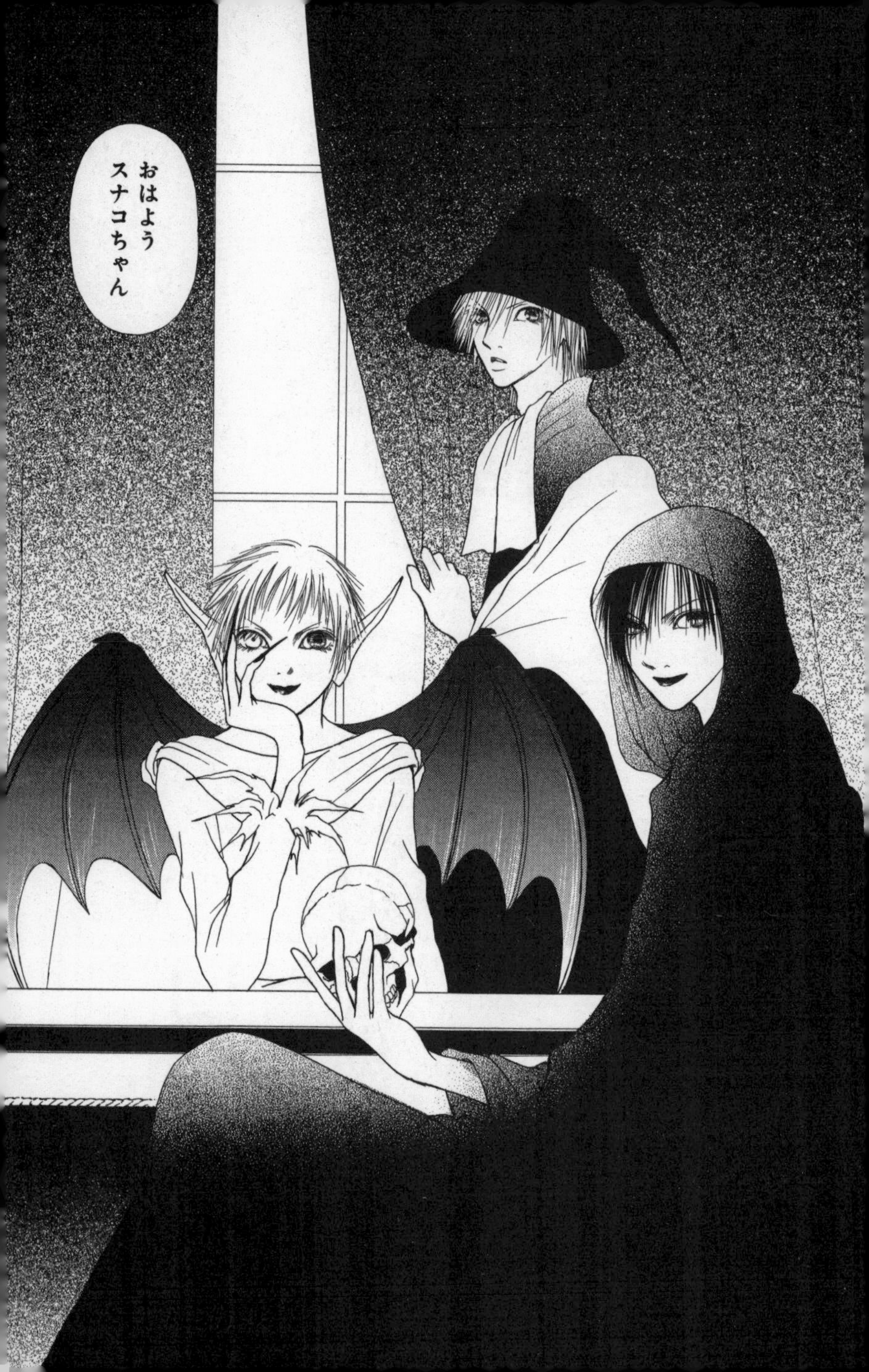
おはよう
スナコちゃん

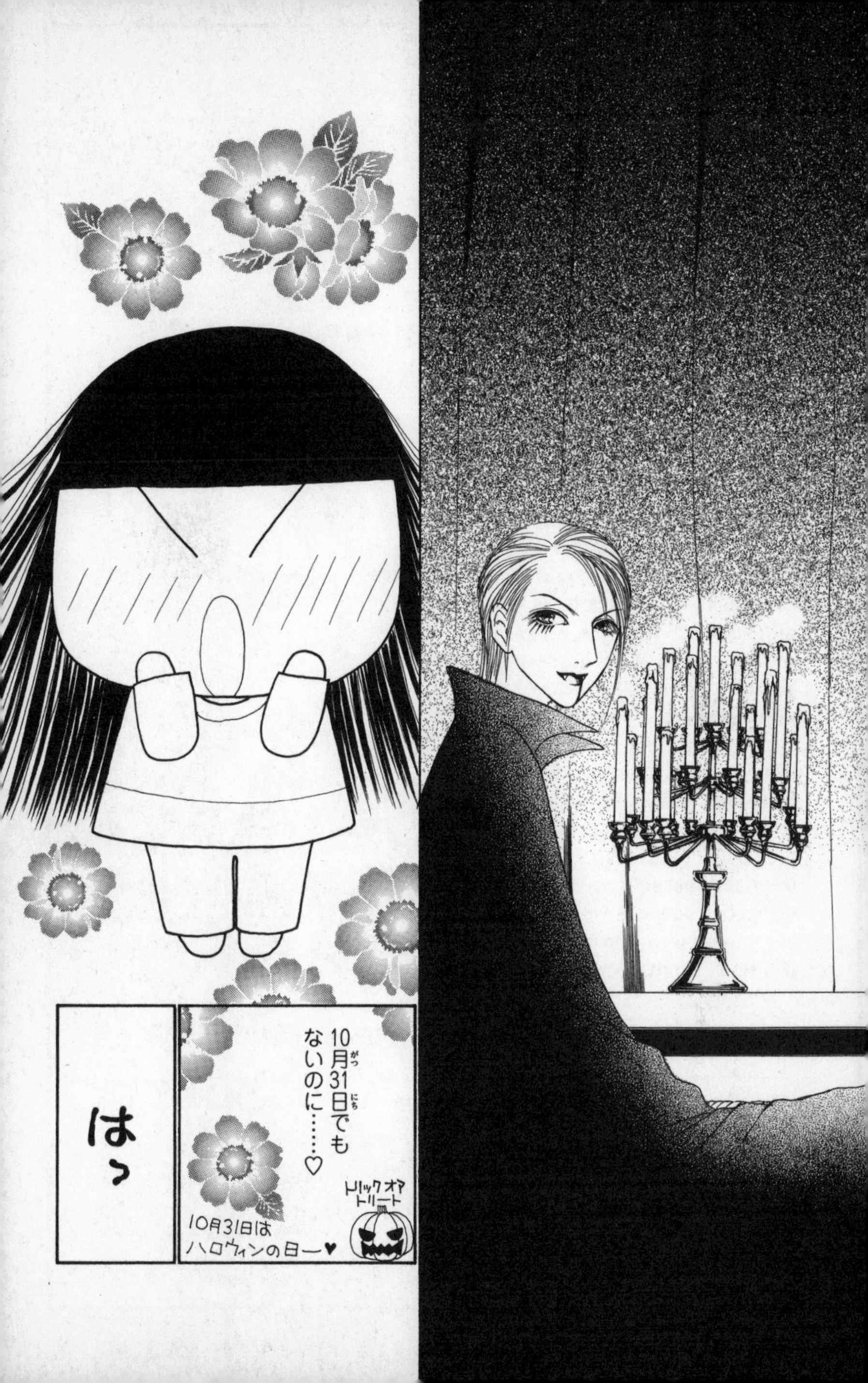
10月31日でもないのに……♡
トリックオアトリート
10月31日はハロウィンの日ー♥
はっ

MY HEAVENLY HOCKEY CLUB

BY AI MORINAGA

WHERE THE BOYS ARE!

Hana Suzuki loves only two things in life: eating and sleeping. So when handsome classmate Izumi Oda asks Hana—his major crush—to join the school hockey club, convincing her proves to be a difficult task. True, the Grand Hockey Club is full of boys—and all the boys are super-cute—but, given a choice, Hana prefers a sizzling steak to a hot date. Then Izumi mentions the field trips to fancy resorts. Now Hana can't wait for the first away game, with its promise of delicious food and luxurious linens. Of course there's the getting up early, working hard, and playing well with others. How will Hana survive?

Special extras in each volume! Read them all!